Political Judgment

Political Judgment

Structure and Process

Edited by
Milton Lodge and Kathleen M. McGraw

Ann Arbor

THE UNIVERSITY OF MICHIGAN PRESS

Copyright © by the University of Michigan 1995
All rights reserved
Published in the United States of America by
The University of Michigan Press
Manufactured in the United States of America
♾ Printed on acid-free paper

1998   1997   1996   1995   4   3   2   1

A CIP catalogue record for this book is available from the British Library.

Library of Congress Cataloging-in-Publication Data

Political judgment : structure and process / edited by Milton Lodge
   and Kathleen M. McGraw.
      p.   cm.
   Includes bibliographical references and index.
   ISBN 0-472-10541-8 (alk. paper)
   1. Political psychology. 2. Public opinion. 3. Voting. 4. Human
information processing. 5. Judgment. I. Lodge, Milton.
II. McGraw, Kathleen M., 1957–
JA74.5.P623   1994
324'.01'9—dc20   94-34167
                                                           CIP

Contents

CHAPTER 1

Introduction

Kathleen M. McGraw and Milton Lodge

There has been a revolution in thinking about thinking, a paradigmatic shift away from the strict stimulus-response behaviorism that dominated American psychology throughout the first half of this century to a recognition in more recent times of the need to look inside the "black box" of the mind for explanations of human behavior. Although historians of science differ as to when the cognitive revolution began (Lachman, Lachman, and Butterfield 1979; Gardner 1985; Markus and Zajonc 1985), 1932 is frequently pointed to as a critical year, with the publication of Bartlett's *Remembering* experiments, showing "schematic" effects on reasoning, as well as Tolman's *Purposive Behavior in Animals and Man,* which posed a direct challenge to behaviorism by demonstrating that rats running a maze developed different "cognitive maps" that facilitated their performance. We, as political scientists, take as our starting point Walter Lippmann's (1922) insight that reality is too complex to be comprehended as is, hence the necessity for people to construct simplified "pictures in the head" to represent the "world outside." These representations of reality (Lippmann called them "stereotypes") are simplified models of the world. The Lippmann-Bartlett-Tolman message is straightforward: to understand how people behave and interact in their environment, one must know how they represent their world.

The notion that information about the world is represented in memory in an organized way and that how this knowledge is "bundled together" affects the way we comprehend and respond to the outside world is not new, dating back to Aristotle (Bartlett 1932). What is new is the treatment of thinking as "information-processing." The information-processing approach to thinking is concerned with identifying the processes by which people acquire, store, retrieve, transform, and use information to perform some intelligent, goal-based activity. This approach sees the individual as a purposive actor whose behavior, while routinely deviating from rational expectations, nevertheless can be viewed as a reasonable response to an experience-based representation of the world.

Let us define more precisely what we mean by "information-processing models" by breaking down the component terms (what follows is drawn heavily from Massaro and Cowan 1993). "Information" is the fundamental building block, referring to the internal representation derived from an external stimulus. Thus, "data," the inputs available in the environment, are distinguishable from "information," or the knowledge within the perceiver. "Information-processing" refers to how information is transformed and modified so that it eventually has some impact on some observable outcome. Finally, "information-processing models" are theories that describe a series of steps or stages through which the processing is accomplished. The goal of the information-processing approach is to understand how some complex behavioral phenomenon, such as casting a vote, is derived from these simpler component processes. Understanding how these basic explanatory processes contribute to some political behavior is also the ultimate justification for utilizing information-processing theories in political science.

The information-processing approach has a number of defining characteristics, with several lists of the key properties that embody the most successful information-processing theories available (e.g., Anderson 1983; Hastie 1986; Lachman, Lachman, and Butterfield 1979; Palmer and Kimchi 1986). For our purposes, three are critical. The first of these is the "physical embodiment" principle (Palmer and Kimchi, 1986), which reflects the assumption that information processing occurs in a physical system, with information embedded in internal memory structures. Several alternative structures have been proposed, and specification of the nature of those internal representations is an important aspect of the information-processing approach (Hastie 1986). The second is an emphasis on processing decomposition, or the breaking down of processing into substages, with the goal of identifying the processes contributing to some observable outcome. Finally, the principle of limited cognitive resources, such as in representational capacity and computational complexity, is crucial, as these cognitive limits place constraints on the performance of the information-processing system.

The decision to publish a volume illustrating the utility of the information-processing approach for understanding political judgment was driven by our firm belief that understanding how citizens make important judgments and decisions such as evaluating candidates, voting, forming opinions on key issues—all among the enduring concerns of political scientists—requires "unpacking the black box" (Lodge, Stroh, and Wahlke 1990). In the absence of an explication of these processes, based upon psychologically informed principles, our discipline is left in the untenable position of being able to predict, but never to understand, how and why citizens act as they do.

The timing is clearly right for such a book, given the high quality of contemporary political psychological research utilizing the information-processing approach. One of our goals in putting together this volume was to bring together some of the foremost practioners of the perspective, and the resulting list of contributors to the volume includes both political scientists and social psychologists, all of whom have been responsible for a number of significant advances in our disciplines' understanding of political cognition. The contributors are united by a commitment to the development of psychologically realistic models of judgment and choice that do not fly in the face of well-established principles and regularities observed in political behavior research.

Adoption of the information-processing approach to the study of political judgment also brings with it a commitment to methodological diversity and innovation. Hence, a second major goal for the book was to bring together, some for the very first time in print, the various methodologies utilized by researchers in this area. Experimentation, not the general purpose public opinion survey, such as the National Election Studies (NES), is clearly the methodological tool of choice, with all of the empirical contributions in this book based, at least in part, on experimental studies. This is not surprising, as the decomposition of complex phenomena into their component, explanatory processes is a task for which experimentation is ideally suited (Kinder and Palfrey 1993). The studies reported in these chapters include a whole array of methodologies and measurement techniques that have the potential for altering substantially the way that political researchers go about their work. These include techniques for measuring how information is stored in memory, such as through reaction times (Berent and Krosnick, Stroh) and recall clustering (Berent and Krosnick, McGraw and Steenbergen, Rahn); consideration of the variability in responses, rather than just the central tendency (Judd and Downing, Feldman); computational modeling (Boynton, Taber and Steenbergen); and process tracing (Lau).

Organization of the Book and Chapter Overviews

The book is organized into two main sections. The common emphasis of the contributions in the first section is on the *representation* of a variety of types of political "stimuli" in memory (e.g., specific candidates, political groups, and political attitudes). The second section of the book is concerned with the *dynamics of information processing,* the contributions united by the goal of specifying, in detail, the cognitive processes that produce a political response, whether it be the evaluation of a political candidate, a vote choice, or articulation of an issue preference. To a large degree, this structure versus process division is artificial, as all of the contributors would agree that consideration of both is necessary for understanding political judgment. The division is primarily based on the empirical focus of the chapters, with those in the first section explicitly concerned with representational measurement, and those in the second more concerned with identifying *how* political judgments and decisions are reached.

Before describing the individual chapters, a few words about terminology. The most widely used, and recently controversial (Kuklinski, Luskin, and Bolland 1991; Lodge, McGraw, Conover, Feldman, and Miller 1991), term used to refer to cognitive structure is *schema*. The appeal of the term appears to rest primarily with its sound historical precedent, and although never a particularly well-specified concept in social psychology, it nonetheless was readily embraced by social, and many political, psychologists, without much concern for definitional precision (Fiske and Linville 1980; Markus and Zajonc 1985). Cognitive psychologists, on the other hand, have grappled much more rigorously with the thorny issues of specifying the nature and role of such large-scale memory representations (Barsalou 1992; Hastie 1986). Although disagreement exists among psychologists and political scientists, the most prominent of the contemporary models conceptualizes the representation of information in memory as an associate network consisting of concepts (nodes) and the associative pathways (links) connecting them (Anderson and Bower 1973; Anderson 1983; Collins and Loftus 1975; Collins and Quillian 1969). In addition to specification of memory structure, associative network models include well-specified principles, such as spreading activation, detailing how information is retrieved and forgotten, made more or less accessible, and so on. (Lodge, in chapter 6, elaborates on these processes in more detail.)

The associative network model has come to be adopted by many political psychologists (Judd and Krosnick 1989; Lodge and McGraw 1991), and it is clearly the structural "currency" of choice for most of the contributors to this volume. So we forewarn readers who may find themselves wondering "where is the schema?" that although the word itself is conspicuously absent from the text, it is conceptually present throughout.[1] In response to those readers who might question whether this omission reflects a movement away from a commitment to cognitive structure, we must underscore the point that the *concept* of schema as an organized memory structure is still vitally important to the understanding of political reasoning and judgment, but that *specification* of the particular form such structures may take demands more precision than the ubiquitous schema term provides.

Finally, the information-processing approach, like political psychology itself, is not yet fully developed, and careful readers will note that there are contradictions between some of the chapters. This is, we think, a natural consequence of an emergent field. It is to the credit of the information-processing approach that the theoretical models make it possible to see where some of the most glaring contradictions lie. We return to a more detailed discussion of such conflicts below.

In chapter 2, Kathleen McGraw and Marco Steenbergen explore how impressions of political candidates are organized in memory. Specifically, they examine the conditions under which two very different representational structures characterize such impressions: one reflecting the basic "stuff" of politics (i.e., policy positions and personal information), the second representing the evaluative implications of information. McGraw and Steenbergen provide a detailed discussion of how memory structures can be measured through recall protocols. Consistent with previous work (McGraw, Pinney, and Neumann 1991), the experimental evidence they report suggests that information about political candidates is much more likely to be organized along the attribute (i.e., policy versus personal) than the evaluative dimension, particularly for the politically sophisticated and when the information is encoded with the goal of forming an impression. The impressions of nonsophisticates, on the other hand, are more strongly shaped by the evaluative implications of the information, a finding that is congruent with Sniderman, Brody, and Tetlock's (1991) recent claim that less sophisticated citizens are particularly likely to reason about politics in an affect-driven manner. McGraw and Steenbergen also explore the judgmental consequences associated with different organizational strategies, focusing on online processing and impression extremity.

Wendy Rahn's contribution in chapter 3 provides a valuable extension to the McGraw and Steenbergen work, in moving beyond the single-candidate case to the more complex two-candidate situation. Rahn argues that whereas some political information environments are structurally simple and highly person-centered (e.g., a candidate's acceptance speech), most are more complex, because people are exposed to information about more than one political candidate at the same time (e.g., in a debate or a political campaign). Drawing on earlier work with her colleagues (Rahn, et al. 1990), Rahn suggests that under these more complex conditions, memory should be organized along the important attributes on which people compare candidates (e.g., partisanship, policies, and personality), rather than organized around the candidates themselves. The results of the experiment she reports provide compelling support for this assertion, with her experimental subjects demonstrating a clear preference for attribute-based, rather than candidate-based, memory organization. Like McGraw and Steenbergen, Rahn is also concerned with the judgmental consequences of cognitive organization, exploring the impact of attribute- and candidate-based organization on candidate evaluation processes.

In chapter 4, Charles Judd and James Downing focus on group stereotypes, a topic that has been largely ignored by contemporary political scientists and political psychologists, despite the central role of groups in political life. Judd and Downing review how scholarly definitions of stereotypes have changed over the past half century. They then develop an innovative theoretical model that distinguishes among three key characteristics that differentiate the representation of ingroups from outgroups, making explicit in this discussion the importance of properly conceptualizing stereotypic accuracy and inaccuracy (see also Judd and Park 1993). First, ingroup stereotypes are more positively valenced than outgroup stereotypes (leading to ethnocentrism and prejudice). Second, outgroup stereotypes tend to be exaggerated, with more members of the outgroup perceived as conforming to the stereotype than is actually the case. Finally, outgroups are perceived to be less variable or dispersed around the central tendency of the stereotype than are ingroups (the outgroup homogeneity principle). Judd and Downing then bring to bear an impressive arsenal of empirical methodologies, including the reanalysis of previous research (Dawes, Singer, and Lemons 1972), analyses of National Election Study data, and an original experiment, to explore the accuracy with which perceivers estimate the political positions taken by members of various social groups. One of the more important conclusions Judd and Downing reach is that the various judgmental biases that result from group stereotypes can take different forms, depending on whether the target of the judgment is the group in the aggregate or an individual member of the group.

In chapter 5, Matthew Berent and Jon Krosnick examine how subjective importance shapes the manner in which attitudes about political policies (e.g., abortion and capital punishment) are organized in memory. Drawing on research suggesting that important issues are associated with deeper, more elaborate information processing, they test the hypothesis that information relevant to important attitudes should be organized in more complex memory structures, in comparison to information for less subjectively important attitudes. This chapter is also notable for the use of multiple methods: it includes four different experiments, each utilizing a different technique for measuring memory organization. Berent and Krosnick find that important attitudes are organized in more elaborate memory structures than are unimportant attitudes, with important attitudes characterized by more organizing dimensions and less reliance on evaluative, or "agreement-based," organization.

In chapter 6, Milton Lodge introduces the second section of the book. Lodge begins his essay by noting a paradox: how is it that the ill-informed voter depicted so pessimistically in much of the empirical literature is able to make such apparently reasonable political judgments? His solution to this paradox is to develop a portrait of the American voter as an "efficient information processor of the 'bounded rationalist' school," who reasons about politics in an "on-line" (Hastie and Park 1986; Lodge, McGraw, and Stroh 1989) rather than "memory-based" manner. Lodge elaborates upon a number of important implications of the on-line model of candidate evaluation, not previously made explicit in the Stony Brook scholars' research, including consideration of the role of affect, anchoring and adjustment processes, reconstructive processes in justifying evaluations, order effects in information impact, and memory decay.

In chapter 7, Charles Taber and Marco Steenbergen make a persuasive argument for incorporating a new methodological tool into the repertoire of political science research, what they label *computational experimentation.* Taber and Steenbergen begin by noting the advantages of two methodologies that have been underutilized by scholars interested in electoral behavior: process-tracing methods from behavioral decision theory and computational modeling. They then propose an innovative blending of the two approaches, arguing that experimental human subjects can be used to provide data inputs (i.e., information used to make a decision) and data outputs (i.e., the decision itself), rather than generating these data randomly, as is the practice in most computational modeling. Various electoral decision rules can be specified as computer models—*electoral robots* in Taber and Steenbergen's terms—in order to test the validity of those rules in a variety of contexts. They formally describe in detail the judgment processes implicit in a number of decision rules that are particularly relevant to the domain of voting behavior. In the final section of the chapter, Taber and Steenbergen describe the results of an initial test of the method to assess the performance of the various decision rules in predicting voting decisions.

Richard Lau's contribution in chapter 8 has much in common with Taber and Steenbergen's work. Lau also draws upon the behavioral decision theory literature in order to introduce a new methodological technique into the study of voting behavior, using the technique to empirically test the validity of a number of prominent models of vote choice. Lau begins by discussing the failure of virtually all models of political behavior to seriously consider how information is acquired and used to choose among alternative candidates, followed by a review of the implicit information-processing assumptions of a number of important theories of voting behavior. He then outlines the benefits of information-search methodologies in behavioral-decision research, at the same time noting the limitations of those methods for capturing the complex, dynamic nature of political campaigns. Lau's innovative solution to these limitations was to develop a "dynamic process-tracing methodology," wherein information about political candidates scrolls across a computer screen. The first experiments utilizing this process-tracing technique are described, and the results interpreted as they reflect upon the validity of the different models of the vote decision outlined at the outset of the chapter.

In chapter 9, Patrick Stroh develops a "pragmatic cognitive miser" model of the candidate-evaluation process, whereby voters work to balance two competing concerns: maximization of the subjective utility, or accuracy, of their vote choice and minimization of the amount of cognitive effort and other resources that must be brought to bear in reaching the decision. Stroh argues that voters seek to resolve the problems inherent in this "accuracy-effort trade-off" problem by focusing on certain types of candidate attributes that consume the least amount of cognitive resources, chief among them character assessments, partisanship, and "easy" issues. Much of Stroh's argument is methodological, in that he claims that the joint consideration of effort and accuracy requires the use of a reaction-time methodology, because reaction time provides a more valid indication of cognitive effort than do survey-based techniques. The results of an experimental test of the model suggest that character assessments, especially judgments of leadership and integrity, provide a particularly efficient means of solving the "accuracy-effort trade-off" problem in the evaluation of political candidates.

The final two chapters in the book provide models of "how" people respond to survey questions, elaborating upon those models within richly nuanced discussions of science and scientific practice. In chapter 10, Bob Boynton argues that theories of question answering must be able to distinguish between actually "having" a preexisting opinion and "constructing one on the spot," in response to an interviewer's query. Boynton advocates computational modeling as a tool to study the cognitive processes underlying "question answering." At the same time, he is properly cognizant of the fact that adoption of this methodology brings with it a radically different way of conceptualizing the research process than the way political scientists have traditionally viewed the enterprise. Boynton then presents a computational model of the survey respondent, drawing upon the artificial intelligence tradition in cognitive science, and associative network models in cognitive psychology. He describes the results of a computational experiment—along the lines of Taber and Steenbergen's technique—wherein subjects' evaluations of a candidate were simulated by a computer model representing the theoretical model. The intriguing result from this study is that reproduction of the subjects' evaluations was substantially improved by adding their "associations that come to mind" when learning of the candidates' stances, in contrast to a simpler model that included only subjects' reactions to the actual descriptions of the candidates.

Stanley Feldman, in chapter 11, is also concerned with developing a model of the survey response that incorporates consideration of the important underlying cognitive processes. Feldman begins with an overview of the two dominant explanations for the "fragility" of survey responses, nonattitudes and measurement error, noting that there is empirical evidence that supports and contradicts both models. He then discusses the difficulties in conceptualizing attitudes and opinions as "true scores" (corresponding to Boynton's notion of actually "having" an opinion). Rejecting this perspective, Feldman proposes a model that conceptualizes many social and political opinions as "distributions of considerations," arguing that in responding to a survey question, people engage in a probabilistic and incomplete memory search of relevant, heterogeneous considerations before formulating a response. Two aspects of Feldman's model deserve to be highlighted here. First, his view of opinions as "distributions of considerations" does not imply that survey responses are random or haphazard, but rather that the range of those considerations—which may be broad or narrow—constrains the probable response. Second, Feldman notes that it is misleading to assume that a single model of the survey response can account for responses to all survey questions. Rather, he suggests, a "true score" model might characterize attitudes involving simple affective evaluations, such as in the case of political figures (as the on-line model implies), whereas more complex opinions, such as toward political issues, may be better understood as a distribution of considerations.

Controversies and Future Directions

We believe the contributions in this volume—theoretically, methodologically, and substantively—indicate that political psychologists are learning how to ask the right questions about political judgment and choice, and learning how to most fruitfully pursue the answers to those important questions. But, at times, the various authors come up with different answers to some of those questions! At this juncture, we briefly lay out a few of those controversial issues, not to engage in fruitless bickering about who is right and who is wrong, but with the goal of highlighting some directions for future research that our authors and others may want to pursue.

1. *When does political sophistication matter?* As Wendy Rahn notes in her chapter, "it has become *de rigueur* for political psychologists to assume that the most important source of heterogeneity in political information processing" is individual differences in sophistication, or knowledge about politics (e.g., Sniderman, Brody, and Tetlock 1991; Krosnick, 1990; Zaller 1992). Rahn and her colleagues, on the other hand, argue that sophistication may not be particularly important in many circumstances (Rahn, Aldrich, Borgida, and Sullivan 1990). The McGraw-Steenbergen and Rahn chapters reach conclusions concerning the relationship between sophistication and memory organization that clearly are at odds with each other:

whereas McGraw and Steenbergen find that when the target is a single political candidate, sophistication is associated with more organized structures in memory, Rahn, in the two-candidate case, finds no relationship between the two. Rahn suggests that in a comparative and redundant information environment (such as in her experiment), sophisticated and unsophisticated people implement essentially the same information-processing strategies. This may be the case, but it is an issue that clearly is deserving of more systematic investigation. More generally, our field will benefit from clearer specification of the conditions under which sophistication shapes political judgment, as well as a firmer understanding of the cognitive processes associated with sophistication differences.

2. *Intracandidate versus intradimension information search and memory organization.* Do voters think about political candidates in a candidate-centered manner—searching for and internally representing information for each candidate as a single gestalt—or do they instead prefer "intradimensional" search and representational strategies, which focus on such critical attributes as partisanship, ideology, and issue positions? Three of the chapters in this volume—Lau, Lodge, and Taber and Steenbergen—adopt the former, intracandidate (also referred to as intraalternative) perspective, whereas Rahn advocates the intradimensional (or intraattribute) view. The empirical evidence is split, with Lau's information-search findings indicating a preference for the intracandidate strategy, while Rahn's memory-organization findings imply a preference for the intradimensional strategy (as with Herstein 1981).

There are numerous differences between the Rahn and Lau studies that might account for the different results, but perhaps the most telling are the assumptions the two make regarding the structure of the political environment in the "real world." Rahn assumes that most political campaigns facilitate comparison of alternatives and that information is redundant, such that citizens explicitly or implicitly are provided with information about a given attribute for all available candidates. Her choice of "mirror image" stimulus candidates is consistent with this assumption. Lau, on the other hand, conceives of political campaigns as unruly, almost chaotic affairs, with information about some attributes available for some candidates, but not others. His dynamic, scrolling information board reflects this assumption. Their empirical results, in turn, are congenial with their underlying assumptions. We suspect both Rahn and Lau are right: in some circumstances, when information is completely available and redundant, intraattribute strategies will dominate. In other circumstances, when this is not the case, intracandidate strategies will be preferred. The challenge, of course, lies in identifying the parameters of the relevant information environment for a given research question. Ultimately, resolution of the conflict will require careful consideration of the nature of the information environment as it exists in various real political contexts.

3. *Compensatory versus noncompensatory decision making.* Three of the chapters in the second section of the book raise the issue of whether vote choices are characterized by compensatory or noncompensatory decision making. In compensatory decisions, trade-offs among attributes occur: although I may not like a candidate's pro-death penalty stance, other policy positions may compensate for it. In noncompensatory decisions, trade-offs are not permissible: if I cannot vote for a candidate who supports the death penalty, then her other attributes are irrelevant. In other words, with compensatory processes, all attributes contribute weight to the decision, whereas with noncompensatory processes, only some, and maybe even very few, attributes contribute weight to the decision. Lodge, and Taber and Steenbergen, argue that candidate evaluation and vote choice are compensatory processes, whereas Lau concludes that, contrary to virtually all models of voting behavior (which implicitly or explicitly posit compensatory decision making), voting decisions are governed by noncompensatory strategies. We, of course, must admit to some intellectual stake in this, because, as Lodge makes clear in chapter 6, the on-line model of candidate evaluation is inherently a compensatory model. Much of the disagreement between Lau and the Stony Brook scholars is operational. That is, the on-line model is compensatory, in that it predicts, and the empirical data indicate, that all information *to which people are exposed* contributes some weight to the evaluation (and it assumes that people prefer candidate-centered formats for learning this information). In contrast, Lau's operationalization of the choice rules in an information-search context, based on behavioral decision theoretic practices, requires that the same information be gathered for each candidate, to count as compensatory. Not surprisingly, in a six-person primary, with constantly shifting information (one of Lau's experimental contexts), the degree of exhaustive search required by this operationalization was negligible. In the absence of strong evidence of compensatory search, Lau concludes that vote choices must be characterized by noncompensatory processes.

This issue, regarding whether vote choices are compensatory or noncompensatory, is not independent of the problem discussed above, regarding the prevalence of intracandidate and intra-attribute processes, and resolution of existing empirical and theoretical discrepancies requires the same approach: careful specification of conceptual parameters, relevant cognitive processes, and appropriate operationalization in empirical work. The behavioral decision theory literature also indicates that variables such as task complexity and information format influence the choice rules that are adopted in various situations (points also echoed by Lau and Rahn). Incorporation of these variables in theoretical models should be a high priority.

4. *Incorporating affect in information-processing models.* It has become commonplace at meetings of political psychologists to set up distinct panels, some dealing with cognition, others dealing with affect and emotion. (We, much to our chagrin, are always placed on the cognition panels.) This seems to us a false, and unfortunate, dichotomy. Although the cognitive models from which political psychologists borrow are often affect-free, affect and evaluation have long been an intrinsic part of political cognition research (see, for example, Fiske 1986; Judd and Krosnick 1989; Lusk and Judd 1988; Sears, Huddy, and Shaffer 1986; Sniderman, Brody, and Tetlock 1991). Many of the chapters in this volume continue this tradition by making explicit the central role of affect in political information processing. Affect, or "hot cognitions," are central to the Lodge and Boynton models, the McGraw-Steenbergen and Berent-Krosnick studies examine the conditions under which memory organization is dominated by evaluative concerns, and Judd and Downing's model provides a means of distinguishing between the affective feelings toward social groups and perceptions of the variability of those groups. We anticipate that political information-processing models will continue to take seriously the role of affect, and look forward to the day when criticisms of "too little affect!" are no longer raised against those adopting the information-processing approach.

5. *The construction of political judgment.* Finally, one of the important themes to emerge from the chapters in this volume is the distinction between "having" a preexisting opinion and "constructing" one on the spot from whatever associations are readily available at the moment the opinion question is asked (Boynton and Feldman articulate these distinctions most clearly). While the mechanisms driving these processes are not yet well understood, the notion that preferences and beliefs are often constructed, not merely revealed by consulting a master list in long-term memory, poses formidable methodological and conceptual consequences for research, whether we rely on survey respondents or experimental subjects. After all, why try to measure what may not exist? It would be foolish to accept unconditionally this pessimistic reworking of Converse's (1964) "nonattitudes" thesis. Rather, the behavioral decision theory literature points to a number of parameters—such as factors associated with the decision, the context, and the individual—that influence the strategies used to construct preferences (Payne, Bettman, and Johnson 1992). In keeping with McGuire's (1983) contextualist perspective on theory testing, a framework that underlies our repeated emphasis on the "conditions under which" various phenomena occur, incorporation of these contingency factors in political

cognition models should be a high priority as a means of delineating when and why "on the spot" opinion construction occurs.

NOTE

1. We certainly did not impose any restrictions on the use of the term *schema*, and we were as surprised as were a couple of early readers that a book dealing with political information processing could completely avoid using it (only Feldman, in chapter 11, even uses the term).

CHAPTER 2

Pictures in the Head: Memory Representations of Political Candidates

Kathleen M. McGraw and Marco Steenbergen

When Bill Clinton announced his candidacy for the presidency, he was an unknown entity to most Americans. His recognition level was low, and few people had an impression of what he was like as a person or political candidate. In the course of the nominating campaign, however, a veritable wealth of information about Clinton was reported by the media. By the time of the 1992 Democratic convention, a reasonable assumption is that the majority of adult Americans recognized his name, knew something—even if very little—about him, and had impressions of him as a presidential candidate. In order for these processes of learning and impression formation to occur, information about Clinton, either as reported by the media or as directly conveyed through personal appearances ("the world outside"), had to be converted into internal memory structures (Lippmann's 1922 "pictures in the head"). Our purpose here is to explore a number of unresolved issues concerning how these memory structures, or impressions, are organized. We examine a number of interrelated questions: Given the wealth of information about candidates available in the environment, to what types of information do people attend? How is that information represented in long-term memory? How does the information and memory structure influence citizens' judgments? Do citizens differing in levels of political sophistication vary in these processes? Because information is central to democratic politics, all of these are issues that are relevant to the study of political behavior.

We undertake several tasks in the chapter. First, we briefly lay out the theoretical framework guiding our work on candidate impressions. Next, we review the substantive and theoretical implications of two different organizational schemes that might characterize political memory, paying particular attention to information processing factors that might influence how impressions of political candidates are formed. We then describe measurement techniques that can be used to infer the organizational structure of impressions. Finally, we describe the results of an experiment designed to explore many of the important unresolved questions we identify.

Impressions as Associative Networks

The phrase "impression formation" implies that social impressions are the result of a dynamic process involving the building of some construct. The theoretical framework guiding our research on this constructive process draws on the family of associative network models popular among cognitive psychologists (Anderson 1983; Collins and Quillian 1969; Hastie 1986), and which have been adopted by political psychologists (Judd and Krosnick 1989; Lodge and McGraw 1991). In such models, knowledge structures in long-term memory are represented as configurations of nodes linked to one another in a network of associations. As initial information about a political candidate is encountered, a "person node" is established in memory (see Sedikides and Ostrom 1988 for evidence of the priority accorded organization along such "person gestalts"). As graphically portrayed in figure 1, as more information is acquired, additional "associative pathways" will be created between the superordinate person node and specific attributes (i.e., the vertical links in fig. 1). Many of the subordinate nodes will also be linked to each other (i.e., the horizontal links in fig. 1). The result of this dynamic building process is an *impression* of the target, "a cognitive representation of what we know and believe about another person" (Hamilton 1989, 239).

There are two critical principles involving impression formation that bear on the issues under consideration here. The first is that the links among the various pieces of information are neither random nor complete. Rather, the impression network reflects the perceiver's effort to impose structure on the assortment of facts that he or she has received. More concretely, links are established among information nodes that are activated simultaneously. Simultaneous activation occurs if the individual consciously recognizes that the nodes are related to each other, actively elaborates upon new information by thinking about it in reference to information already stored in the structure, or if external events somehow connect pieces of information that the individual may not spontaneously activate together.

The second principle is that information tends to be organized into conceptually similar clusters. A major focus of our research lies in identifying the dimensions that are used to organize those memory clusters. Let us return to the Bill Clinton example. When he first pierced our hypothetical citizen's consciousness, perhaps the first piece of information that was learned was that Clinton was a Democratic candidate for president. If sufficiently motivated, our citizen would make the mental effort to construct a memory structure, or impression, for Bill Clinton, and link that first piece of information to the superordinate person node. Imagine that over the course of the nominating campaign, the following additional attributes about

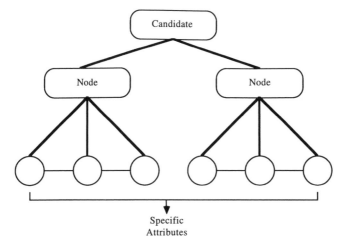

Fig. 1. Associative network structure

Bill Clinton were learned (that is, attended to and retained in long-term memory), in the following sequence: (1) he was a long-time governor of Arkansas; (2) he supports abortion rights; (3) he is in favor of tax relief for the middle class; (4) he is in favor of national health care; (5) he has been charged with marital infidelity; (6) he avoided military service during the Vietnam War; (7) he supported the United States's involvement in the Gulf War; (8) he supports capital punishment; (9) he has a reputation for trying to please everybody; (10) he is in favor of education reforms; (11) he plays the saxophone; (12) he was a Rhodes scholar.

How would these twelve pieces of information be organized in the impression network? A number of possibilities exist. We have chosen to focus upon two different organizational schemes that are relevant to enduring theoretical puzzles in the study of voting behavior. The first representational scheme, illustrated in figure 2a, differentiates between policy positions and personal attributes. Two distinct clusters are evident, one for Clinton's specific policy positions (e.g., stances on health care, capital punishment, etc.), the other for personal information (e.g., previous political experience, marital fidelity, musical hobby, etc.). In an earlier study, we examined a variety of ways in which political impressions could be organized (McGraw, Pinney, and Neumann 1991). The results of that study indicated that impressions tend to be organized according to this scheme, with two distinct clusters differentiating between policy positions and personal attributes stored in memory. Moreover, this representational scheme was most evident among political sophisticates, which would be expected. Within the associa-

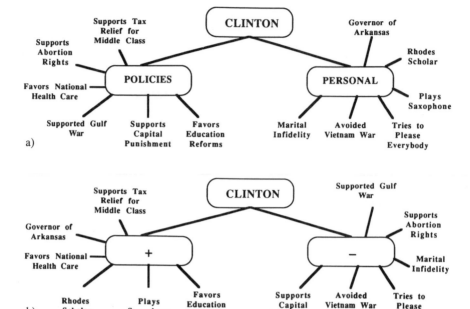

Fig. 2. Organizational schemes: a, by attribute type; b, by evaluative implications

tive network framework, it is reasonable to expect that because sophisticates are more involved in and knowledgeable about political affairs, they will have more nodes represented in memory, more and stronger links among the nodes, and, as a result, more systematic and better organized memory structures (Judd and Krosnick 1989).

An alternative representational strategy is not concerned with the substance of information, and, instead, based upon the evaluative implications drawn from the information. Simply, our citizen may encode and organize the information about Clinton in terms of its evaluative implications, with separate clusters for positive and negative information, as illustrated in figure 2b. "Positive" and "negative" are subjectively defined here and in the empirical results described below—it is the individual's personal affective reaction to the attributes that dictates the valence. We assume, as do most political network theorists, that affective "tags" are part of the attribute nodes (Fiske and Pavelchak 1986; Fiske 1986; Judd and Krosnick 1989; Lodge and McGraw 1991). The supposition of evaluative organization goes farther, in that it suggests that valence may exert a primary organizational influence on impressions. (Berent and Krosnick, in their work on policy attitude structure reported later in this volume, use the term "agreement-based structure" for this representational scheme.) As we shall detail below, there has been relatively little work on whether impressions are organized primarily along affective lines, with our own work on this topic yielding mixed results.

Theoretical and Substantive Implications of the Two Representational Structures

At this point, we consider some of the important questions that are raised when considering whether candidate impressions are organized along the personal-policy attribute dimension or the evaluative dimension.

Personal and policy attributes. Researchers and politicians have long wondered "Do voters vote for the person or for the policies?" In other words, are personal attributes or policy positions more important determinants of voters' decisions (Brady 1990)? Not surprisingly, there have been historical trends in how political scientists have answered this question. Dominated by rational choice models, the 1960s were characterized by an emphasis on issues as the determinant of the vote (see Kessel 1972 for a review of the issue-voting literature of this period). The increasing attention to social psychological models in the 1980s, on the other hand, resulted in a spate of research on the assessment and impact of political (usually presidential) character, focusing on the importance of personality traits in the candidate evaluation process (e.g., Kinder 1986; Kinder et al. 1980; Lau 1986, 1989; Markus 1982; Miller, Wattenburg, and Malanchuk 1986; Rahn et al. 1990; Stoker 1993; Stroh in this volume; Sullivan et al. 1991). A common theme of this research tradition is that just as impressions of "ordinary" people are largely trait-based, particularly for the case of impressions formed over an extended period of time (Park 1986), so, too, are the impressions of "nonordinary" political people. Most recently, researchers have accorded traits an even more important status, suggesting that trait inferences are made automatically, on the basis of issue positions (e.g., Rahn et al. 1990; Rapoport, Metcalf, and Hartman 1989).

In our view, it is unfortunate that the emphasis in the voting behavior literature on the relative impact of traits and issues on candidate evaluations has neglected serious consideration of how citizens process and represent the varieties of available information in order to form impressions of candidates. As we noted earlier, differentiating between policies and personal attributes appears to be a critical factor in the political impression formation process (McGraw et al. 1991). Why might this be a particularly useful—and commonly used—organizational strategy? One possible reason is that issue stances and personal information are the basic "stuff" of politics that are widely reported by the media. Citizens may come to learn through exposure to the media that these are the two critical dimensions on which candidates can and should be evaluated. Moreover, if as Lau (1986, 1989) has suggested, issues and candidate personality are two of the key generic schemata by which people appraise political stimuli, differentiating between these two types of attributes in regards to a specific political figure may provide a particularly efficient means of simplifying the evaluation process. Finally, differentiating between issues and personal information may serve distinct instrumental functions. That is, separate storage of issue positions may serve the utilitarian function of maximization of self-interest (Downs 1957), whereas separate storage of personal information, particularly character traits, may serve the instrumental function of allowing the citizen to predict the candidate's probable future performance in office (Kinder 1986; Page 1978).

Distinguishing between personal and policy information, as well as consideration of the evidence that sophistication is associated with the use of that representational scheme (McGraw et al. 1991), brings to mind a provocative set of results reported by Miller et al. (1986) and Lau (1986). Both found that better-educated citizens (education being a reasonable surrogate measure for sophistication) were more likely to make reference to personal characteristics in the open-ended "like-dislike" NES study questions. The conclusion that "elections are more likely to be 'personality contests' for college-educated voters" (Miller et al. 1986, 527) is provocative because it is contrary to the long-accepted and intuitively plausible "cognitive capacity" hypothesis proposed by Converse (1964). Namely, Converse suggested that better-educated people should be more likely to attend to policy information—in comparison to other types of information, and in comparison to the less educated—because the complexities of issue politics require a sufficient level of ability and motivation which would characterize only the most sophisticated citizens.

Although the results of these two studies (Lau 1986; Miller et al. 1986) are provocative and clearly counter to the cognitive capacity hypothesis, the NES survey data on which they are based compromise the confidence with which those conclusions can be accepted. That is, the NES data do not permit control for exposure to different types of information, nor do the "like-dislike" questions rigorously tap into the information that is available in long-term memory (in fairness, they were never intended to be used as memory measures). Thus, the status of the predictions linking sophistication with greater attention to policy (Converse 1964) or personal (Lau 1986; Miller et al. 1986) information is still an open question, one that we explore in a context where information exposure can be controlled, and what is available in memory rigorously assessed.

The evaluative dimension. It is widely accepted in social and political psychology that the processing of the evaluative implications of information is pervasive. For example, people appear to automatically process (before conscious recognition occurs) the subjective evaluation of social stimuli (Bargh et al. 1988; Fazio et al. 1986)), with negatively valenced information automatically attracting more attention than positively valenced information (Pratto and John 1991; see also Fiske 1980). Negative information also carries more weight in social (Skowronski and Carlson 1989) and political (Lau 1982, 1985) judgments. In addition to the automatic processing of the evaluative implications of information, a number of theoretical formulations suggest that affect is a feature attribute that may exert some organizational influence in memory (see Fiske and Taylor 1991 for a review). Similar assertions exist in the political psychology literature. For example, Judd and his colleagues (Judd and Krosnick 1989; Lusk and Judd 1988) have called for the incorporation of evaluative features into what have traditionally been affect-free representational models (see Sears, Huddy, and Shaffer 1986, and Sniderman, Brody, and Tetlock 1991 for additional arguments for incorporating affect into models of political judgment).

We take as a given that the evaluative processing of information is pervasive. Accordingly, it is only natural to pursue the question of the extent to which information is organized in memory along the evaluative dimension (as in fig. 2b). We have conducted a series of studies aimed at determining if and when evaluative organization occurs, with mixed results. The study on memory for a political candidate described earlier did not reveal any evidence of evaluative organization (McGraw et al. 1991). In contrast, evaluative organization was evident in a study examining memory for information about a public policy (taxes; McGraw and Pinney 1990). In accounting for the discrepant findings, an important procedural difference between the two studies (in addition to stimulus domain) must be considered, as it points to what may be a necessary condition for the occurrence of evaluative organization. In both studies, subjects were instructed to form an impression of the target (candidate or policy). However, in the tax policy study, subjects were also required to explicitly rate the information on an evaluative dimension as the information was learned, whereas in the candidate study, no such rating was elicited.

Assessing the impact of explicitly "rating" information along the evaluative dimension as it is encountered has both methodological and broader substantive implications. It is well known that the goals people have at the time they receive information have a tremendous impact on cognitive processes. The impression-formation goal, in particular, arguably the most common in social settings (Hastie and Park 1986), has pervasive effects, including enhanced recall, increased organization of impressions into psychologically meaningful categories, and facilitation of on-line processing (see Hastie, Park, and Weber 1984; and Fiske and Taylor 1991 for reviews). However, little is known about the actual mechanics of the encoding process during impression formation. How exactly is the stimulus information transformed into the mental representation? The instructions used to activate the impression-formation goal in experimental research vary across studies, but they typically involve, implicitly or explicitly, a prompt to evaluate the target along either a specific (e.g., suitability as a job candidate; Hastie and Park 1986) or global (e.g., likability; Lodge, McGraw, and Stroh 1989) dimension. Regardless of the dimension, the inherent evaluative aspect of impression formation would seem to implicate encoding information in terms of affective—positive and negative—reactions. If so, it is possible that experimental instructions that explicitly require evaluative encoding may actually elicit impression-formation processes that parallel their "natural" occurrence. On the other hand, it is equally plausible that the intrusiveness and artificiality of the procedures disrupt spontaneous impression-formation processes. One of the major purposes of the experiment described below was to examine the consequences of explicit evaluative encoding instructions, in order to determine whether this procedure disrupts or parallels "natural" (i.e., in the absence of experimental instructions) impression-formation processes.

The role of thought. Impressions are not stable structures, but rather, are continuously updated as new information is acquired. Moreover, even in the absence of exposure to new information, impressions are frequently modified, particularly if the individual thinks about the content of his or her impression. Consideration of role of thought is particularly important in the realm of politics, because, after all, (some) people reflect upon and talk about political candidates. Thinking about a candidate, once the impression has been formed, should result in a more cohesive and better organized structure, because the frequency and recency of activation principles (Fazio 1989) posit that the aspects of the impression structure that are thought about (brought into short-term memory) become stronger and more accessible (see also Tesser 1978).

Moreover, the social psychological literature suggests that the impact of subsequent thought should be particularly evident along the evaluative dimension. Theories of cognitive consistency suggest that a key principle for organizing and modifying attitudes is consistency along the "good/bad" dimension. Thinking about an attitude should lead one to try to resolve evaluative inconsistencies, because the experience of inconsistency is unpleasant. There is support for this hypothesis in the social psychological literature, with thought resulting in more extreme or polarized judgments because the underlying cognitive representation becomes more evaluatively consistent (Tesser 1978; Chaiken and Yates 1985). The thought-induced polarization effect is also facilitated by well-developed knowledge structures (or sophistication; Tesser and Leone 1977; Chaiken and Yates 1985; Lusk and Judd 1988).

Measurement of Memory Structure

A variety of measurement techniques can be used to infer how impressions are organized in memory. The two most common are response latencies (or reaction times; see Fazio 1990 for a good introduction) and the analysis of clustering patterns in free recall. We focus on the latter in this chapter.

Clustering in recall: The adjusted ratio of clustering measure. Associative network models assume that the manner in which information is organized in memory will affect the way in which it is later recalled. The process is modeled as follows: Following a prompt—either self-instigated or from an external source—to remember information about a political figure, the superordinate person node is accessed, and the vertical pathways traversed to recall the first piece of information. The nodes and links have different strength values associated with them that represent the accessibility from long-term memory—that is, the ease with which the information can be retrieved (Anderson 1983; Judd and Krosnick 1989; Lodge and McGraw 1991). Nodes with higher strength values have a greater probability of recall. These strength values are a function of a number of factors, including the frequency and recency of prior activation (Fazio 1989) and the subjective importance of the information (Krosnick 1989). After the first item is recalled, the retrieval process is assumed to traverse along the links in the network, with the sequence of recall determined by the strength of the associative pathways. If attributes have been organized in systematic clusters, then attributes from the same cluster should be recalled in succession, because links among those attributes exist. If information has been organized along the evaluative dimension, as in figure 2b, this process implies that positive items should be clustered systematically in one part of the recall sequence, and negative items in another part.

The adjusted ratio of clustering (ARC), proposed by Roenker, Thompson, and Brown (1971), is a measure of categorical clustering in free recall that has proven to be particularly useful in inferring memory organization in social psychology (Ostrom et al. 1981; Srull 1984), and increasingly in political psychology (Berent and Krosnick in this volume; McGraw and Pinney 1990; McGraw et al. 1991; Rahn in this volume). The ARC measures the extent to which information from the same category is recalled in sequence, beyond the level that would be expected by chance. The formula used to calculate the ARC score is:

$$ARC = [R - E(R)] / [MAX\ R - E(R)$$

where R is the number of within-category repetitions, $E(R)$ is the number of category repetitions expected by chance, and $MAX\ R$ is the maximum number of possible repetitions. $MAX\ R$ is equal to the total number of items recalled, N, minus the number of different categories that were recalled, k. $E(R)$ is equal to $[\Sigma m(i)^2/N] - 1$, where m is the number of items recalled from each category i.

Imagine that when we asked our hypothetical citizen to recall what she knows about Clinton, she "output" the twelve attributes listed earlier, and the evaluative features of the information she recalled (in sequence) would be represented as:

$$+, +, +, +, -, -, -, -, +, +, -, -.$$

The total number recalled, N, is equal to 12. The number of categories, k, is equal to 2, for recall of at least one item from each of the two valence categories. The maximum number of possible repetitions, $MAX\ R$, is equal to $N - k$, or 10. The number of observed repetitions, R, in this protocol is equal to 8. The expected number of repetitions, $E(R)$ is equal to $[(6^2 + 6^2)/12] - 1$, or 5. Substituting the appropriate values yields an ARC score along the evaluative dimension of .60.

Imagine that the same recall protocol can also be represented according to the substantive, or attribute, dimension (where I = issue and P = personal):

$$I, P, P, P, I, I, P, P, I, I, I, P.$$

Many of the parameters remain the same: $N = 12$, $k = 2$, $MAX\ R = 10$, and $E(R) = 5$. The observed number of repetitions here, however, is equal to 6. Substituting the appropriate values yields an attribute ARC score of .20.

How would these two values be interpreted? The ARC formula sets chance clustering at 0 and perfect clustering at 1. The .20 attribute ARC reflects a level of clustering that does not differ much from what would be expected by chance (although an aggregate mean of .20 with a large enough sample size and small enough variance may differ significantly from the chance value of 0).[1] The same protocol, on the other hand, reveals more systematic clustering along the evaluative dimension. We would conclude that this person's impression of Bill Clinton is organized along the evaluative, rather than the attribute, dimension.

A few additional points about the advantages and disadvantages of the

ARC measure. First, it tends to be independent of amount of recall, making it useful for comparing clustering among conditions varying in total recall (Murphy 1979). Second, the measure corrects for the number of organizational categories (k), making it possible to compare organizational schemes based on different numbers of categories. Third, the ARC assumes a unidimensional representation, meaning that organization, for example, along the evaluative or attribute dimensions can be examined separately but not simultaneously. Fourth, it is not a symmetrical indicator, as there is no absolute lower bound of -1.0. Negative scores are difficult to interpret, in that they suggest that the individual is using an organizational strategy different than the one posited by the investigator. Finally, and related to the last point, the ARC is not particularly amenable to exploratory analyses. Rather, the conceptual dimensions must be specified a priori by the investigator; the dimensions do not "emerge," as in Q-sort analyses (Brown 1980), nor are they left unspecified and idiosyncratic, as in the Scott sorting methodology (Scott, Osgood, and Peterson 1979).

Evaluative consistency. In addition to recall clustering, research on the representation of evaluative beliefs has utilized a second conceptualization, evaluative consistency (Judd and Lusk 1984; Lusk and Judd 1988). Evaluative consistency measures the extent to which an impression is characterized by a predominance of *either* positive *or* negative information. As with the ARC index, the measure is based on patterns evident in recall protocols. Following Lusk and Judd (1988), evaluative consistency can be measured by summing the number of positive attributes that are recalled about a candidate and subtracting the number of recalled negative attributes. This difference score is then divided by the total number of recalled attributes. Large positive values of this ratio are indicative of an impression dominated by positive attributes, whereas large negative values reflect an impression dominated by negative attributes. The absolute value of the ratio results in a direction-free indicator of evaluative consistency. The lower bound of the measure is 0, the upper bound is 1, and higher values reflect a predominance of either positive or negative information in memory, whereas lower values reflect evaluatively balanced memory structures.

Although we do not know of any previous investigations that have compared the two, evaluative consistency and evaluative clustering are logically independent. That is, the extent to which information is organized into positive or negative clusters does not reveal whether one type predominates over the other. For example, the recall protocol describe above, which evidenced a fairly substantial degree of evaluative clustering, would yield an evaluative consistency score of 0, because equal numbers of positive and negative attributes were recalled.

Overview

We conducted an experiment to explore these important issues concerning the structure of political impressions. In order to be able to control for the information to which people are exposed, a hypothetical candidate was created. The subjects learned about this candidate's attributes under a variety of conditions. Specifically, we manipulated the encoding task in order to explore the impact of explicitly rating the information along an evaluative dimension with impression-formation instructions not including that rating procedure. In addition, the task intervening between exposure and recall was varied in order to examine the impact of thought on memory and judgment processes. We also measured the subjects' level of political sophistication, in order to control for that important individual characteristic. We then examined the impact of these three information-processing factors—encoding task, thought, and sophistication—on the manner in which the candidate's attributes were organized in memory, focusing on the attribute type (policy versus personal information) and evaluative dimensions.

Method

The experimental subjects were 104 undergraduates enrolled in political science courses. They were randomly assigned to one of the six conditions representing the 3 (Encoding Task) × 2 (Intervening Task) between-subjects design (the manipulations are described fully below). The stimulus materials were identical to those used in our earlier candidate memory study (McGraw et al. 1991). The initial instructions stated that the purpose of the study was to examine how ordinary citizens learn about political candidates, that they would be learning about a candidate for Congress from eastern New York state named Howard Wilson, and that the information had been gathered from a candidate report provided by the League of Women Voters, "a nonpartisan organization whose goal is to provide voters with accurate and objective information about political candidates."

The encoding task manipulation was then implemented. Subjects in the *impression formation with evaluative encoding* condition (IF + EVAL) were told, "While you are reading the information, you should try to form an impression of Mr. Wilson—think about how much you like or dislike him as a candidate. On each card, you will find a rating scale, where the 'very −' means 'very negative' and 'very +' means 'very positive.' After you read each statement, you should indicate your reaction to it on the rating scale provided on the card." The scale had seven labeled response alternatives, anchored with "very +" and "very −."

Subjects in the *impression formation only* condition (IF ONLY) were given the identical impression formation instructions. However, they were not asked to react to the statements along any specified dimension. Thus, these subjects share the same processing objective with the IF + EVAL subjects, but they were not given any instructions specifying how they were to accomplish that goal. Consequently, we will be able to compare the impact of the evaluative rating procedure with impression formation not requiring that somewhat intrusive technique.

Finally, subjects in the *clarity encoding* condition (CE) were told, "While you are reading, you should think about whether each statement is a clear or ambiguous description of the candidate. After you read each statement, you should indicate your reaction to it on the rating scale provided on the card." Assessing the clarity of each piece of information has been found to inhibit the activation of the impression-formation goal (Lichtenstein and Srull 1987; Lodge, McGraw, and Stroh 1989). Inclusion of this condition allows for tests of the impact of the impression-formation objective on memory and judgment processes.

A packet of sixteen shuffled cards, each containing a single declarative sentence, was provided, and the subjects were asked to read through the cards one at a time, at their own pace. The random order of the shuffled cards eliminates the possibility of systematic order effects. The information consisted of eight issue positions (e.g., "Wilson is in favor of increasing funding for student loans") and eight personal attributes (e.g., "Wilson commands the respect of those who meet him"). The statements were completely balanced, in terms of evaluative (eight positive and eight negative) and partisan (eight stereotypic Democratic and eight stereotypic Republican) implications. The candidate himself was not identified as belonging to either party.

After the cards had been read, the intervening task manipulation was implemented. Subjects in the *thought* condition were told, "We have found that at this point in the experiment, people find it useful to have some time to think about the information they have learned .... Please use the next few minutes to think about the information you have just learned, and how it fits with your overall impression of Howard Wilson." In contrast, subjects in the *distractor* condition were told, "We have found that at this point in the experiment, people find it useful to let the information settle by completing a very different kind of task .... We would like you to use the next few minutes by listing as many of the fifty United States as you can."[2]

Both intervening tasks lasted three minutes. When that period was over, the subjects were asked to recall as much of the information about Wilson as possible; there was no time limit. They then responded to a number of questions that assessed impressions of the candidate, ratings of the sixteen statements on a number of dimensions, and indicators of political knowledge. Impressions were measured through two questions: "Overall, how favorable is your impression of Wilson?" and "How likely is it that you would vote for Wilson?" As the responses to these two questions were highly correlated ($r = .62$), they were averaged to created the impression variable. Consistent with recent recommendations (Fiske, Lau, and Smith 1990; Zaller 1990), we rely on political knowledge as an indicator of political sophistication. The political knowledge items required correct identification of the partisan affiliation of ten prominent political figures. The number of correct responses were summed and the resulting scale split at the sample median to form groups that were high and low in sophistication.

Results

Unless otherwise noted, the data were analyzed via 3 (Encoding Task) × 2 (Intervening Task) × 2 (Political Sophistication) analyses of variance (ANOVAs). When appropriate, the dependent variables were incorporated as repeated measures in multivariate ANOVAs.

What Kind of Information Is Recalled?

We begin by examining the overall amount, as well as the kind, of information (policy versus personal, and positive versus negative) that was recalled under the different processing conditions. The raw recall data were converted to percentages, reflecting the percentage of the available information of each type that was recalled.[3] The relevant results are summarized in table 1. We start with the impact of the Encoding Task. Consistent with previous research, recall was greater when the impression-formation processing objective was activated than when impression formation processing was inhibited through the clarity rating task ($F[2,92] = 30.33$, $p < .001$). This pattern holds for the probability of recalling each of the four more specific types of information (the main effect of encoding for each of those variables significant to at least the .001 level). Interestingly, the evaluative rating task accompanying the impression-formation goal neither hampered nor helped recall; in no instance did recall differ in the two impression-formation conditions.

    Turning now to the impact of sophistication: sophisticates tended to recall more information than nonsophisticates, although the effect was weak ($F[1,92] = 2.95$, $p < .09$). Although overall policies were more likely to be recalled than were personal attributes ($M = 55$ percent and 50 percent, respectively; MANOVA $F[1,92] = 4.48$, $p < .01$), this effect was contingent upon level of sophistication (Sophistication × Recall Measure interaction

$F[1,92] = 8.37$, $p < .01$). As table 1 indicates, sophisticates were equally likely to recall policy and personal information, whereas nonsophisticates were more likely to recall policy information over personal information. An alternate way of thinking about this interaction effect is evident from the correlational data. Specifically, sophistication (as a continuous variable) was positively related to recall for personal information ($r = .18$, $p < .05$), but negatively related to recall for policy information ($r = -.22$, $p < .05$). Thus, contrary to Converse's "cognitive capacity hypothesis" (1964), but consistent with the analyses of the NES data reported by Miller et al. (1986) and Lau (1986), in an information environment in which both types of information were equally available, sophisticates were more attentive to personal information, whereas nonsophisticates were more attentive to policy information.

Overall, negative information had an advantage in memory, relative to positive information ($M = 56$ percent and 50 percent, respectively; MANOVA $F[2,91] = 4.79$, $p < .05$), consistent with previous studies indicating that negative information attracts more attention than positive information (Fiske 1980; Pratto and John 1991). As with the attribute type analysis, this pattern was not affected by the manipulated processing factors, but was contingent upon sophistication (interaction $F[1,91] = 5.28$, $p < .05$). Although both groups were more likely to recall negative information, the memorial advantage of negative information relative to positive information was greater among nonsophisticates.

Finally, none of the recall variables were significantly influenced by the intervening task manipulation (that is, thought), as a main effect or in interaction with the other two predictor variables.

TABLE 1.   Recall as a Function of Encoding Task and Level of Sophistication

	Encoding Task			Sophistication Level	
	IF ONLY	IF + EVAL	Clarity	Low	High
Total					
recall	.58	.56	.42	.51	.54
Attribute type:					
Policy	.61	.56	.46	.56	.54
Personal	.54	.56	.38	.46	.54
Evaluative type:					
Positive	.57	.58	.38	.51	.49
Negative	.63	.62	.42	.58	.53

Note: Entries are the mean percentage of items recalled overall and the percentage for each attribute and evaluative type.

How is information organized in memory?

Memory organization was assessed through both the clustering and evaluative consistency measures described earlier. We consider the results concerning clustering in recall first. Two different ARC scores were computed from each subject's recall protocol: (1) an evaluative ARC score, based on three categories (positive, negative, and neutral), subjectively defined; and (2) an attribute ARC score, based on two categories (personal and policy information), objectively defined. The ARC scores were analyzed as repeated measures in a multivariate ANOVA; the results are summarized in the top two panels of table 2.

TABLE 2.   Organization in Memory as a Function of Encoding and Intervening Tasks

	DV = Attribute ARC		
	Intervening Task		
Encoding Task	Thought	Distractor	Marginal
IF ONLY	.38[a]	.17	.28[a]
IF + EVAL	.44[a]	.28[a]	.37[a]
Clarity	.12	.03	.07
	.32[a]	.16[a]	.24[a]
	DV = Evaluative ARC		
	Intervening Task		
Encoding Task	Thought	Distractor	Marginal
IF ONLY	.16	.15	.15
IF + EVAL	.22	−.03	.11
Clarity	.01	−.05	−.02
	.13	.05	.08
	DV = Evaluative Consistency		
	Intervening Task		
Encoding Task	Thought	Distractor	Marginal
IF ONLY	.17	.26	.22
IF + EVAL	.17	.20	.19
Clarity	.37	.26	.31
	.23	.24	.24

Note:
[a]Mean ARC scores significantly different from chance clustering at the $p < .05$ level.

A number of effects are noteworthy. The first is the influence of encoding task. Consistent with previous research, the two impression-formation conditions resulted in better memory organization (collapsing across both ARC measures, $M = .21$, and .24 for the IF ONLY and IF + EVAL conditions, respectively) than the clarity encoding task ($M = .01$, $F[2,91] = 3.23$, $p < .05$). In no instance was a significant degree of organization evident when the impression-formation objective was inhibited. Organization was also enhanced with the opportunity to think about the information prior to recall, in contrast to being distracted ($M = .23$ and .08, respectively; $F[1,91] = 4.25$, $p < .05$), consistent with the argument that thought results in a tighter and stronger organization of stimulus attributes (Tesser 1978). The encoding and intervening task factors did not interact.

What do the data indicate about the prevalence of organization along the attribute and evaluative dimensions? Across all conditions, information was more likely to be organized along the attribute dimension than the evaluative dimension (ARC $M = .24$, and .08, respectively; $F[1,91] = 7.95$, $p < .01$), consistent with the results of our earlier study (McGraw et al. 1991). Of particular importance for the present undertaking is the finding that this pattern did *not* vary under the different encoding tasks (Encoding Task × ARC Measure interaction $F < 1$), indicating that organization along the evaluative dimension was *not* enhanced by the evaluative encoding task.

The dominance of organization along the attribute dimension was most evident among sophisticates (ARC Measure × Sophistication interaction $F[1,91] = 4.91$, $p < .05$), also replicating previous results (McGraw et al. 1991). Sophisticates exhibited significant levels of attribute clustering, and essentially no evaluative clustering ($M = .30$ and .03, respectively). In contrast, nonsophisticates demonstrated less systematic evidence of organization along the attribute dimension ($M = .19$, $p < .05$), and more evidence of organization along the evaluative dimension ($M = .13$, $p < .05$). In fact, the only condition in which a significant amount of evaluative clustering was evident was in the IF ONLY encoding condition among nonsophisticates ($M = .32$; this value also differs reliably from the amount of evaluative clustering, $M = .03$, observed in the rest of the sample, $t[101] = 2.40$, $p < .05$). Thus, to the extent evaluative memory organization was evident, it tended to occur among the less sophisticated, who processed the information with the goal of forming an impression.

Evaluative consistency. The measure of evaluative consistency was computed as proposed by Lusk and Judd (1988), and as summarized above. The first result of note is that evaluative consistency was independent of the clustering scores ($r = .05$ and .18, both nonsignificant, for the attribute and evaluative ARC scores, respectively). Thus, the two types of measures provide distinct information about the organization of information in memory.

As evident from the data presented in the bottom panel of table 2, memory was more evaluatively consistent in the CE condition than in the two impression formation conditions ($F[2,92] = 3.05$, $p < .05$). Thus, while impression formation increased the likelihood of organization into conceptually similar clusters (as evident from the ARC score analyses), it also *minimized* the extent to which memory was dominated by recall of valenced—either positive or negative—information. Because both the ARC scores and evaluative consistency are measures of memory organization, this reversal may appear to be paradoxical. However, consideration of the deliberately balanced nature of the stimulus materials used in this study can account for the evaluative consistency results. To the extent that impression formation requires a careful consideration of the evaluative implications of all available information, memory for this particular candidate should have been balanced when the impression-formation objective was activated, because he was characterized by an equal number of positive and negative attributes. This was the case. In circumstances when the information environment is more slanted toward eliciting primarily positive or negative evaluations of the individual attributes, we would not expect this relationship to hold. In other words, evaluative consistency under impression-formation conditions should parallel (although not necessarily in a strictly veridical fashion) the information environment.

This interpretation also suggests attentional mechanisms are an important determinant of evaluative consistency, in that the subjects had to focus their attentional resources on the individual attributes when forming impressions of the candidate. A significant Encoding Task × Sophistication interaction ($F[2,92] = 3.83$, $p < .05$) is consistent with this line of reasoning. Evaluative consistency among nonsophisticates did not differ in the three encoding conditions. In contrast, sophisticates, who presumably possess the attentional capacities and motivation to process information carefully, exhibited relatively balanced memory in the two impression-formation conditions ($M = .17$ for both) and a substantial degree of evaluative consistency in the CE condition ($M = .41$).

Finally, although the ANOVA did not reveal any significant differences due to the intervening task factor, a subsequent inspection of the cell means revealed a pattern that is also congruent with the attentional argument outlined above. Compared to the level of evaluative consistency observed in the distractor task conditions (which did not vary as a function of processing objective, $M = .24$), given the opportunity to think about the candidate *increased* evaluative consistency when the impression formation goal was inhibited (CE $M = .37$), but *decreased* evaluative consistency when the impression-formation goal was activated (M for the two IF conditions = .17; the difference between these two means within the thought condition is significant; $t[52] = 3.16$, $p < .01$). Although the thought-induced polarization literature suggests that thought should increase the evaluative consistency of information stored in memory (Chaiken and Yates 1985; Tesser 1978), our results indicate that, in a balanced information environment, thought following impression formation minimizes evaluative consistency. In sum, it appears that the nature of the information environment, in conjunction with information-processing goals, places constraints on the thought-induced polarization effect (Lieberman and Chaiken 1991).

Does Organization Matter? Judgmental Consequences

Although it is generally agreed that the study of cognition should be able to inform us about the determinants of important decisions and behaviors, social memory research has only recently begun to turn to questions of how judgments, inferences, and choices are derived from cognitive representations (Ostrom 1989). We explored two important judgment processes: on-line processing and impression extremity.

On-line processing. An important recent distinction in the candidate-evaluation literature has been whether and when evaluations are made "on-line" (at the time information is acquired) or are "memory-based" (computed at the time a judgment is required; Hastie and Park 1986; Hastie and Pennington 1989; Lodge et al. 1989; McGraw, Lodge, and Stroh 1990; see Lodge in this volume for a discussion). We have already seen that sophisticates are more likely to recall personal information and less likely to recall policy information when both are equally available. If sophisticates view personal attributes as more important and/or informative, they should also accord those factors more weight in the judgment process. We estimated the prevalence of on-line and memory-based processing in the standard fashion, but created separate indicators for personal and policy information.[4] The impact of the two sets of memory-based and on-line processing indicators on evaluations of the candidate was then examined. The results of those analyses are summarized in table 3.

The sample sizes are small, resulting in marginal significance levels. Nevertheless, the results are suggestive. Consistent with the results presented earlier, on-line processing among nonsophisticates was dominated by the policy information, whereas on-line processing among sophisticates was dominated by personal information. The recalled information of either sort had a negligible impact on the impressions, providing, as would be expected (Hastie and Park 1986; Lodge et al. 1989), little evidence of memory-based processing when impression formation was an objective.

Impression extremity. What of the judgmental consequences associated with evaluative organization? Because the organization measures are direction-free indicators, there is no reason to expect any of them to be related to final evaluations per se. Rather, these indicators are more likely to be related to the extremity of those evaluations. A fairly extensive literature suggests that the evaluative structure of an impression is associated with the extremity of social judgments, albeit in complex ways (see Lusk and Judd 1988 and Millar and Tesser 1986 for reviews). For example, the thought-polarization phenomenon described above is mediated by evaluative consistency (Tesser 1978; Chaiken and Yates 1985). In the political realm, sophisticates exhibit more evaluatively consistent impressions of political figures; evaluative consistency, in turn, is associated with more extreme candidate evaluations (Lusk and Judd 1988). Impression extremity is relevant to models of voting behavior, because it is an indicator of the strength of the voter's attitude toward the candidate. Attitude strength, in turn, is an important determinant of subsequent behavior (Krosnick and Abelson 1991).

An impression extremity measure was created by folding the impression dependent variable at the sample mean, which coincidentally was equivalent to the scale midpoint. The relationship between the three memory organization measures and impression extremity was then explored. Consistent with much of the data presented to this point, preliminary analyses suggested that the relationship between the two evaluative organization measures and impression extremity varied as a function of level of sophistication. Accordingly, we estimated the following equation, which incorporated the appropriate interaction terms between sophistication and the evaluative representational measures:

Impression Extremity = $\beta0$ + $\beta1$ Percentage Recalled + $\beta2$ Sophistication + $\beta3$ Intervening Thought + $\beta4$ Evaluative Consistency + $\beta5$ Evaluative ARC + $\beta6$ Attribute ARC + $\beta7$ Sophistication × Evaluative Consistency + $\beta8$ Sophistication × Evaluative ARC + error.

TABLE 3.   On-Line and Memory-Based Processing, as a Function of Information Type and Political Sophistication

	Low Sophisticates	High Sophisticates
On-line indicators		
Personal information	−.04	.31*
Issue information	.24*	.07
Memory-based indicators		
Personal information	.08	−.05
Issue information	.01	−.10

Note: The entries are third-order partial correlation coefficients between each of the predictor variables and impressions of the candidate, controlling for the effects of the remaining three predictors. Subjects in the clarity encoding condition were omitted from these analyses.

* $p < .15$

The results are summarized in table 4.

The results are suggestive of the manner in which evaluative organization is related to impression extremity. Across all subjects, clustering along the evaluative dimension tended to be associated with more extreme impressions, particularly—as the marginally significant negative interaction suggests—among the nonsophisticated. On the other hand, evaluative consistency was weakly associated with more extreme impressions among sophisticates, consistent with Lusk and Judd's (1988) findings. Inspection of the within-cell correlation matrix revealed that the evaluative consistency-judgment extremity relationship among sophisticates was particularly prominent following thought ($r = .50$), but nonexistent after the distractor task ($r = .02$). In short, both evaluative organization measures tended to be associated with more extreme impressions, with the measure-specific effects dependent upon level of sophistication.

Discussion

The results of this experiment shed light on the impact of three important information processing factors—encoding, subsequent thought, and sophistication—on the structure of impressions of political candidates. Consistent with the results of a number of studies in the social psychological literature, activation of the impression-formation goal in this study had a variety of consequences. These included enhanced recall and more organized impressions, as well as impressions characterized by more evaluative balance, suggesting that the impression-formation goal focused attention on the balanced nature of this particular candidate's attributes.

The interesting, albeit null, result involving information encoding is that there were *no* discernible differences between the two impression-for-

TABLE 4. Memory Organization and Impression Extremity

Predictors	B/SE	Beta
Percentage recalled	−.23/.78	−.04
Sophistication	.01/.04	.04
Intervening thought	−.06/.17	−.05
Evaluative consistency	−.43/.77	−.12
Evaluative ARC	.54/.33	.37*
Attribute ARC	−.04/.19	−.03
Soph. × evaluative con.	.17/.16	.26
Soph. × evaluative ARC	−.09/.06	−.34*

Note: The entries in the first column are unstandardized regression coefficients, with standard errors; the entries in the second column are standardized regression coefficients. Subjects in the clarity encoding condition were omitted from these analyses.

* $p < .12$

mation conditions. Requiring the subjects to rate the candidate's attributes as they were initially encountered along the evaluative dimension did not disrupt the more "natural" impression-formation processes in any way. This is consistent with the view that processing information in terms of its evaluative implications is an integral and automatic part of impression formation. In terms of methodological implications, our recommendation is ultimately one of using common-sense. On the one hand, these data suggest that the "rating-while-learning" procedure, along the evaluative dimension, does not disrupt normal impression-formation processes, and if time is a scarce commodity, this information could be obtained with this procedure at initial exposure. On the other hand, researchers concerned with the external validity of their procedures would be well advised to be wary of using the technique, because, after all, people in the "real world" do not come equipped with seven-point rating scales, and it is usually a fairly simple matter to obtain the same information in a less artificial manner later in an experimental session.

If evaluative encoding is indeed an inherent aspect of impression formation, how can we account for the fact that this study yielded little evidence of clustering along the evaluative dimension, even under a condition (IF + EVAL) that should have been particularly conducive to the production of that organizational pattern? At this juncture (given the similar absence of evaluative clustering in the McGraw et al. 1991 study), we would have to conclude that the evaluative dimension does not exert a dominant influence on the organization of impressions of political candidates.[5] To the extent that people care about a variety of characteristics of their potential leaders—prior experience, character, issue positions, appearance, linkages to various social groups—a simple evaluative organizational scheme apparently serves no useful purpose in structuring political impressions.

Because impressions are dynamic structures that can be modified even without exposure to new information, we also explored the impact of subsequent thought. Though its effects were not nearly as pervasive, thought exerted an influence similar to the impression-formation processing objective, particularly in terms of producing a more organized and evaluatively balanced impression network. Thus, the more one thinks about a political candidate, the more coherent and organized the impression becomes. In addition, replicating Lusk and Judd's (1988) earlier results, thought appears to strengthen the relationship between evaluative consistency and impression extremity among sophisticates.

Probably the most striking results from this experiment are those involving individual differences in level of political sophistication. As Iyengar has noted, "political choice is inherently reductionistic" (1990, 181). Our data suggest that level of sophistication plays a crucial role in determining which strategy is used to reduce the complexity involved in such choices. Several results support the conclusion that the impressions of nonsophisticates are strongly shaped by the evaluative implications of information. First, to the limited extent evaluative clustering in memory was evident, it occurred among the nonsophisticates, who had the goal of forming an impression. Moreover, the relationship between evaluative clustering and impression extremity was more evident among these subjects. Third, they were more likely to recall a preponderance of negative information (relative to positive information), suggesting that less sophisticated citizens may be more subject to negativity biases in political judgment (Lau 1982, 1985). The role of affect among nonsophisticates is also consistent with evidence that these individuals are more subject to projection biases, in comparison to sophisticates (Lodge et al. 1989). More generally, these data support the claim of Sniderman et al. (1991) that nonsophisticates are particularly likely to reason about politics in an affect-driven manner: "So far as the less sophisticated are concerned, affect can serve as a calculational crutch" (Sniderman et al. 1991, 8). The term *crutch,* of course, has a pejorative connotation, one that Sniderman et al. (1991) do not intend, as the remainder of their treatment is admirably evenhanded in its consideration of differences due to sophistication. Rather, their point, which is supported by our research, is that nonsophisticates use affect as a heuristic to simplify their political world.

Sophisticates, on the other hand, appeared to be less "distracted" by evaluative concerns. Rather, their impressions were predominantly organized around the basic "stuff" of politics, namely, policy positions and personal characteristics. One of the most intriguing results from this study involves the differences between high and low sophisticates in the recall and use of these two types of information. Namely, sophistication was associated with increased recall of personal attributes and diminished recall of policy information. Moreover, personal attributes dominated on-line processing among sophisticates, whereas policy information dominated on-line processing among nonsophisticates. These findings have relevance for democratic theory, which, either implicitly or explicitly, has posited that policy stances ought to drive citizens' voting decisions. The clearest expression of this can be found in rational choice models, particularly in the guise of spatial theories of voting (see Enelow and Hinich 1984; Wahlke 1991). At the same time, however, theorists have been skeptical about whether ordinary people are capable of such policy-based reasoning (Schumpeter 1950). The expectation thus established is that while every citizen ought to pay attention to issue politics, only the most sophisticated are capable of doing so. In short, attainment of the democratic ideal is reserved in practice—so theory suggests—for the most sophisticated citizens.

But in our study, we find evidence for exactly the opposite: it is not sophisticates who recall polices and bring them to bear on candidate evaluations, but the nonsophisticates who do so. This suggests that ordinary people may be able to deal with policy issues, broadening the applicability of the democratic ideal. On the other hand, the evidence that sophisticates do not primarily focus on policies (see also Lau 1986; Miller et al. 1986) casts doubt on the normative power of this ideal. Sophisticates may not pay much attention to the issues, perhaps because they realize that politicians oftentimes merely take positions (Mayhew 1974), and do not live up to their promises. For the sophisticated citizen, personal characteristics may be a much more reliable cue about a candidate's potential as a politician than the issues he or she espouses. Because our college-aged subjects have come of age in an era when media coverage of political campaigns is increasingly dominated by personality and character issues, it seems probable that sophisticated citizens (who pay more attention to media coverage of campaigns) may learn to focus on personal characteristics from the media. In short, the picture that emerges from this study is that sophisticated citizens may not see the democratic ideal of issue politics as particularly valid in contemporary democracy.

All told, we are increasingly persuaded that individual differences captured by the sophistication construct are a critical determinant of impression-formation processes, in particular, and political reasoning, in general (see Rahn et al. 1990, for a contrary view). We concur with Sniderman et al. (1991) that the "presupposition of causal heterogeneity" due to sophistication is likely to be a fruitful principle in future research on political reasoning.

Our data also begin to shed some light on the consequences of mental representations for candidate evaluations, in particular, the extremity of those evaluations. Ironically, the dominant organizational strategy in this study (differentiating between personal and policy information) had no impact on impressions, as far as we were able to ascertain. This is actually not surprising. Because evaluations of candidates are by definition primarily affective judgments, operationalizing the attribute-type memory structure in a manner devoid of affective connotations, as we have done, would not be expected to reveal a direct and simple relationship to those judgments. However, evaluative organization, both in terms of clustering and consistency, was associated, albeit weakly, with impression extremity. The evaluative consistency-impression extremity relationship evident among the sophisticated subjects has been demonstrated previously (Lusk and Judd 1988), and is probably due to the overall evaluative redundancy of the attributes stored in memory. The evaluative clustering-impression extremity relationship—with the caveat that this organizational strategy was rare—may lead to more extreme evaluations, because the evaluative implications of the information are doubly encoded: as the "headers" on the subordinate clusters and as the individual attribute "tags." Although our interpretation is speculative, the result itself is important, because there have been few attempts to link ARC scores with judgmental or behavioral consequences in the social or political person memory literatures (Rahn in this volume is an exception).

A final implication of our research concerns the constraints imposed by the information environment on impression-formation processes. This is an obvious, but frequently overlooked, proposition (see Rahn in this volume for a discussion). Our hypothetical candidate was deliberately portrayed to be balanced, in terms of the types of attributes made known about him and the evaluative connotations of those attributes. Consequently, the resulting impressions were, for the most part, evaluatively balanced, reflecting a more or less veridical representation. Similarly, memory structures differentiating between personal and policy information are only possible if citizens are exposed to a sufficient amount of information about both of these types of attributes. Determination of the "veridicality" of political impressions, and consideration of the conditions under which impressions systematically deviate from that criterion necessarily require evidence about the nature of the information environment. A real challenge for extending research on memory for candidates in the world of real politics lies in specifying the types of information citizens encounter in the course of forming impressions about those candidates.

Recommendations for the Future

In this final section, we briefly recommend two issues that future research might profitably address, as we view our work as only a preliminary attempt at specifying how information about political candidates is represented in memory. The first issue concerns the assessment of hierarchical memory structures. If, as our research indicates, impressions of political candidates are structured along the policy, versus personal, attribute dimension, it is certainly plausible that these two categories are, in actuality, superordinate nodes under which more specific subclasses of information are organized. The subcategories for policy information might include separate clusters for foreign policy, domestic, and "moral" issue stands, whereas the subcategories for personal information might include separate categories for family, professional background, and the core dimensions of political character inferences (i.e., competence, leadership, integrity, and empathy; Kinder 1986).

Our stimulus materials were not sufficiently complex to examine these possibilities, but we anticipate that research designed to examine hierarchical memory representations will yield valuable insights.

A related issue reflects a limitation of the ARC measure. Specifically, the ARC score requires the experimenter to define nonoverlapping conceptual categories (i.e., policies versus personal information, positive versus negative attributes), and the simultaneous consideration of multiple categories is not possible. Political impressions may be more complex than this "either-or" conceptualization implies. Friendly (1977, 1979) has developed an alternative memory organization measure that overcomes this problem. The technique results in a hierarchical tree structure similar to that obtained through multidimensional scaling techniques (see Srull 1984 for further discussion). Although, to our knowledge, this technique has not been used in either social or political cognition research, it would appear to be capable of determining the existence of impressions organized according to multiple, overlapping conceptual categories.

In conclusion, our hope is that the issues we have discussed in this chapter, and the analyses we reported serve as a heuristic tool to stimulate further empirical work on representational issues in the political realm. Such work will simultaneously enrich theories of candidate evaluations, of concern to political scientists, and theories of impression formation, of concern to social psychologists.

NOTES

This research was facilitated by a Dr. Nuala McCann Drescher award to Kathleen McGraw. We are grateful to Milton Lodge for his helpful comments on a previous version of this chapter.

1. In determining whether a sample ARC mean is significantly different from the chance level of 0, 95 percent or 99 percent confidence intervals are constructed. If the lower bound of the confidence interval is greater than 0, the conclusion that the observed level of clustering is significantly different from chance is warranted.

2. These instructions have been used with success in other experimental studies (cf. Wyer, Budesheim, and Lambert 1990).

3. In these and subsequent analyses, the evaluative measures are based on the individual subjective ratings of the information, not aggregate ratings. Accordingly, the positive and negative recall percentage variables are based on the number of each type recalled divided by the total number of the information statements the subject evaluated as positive or negative. These two variables do not average into, or directly correspond to, the total recall variable, because items evaluated as neutral (neither positive or negative) were omitted from the analyses.

4. The on-line measure for personal information is the mean of the evaluative

ratings of all the presented personal attributes, whereas the on-line measure for the policy information is the mean of the evaluative ratings of all presented policy positions. Similarly, the memory-based measure for personal information is the mean of the evaluative ratings of just the personal information that was recalled, whereas the memory-based measure for policy information is the mean of the evaluative ratings of just the policy information that was recalled. We restricted these analyses to the two impression-formation conditions, as activation of the impression-formation processing objective is a necessary condition for on-line processing (Hastie and Park 1986; Lodge et al. 1989).

5. Evaluative organization in memory for information related to policies or other nonpersonal attitude objects may be more common, a conclusion that is consistent with the McGraw and Pinney (1990) results. See Berent and Krosnick (in this volume) for a discussion of the literature pertaining to the evaluative organization of attitude structures.

CHAPTER 3

Candidate Evaluation in Complex Information Environments: Cognitive Organization and Comparison Processes

Wendy M. Rahn

Vote choice is a complicated decision task. Particularly in visible elections such as the race for the presidency, citizens are exposed to considerable information, however incidental (Popkin 1991), about the two major party nominees. Over the course of a campaign, this information will involve various dimensions of appraisal: governmental performance; policy differences; partisan images; and the background, experience, families, and personal qualities of the candidates themselves. Constrained by well-known limitations on information processing and usually lacking in motivation, the voter would seem to have a rather acute problem in integrating information in a way that is useful for political decision making.

As documented by behavioral decision literature on choice processes (see Hogarth and Einhorn 1992; Payne, Bettman, and Johnson 1990) and the social cognition literature on person impressions (see Fiske and Taylor 1991), information-processing strategies are adapted to task characteristics. Task complexity often requires that individuals forgo more comprehensive strategies in favor of routines that are less taxing on cognitive resources, unless individuals are particularly expert in a domain or are highly motivated. My collaborators and I have suggested that the complexity of political choice leads voters to simplify the task of candidate appraisal by relying on strategies they have developed for use in everyday life (Rahn et al. 1990). An important component of our model is an argument that voters are aided in task simplification by features of the political environment, in some circumstances. Our model assumes that voters will adopt a cognitive strategy that leads them to summarize the more specific information they acquire about the candidates into a series of trait judgments. These trait judgments, in turn, produce affective reactions, which then lead, in a straightforward way, to a voting decision.

In the original statement of our model, we were not explicit about the

43

processes by which the more specific information voters learn about candidates is transformed into the more abstract trait and affective judgments that ultimately drive vote choice. A number of different theoretical relationships between memory and judgment are consistent with our model and our empirical evidence. Conceivably, though unlikely for most voters, in our view, the entire process could be memory-based, in which only the episodic information voters learn about the candidates is stored in memory. Trait judgments would have to be computed from the recall of specific information, and, in turn, global evaluations would be extracted from the trait judgments. A "pure" on-line strategy is also possible: both trait judgments and affect could be generated at the time of information acquisition. Using this processing strategy, an evaluation tally would be constantly updated in memory, and voters would simply retrieve their tallies in order to make their choices.

As noted by Hastie and Pennington (1989) and Lodge (in this volume), the on-line versus memory-based distinction is overly simplified. Our model, for example, is also consistent with the hybrid strategy in which voters abstract trait judgments on-line from the information they receive about candidates (see Park 1989). However, the generation of summary evaluative judgments may be delayed until sometime later, in which case voters would retrieve the trait judgments from memory, but not the raw input data, and compute judgments based on these personality inferences. Hastie and Pennington (1989) refer to this type of process as an inference-memory-based judgment. In another hybrid model, on-line judgments and specific information may be recalled together, in order to make decisions. Consistent with this latter possibility, in our survey work we found that overall summary affect toward the candidates was not sufficient to account for all of the variance in voters' choices (see Rahn et al. 1990). Party identification still had a direct effect on choice, unmediated through trait judgments and affect.

Recent experimental and survey evidence confirms that there is likely to be considerable heterogeneity across voters in the relationship between memory and judgment. For example, in experimental studies, political sophisticates have been shown to process more on-line than novices, when exposed to information about an unfamiliar candidate (McGraw, Lodge, and Stroh 1990; Rahn, Aldrich, and Borgida 1992). Using data collected during the 1990 gubernatorial election in Ohio, Jon Krosnick, Marijke Breuning, and I have shown that voters who delay their decisions are more likely to use memory-based processes to arrive at their candidate evaluations, in comparison to voters who reached their decisions early in the campaign (Rahn, Krosnick, and Breuning 1992).

If there are some voters for whom candidate evaluations are produced through memory-based processes, then an important next step in understanding how these types of judgments are produced is examining how memory for candidate information is organized. If all voters were to process information completely on-line, there would seem to be little use in studying the role of cognitive organization in candidate evaluation, for organization would have no mediational role in candidate evaluation under such circumstances. To the extent that candidate judgments have some memory-based components to them, however, voters' memory representations for political candidate information have the potential to affect how voters arrive at their overall assessments and make their choices. The next section develops this more argument fully. I will present some hypotheses about what factors influence the organization of political candidate memory and some arguments about why organization might be important for candidate-evaluation processes. I then present an experiment designed to test some of these ideas, and present the results of this investigation. I conclude with some general remarks about the current state of cognitive models of vote choice processes.

Context and Candidate Evaluation

Voters acquire information about political candidates in a variety of settings. As we have argued elsewhere, processes of candidate evaluation may be importantly conditioned by features of the context (see, further, Rahn et al. 1990; Sullivan et al. 1990). For example, the impact of the quantity and quality of information has been discussed by several students of vote choice. Without sufficient information, voters cannot form well-defined impressions of the candidates. This seems to be the challenger's fate in many races for the U.S. House (Jacobson 1992), and in some uncompetitive Senate elections (Westlye 1991). Furthermore, if candidates are ambiguous about their policy positions, there is more berth for misperception biases and cognitive heuristics to operate (Page and Brody 1972; Krosnick 1990a; Stroh 1989).

In addition, a more subtle constraint imposed by the context of candidate evaluation may inhere in the *structure* of information. Some information environments are simple. For example, a presidential nominee's acceptance speech, while often containing considerable information, is nevertheless highly person-centered. By contrast, consider the setting of a political candidate debate. The debate context is more complex, not only because the volume of information may be greater, but also because a debate features at least two people presenting information on a number of different dimensions, usually in some alternating format. Early televised debates among the contenders for the 1992 Democratic nomination, for example, included as many as six participants.

Political candidate debates are examples of multiperson, multiattribute environments. Social psychological research suggests that the processing of information in these more complex settings may differ from the processing of information in simpler environments (see, e.g., Pryor and Ostrom 1981; Devine and Ostrom 1985; Sedikides, Devine, and Fuhrman 1991). The picture that emerges from this literature is that in processing multitarget information, individuals match their cognitive strategies to the aspects of the task environment, including the structure of information.

When individuals receive information about only one person, it is usually assumed that this information is organized into a person category, a knowledge structure stored in memory in which the information about the target is connected to a single, superordinate "person node" (see McGraw and Steenbergen, in this volume). Various information-processing tasks, such as memory for the information and judgments about the stimulus person, are facilitated by this type of cognitive organization. It is less clear that this person-based preference for cognitive organization extends into multiperson settings; other "organizing principles" may suggest themselves. Rather than individuating multiple targets in memory, perceivers, for example, may use attributes about people (e.g., gender or occupation) or relationships (e.g., married couples) as a way to organize the information about the people they meet (see Sedikides, Olsen, and Reis 1993). In these sorts of representational structures, person nodes would be subordinate to other kinds of cognitive categories.

John Pryor, Thomas Ostrom, and their colleagues have conducted a number of studies designed to investigate whether person-based cognitive organization is a "privileged" strategy in multitarget settings (for a comprehensive review, see Sedikides and Ostrom 1988). While there is some disagreement over whether cognitive organization according to person schemas is naturally favored over other structural possibilities (see Sedikides and Ostrom 1988, 1990; Mullen and Cooper 1989), a number of studies have located factors that affect the extent to which complex social information is organized into separate person categories. Perceivers' processing objectives (Srull 1983; Sedikides, Devine, and Fuhrman 1991); the structure of the stimulus information, in particular, whether the information is blocked around individual targets or blocked around descriptive attributes or categories (Srull 1983; Devine and Ostrom 1985; Sedikides, Devine, and Fuhrman 1991); whether targets are familiar (Pryor and Ostrom 1981; Pryor et al. 1982; Pryor et al. 1983); and the number of targets and the attributes per target contained in the stimulus field (Srull 1983) all appear to influence the degree to which multiple targets are individuated in memory.

Given that most vote-choice settings are at least dual-target environments, social cognition research suggests that candidate-based cognitive organization may not be the only viable representational strategy. The obvious alternative to candidate-based cognitive organization would be organization based on the attributes on which people compare candidates. As we suggested in our model, these attributes are likely to be partisanship, ideology, policies, and personality characteristics (Rahn et al. 1990). Our model specifically postulates that voters will make comparisons across these attribute dimensions. In decision-theoretic terms, we assume an additive-difference, or intradimensional, decision process (Tversky 1969; Svenson 1979; see also Lau in this volume for a review of other vote-choice models and their assumptions about the nature of candidate comparisons). Thus, we would predict that voters' memory organizational strategies should be more attribute- than candidate-based.

Very little research in political psychology has examined the memory organization of complex political stimuli. The research reported by McGraw and her colleagues (McGraw, Pinney, and Neumann 1991; McGraw and Steenbergen, in this volume) is an exception. However, their studies have involved only a single political candidate, and thus do not address the question under consideration here, namely to what extent voters use a candidate-based or attribute-based organization strategy.

The social cognition research on multiperson environments has examined several variables that might influence organizational processes. The research I report below investigated three: information-processing goals, information structure, and political expertise. Thus, the first section following the description of research methods treats cognitive organization as a dependent variable. In the following section, I then examine the consequences of cognitive organization for processes of candidate evaluation.

Methods

The study described more fully below used written descriptions of fictitious political candidates as stimulus material. The experiment featured two manipulated independent variables, information structure and information-processing goals, each of which has been shown in social cognition studies to affect cognitive organization.

Two political candidates, John Vanderkenning and Larry Drake, were described by fourteen attributes: seven biographical items, six issue position descriptions, and one statement about political party affiliation. The descriptions were based on video stimulus materials developed in our research program (see Rahn 1990). Each attribute was written as a statement about the particular candidate (e.g., Larry Drake is running for office as a Democrat) and was printed on a 3 × 5 index card. In the *person-focused* condition, all fourteen items about one candidate appeared before the fourteen items pertaining to the other candidate. The *attribute-focused* condition featured alternations between candidates within the fourteen types of descriptive features. The order of candidates was counterbalanced across subjects in both the person- and attribute-focused conditions. In both the person- and attribute-focused conditions, the biographical information came first, the statement about party affiliation came in the middle, followed by the policy items. The six policy dimensions involved two issues, defense and social services, that previous research has suggested are highly diagnostic of partisanship, three issues that are mildly diagnostic (schools, business climate, and farm policy) and one issue, trade policy, for which partisan expectancies are rather weak (see Rahn 1993). Each candidate's policy positions were congruent ideologically.

The information-structure manipulation also contained a *random* condition. Here, the twenty-eight statements were arranged in one random, order held constant across subjects in this condition. Randomization of the twenty-eight statements resulted in a presentation format in which no more than three attribute items about a given candidate appeared in succession. In addition, the two items of information pertaining to one attribute category never appeared contiguously. For example, the statement "John believes that we should get people off of welfare and into the workplace" was not followed by the statement that "Larry believes that we have cut back too much on government services."

The administration of the experiment occurred as follows. Subjects were first provided with instructions about how to approach the task. Approximately one-quarter were told to form an *impression* of each of the candidates without worrying too much about memorizing the information. Another quarter was told to *memorize* the information, as they would be asked about it later. In the third goal condition, subjects were told to read the information as if they were a voter attempting to make a *vote choice*. And finally, in the *control* condition, the remaining subjects were given no further instructions, beyond reading the information carefully. After the goal induction, subjects read the candidate information contained on the index cards. After they were finished reading, they completed an eight-minute distractor test, after which they rated each of the candidates on seven-point liking scales. A free recall task followed these judgments. Subjects were given ten minutes to recall as much of the information as they could. Upon completing the recall task, subjects were instructed to score each item they had recalled for its evaluative significance—positive, negative, or neutral. When subjects finished with the rating of their recall, they filled out a questionnaire concerning their impressions of the candidates, their perceptions of the candidates' issue positions, and standard demographic items.

The recall protocols were scored for a variety of information. For the purposes of the analysis presented in this chapter, each item recalled was coded for the candidate to which it referred and the descriptive feature remembered. Initially, a subset of the protocols was selected to be coded independently by three coders. Percentage agreement among coders for these two dimensions averaged over 95 percent, so the remainder of the protocols were simply divided among them.

Procedure. 309 students enrolled in an introductory political science class participated in the experiment in exchange for course credit. At the beginning of the semester, students filled out an omnibus political attitude survey. This questionnaire included items designed to measure political sophistication and students' policy preferences. Two months later, the students participated in the actual experiment. Sixteen experimental sessions were run during regularly scheduled discussion sections. Information-processing goal conditions were randomly assigned to discussion sections, while information-structure conditions were randomly assigned to individuals. Upon arriving, students were seated and given a packet containing a stack of index cards, a questionnaire, and a booklet in which to record their memory for the information contained on the cards.

An experimenter blind to the hypotheses under investigation read instructions to the participants. Subjects followed along in their questionnaires. Subjects were then paced through the twenty-eight index cards at a rate of ten seconds per card. Past research on reading time has shown this is sufficient time to adequately process short descriptive statements (see Bargh and Thein 1985). After subjects were done reading the candidate descriptions, they performed a distractor task, made their overall evaluations of the candidates, completed the free recall assessment, and then filled out the questionnaire.

Cognitive Organization as a Dependent Variable

Expectations. Numerous studies in social cognition have attempted to link individuals' information-processing goals with different cognitive strategies (see, e.g., Hamilton, Katz, and Leirer 1980; Srull and Wyer 1986). In multi-target settings, tasks such as impression formation might be thought to lead to more individuation of target persons in memory than other goals, such as memorization. This hypothesis, however, has met with mixed success (See Pryor et al. 1982; Sedikides, Devine, and Fuhrman 1991; c.f., Srull 1983). The literature on goals and information processing has not directly addressed how the task of choice might affect memory organizational strategies. In our view, political-choice tasks motivate dimensional evaluations of the competing candidates; therefore, I expected attribute organization to be most pronounced in the vote choice condition of the experiment. In addition, we argue that for individuals qua voters, impression formation is a subgoal executed in the service of the more fundamental political task of choosing. Thus, in contrast to the typical social cognition hypothesis, I also expected to see significant attribute organization in the impression-formation condition. It is not clear how memorization should affect organizational strategies, although Srull (1983) suggests that memorization should result in information organized by how it was originally presented. Memory set subjects, therefore, should be most affected by presentation format. Finally, the three explicit goal conditions of the experiment (impression formation, memorization, and vote choice) should motivate more systematically organized cognitive representations than the control condition.

Experimental manipulations of information structure consistently produce differences in cognitive organization. Information structures that focus attention on persons, rather than attributes, result in more person organization than structures that highlight attributes instead of persons (see, e.g., Pryor et al. 1982). Therefore, subjects in the person-focused condition should show more candidate-based memory organization than subjects in either the attribute-focused or random conditions.

Political expertise usually is viewed as having important consequences for political information processing. Indeed, it has become de rigueur for political psychologists to assume that the most important source of heterogeneity in political information processing is individual differences in this construct (see, e.g., Sniderman, Brody, and Tetlock 1991). Sniderman, Griffin, and Glaser (1990), for example, suggest that the politically knowledgeable make intradimensional comparisons of candidates, while the less knowledgeable follow a candidate-based, specifically, incumbent-centered, comparison route. On the other hand, we have made the claim that sophistication may not be terribly consequential for vote choice processes in some circumstances (Rahn et al. 1990).

The memory-organization and behavioral-decision literatures also contain contrary expectations regarding the impact of individual differences. McGraw and Steenbergen (in this volume) and McGraw, Pinney, and Neumann (1991) found that political sophistication does affect how political-candidate information is represented in memory. Both of their studies, however, involved a single-candidate stimulus environment, so sophistication has yet to be studied in a dual-target, vote choice setting. Some social cognition research on multitarget environments suggests that familiarity with the targets promotes person-based memory organization. While both sophisticates and nonsophisticates in my experiment would have been equally unfamiliar with the two candidates, the sophisticates would perhaps have had more experience with the task of candidate evaluation in general, and thus, according to the familiarity hypothesis, might be expected to organize information according to persons.

Some studies in the behavioral decision theory literature support the notion that the processing of multiattribute, multialternative information may be affected by prior experience with a task. In an information search study, Bettman and Park (1980) found that knowledgeable consumers tended to process information by brand, a product analog of candidate-based processing, while less knowledgeable customers searched first by dimension, and then switched to brand-based processing. Jacoby and colleagues (Jacoby et al. 1987), on the other hand, found that better performing stock analysts processed information about multiple stock options intradimensionally, while the poorer performing analysts processed information within each alternative, rather than across dimensions. Given conflicting guidance from these various research findings, I simply tested whether sophistication is associated with a particular organizational strategy.

To examine these expectations, two types of ARC scores were computed for each subject (see McGraw and Steenbergen in this volume; Ostrom, Pryor, and Simpson 1981). The *candidate-ARC* score indicates the degree to which subjects' recall showed candidate-based clustering. It is based on the number of within-candidate repetitions in free recall, relative to what would be expected by chance. If subjects had individuated the candidates in memory, then their candidate-ARC scores would be positive. I also computed an *attribute-ARC* score. The attribute-ARC score is based on the number of within-attribute repetitions in subjects' free recall protocols. For example, if a subject recalled that Larry was a Democrat, followed by John was Republican, this would have been scored as one attribute repetition. Given the stimulus configuration, the number of within-attribute repetitions could have ranged from zero to fourteen. Note that between-candidate transitions in subjects' recall are not necessarily within-attribute repetitions.

The correlation between the two types of ARC scores is quite negative ($r = -.86$), indicating that positive candidate-ARC scores are associated with negative attribute-ARC scores. Candidate-based and attribute-based organization strategies appeared to have competed with one another, a competition inherent in the structure of the stimulus materials.

I tested the hypotheses introduced above with a 4 (impression, memory, vote choice, control) $\times$ 3 (random, person, attribute) $\times$ 2 (novice, expert)[1] $\times$ 2 (candidate-ARC, attribute-ARC) multivariate analysis of variance, treating the last factor as a within-subject, repeated measure of the dependent variable. Neither task nor expertise had significant main effects ($F < 1$), nor did they reliably interact with each other, with information structure, or with the different types of ARC scores (all $p > .14$)

The failure of both task and expertise to influence cognitive organization requires some comment, particularly given the fact that in the single-candidate studies by McGraw and her colleagues, these two variables have been shown to affect memory organization.[2] A number of explanations for the failure of the goal manipulation are possible. First, the social cognition literature itself is littered with null or mixed results about the impact of information-processing goals on cognitive organization (see, e.g., Pryor et al. 1982; Sedikides, Devine, and Fuhrman 1991). Thus, in *multitarget* environments, the specific linkage between goals and memory organizational strategies is not firmly established, either theoretically or empirically. My results, when viewed in the context of these studies, are not unusual. Moreover, I believe that the lack of significant differences for the goal variations is related to the "natural" task that is implied by the nature of the information environment in the experiment. The very presence of comparative information about two political candidates may trigger the same organizational strategy, regardless of the overt task instructions.[3] Given a two-candidate information environment, it may be difficult to override individuals' tacit goal with alternative instructions, but further research is needed to evaluate whether this conclusion is robust across other manipulations of task and structure.

While perhaps surprising, given conventional wisdom in political psychology regarding the pervasiveness of sophistication differences, the unimportance of sophistication in the present experiment is quite consistent with the predictions of our model of candidate appraisal. We have argued that the "deficiencies" of nonsophisticates may be partially compensated for by the political environment (see Rahn et al. 1990). While not gainsaying the important expertise differences that have been discovered by others, we have argued that the task of vote choice, as well as the informational setting in which people make certain kinds of political choices, can reduce the importance of individual differences in sophistication. According to our argument, in comparative information environments, such as the one featured in the present experiment, both the sophisticated and the less sophisticated should be able to implement essentially the same information processing strategies. Comparative information environments compensate for differences in voters' cognitive resources by making it easier to compare the two alternatives. When information is available about each candidate on the same dimensions of appraisal, voters can compare each candidate along the same attribute (e.g., trade policy). However, in environments in which there is unique information available about one or both candidates (e.g., a voter knows one candidate's position on trade policy and the other candidate's position on school funding, but does not have the information for both dimensions for both candidates), then the task becomes much more difficult (see Tversky 1969; Slovic and MacPhillamy 1974). Thus, by the logic of our model, the expressly comparative structure of the stimulus materials should have worked to diminish the importance of sophistication differences. Given a different informational configuration, however, sophistication would be expected to play a more important role.

Another reason for the lack of sophistication differences in the present experiment may be due to the redundancy of the policy attributes with the candidates' partisanship. In making our original claims about the relative unimportance of sophistication for vote choice, we stressed that an important feature of many recent presidential elections has been the redundancy of the information to which voters are exposed. The changes within the two parties that have resulted in more ideological campaigns, the logic of two-party competition, and the media's portrayal of the candidates have produced a context in which the political attributes of each candidate are highly correlated, or redundant. A subset of attributes, then, conveys nearly the same information as the full set, and information about the political characteristics of one candidate implies something about the other. Thus, redundancy can be a property of the stimulus environment, not just a characteristic of political sophisticates' knowledge structures (as in Lusk and Judd 1988). Cue redundancy simplifies many aspects of choice and judgment processes (see Einhorn, Kleinmuntz, and Kleinmuntz 1979).[4]

Of course, one can never prove the null hypothesis; I have merely failed to reject it in this particular case. However, our argument that the context of choice may be more consequential for information-processing strategies than the individual characteristics of voters finds some support in other results from the ARC-score analysis. As expected, information structure had a significant impact on the measures of cognitive organization ($F[2,262] = 26.5$, $p < .000$). Person organization was significantly greater in the person-focused condition and attribute organization was most pronounced in the attribute-focused condition. Consistent with our claims that vote choice involves an intradimensional comparison strategy, subjects showed a marked preference for attribute- rather than candidate-based organization ($F[1,262] = 125.0$ $p < .000$).

Interestingly, the analysis also revealed a highly significant interaction between type of ARC score and information structure ($F[2,262] = 41.6$, $p < .000$). Table 1 displays the relevant condition means. Every structure condition resulted in more attribute organization than would be expected by chance alone.[5] The interaction between type of ARC score and information structure arises because the attribute-ARC score in the person-focused condition is positive, indicating that even in an informational configuration inhospitable to attribute organization, subjects nonetheless adopted some degree of attribute organization in memory.

If we restrict our attention to the person- and attribute-focused conditions, my results closely follow Herstein's (1981) findings regarding voters' information search patterns. In his experiments, he presented subjects with information about two political candidates, arranged in two different displays. In his candidate-salient display, the attribute information about each candidate was grouped around each candidate, similar to my person-focused condition. The item-salient display, on the other hand, positioned the attribute information together. Two of his findings are of interest. First, information search was mostly intraitem, rather than intracandidate. However, the item-salient display significantly facilitated intraitem search, while the reverse was true for the candidate-salient display, precisely the sort of results I obtained using memory organizational measures. Information search and information retrieval may be closely linked processes, and both are affected by presentation format. Other studies have uncovered similar information search differences due to presentation format (see Bettman and Kakkar 1977; for a review, see Ford et al. 1989). To a large extent, information retrieval may simply reflect the way information was initially acquired, and in information search studies, these acquisition operations appear to be strongly influenced by the way in which information is presented (see also Tversky 1969).

Presentation format, however, cannot explain the results obtained in the random structure condition. Given no "clues" in the structure of the information about how to encode and organize it, subjects' ARC scores nevertheless reveal that they imposed an attribute-based organization upon it. The candidate-ARC score cannot be reliably distinguished from zero; the attribute-ARC score, however, indicates high levels of attribute-based clustering. Nor can presentation format account for the positive attribute-ARC scores in the person-focused condition. The positive attribute-ARC scores in both the random and person-focused conditions suggest that attribute-based organization may be a default strategy in political choice settings characterized by fully comparative information environments.

The high degree of attribute-based organization in subjects' recall is

TABLE 1.   Mean Candidate-ARC and Attribute-ARC Scores by Information Structure

	Type of ARC Score	
Structure	Candidate-ARC	Attribute-ARC
Random	−.06	.50*
Person-focused	.34*	.35*
Attribute-focused	−.40	.73*
Column mean	−.04	.52*
N	308	305

Note: * indicate that the mean ARC score is significantly greater, $p < .05$, than would be expected by chance.

not only consistent with our vote choice model, but with studies of nonpolitical decision making, in which a preference for attribute-based processing has been found (e.g., Rosen and Rosenkoetter 1975; Russo and Dosher 1983). No doubt the informational configuration provided to subjects in the present experiment made a comparative organizational strategy relatively easy. Not only were the candidates' positions effectively "mirror images," but their platforms were congruent with ideological expectancies. The alternatives were quite dissimilar, and various process-tracing studies, including Herstein's (1981), suggest that dissimilar alternatives make binary choice tasks easier (see also Bockenholt et al. 1991). Certainly not all political information environments are as congenial to intradimensional processing as the stimulus configuration of the experiment. However, all else equal, attribute-based processing strategies are easier to implement in choice settings than alternative-based, or additive, strategies (Tversky 1969; Russo and Dosher 1983). So, unless the information environment is configured in such a way as to make an alternative- (i.e., candidate-) based strategy easier or to make an attribute-centered strategy more costly (e.g., as it would be in a candidate-focused display format), attribute-based strategies are likely to dominate.

Even though attribute-based processing may be a preferential strategy, context and other task contingencies clearly affect individuals' decisions about how to decide. The sensitivity of strategy choice to environmental constraints probably accounts for the divergence between my memory organizational findings and Lau's (in this volume) information search results. He finds about equal amounts of intracandidate and intradimensional search in a static information environment, a display condition that did not militate against using either strategy. However, in the dynamic, or "scrolling," version of the information display, it would have been extraordinarily difficult for subjects to implement an intradimensional strategy. Given that there were many more attributes than candidates, it is much more likely that information pertaining to a given candidate would appear close together than that information about different candidates on the same attribute would be located in close proximity.

Lau is certainly correct in claiming that political information environments are much more unruly than product displays in supermarkets. Yet, the political world is not without structure. Candidates' advertising, for example, is quite often "comparative" in nature, explicitly or implicitly providing the viewer with information about both candidates. The most widely watched political information events of the 1992 campaign, the three presidential debates, also were highly attribute-focused, comparative environments. Many newspapers publish candidate by policy position matrices during political campaigns, and television news stories often have a comparative structure to them, especially during the general election campaign, as the coverage becomes more policy-oriented. Other political information events, of course, are more candidate-focused. The infomercials broadcast by Ross Perot during the 1992 campaign or the presidential nominees' acceptance speeches, given their structure, encouraged intracandidate processing strategies.

In addition, while information search and memory organization patterns may both indicate something about decision strategies, they should not be viewed as interchangeable measures. Memory organization measures and information search indicators deal with different phases of information processing. The subjects in my study were not permitted to engage in selective attention, an unnatural manipulation to be sure, but one typically employed in memory organization studies. To my knowledge, there have been no studies in which information acquisition patterns were compared to memory organization measures. In decision-theoretic studies, it is assumed that subjects' search patterns, whether indicated by eye fixations (e.g., Russo and Dosher 1983), verbal protocols (e.g., Bettman and Park 1980), or manual information-seeking responses (Lau in this volume; Herstein 1981), are indicative of decision strategies. Subjects are asked to make judgments or choices during the acquisition process, or immediately after being exposed to the information. To the extent that judgments and choices are made on-line, information search patterns are probably good indicators of individuals' information-processing strategies. However, not all decision makers process information on-line. If decision making requires the retrieval of specific information from memory, then memory organizational processes may be more consequential for decision strategies than information-acquisition processes. Addressing this hypothesis would require the integration of the information search and memory organization literature, two areas of information-processing research that have been rather isolated from one another to date.

To summarize the results so far, I have found that information structure has a powerful effect on cognitive organization. Person-focused structures facilitated candidate-based organization, while attribute-focused structures encouraged an attribute-based organizational strategy. Nonetheless, subjects demonstrated an unambiguous preference for attribute-based organization. Information-processing objectives and political sophistication had no reliable effects on cognitive organization, either as main effects or in interactions.

Cognitive Organization as an Independent Variable

The research on the antecedents of cognitive organization has been much more plentiful than the research on its consequences. In part, this is because cognitive organization will not mediate other cognitive responses and social judgments, unless these tasks require the retrieval of specific information from memory (see Devine and Ostrom 1985). If most judgment tasks are executed on-line, then cognitive organization may be irrelevant to understanding these processes. Differences in cognitive organization may simply be the by-products of other cognitive activity that occurs at encoding, activity that may be influenced by such things as presentation focus (see Herstein 1981; Devine and Ostrom 1985), processing objectives (Lodge, McGraw, and Stroh 1989), political sophistication (McGraw, Lodge, and Stroh 1990; McGraw and Steenbergen in this volume), and information search strategies. However, not all candidate evaluations are produced through on-line processes. To the extent that evaluations are constructed through memory-retrieval processes, different types of organization may have an impact on how these judgments are computed, and the confidence with which they are held. Indeed, one reason that McGraw and Steenbergen (in this volume) found that memory organization played a role in evaluative extremity only for nonsophisticates may be due to the fact that nonsophisticates are more likely to be memory-based processors, and, thus, memory organization has more potential to mediate judgmental processes under such circumstances.

Despite the rather undeveloped state of the social-cognition literature, I nevertheless can offer a few tentative hypotheses about the likely impact of cognitive organization. Cognitive organization will still have some consequence for such obviously memory-based tasks as recall and recognition, regardless of whether overall judgments are produced through on-line or memory-based processes (Ostrom et al. n.d.). In the present experiment, person-based memory structures should have facilitated the recognition and recall of the information presented. I base these predications on the notion that, in the context of the present experiment, high degrees of person organization imply that only two cognitive categories—one for each candidate—needed to be accessed to accomplish recall and recognition tasks. In contrast, if memory was organized according to attributes, more "nodes" had to be accessed for these retrieval operations. Thus, high attribute organization would not contribute to memory performance.

The amount of recall was measured by the number of items subjects recalled during the free recall exercise. Recognition memory was measured by the number of correct matches subjects made in a matching test embedded in the questionnaire. Here, subjects were provided with the 28 statements randomly arranged (and in a different random order than in the random structure condition) without the candidates' names attached. Subjects had to match the statement to the correct candidate.

In an earlier paper (Rahn 1992), I demonstrated that information-processing goals and political expertise both influenced the amount of information subjects were able to recall. Thus, in order to test the hypothesis that person organization facilitates memory, these other variables must be controlled. Moreover, given the strong correlation between information structure and organization in table 1, any effects due to information structure must also be held constant, in order to claim a mediational role for memory organization. Accordingly, I performed an analysis of covariance in which the effects of goals, expertise, and structure were partialled out before testing the significance of variations in memory organization. For the ANCOVA, subjects' candidate-ARC and attribute-ARC scores were trichotomized into high, medium, and low levels. Table 2 presents recall and recognition scores by the different levels of organization, expressed as deviations from the grand mean, adjusted for the effects of the other variables. As expected, only candidate-based organization had a reliable impact on memory in the expected direction, but its effects were limited to facilitating recall. Recognition memory performance appears to have been little influenced by memory organization, once the other independent variables were controlled. High attribute organization significantly hampered subjects' abilities to recall the information. This finding is due, in part, to the strong negative correlation between attribute- and candidate-ARC scores.

Though the social cognition literature does not provide much guidance on how memory organization influences choice strategies, I hypothesize that it affects the ways in which political candidate comparisons are constructed, when such evaluations are memory-based. In particular, attribute-based organization should facilitate intradimensional comparisons of the candidates, whereas person-based organization should be more compatible with a candidate-based, or interdimensional, comparison. In other words, cognitive organization has the potential to mediate whether a voter follows an additive difference comparison strategy (such as postulated in Rahn et al. 1990) or

TABLE 2. Recall and Recognition Memory by Cognitive Organization

	Recall Memory (grand mean = 17.7)		Recognition Memory (grand mean = 24.7)	
	Candidate-ARC	Attribute-ARC	Candidate-ARC	Attribute-ARC
Low	−.14	.62	−.12	.16
Medium	−.69	.09	−.25	.29
High	.83	−.71	.37	−.45
F	4.11**	2.83*	1.40	1.80
N	288	286	288	286

Note: Entries are deviations from the grand mean, adjusted for the effects of the covariates.
* $p < .10$.
** $p < .05$.

an additive rule. In the former strategy, the candidates are compared along each dimension, and these evaluative differences are summed across dimensions to produce a choice. In the latter strategy, overall evaluations are computed separately for each candidate, and then compared to determine the choice.

Testing this hypothesis is difficult, for a couple of reasons. As noted above, cognitive organization may be the product of different on-line comparison strategies, rather than a mediator of such processes. If individuals evaluate candidates on-line, and, therefore, information integration occurs at the time of encoding, then cognitive organization may be epiphenomenal. Indeed, previous research has shown that presentation format does encourage different kinds of on-line evaluations. Herstein (1981), for example, found that person-centered displays encouraged on-line global evaluations of political candidates, whereas attribute-centered displays encouraged specific evaluations based on attributes. If all candidate evaluation activity occurs at encoding, then any relationship between cognitive organization and type of comparison strategy would be spurious, due simply to the correlation between memory organization and presentation format.

An easy way to avoid confounding presentation format with cognitive organization is to focus attention on those individuals in the present experiment for whom presentation format is irrelevant, namely those subjects in the random structure condition. In addition, I found in an earlier analysis that the relationship between recall memory and judgment was significantly stronger in the random structure condition (Rahn 1992), suggesting that individuals in this condition were more likely to construct candidate judgments using memory-based processes. Thus, should differences in cognitive organization produce the hypothesized effects among these individuals, I can claim with more justification that its effects are mediational, rather than merely derivative.

A second problem with evaluating the hypothesis is how to operationalize candidate-based and attribute-based comparison strategies. While the memory organization data clearly indicate that subjects preferred attribute-based organization, how do we know that differences in organizational strategy actually result in qualitatively different comparison strategies? One way to examine this question is to fit a candidate-based model of vote choice to groups of individuals who organize the information in different ways. If cognitive organization influences how candidates are compared, then models that predict independent, separately constructed candidate evaluations should fit better under conditions of strong person organization. If strong attribute organization promotes intradimensional comparisons, then a model that specifies that voters produce candidate evaluations one candidate at a time should not fit as well. The null hypothesis with this kind of operationalization becomes that the candidate-based model fits equally well under conditions of high-person and high-attribute organization.

I tested my expectation using a regression model that treated subjects' overall evaluations of John and Larry, as measured by seven-point like-dislike scales, as two separate dependent variables. Two independent variables, policy similarity and party identification, were used to predict the overall candidate judgments.

In order to fit a candidate-based comparison model, the independent variables had to be constructed in such a way as to avoid implying an intradimensional comparison of the candidates. I constructed a policy similarity variable for each candidate, using pretest data on subjects' political predispositions. These two similarity variables—one for each candidate— were based on subjects' ratings of their positions on several political issues included in the political survey they completed two months before the experiment. Five of these issues—trade, defense spending, farm policy, social service spending, and education—were ones on which the candidates in the experiment took positions. Because subjects' predispositions regarding these issues were obtained several weeks before the actual experiment, they are uncontaminated by any persuasion effects that might have resulted from exposure to the candidate information.

In the pretest, subjects rated their own attitudes toward these policies on seven-point scales. For each issue, subjects were given a policy similarity score. If their attitude fell on the Republican side of the scale, subjects received a score of 1, indicating similarity to John. If a subject's attitude rating was closer to Larry's (the Democratic) position, on the other hand, the subject received a similarity score of -1. If subjects rated their attitude at the middle of the issue scale, at position 4, or they didn't have an attitude on the issue, they received a similarity score of 0 for that issue. To obtain the similarity score for John, the number of issues for which subjects had similarity scores of +1 were counted; for Larry, the number of issues for which subjects had similarity scores of -1 were counted. For each candidate, then, the policy similarity variable has a range of 0 to 5, with 5 indicating maximum similarity to the candidate.

The similarity variable is specific to each candidate, and as constructed, does not involve a comparison of which candidate is closer to the subject. Computing a candidate-specific measure of party identification requires a slight departure from the way party-identification is usually treated in vote choice models. The full party identification scale (even in its three-point version) implicitly incorporates a comparison. Rather than using party identification in this fashion, I treated it as a dummy variable, scored 1 if subjects shared the candidate's partisan affiliation, 0 otherwise. Thus, in the regression equations predicting evaluations of John, Republican identifiers were given scores of 1. In the equations predicting evaluations of Larry, Democratic identifiers were given a score of 1. There are, then, two different party identification variables, one for each candidate. Given the construction of the independent variables, party identification and policy similarity should be positively related to subjects' overall assessment of each candidate.

Overall candidate evaluations were regressed on party identification and policy similarity for each candidate. These analyses were performed separately for subjects in the random condition with high candidate-ARC and high attribute-ARC scores. Limiting the analysis to only those subjects in the random condition with high ARC scores significantly reduces the statistical power of the analysis. Nonetheless, in table 3 we see that my expectations were strongly confirmed. Candidate evaluations, treated separately, are not predicted well under conditions of high attribute organization. The equations do significantly better when subjects organized information according to candidates, especially so in the case of John, the Republican candidate.[6] These results are consistent with the hypothesis that person-based organization facilitates a process whereby individuals compute evaluations of the candidates separately, making their choices based on a comparison of these overall judgments. Attribute-based organization, however, does not appear to be conducive to this type of comparison process, at least as measured by the poor fit of the candidate-based model.

To summarize the results of this section, I found support for the notion that cognitive organization does matter for processes that involve retrieval of candidate information from memory. Individuals with strong person-based organization performed better on the recall memory task. In addition, candidate-centered memory representations appeared to mediate a candidate-based comparison strategy under conditions conducive to memory-based processing.

Even though candidate-based organization results in superior performance in a memory test, it is difficult to say which type of cognitive organization might be more desirable, all else equal. For a subset of voters, those who process information on-line, cognitive organization does not mediate the production of candidate judgments, although it may be an after-the-fact indicator of judgment strategies. For the remainder, attribute-based organization may facilitate task simplification. Tversky (1969) and others have suggested that attribute-based comparison strategies are simpler than comparisons based on constructing independent evaluations of each alternative, a processing strategy I have been calling candidate-based, and that others have called "holistic" (e.g., Rosen and Rosenkoetter 1976; Russo and Dosher 1983). As we argued earlier (Rahn et al. 1990), the political environment also facilitates this type of task simplification by presenting voters with information about the candidates in a comparative format. We have also seen in the results presented here that comparative information environments strongly promote attribute-based cognitive organization. On the other hand, Tversky (1969) also notes that attribute-based strategies can result in preference reversals (see also Stroh and Moskowitz 1992), even in the two-alternative case where complete information about all dimensions is available. Given my results that individuals preferred attribute-based organization, it would seem that voters' task-simplification strategies are at odds with normatively desirable properties of choice. On the other hand, given information costs and the small rewards associated with voting, perhaps voters' simplifying strategies are "good enough" in the long run, and, in fact, may be better suited to the informational configuration of the political environment.

Discussion

Political psychologists have made important strides in recent years in unpacking the "black box" of political candidate evaluations (Lodge, Stroh, and Wahlke 1990). However, this theoretical progress has often meant ab-

TABLE 3.   Predicting Single-Candidate Evaluations by Cognitive Organization, Random Structure Condition Only

	High-Attribute ARC (attribute-ARC > .76)		High-Candidate ARC (candidate-ARC > .25)	
	B	beta	B	beta
John evaluations				
Policy similarity	.04	.03	.57*	.36
	(.38)		(.29)	
Party identification	.55	.22	1.67**	.49
	(.58)		(.67)	
R^2	.05		.43	
N	21		21	
Larry evaluations				
Policy similarity	.11	.10	.33	.23
	(.26)		(.28)	
Party identification	1.23*	.40	1.33**	.34
	(.70)		(.61)	
R^2	.15		.33	
N	20		22	

Note: Standard errors are in parentheses.
* $p < .10$.
** $p < .05$

stracting away from the context in which political-candidate evaluation occurs. Models of political information processing that have been developed for the appraisal of single candidates (e.g., Lodge, McGraw, and Stroh 1989; Wyer et al. 1991) ignore the complexities that arise when voters must compare candidates in order to choose. The information environment in which vote choice decision making occurs is quite complicated, typically involving at least two, if not more, multidimensional alternatives. Integrating this information in a way that is useful for *choice* is difficult for the voter. Certainly not all political information processing tasks involve choice, nor are all political-choice settings equally comparative. My point, however, is that further progress in this area will require researchers to pay as much attention to the task environment as they have to individual differences (see also Riggle 1992).

I have suggested in this chapter that exploring the cognitive representation of multicandidate information is one way to begin investigating the nature of these comparison processes. The results presented here demonstrate that cognitive organization is reliably influenced by the way information is structured. However, individuals also revealed a spontaneous preference for attribute-based organization, something that may help them to simplify the process of integrating information about multidimensional alternatives. When judgments are memory-based, the different ways of representing multicandidate information may also mediate voters' candidate comparison strategies. Whether viewed as an independent or dependent variable, cognitive organization adds to our understanding of the processes by which voters choose. Obviously, the representational structure of "real" multicandidate information is more complex than the candidate-based and attribute-based strategies I have investigated. I join McGraw and Steenbergen (in this volume) in calling for more research into, and alternative measures of, the cognitive organization of candidate information.

The temptation of a "black box" is, of course, that once opened, it will become Pandora's box, as empirical findings proliferate. Volumes such as this one are important for imposing some theoretical coherence on this burgeoning area of research. As I see it, the challenge that confronts those of us working from an information-processing orientation is to integrate the now-emerging constructivist view of political cognition with the aggregate regularities that are observed in real electoral behavior. This chapter has tried to suggest that the structure of the political environment may be one element linking intrapsychic processes to observed outcomes. The relationship between the informational structure of the political environment, on the one hand, and the representational structure of political cognition, on the other, however, remains relatively uncharted terrain. Political psychologists are uniquely poised to fill in the rest of the map.

NOTES

The research reported in this chapter was supported by National Science Foundation Grant SES-9296046 and the University of Wisconsin Graduate School Research Committee. Neither of these institutions bears responsibility for the analyses and interpretations presented. I thank Constantine Sedikides for his generous assistance and the editors and Gregory Diamond for their comments on earlier drafts.

1. I measured expertise with an additive, equally weighted index of 3 variables: political knowledge, behavioral experience with politics, and self-reported interest in politics. A median split was used to define the two sophistication groups.

2. Both task and expertise had effects on other kinds of memory variables, as discussed in an earlier paper (Rahn 1992). Consistent with the findings in McGraw and Steenbergen (in this volume), experts recalled more information than novices. In addition, memorization goals resulted in significantly lower levels of overall recall, consistent with many social cognition studies (see, e.g., Hamilton, Katz, and Leirer 1980). A significant interaction between expertise and task qualified both of these effects, however. The politically less sophisticated were especially hampered by memorization goals, particularly in comparison to their recall performance in the impression-formation condition, where no sophistication differences in the amount of recall were apparent. The politically sophisticated were much less affected by the different goal manipulations, consistent with the notion that they have more flexibility in their cognitive capacities, and, thus, are less encumbered by environmentally induced demands.

3. Demand characteristics as an explanation for the lack of differences among the different processing goals can be rejected. Even though the subjects were college students who, because of the very academic-like setting (discussion sections), may have anticipated a memory "test," results presented elsewhere demonstrated that the goal manipulations did have effects on other aspects of memory performance (Rahn 1992; see also n. 3).

4. Because redundancy (or partisan consistency) was not manipulated in the present experiment, its role in cognitive organization cannot be tested. The results presented in Pryor, Kott, and Bovee 1984 suggest that information redundancy facilitates person-based organization, a hypothesis that I am pursuing in another study.

5. By Neuman-Keuls post hoc comparisons, mean attribute-ARC scores in the three structure conditions are significantly different.

6. To test the claim that judgments have to be memory-based in order for memory organization to play a significant mediational role, I conducted the same analysis shown in table 3 for subjects in the person- and attribute-focused information structure conditions. While the candidate-based comparison model does fare better for those individuals with high candidate-ARC scores, the improvement in the fit of the model is not nearly as dramatic as we see in Table 3. For John, the R^2 improves from .17 to .27. For Larry, the difference in R^2 is even smaller. For the high-attribute equation, the R^2 is .29, only improving to .33 for the high candidate-ARC equation. These results suggest that memory organizational differences do not play a large role when judgments are constructed on-line.

CHAPTER 4

Stereotypic Accuracy in Judgments of the Political Positions of Groups and Individuals

Charles M. Judd and James W. Downing

Many political judgments are largely stereotypic judgments. In the political realm, we categorize others by the positions we believe they hold and the affiliations and allegiances we believe they espouse. We tend to know whom we agree with and whom we disagree with, and we have beliefs about what both sorts of groups are like.

Group stereotypes have received a tremendous amount of attention in social psychology in the last half century. Yet relatively little of this attention has been devoted to stereotypes in the political arena and their role in influencing political judgments and political behaviors. It is our intention in this chapter to examine certain kinds of political judgments using the conceptual and methodological tools that recent research on social stereotyping has to offer. We do not intend to comprehensively review the stereotyping literature or examine all possible connections that might be made to the political arena. Rather we will selectively focus on certain issues in stereotyping research that seem particularly relevant to political judgments and that have occupied our interest over the last few years. We start with some historical observations about the changing definitions of social stereotypes over the course of the last seventy years. We then examine some recent theoretical and empirical work on stereotypic judgments. This work, then, informs the main text of the chapter, which is devoted to an examination of the accuracy of stereotypic judgments of positions espoused by political groups and individuals.

Definitions and Dimensions of Social Stereotypes

Social psychologists first began to think seriously about group stereotypes as a result of Walter Lippman's influential book, *Public Opinion,* published in 1922. According to Lippman, group stereotypes are prejudicial generalizations about social groups, since they tend to be illogically derived from observation, held rigidly, and erroneous in content. Early empirical work on group stereotypes reflected these definitional assumptions. Katz and

Braly (1933) asked judges to identify sets of attributes that are "most typical" of various ethnic and social groups. The agreement among judges in these judgments and their apparent ease in applying general trait terms to entire social categories led these researchers to define a stereotype as "a fixed impression which conforms very little to the facts it pretends to represent" (Katz and Braly 1965, 267).

Due to the pioneering work of Gordon Allport (1958) and Henri Tajfel (1969) and influenced by the cognitive renaissance in psychology of the 1960s and 1970s, a redefinition of stereotypes gradually took hold. This redefinition saw them as social categories, similar to object categories, defined by a set of features that are presumed to be more or less characteristic of group members. As such, stereotypes are probabilistic generalizations about a group or class of people, no more illogical or erroneous than generalizations about any other sort of category that perceivers might construct and find useful (e.g., the categories of chairs or dogs, for instance). Thus, the judgment that Democratic political candidates tend to support deficit spending for social welfare programs is really no different, conceptually, from the generalization that cocker spaniels tend to be affectionate. Both are probabilistic statements about a category of objects and therefore qualify as stereotypes, although this term is normally confined to probabilistic generalizations about categories of people, rather than about categories of dogs.

As a result of this definitional shift, a new set of theoretical questions aroused researchers' interest. Rather than simply describing the content of stereotypes, as earlier empirical work had tended to do, more cognitively oriented researchers tend to focus on process issues concerning the origin of stereotypes (e.g., Hamilton 1981), their influence on information processing and judgment (e.g., Rothbart 1981), and situations under which disconfirming information leads to stereotype change (e.g., Weber and Crocker 1983). Differences in the structure of stereotypes as a function of whether or not the perceiver is a member of the stereotyped group (i.e., ingroup-outgroup differences) have also received considerable attention (e.g., Brewer and Lui 1984; Park and Rothbart 1982; Park, Ryan, and Judd 1992). Finally, the issue of whether or not stereotypes are exaggerations and overgeneralizations became an issue that could be examined empirically, rather than being included as a defining characteristic of stereotypes. Hence, recent work has focused on the question of stereotype accuracy, particularly ingroup-outgroup differences in accuracy (e.g., Judd, Ryan, and Park 1991; Judd and Park 1993; Jussim 1991).

A great deal of this research can be summarized by conclusions about three primary characteristics that differentiate ingroup stereotypes from stereotypes of outgroups. First, extensive evidence exists that ingroup stereotypes tend to be more positively valenced than outgroup stereotypes. This difference, known as ethnocentrism, has been shown to exist even when group membership is defined arbitrarily and randomly (Brewer 1979). Such evaluative differences are found both when judgments are made about the groups as a whole and when they are made about individual members of groups. Ingroups and their members tend to be more positively evaluated than outgroups and their members.

A second difference is that a larger percentage of outgroup members are seen as conforming to the group stereotype, and a smaller percentage as deviating from it, than is the case with the ingroup (Park and Judd 1990; Park and Rothbart 1982). In other words, given a stereotype of what the group, as a whole, is like, the outgroup is judged to be more stereotypic, on average, than the ingroup. Equivalently, the outgroup stereotype is more extreme than is the ingroup stereotype. To illustrate, suppose that Democratic politicians are judged, on average, to support deficit spending for social welfare programs. A Republican judge will tend to think that this is more true, or truer for a larger percentage of Democratic politicians, than will a Democratic judge. For the former judge, the Republican, the stereotyped group is an outgroup and the judgment is more stereotypic than is the case when the judge is a Democrat and the judged group an ingroup. Interestingly, this difference seems to be found only when judgments are made about groups as a whole, and not when judgments are made about concrete individuals who are known to be group members. Thus, it is not necessarily true that the Republican judge will predict a particular Democratic politician to be more in favor of deficit spending for social welfare than will a Democratic judge. The difference seems to emerge only when the judgments are made at the group level.

Finally, ingroups are judged to be more variable, or dispersed around their perceived central tendency, than are outgroups (Park and Judd 1990; Linville, Fischer, and Salovey 1989). Suppose our Democratic and Republican judges were asked to form a frequency distribution of where each thought one hundred typical Democratic politicians stood on the issue of deficit spending for social welfare programs. The frequency distribution of the Democratic judge would tend to be more spread out, or dispersed, than the frequency distribution constructed by the Republican judge. This difference and the stereotypicality difference defined in the previous paragraph are easily confused, even though it turns out they are empirically nearly independent of each other. The stereotypicality difference concerns the perceived central tendency of the distribution: the Republican judge would think that the average sentiment of Democratic politicians on this issue was more extremely supportive than would the Democratic judge. The dispersion difference we have just defined concerns not the extremity of the perceived central tendency, but the perceived dispersion of the group around that central tendency. Again, like the difference in stereotypicality, this ingroup-outgroup difference seems to emerge only when judging the group as a whole. If our judges were asked to judge the positions of individual Democratic politicians whom they knew as individuals, a difference in the perceived dispersion of these judgments probably would not emerge (Judd and Park 1988).

The above differences are all relative differences between ingroup stereotypes and outgroup stereotypes. Ingroup judges tend to see the group as more positive, less stereotypic, and more dispersed than outgroup judges. The first difference seems to emerge when judgments are made about the group as a whole, as well as about its individual members. The second and third differences only seem to emerge when thinking about the group as a whole.

In addition to these relative differences, the question of the accuracy of social stereotypes can be asked with respect to all three components (Judd and Park 1993). Not only can we examine whether outgroup judges see a group more negatively than do ingroup judges, but, assuming some criterion for assessing accuracy, we can also ask whether outgroup judges see the group more negatively than they should. Similarly, we can ask not only about ingroup-outgroup differences in perceived stereotypicality, but also about whether judges see outgroups more stereotypically than they actually should, again given some criterion of where the group actually stands on the attributes in question. Finally, we can ask not only about ingroup-outgroup differences in perceived dispersion, but also about whether judges see outgroups as less dispersed than they actually should, again given some criterion on the actual dispersion of the group.

Each of these forms of stereotype inaccuracy have interesting implications. The first, seeing a group more negatively than one should, can be defined as *prejudice* toward the group and its members. Behavioral consequences, in the form of discrimination, should ensue at both the group and individual levels. The second sort of inaccuracy might be seen as an *exaggeration* of the group stereotype. The group is expected, on average, to be more strongly stereotypic than is, in fact, the case. Finally, the third sort of stereotypic inaccuracy can be seen as an *overgeneralization* about the group, seeing it as more homogeneous than is warranted. In theory at least, these three forms of stereotype inaccuracy are conceptually independent of each other. In practice, it may be that relations exist among them. Thus, one might expect individuals who are prejudiced toward a group (the stereotype is more negative than it should be) to exaggerate the group stereotype (the group stereotype is more extreme than is warranted) and to overgeneralize about the group (the group is perceived to be more homogeneous than it is).

Stereotypic Judgments of Political Positions

In the political realm, voters and informed citizens routinely make judgments about political groups and political candidates. These judgments have been of considerable interest to political scientists, since group affiliations, particularly party affiliations, and candidate judgments largely determine voting behavior. Judgments are made about the attributes of political groups and candidates along a variety of dimensions. Of these, the most salient and the most studied are judgments of the locations of political groups and candidates along ideological dimensions, judgments of the policy positions espoused by political interest groups, and candidates.

From the point of view of the issues that we have highlighted from the recent literature on social stereotyping, the political arena is, in many ways, an ideal setting in which to study stereotypically based judgments of ingroups and outgroups. The American two-party system and the ideological opposition between competing political groups means that on any issue there are generally well defined ingroups and outgroups. In addition, it is relatively easy to identify attributes (i.e., issues and policies) that are stereotypic or counterstereotypic of each group. Thus, for instance, if the group to be judged consists of Democratic politicians, then agreement with various liberal policies and issue stances would generally be seen to be stereotypic, while agreement with conservative positions would be seen as counterstereotypic.

In fact, a number of studies have attempted to evaluate the accuracy of ingroup and outgroup judgments in the political realm, focusing on biases in the judgments of political actors' (typically candidates') policy positions, where those actors are defined as ingroup members if the judge likes or agrees with them or as outgroup members if the judge dislikes or disagrees with them (e.g., Brent and Granberg 1982; Conover and Feldman 1982; Granberg and Brent 1974; Kinder 1978).

Consistent with notions about psychological balance (Heider 1958) and assimilation and contrast tendencies in social judgment (Sherif and Hovland 1961), the dominant theoretical question that has guided this work on accuracy in judging the positions of political actors concerns whether those judgments are influenced or biased by the judge's own positions and whether or not the actors or targets being judged are in the judge's ingroup or outgroup. Relatively simple applications of these theoretical points of view suggest that judges should judgmentally assimilate to their own preferred positions the perceived positions of ingroup or liked candidates, and judgmentally contrast away from their own positions the perceived positions of outgroup or disliked candidates. In terms of the stereotypic inaccuracies defined earlier, this would amount to stereotypic exaggeration of both in-group and outgroup candidates.

Empirical examinations of this hypothesis have generally involved computing measures of association between the judge's own position and the judged position of the target candidate separately for judges who generally like and those who generally dislike the candidate (Conover and Feldman 1982; Granberg and Brent 1974; Granberg and Jenks 1977; Kinder 1978). If the positions of liked candidates are assimilated to the judge's own point of view and those of disliked candidates are contrasted away, then it would seem that positive relationships should be observed between the judge's position and his or her judgments in the case of liked candidates, and negative relationships in the case of disliked candidates. In general, this pattern of association has been reported in the literature, lending support to the notion that the judge's own political stances are a source of influence in judging the espoused positions of political actors, and that different sorts of judgmental biases exist in ingroup judgments than in judgments of the outgroup.

In addition to the general level of support that these studies have offered, it has also frequently been noted that the negative associations found for disliked candidates are typically quite a bit smaller (in absolute value) than are the positive associations found in judgments of liked candidates' positions. Granberg has repeatedly documented such asymmetries, as have both Kinder and Conover and Feldman. These researchers have concluded from these asymmetries that the judgmental biases induced by one's own position are stronger in the case of judgments of liked candidates' positions than they are in the case of judgments of disliked candidates'. In the terms we borrowed earlier from the stereotyping literature, the conclusion seems to be that stereotypic inaccuracies are greater in the case of ingroup targets than outgroup targets. This conclusion is both somewhat surprising and contradictory of the stereotyping literature that has documented ingroup-outgroup differences in stereotype accuracy (Judd, Ryan, and Park 1991). The stereotyping literature suggests that stereotypic judgments are generally more accurate in the case of ingroup judgments than they are in case of outgroup judgments. For reasons of simple propinquity and familiarity, it makes sense that we should make less biased judgments for ingroup targets than for outgroup targets. And yet, the suggestion in the literature on biases in judgments of the policy positions of political candidates suggests greater bias in such judgments for liked, familiar, and ingroup candidates than for ones who are disliked and less familiar.

Judd, Kenny, and Krosnick (1983) have written a methodological critique of the empirical work that has examined associations between the judge's position and his or her judgments of liked and disliked candidates' positions. Their principle argument is that differences in the absolute value of relationships between judgments of liked candidates and judgments of disliked candidates are very difficult to interpret, in light of the fact that errors of measurement in assessing the judge's own position and his or her judgment of the candidate's position are probably positively correlated. Such a positive correlation between the two errors of measurement, induced by individual differences in scale usage (among other things), results in associations that are positively biased, both in the case of liked and disliked candidates. The resulting bias leads one to overestimate the absolute magnitude of associations in the case of liked candidates and to underestimate the absolute magnitude of associations in the case of disliked candidates.

Although Judd et al. (1983) focus their empirical efforts on overcoming this problem of correlated measurement error, a second problem that they mention is more central to the present chapter. They suggest that conclusions about bias in judgments of positions of candidates are necessarily problematic, in the absence of a criterion with which those judgments can be compared. In other words, in none of this work does the researcher know the actual position of the political candidate. Without this, it seems very difficult to say that judgments are biased and to compare the magnitude of bias. One can rightly say that judges' positions on an issue influence their judgments of a candidate's position, but one cannot easily talk about there being a bias when there is not a criterion of accuracy. Although approaches to the assessment of accuracy, in the absence of a criterion by which accuracy is defined, are certainly possible, accuracy assessment, even in the presence of a criterion, is sufficiently difficult (see the literature on accuracy assessment—Cronbach 1955; Funder 1987; Judd and Park 1993; Kruglanski 1989; Swann 1984). The issues become all the more tangled, in the absence of a criterion, and conclusions about the presence and relative size of bias in judgments must remain only very tentative.

In the following sections of this chapter, we report on some recent empirical work that has examined judgments of others' political positions when the actual positions of those others who are judged are known, admittedly with some error. Thus, the work that we will be reporting examines the accuracy of judgments of ingroup and outgroup targets (i.e., liked or agreeable individual political actors and groups, on the one hand, and disliked or disagreeable individual political actors and groups, on the other) in the presence of a criterion concerning the actual positions espoused by those targets. In this way, we will be examining biases in stereotypic political judgments using methods that have been used to assess stereotypic accuracy more broadly. We will then reconsider the conclusions about biases in the judgment of others' political positions, based on these studies that include criterion measures.

A preliminary and not terribly precise distinction can be made concerning the basis of communication between the judge and the target that underlies the accuracy of judgment. Two factors can be identified that should affect the accuracy of judgment of a target's political positions. The first concerns the judge's expectations about the target group that influence his or her judgments, in the absence of any specific information from the target about the positions to be judged. Such expectations constitute stereotypic biases, that can only be assessed prior to any explicit communication between the judge and the individual target that is judged. Once there is explicit communication about the target's positions, then the effects of these expectations are confounded with biases that operate on the processing of the communicated information about the target's positions. In other words, judgments about the target's position may be inaccurate both because of prior expectations about the target and because of information-processing biases that affect the interpretation of any explicit message from the target to the judge concerning the to-be-judged positions.

Biases in Political Position Judgments in the Absence of Explicit Communication

We report two studies that may be seen as examining the effects of stereotypic expectations on judgments of a target's political position. In neither study can we strictly argue that there has not been explicit communication between the target and the judge. But we prefer to think that these two studies demonstrate the role of stereotypic expectations, because any communication was prior to and outside of the confines of the study itself. As we indicated previously, the distinction between the role of stereotypic biases and biases in processing communications from the target to the judge is not always as precise as we might like.

In 1972, Dawes, Singer, and Lemons reported a study in which they asked subjects who were either "hawks" or "doves" on the Vietnam War to construct two sets of attitude statements: those that they would expect to be endorsed by typical "hawks," and those that they would expect to be endorsed by typical "doves." The resulting four sets of statements (i.e., two sets of ingroup-generated statements [typical dove statements generated by doves and typical hawk statements generated by hawks] and two sets of outgroup-generated statements [typical dove statements generated by hawks and typical hawk statements generated by doves]) were then given to a new set of hawk and dove subjects, who were asked to judge the appropriateness of the statements that were generated to be typical of their group. Subjects in this second set judged the appropriateness of the statements as descriptors of their own stands on the war, judging each on a scale anchored with the endpoints "more extreme than my own position" and "more moderate than my own position." In sum, the first set of subjects were the judges (to translate the design into our judges and targets terms), generating statements that they believed would be endorsed by typical ingroup and outgroup targets. The second set of subjects, although they judged these statements, were actually the targets, and the accuracy of the generated statements was assessed by asking these target subjects if the generated statements were appropriate descriptors of their points of view or whether they were too extreme or too moderate. Of course, these target subjects were not informed of whether a particular statement was generated by a hawk or a dove subject.

The judgments of the second group of the target subjects revealed a pronounced ingroup-outgroup difference in whether or not the generated statements were seen as too extreme for the group for whom they were generated. Statements that were generated to be typical of the outgroup (regardless of whether they were hawk statements generated by doves or dove statements generated by hawks) were consistently judged to be too extreme by the target subjects. Statements generated to be typical of the ingroup were not seen as too extreme, and were judged more appropriate by members of the target group for which they had been generated.

These results seem to be somewhat at odds with the conclusions reached from the research reviewed earlier, where attempts were made to assess judgmental accuracy in the absence of a criterion. There, the conclusion seemed to be that there was greater inaccuracy in judging the positions of a target with whom one agreed (greater assimilation of those positions) than the positions of a target with whom one disagreed.

Interestingly, the Dawes et al. results are entirely consistent with the research on stereotypic inaccuracies in group judgments reviewed at the start of the chapter (Judd, Ryan, and Park 1991). In that work, outgroup stereotypes tended to be stereotypic exaggerations of the actual nature of outgroups, while ingroup stereotypes typically were less exaggerated. In sum, although the Dawes et al. study seems to contradict earlier work on biases in the judgment of others' preferred policy positions, it is entirely consistent with work on ingroup-outgroup differences in stereotypic accuracy, where criterion measures have been used to assess accuracy.

The Dawes et al. (1972) study represents an advance over other studies that have explored biases in the judgment of targets' political positions in the absence of a criterion. However, the measurement of the criterion is certainly not without its problems in this study. The second set of target subjects, those providing the criterion, was certainly not a representative sample of all hawks and doves. It is entirely possible that this criterion sample was actually less extreme in their political positions than the population of hawks and doves in general or the population that the judges had in mind when generating the attitude statements. Accordingly, although the results of this study are of considerable interest, a replication seems in order, in which the criterion is measured from a representative sample of the target groups.

Using data from the 1976 National Election Study conducted by the Institute for Social Research at the University of Michigan, we have recently explored how Democratic and Republican judges perceive the political positions of Democratic and Republican target groups on a set of political attitude items standardly used in the National Election Studies (see Judd and Park 1993). We compared the judgments of respondents with a criterion constructed from the attitude responses that self-identified Republican and Democratic respondents to the survey made on the same attitude items.[1] Since the sample (presuming complete data) is a stratified random sample of all voting-age United States residents, we can presume that the mean self-ratings of attitudes on these items by individuals who represent themselves as Democrats and Republicans are unbiased estimates of the means of their respective populations.[2]

Table 1 presents the ten political issues on which both self-reported attitudes and judgments of Democratic and Republican target groups were made. All responses were given on seven point scales, where an ideologically liberal answer was represented as a one and a conservative one as a seven. Thus, higher responses are seen as stereotypic of the Republican targets and counterstereotypic of Democratic ones; low responses are considered to be stereotypic of Democratic targets and counterstereotypic of Republican ones. To examine the accuracy of judges' estimates of where most of the party is seen to be, simple discrepancy scores were computed for each judge on each issue between his or her judgment of each target group and the mean of the self-reported responses of all individuals who indicated that they were either Democrats or Republicans. Self-reported attitudes of individuals who indicated no party affiliation were not included in constructing the criterion means.

Since the issue of interest here is whether the stereotypicality of the groups is overestimated (as was found in the case of outgroup judgments in the Dawes et al. 1972 study), the discrepancy scores were computed in all cases so that positive values indicate that the target group is seen more stereotypically than is, in fact, the case. Thus, in the case of the Republican targets, the criterion mean was subtracted from the judge's estimate. (Thus, positive discrepancies indicate that the target's conservativeness is overestimated.) For the Democratic targets, the judge's estimate was subtracted from the criterion mean. (Thus, positive discrepancies indicate that the target's liberalness is overestimated.) The mean values of these discrepancies, aggregating across both judges and items, are presented in the top half of table 2, broken down by judge and target party affiliations.

The most striking thing about these means is that they are all positive for the Democratic targets and negative for the Republican ones. All judges, regardless of their affiliation, overestimated the liberalness of the Democratic targets and underestimated the conservativeness of the Republican

TABLE 1. Issues in 1976 NES Political Attitude Data

Government Guaranteed Job
  1 = Government see to job and good standard of living
  7 = Government let each person get ahead on his own

Rights of Accused
  1 = Protect rights of accused
  7 = Stop crime regardless of rights of accused

School Busing
  1 = Bus to achieve integration
  7 = Keep children in neighborhood schools

Government Aid to Minorities
  1 = Government should help minority groups
  7 = Minority groups should help themselves

Federal Medical Insurance Plan
  1 = Government insurance plan
  7 = Private insurance plans

General Lib/Con Ideology
  1 = Extremely liberal
  7 = Extremely conservative

Urban Unrest
  1 = Solve problems of poverty and unemployment
  7 = Use all available force

Legalization of Marijuana
  1 = Make use of marijuana legal
  7 = Set penalties higher than they are now

Tax Rate Reform
  1 = Increase the tax rate for high incomes
  7 = Have the same tax rate for everyone

Women's Role
  1 = Women and men should have an equal role
  7 = Women's place is in the home

targets. In other words, there is a general tendency in these judgments to overestimate the liberalness of both target groups; as a result the Democratic targets appear to be seen more stereotypically and the Republican targets less stereotypically than they are.

In addition to this overall estimation of target group liberalness, there is a reliable ingroup-outgroup effect (i.e., judge group by target group interaction, treating the former factor as between-subject and the latter as within-subject) in these data, $F(1,1100) = 54.74$; $p < .001$. In the case of the Democratic targets, Democratic judges show less overestimation of liberalness (i.e., less stereotypicality) than do Republican judges. In the case of Republican targets, Republican judges show more overestimation of liberalness (i.e., less stereotypicality) than do Democratic judges. Thus, over and above the systematic overestimation of liberalness, ingroup judgments were less stereotypic than were outgroup judgments.

To explore whether strength of affiliation with one's ingroup moderates the above ingroup-outgroup difference, we included the judge's self-report of whether he or she was a strong or not very strong party affiliate as an additional factor in the analysis.[3] The mean discrepancy scores that result when this additional factor is included are presented at the bottom of table 2. As expected, the triple interaction (judge party by target party by strength of judge's party affiliation) was reliable in these data, $F(1,1100) = 5.30$; $p < .05$. The direction of this triple interaction indicates that the ingroup-outgroup difference (with ingroups judged to be less stereotypic than outgroups) is stronger among judges who indicate a strong party affiliation than among judges who indicate they are more weakly affiliated.

In many ways, these data are consistent with the results presented earlier from the Dawes et al. (1972) study. Namely, in these national survey

TABLE 2.   Mean Stereotypicality Discrepancies 1976 NES Political Party Judgments

Judge's Party	Target Party	
	Democrat	Republican
Democrat	.68	−.3
Republican	1.04	−.53
(Including strength of party affiliation)		
Strong Dem.	.70	−.24
Not Very Strong Dem.	.66	−.41
Strong Rep.	1.31	−.40
Not Very Strong Rep.	.85	−.62

data, we found that the stereotypicality of outgroup target judgments was overestimated relative to the stereotypicality of ingroup target judgments. For Democratic targets, this means that Democratic judges saw them as less extremely liberal than did Republican judges. For Republican targets, Republican judges saw them as less extremely conservative than did Democratic judges. In addition, the strength of the judge's party affiliation moderated this ingroup-outgroup difference, such that the ingroup-outgroup difference in stereotypicality was greater for judges who indicated stronger party affiliations. The one complicating factor is that all judges overestimated the liberalness of all target groups. Thus, in an absolute sense, we cannot say that the judgments of Republican targets were more extremely stereotypic than the criterion. Even the outgroup judges saw the Republican targets as less conservative than they were. This tendency to provide target estimates that are too liberal for all target groups illustrates one of the major problems in assessing the accuracy of judgments by computing discrepancy or difference scores between judgments and the criterion (see Cronbach 1955; Judd and Park 1993). A tendency to see all target groups as relatively liberal, and more liberal than one judges oneself to be, on average, may simply represent a response set that exists independent of other forms of accuracy of judgment. Such a response set complicates the interpretation of these sorts of discrepancy scores as indices of accuracy of judgment. As Cronbach has effectively argued, one may systematically overestimate or underestimate a criterion (thus yielding large discrepancy scores) while, nevertheless, being very sensitive to variation in the criterion from one judgmental domain or question to another.

To overcome this response set problem, and to assess accuracy in the sense of sensitivity of judgments to variation in the criterion across items, within-judge sensitivity correlations were computed as an additional measure of accuracy of judgment. To compute these correlations, we took each judge's estimates of where he or she thought most party members stood on the ten issues and correlated those judgments with the criterion means on the ten issues, computing the correlation across the ten issues. Higher correlations indicate greater sensitivity of the judge to variation in the criterion from item to item. They indicate that judges are able to accurately report variations across the issues in how liberal or conservative the target group actually is.

Mean sensitivity correlations, broken down by judge's party and target group party, are given in figure 1. These means were computed by transforming each judge's accuracy correlations (one for each target group) into Fisher z statistics (to reduce the skew in the distribution of correlations), computing the mean of the Fisher z's, and then doing an inverse or reciprocal transformation on this mean to return it to the correlation metric. As in the analysis of the discrepancy scores, these correlations show a strong ingroup-outgroup effect (judge party by target-group party interaction), $F(1,237) = 12.23$; $p < .001$, such that ingroup judgments are substantially more accurate than outgroup judgments. The mean accuracy correlation for ingroup judgments equals 0.285; for outgroup judgments, the mean is 0.180. This accuracy difference means that judges are more sensitive to differences from issue to issue in where the ingroup targets stand than inwhere the outgroup targets stand.

As we did with the discrepancy scores, we also included self-reported strength of judge's party affiliation as an additional between-subjects factor in the analysis. The mean sensitivity correlations, broken down by judge's party, target group party, and strength of judge's party affiliation, are given in figure 2. Once again, we find that the triple interaction is reliable, $F(1,237) = 7.62$; $p < .01$, indicating that the magnitude of the ingroup-outgroup difference in accuracy is greater in the case of judges who strongly affiliate with their party than in the case of judges who are more weakly affiliated. For judges who indicate a strong party affiliation, the mean ingroup correlation is 0.335 and the mean outgroup correlation is 0.120. For those who indicate a weaker affiliation, the mean ingroup correlation is 0.235 and the mean outgroup correlation is 0.200.

These sensitivity correlations nicely replicate the ingroup-outgroup difference found in the discrepancy analyses and lead to the conclusion, once again, that judgments of positions of ingroup targets are more accurate than are judgments of positions of outgroup targets. Particularly interesting in these data is the fact that this ingroup-outgroup difference is moderated by strength of the judge's party affiliation, such that stronger party affiliates are more accurate in their ingroup judgments than are weaker affiliates, and are actually less accurate in their outgroup judgments than are weaker affiliates. This last result is quite intriguing, for we know that individuals who report stronger party affiliations also tend to be more involved in politics in general, more knowledgeable about political issues and groups, more likely to read about politics, and so forth (Campbell, Converse, Miller, and Stokes 1960; Kinder and Sears 1985; Lusk and Judd 1988; McClosky and Zaller 1984). Thus, because of these differences in knowledge, we might have expected stronger party affiliates to be more accurate in their judgments of both the ingroup and the outgroup than those who affiliate with their party more weakly. But what we find is that, in spite of their greater knowledge and involvement in the political domain, the stronger party affiliates are actually less accurate in judging the positions of the outgroup party than are those who have weaker party ties. Being a party loyalist appears to increase the accuracy of ingroup judgments and to decrease the accuracy of outgroup judgments.

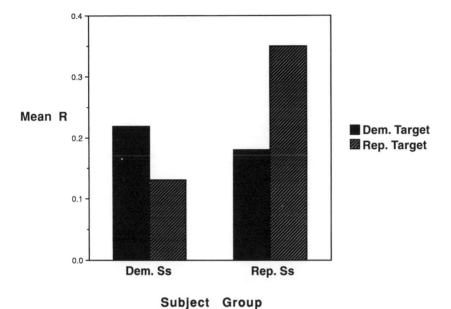

Fig. 1. Mean sensitivity correlations of political party judgments

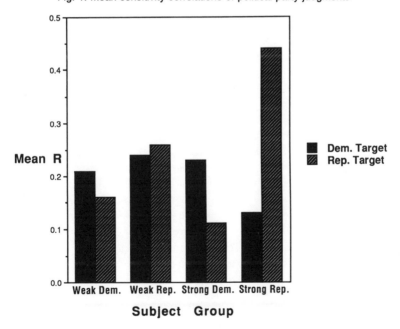

Fig. 2. Mean sensitivity correlations in political party judgments

Biases in Political Position Judgments, Given Explicit Communication

The above studies all involve stereotypic biases in the judgment of policy positions attributed to ingroups and outgroups without any attempt to control or examine the sorts of information that judges have at their disposal in making their judgments. We assume that these biases derive from differences in how information is processed and retrieved about the positions they are judging, but it is difficult to verify this assumption in the absence of explicit control over the information on which judges' estimates are based. It is also possible, of course, that the ingroup-outgroup differences that we have documented derive from differences in the messages that targets actually communicate to ingroup and outgroup judges, rather than differences in how those messages are processed.

To examine our assumption that the biases in judgments derive from differences in information processing, experimental procedures are necessary in which we can strictly control the information that targets communicate about their positions to judges. We need to construct a situation in which judgments are made of the positions of ingroup and outgroup targets, holding constant what actually is communicated by the targets about their positions to the ingroup and outgroup judges. We have recently completed a study (Downing 1991) in which this was done. Videotaped interviews were conducted with eight target individuals about their views on abortion. A set of standard interview questions was used for all targets, asking them what their overall position on the issue was, why they held the position they did, how important the issue was to them, and any reservations or qualifications they might make about the position they took on the issue. The interviews were very short, lasting an average of three minutes.

The eight target individuals were chosen so that four of them were generally pro-life (i.e., antiabortion) and four of them pro-choice (i.e., proabortion rights). Within each group of four there were two male and two female targets, and an effort was made to assure some variation in espoused positions between targets within the two groups. After being interviewed, the eight target individuals completed various questionnaire measures on which they indicated their attitudes on the issue of abortion. These self-ratings served as the accuracy criterion in examining the judgments made by individual judges who viewed the videotaped interviews.

An additional 68 individuals (37 females and 31 males) served as judges in the study. They first completed an attitude questionnaire, including the same questions on the abortion rights issue as those completed by the targets. They then watched the 8 interviews (in one of two different random orders), keeping notes if they wished about what each person said. Notes were allowed in order to help the judges distinguish the targets from each other. Following all eight interviews, the judges were shown still photographs of each of the target individuals and asked to judge the position on abortion rights that each espoused, using the same set of questions as both they and the targets had used to indicate their own attitudes on the issue. They were allowed to keep the notes they had made during the interviews while completing these judgments.

The resulting judgments of the target's positions were analyzed as a function of whether the target was generally in favor of or opposed to abortion rights, whether the judge was generally in favor of or opposed to abortion rights, and the extremity of the judge's own position on the issue.[4] The first two of these variables were dichotomous; the final was treated as a continuous variable in the analyses. The interaction between the first two factors, in that is, target's position and judges' positions—is equivalent to the ingroup-outgroup distinction or the distinction between judgements made of agreeable targets and judgments made of disagreeable targets.

It is important to note that the judgments in this study are judgments about the positions espoused by target individuals, rather than about the positions attributed to the ingroup or outgroup as a whole. In the beginning of this chapter, we reviewed recent work on stereotype accuracy and made the argument that judgmental biases that ensue from stereotypes can take different forms, depending on whether judgments are made at the group level, about ingroups and outgroups as aggregates, or whether judgments are made about individual group members and then those judgments are aggregated across the individual ingroup and outgroup targets. We return to this point following our discussion of the results of this experiment.

The initial dependent variable that we analyzed was the judged extremity of the targets' positions, aggregating across the four pro and four anti targets. Higher values on this dependent variable indicate that the targets were seen to be more extreme in their positions, either in the pro-life direction (if they opposed abortion rights) or in the pro-choice direction (if they favored it). Mean extremity scores for the target judgments as a function of ingroup-outgroup and judge's own extremity (dichotomized for purposes of presentation of the mean values) are given in figure 3. As these means show, there was a large main effect of extremity of judge, $F(1,65) = 62.09$; $p < .001$, a reliable ingroup-outgroup difference, $F(1,65) = 12.39$; $p < .001$, and a reliable interaction between judge's extremity and the ingroup-outgroup difference, $F(1,65) = 12.54$; $p < .001$. In general, judges who were themselves more extreme saw the targets as espousing more extreme points of view. This main effect parallels similar judgmental effects shown in previous work (Judd and Johnson 1981). In addition, and consistent with the ingroup-outgroup judgmental differences discussed earlier, outgroup targets

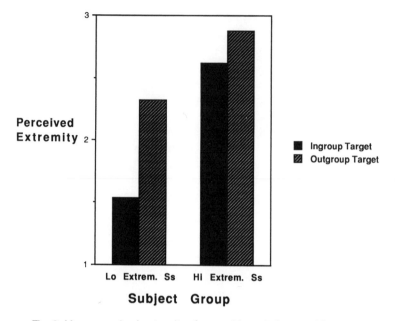

Fig. 3. Mean perceived extremity of agreeable and disagreeable targets

were seen as espousing more extreme points of view than were ingroup targets. In other words, outgroup targets were seen more stereotypically than were ingroup targets. Somewhat surprising was the interaction. As the means show, the difference in the perceived extremity of ingroup and outgroup targets was more pronounced in the case of judges who were themselves less extreme than in the case of judges who were more extreme. Expressed the other way around, the effect of judge's own extremity on the perceived extremity of the targets was greater for ingroup targets than for outgroup ones.

Parallel effects emerged when the dependent variable incorporated the criterion of each target's self-rating into a discrepancy score between the judge's rating of the target and the target's self-rating on the issue. As in the National Election data presented earlier, discrepancy scores were computed so that positive values indicated greater stereotypicality in judgments than in the criterion (i.e., pro-life targets seen as more pro-life than they are; pro choice targets seen as more pro choice than they are). From the mean values that are presented in figure 4, it is apparent that judges generally underestimated the stereotypicality of all targets. We suspect that this underestimation may simply be due to the fact that a three-minute interview did not allow targets sufficient time to convey the depth of their conviction

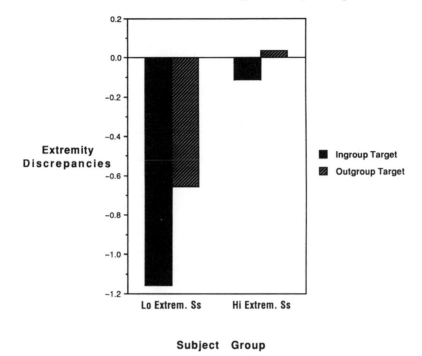

Fig. 4. Perceived-actual discrepancies in extremity

on the issue. Judges' estimates of where the targets stood were thus regressive in the sense that their uncertainty about where the targets stood led them to relatively moderate judgments of their positions. As the means in figure 4 show, there was a strong main effect of extremity of judge, $F(1,65)$ = 56.87; $p < .001$, a reliable ingroup-outgroup difference, $F(1,65) = 6.55$; $p < .02$, and a reliable interaction between judge's extremity and the ingroup-outgroup difference, $F(1,65) = 5.89$; $p < .02$. In spite of the absolute underestimation of the stereotypicality of all targets, it is still the case that outgroup targets were seen more stereotypically by all judges, that more extreme judges saw the targets more stereotypically, and that the ingroup-outgroup difference in stereotypicality was particularly pronounced among less extreme judges.

To overcome the problems inherent in the use of discrepancy scores as measures of accuracy, we also examined within-subject accuracy correlations computed between each judge's estimates of the targets' positions and the targets' self-expressed positions. Note that these accuracy correlations are rather different from those that we computed in the case of the political party judgments when we examined the National Election study data. There we computed correlations between each judge's estimate of where the target group stood as a whole and the criterion for the target group across the ten issues that were assessed. In the present situation, we computed a correlation between the judgment of an individual target's attitude and the target individual's self-reported attitude, computing the correlation across the four targets within a group on a single issue. Thus, there are two fundamental differences between these correlations and those reported earlier. Earlier, the correlations referred to judgments about a group of individuals, and were computed across issues. Here, the correlations refer to judgments of individuals, and are computed across individuals on one issue.

As the above discussion makes clear, two separate accuracy correlations were computed for each judge, one for the set of pro-life targets and one for the set of pro-choice targets. These were analyzed using the same factors as those employed in the analysis of the judgments and judgment discrepancy scores already reported. Figure 5 presents the mean accuracy correlations as a function of ingroup-outgroup and the extremity of the judge's own position on the issue. The first thing to note about these means is that the correlations are exceedingly high. Judges showed remarkable ability to pick up the differences among the four targets in each group. Doubtlessly this was due, in part, to the fact that they kept notes during the interviews and could refer to these notes when making their judgments. Nonetheless, it was still necessary to translate what they had heard into a scale rating that reflected the target's own scale rating. The resulting correlations are impressively high.

The analyses of these accuracy correlations revealed both a reliable ingroup-outgroup difference, $F(1,65) = 9.75$; $p < .01$, and a reliable interaction between ingroup-outgroup and the extremity of the judge's attitude, $F(1,65) = 6.90$; $p < .02$. As the means in figure 5 show, judgments display more accuracy for outgroup targets than for ingroup ones. This difference was primarily due to judges who were not very extreme in their own attitudes. More extreme judges showed little difference between agreeable and disagreeable targets. Thus, contrary to the results using the accuracy correlations from the National Election study data, here we find more accurate judgments for the outgroup than for the ingroup, although this difference is only found for relatively moderate judges (i.e., judges who are not as invested in and extreme about their position on abortion rights).

Integration and Conclusions

From the studies we have reviewed, four primary conclusions emerge concerning the accuracy with which judges estimate the political positions of target groups.

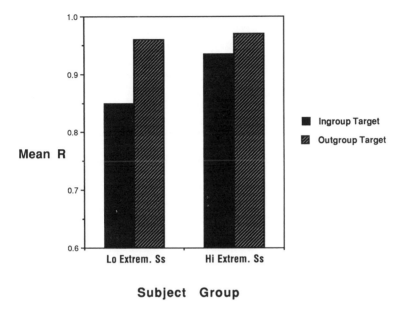

Fig. 5. Mean accuracy correlations across targets

1. The stereotypicality or extremity of outgroup targets, or targets with whom the judge disagrees, is overestimated, relative to ingroup targets. This seems to be true both for judgments at the group level and for judgments of individuals who are members of the ingroup and outgroup. It also seems to be found even when the content of what is communicated by the target to the judge is held constant.

2. Judges' own extremity on the issue being judged and the strength of their affiliation to their ingroup seem to moderate the degree to which they see ingroup and outgroup targets stereotypically. Judges who are themselves relatively extreme on an issue tend to see individual others as relatively extreme on an issue, both others with whom they agree and others with whom they disagree. Judges who identify more strongly with their ingroup tend to overestimate the stereotypicality of the outgroup as a whole, compared to judges who are more weakly affiliated with their ingroup.

3. Judgments of where the ingroup as a whole stands on issues are more accurate, in the sense of sensitivity to differences from issue to issue, than are their judgments of where the outgroup as a whole stands on those issues. This difference also seems to be more true for judges who profess stronger affiliations with their ingroup.

4. Judges are more accurate in judging differences between the posi-

tions of individual outgroup members on an issue than they are in judging differences among individual ingroup members, although this accuracy difference is smaller as judges themselves adopt more extreme points of view.

Although these results are quite consistent with other work on the accuracy of stereotypic judgments, they seem to be rather inconsistent with earlier work that has explored biases in the judgments of others' policy positions in the absence of criterion measures. That work, reviewed earlier in this chapter, suggested that such biases were more potent in the case of agreeable targets than in the case of disagreeable ones. The research that we have reviewed suggests something rather different. The tendency to see others stereotypically, both in the political positions they espouse, and in the traits they are seen as possessing (Judd, Ryan, and Park 1991), seems to be greater in the case of outgroups (i.e., groups with whom one disagrees) than in the case of ingroups. Thus, across the three studies we have presented, outgroup political positions are always seen as more extreme or more stereotypic than are ingroup political positions. Admittedly, they are not always seen as extreme or as stereotypic as are the normative criteria with which the judgments are compared. Nevertheless, given the difficulties of assessing the criterion and the problems that response biases pose for the interpretation of discrepancy scores (Judd and Park 1993), the consistent ingroup-outgroup difference in stereotypicality is of considerable interest.

The second conclusion, that the degree to which judges overestimate the stereotypicality of ingroups and outgroups depends on the subject's own extremity on the issue and the strength of his or her affiliation with the ingroup is consistent with past work (Judd and Johnson 1981), and expected from theoretical models of group identity (Tajfel and Turner 1986). In general, it seems that individuals who adopt extreme positions on issues tend to see the world as more polarized on that issue than individuals who adopt more moderate positions (Judd and Johnson 1984). In addition, individuals whose identity is more closely tied to their group seem to manifest stronger stereotypes, particularly of the outgroup, than individuals who affiliate less strongly with the ingroup.

The third and the fourth conclusions that we have reached, both based on within-subject accuracy correlations, seem superficially to contradict each other. The third one argues that judges are more sensitive to differences between issues in where the ingroup stands on those issues than in where the outgroup stands on those issues. This would seem to indicate greater accuracy in judging the positions of ingroups than those of outgroups. The fourth conclusion, on the other hand, suggests that judges are more sensitive to individual differences in the positions espoused by outgroup or disagreeable others than they are to individual differences among agreeable others, thus, seemingly suggesting greater accuracy in outgroup judgments than in ingroup ones.

In fact, however, these two conclusions need not be contradictory. If one allows that accuracy in judging a group of individuals is not necessarily the same thing as accuracy in judging individual group members, then these two conclusions are simultaneously consistent with past work. To see how these two conclusions need not be contradictory, consider first that the accuracy correlations in the two cases are computed in rather different ways. The third conclusion is based on accuracy correlations computed between where either the ingroup or outgroup as a whole is judged to stand and the mean of the ingroup or outgroup self-ratings, computed across issues. It suggests that judges are better in reporting differences in positions across issues for their own group than for a group with whom they disagree. On the other hand, the accuracy correlations that underlie the fourth conclusion are based on judgments of individual group members, computing the relationship between those judgments of individuals and the individuals' own self-ratings, across the four individuals in the ingroup or the outgroup. These correlations suggest that judges are better at discriminating among individual targets in the positions they espouse in the case of outgroup targets than in the case of ingroup ones.

Interestingly, these two sets of results are consistent with earlier work on stereotypic judgments of group members provided at either the individual level or the group level (Judd and Park 1988). Judd and Park examined group stereotypes in a modified minimal group situation (i.e., individual subjects were randomly assigned to one group or the other, and no realistic group differences, in fact, existed). Judd and Park showed that when making judgments about groups as a whole, that is, the ingroup and the outgroup, subjects showed a tendency to underestimate the diversity within the outgroup as a whole relative to their judgments of the ingroup. Thus, when thinking about the group as a whole, there seemed to be insufficient allowance for the diversity of outgroup members and overestimation of the potency of the outgroup stereotype. At the same time, when given a memory test for the statements made by individual group members, subjects showed more accurate cued recall memory for individual outgroup members than individual ingroup members. Apparently, at the level of the individual, the subjects were better able to discriminate among outgroup members than among ingroup members.

In combination, these two effects paint a fascinating picture of the way in which outgroup judgments differ from ingroup judgments. On the one hand, when thinking about the group as a whole, outgroups tend to be seen more stereotypically and extremely than ingroups. One "lumps them all together" and presumes that they all fit the stereotype. Thus, they are seen as adopting more disagreeable positions than they in fact do, and differences between issues in the positions they are judged to adopt are minimized. On the other hand, when confronted by individual outgroup members who have actually communicated information about themselves as individuals, more attention may be devoted to outgroup members than ingroup members, and one may be better able to retain individuating information about them than in the case of ingroup members. Perhaps because of a defensive posture that keeps one "wary of the moves of the enemy," one is simultaneously more sensitive to variations within that enemy while, nevertheless, lumping them altogether and thinking of them all, as a group, as more villainous than they are. The political world is seemingly guided by such stereotypic postures and judgments.

NOTES

The research reported in this chapter was supported by grants BNS-8819372 from the National Science Foundation to the first author and R01 MH45049 from the National Institute of Mental Health to Bernadette Park and Charles M. Judd.

1. Brady and Sniderman (1985) have also reported analyses of these data, comparing judgments with criterion measures constructed from self-reported attitudes. Although they were certainly concerned with accuracy issues, their work differs from ours in a number of important ways. First, their assessment of accuracy involves correctly perceiving which side of an issue various political groups line up on, whereas our measures involve deviations from and correlations with estimates of means of the respective populations. Second, their primary motivation was to develop a model of attitude attribution incorporating affective concerns, whereas our research is primarily concerned with ingroup-outgroup differences in accuracy and bias.

2. Admittedly, the criterion here suffers from other problems that are not overcome by the fact that a representative sample of the target population has been used. Two major concerns are important. First of all, the judgment questions asked respondents to identify what they judged to be the typical positions on each issue of the Democratic and Republican parties, rather than the typical positions of self-identified Democrats and Republicans. Thus, the targets of these questions may be different from targets from whom we have measured the criterion. Second, it is certainly debatable whether self-reported attitudes (the mean of which constitutes our criterion) necessarily represent unbiased estimates of a target individual's actual attitudes. Certainly, self-presentational and reporting biases may affect responses. It seems reasonable, however, to think that if a survey respondent believes that his or her responses will remain confidential, self-presentation effects can be minimized. In addition, considerable work suggests that individuals may not, in fact, have well-formulated attitudes on these sorts of political issues (e.g., Campbell, Converse,

Miller, and Stokes 1960; Converse 1964; Converse 1970), or may not have ready access to whatever sentiments they have (e.g., Fazio 1989). It is not our intention to suggest that criterion assessment is an easy task or that we would ever be completely confident in the criterion that we use. We simply wish to argue that without some attempt at criterion assessment, it is nearly impossible to ask questions about the accuracy with which the political positions of target individuals are judged.

3. The exact wording of the question used is "Would you call yourself a strong (Republican or Democrat) or a not very strong (Republican or Democrat)?."

4. These extremity scores were computed by taking the absolute difference between each person's espoused position on the issue and the scale midpoint.

CHAPTER 5

The Relation between Political Attitude Importance and Knowledge Structure

Matthew K. Berent and Jon K. Krosnick

Political scientists have long maintained an interest in the structure of cognitive elements in the minds of citizens. Certainly the most prominent literature on this topic has examined the degree to which citizens' attitudes on specific policy issues are organized or structured by overarching ideological principles. It is now clear that some citizens evidence substantial ideological organization, while others manifest little, if any (for a review, see, e.g., Judd and Krosnick 1989). Important motivation for this literature has come from the belief that the structure of an individual's attitudes is influenced by political context (Nie, Verba, and Petrocik 1979), and that such structure has important implications regarding political decision making and behavior. Thus, differences between voters in terms of attitude structure can help us understand differences in political information-processing and action patterns.

More recently, political psychologists have become interested in a different sort of cognitive structure: the organization of beliefs about a single political object. This interest has been partially sparked by growing attention in social and cognitive psychology to information processing and knowledge structures. In political science, the most often used concept in this area has been that of schemas. Although some political psychological analyses using the schema concept have made little use of the structural notion inherent in it (see, e.g., Kuklinski, Luskin, and Bolland 1991), others have paid greater attention to belief structure, to valuable ends (e.g., McGraw, Pinney, and Neumann 1991; Lusk and Judd 1988). Our goal in this chapter is to bring together the notions of cognitive structures and knowledge organization with the concerns and ideas of attitude theories in order to yield new and useful insights into political attitude functions.

Specifically, we will explore the relation between one dimension of political attitudes, attitude importance, and the organization of attitude-relevant knowledge in memory. And our focus here is on one particular type of political attitude: preferences regarding the policies that government should and should not implement. We will first introduce the concepts of attitude importance and knowledge organization and suggest why they might be related in the case of policy attitudes. Then, we will describe the results of four experiments that explored the relation between policy attitude importance and knowledge organization.

Attitude Importance

Political scientists and psychologists have come to recognize, during the last two decades especially, that all attitudes are not created equal: some are stronger than others. Although strength has not been precisely defined over the years, Petty and Krosnick (n.d.) have recently proposed a definition that seems faithful to most prior uses of this term. According to their perspective, strong attitudes have four defining features: (1) they are quite resistant to change; (2) they are highly stable over time; (3) they have strong impact on the processing of relevant incoming information; and (4) they have strong impact in shaping relevant behaviors.

Several different attributes of attitudes have been used over the years to differentiate strong attitudes from weak ones. These include affective-cognitive consistency (Rosenberg 1956, 1968), ego-involvement (Sherif and Cantril 1947; Sherif, Sherif, and Nebergall 1965), affective intensity (Cantril 1944, 1946), certainty (Budd 1986; Budd and Spencer 1984; Cantril 1944; Davidson, Yantis, Norwood, and Montano 1985; Ewing 1942; Holtz and Miller 1985; Krosnick and Schuman 1988), and extremity (Ewing 1942; Judd and Johnson 1981; Tannenbaum 1956; Tesser 1978). In general, research investigating these dimensions has found that attitudes typified by high affective-cognitive consistency, intensity, certainty, and so on, do indeed tend to be more crystallized and consequential than weak attitudes (for a detailed review, see Krosnick, Boninger, Chuang, Berent, and Carnot, n.d.).

In this chapter, we focus on one such dimension of attitude strength: attitude importance. Attitude importance refers to the subjective personal importance an individual attaches to an attitude object. Two components of this definition merit some brief attention. First, attitude importance is subjectively determined. Although the objective relevance of an attitude object to an individual's life often influences attitude importance, such relevance does not define importance. That is, people can attach a great deal of importance to issues that don't affect them, and they can attach very little importance to issues that do involve them. Second, importance, as we study it, is inherently personal. It deals with how important an attitude object, such as a political issue, is to the individual who possesses an attitude toward it. As such, attitude importance does not involve judgments of the significance of the object for people in general. Thus, even though a person may recognize that an issue is important for the country as a whole, her or his attitude will be described as unimportant if she or he does not care about the issue personally.

Attitude importance, as a subjective and personal dimension of attitude strength, has been the focus of a substantial body of research (Cantril 1944; Festinger 1957; Krosnick 1988a, 1988b, 1989, 1990b; Madsen 1978; Tourangeau, Rasinski, Bradburn, and D'Andrade 1989a, 1989b). As with other attitude dimensions related to strength, the consequences of attitude importance can be observed across a variety of domains. More important attitudes lead to better memory for relevant information (Berent 1990), are more stable over time (Hahn 1970; Krosnick 1988b; Schuman and Presser 1981), are more resistant to change (Borgida and Howard-Pitney 1983; Fine 1957; Gorn 1975; Howard-Pitney, Borgida, and Omoto 1986; Powell 1977; Rhine and Severance 1970), are more accessible in memory (Krosnick 1989), and have more influence on perceptions of candidates' attitudes (Granberg and Seidel 1976; Holtz and Miller 1985; Krosnick 1988a; Marks and Miller 1982), on preferences for particular candidates (Aldrich and McKelvey 1977; Clore and Baldridge 1968; Granberg and Holmberg 1986; Krosnick 1988a; Tedin 1980), on other political attitudes (Budd 1986; Hoetler 1985; Judd and Krosnick 1989; Kaplan 1980; Young, Borgida, Sullivan, and Aldrich 1987), and on political behavior (Jaccard and Becker 1985; Krosnick 1988a; Rokeach and Kliejunas 1972; Schuman and Presser 1981).

Attitude Importance and Elaborative Processing

In this chapter, we explore another possible consequence of attitude importance that may, in part, account for some of these previously documented effects of importance. Specifically, we suspect that attitude importance may inspire deeper processing of attitude-relevant information, which, in turn, yields more refined organization of that information in memory. To explain the basis for this hypothesis, we must begin by considering the various ways in which people can process incoming information.

A popular assumption among social and cognitive psychological researchers is that people are limited information processors (e.g., Fiske and Taylor 1991; Schneider and Shiffrin 1977; Shiffrin and Schneider 1977; Taylor 1981; Tversky and Kahneman 1974; Wyer and Srull 1986). That is, people are unable (or perhaps unwilling) to expend the cognitive effort necessary to extensively process all information to which they are exposed. Consequently, individuals may extensively and deeply process some select classes of information, employ heuristics or other shortcuts when processing other classes of information, and completely ignore still other classes of information.

Different levels of information processing require different amounts of cognitive effort. At the most superficial level, individuals may simply perceive the presence of a stimulus. Processing information at such a shallow level requires very little cognitive effort. At a somewhat deeper level, individuals may both perceive a stimulus and interpret its meaning, the latter step requiring more effort. At a still deeper level, individuals may perceive, interpret, and evaluate stimulus information. At this deep level of processing, which requires even more effort, individuals elaborate on new information by relating it to the knowledge they have already stored in memory (Craik and Tulving 1975; Reder and Anderson 1980; Wyer and Srull 1980, 1986). In effect, they are asking themselves: Do I already know this? How does it compare to things I already know? Does it support or challenge my attitude?

If people are, indeed, cognitive misers, it follows that only individuals with unusual motivation will engage in such elaborative processing (see, e.g., Petty and Cacioppo 1986). A natural question is then: When are people motivated to engage in effortful processing? One possible answer is that people will do so when a stimulus is relevant to an attitude that the individual considers highly personally important. As we noted earlier, attaching personal importance to an attitude leads individuals to expend extraordinary effort in using that attitude when perceiving others' attitudes, when forming attitudes toward others, and when performing relevant behaviors. By the same token, personal importance may lead individuals to expend greater cognitive effort when processing new relevant information.

One set of recent studies suggests that individuals are, indeed, more motivated to extensively and elaboratively process new information when it is relevant to personally important attitudes. Berent (1990) found that individuals recalled and recognized information relevant to important attitudes better than they recalled and recognized information relevant to unimportant attitudes. Furthermore, this relation between importance and memory was mediated by selective elaboration of attitude-relevant information. When the opportunity for elaboration was removed, the memorial advantage of information relevant to important attitudes disappeared. Thus, when presented with several pieces of information concerning different political issues, individuals apparently devote more cognitive resources to the elaboration of information that is relevant to personally important attitudes.

The Organizational Consequences of Elaboration

Our primary interest in this chapter is in the possibility that this selective elaboration influences how political information becomes organized in memory. In order to understand this possible effect, we must first establish a model of memorial organization. In this context, we have found it most useful to think in terms of the associative network conceptualization popular among cognitive psychologists (Anderson 1983; Anderson and Bower 1973; Collins and Loftus 1975; Collins and Quillian 1969; Quillian 1969). Within this framework, knowledge organizations are composed of two basic components. First, knowledge organizations contain individual pieces of knowledge, defined in the most generic sense. A single piece of knowledge may refer to any of several constructs, such as the cognitive representation of an object, a piece of factual information, a belief, or some value of a dimension. Second, knowledge organizations contain links between these individual pieces of knowledge.

Links between individual pieces of knowledge are not built randomly. Rather, they are built between pieces of knowledge that an individual recognizes to be somehow related to one another by virtue of relevance to some dimension. For example, one might believe that people who are antiabortion are typically old; one might also believe that antiabortion people are typically religious. Thus, these two beliefs might be perceived to be related, by virtue of the fact that they both refer to characteristics of people who oppose abortion. Two such beliefs would then be linked in memory to a node representing the characteristic or dimension they have in common (i.e., relevance to the characteristics of antiabortionists). This dimension node would then be linked to the node representing the attitude object. In this way, beliefs and factual information about an object that share some value of a dimension are linked to the object indirectly, via their links to the dimension.

To understand this notion more graphically, in the case of political attitudes, consider individuals whose knowledge about an object is poorly organized. In the extreme, such individuals have not noted any relations among the beliefs and pieces of information they have about an object. Figure 1 illustrates how a person might store his or her knowledge about the attitude object of abortion in this fashion. The person has several pieces of knowledge about abortion, but has not noted that some of them are somehow related to one another. Consequently, dimensions around which other individuals might organize knowledge relevant to abortion are absent from this individual's knowledge structure. Beliefs and pieces of information are linked only with the attitude object.

In contrast to this scenario, consider an individual whose knowledge about abortion is highly organized. Figure 2 illustrates how the same bits of knowledge included in the preceding illustration might be stored in a more structured fashion. Here, the beliefs and pieces of information are organized around a variety of dimensions: philosophical arguments, rights

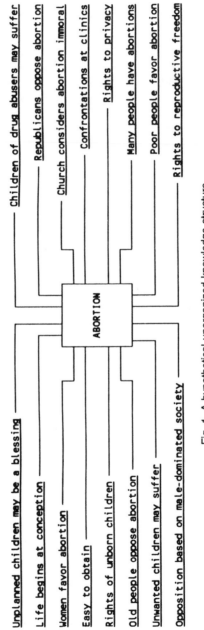

Fig. 1. A hypothetical unorganized knowledge structure

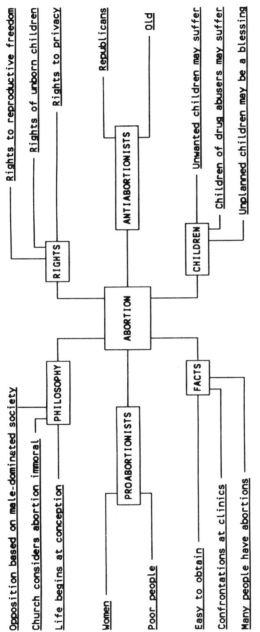

Fig. 2. A hypothetical organized knowledge structure

involved, typical proabortionists, typical antiabortionists, veridical facts, and implications involving children. Thus, within this framework, more organization refers to the use of more dimensions to organize subjectively related beliefs and information one has about an object.

This sort of refined organization is only likely to evolve if a person spends a great deal of time thinking about the information. Such cognitive elaboration presumably involves evaluating and relating new information to knowledge already stored in memory. The more one thinks about a new piece of information, the more likely he or she is to recognize what it has in common with previously stored knowledge. As a result, the person may incorporate the new information into the structure, either by linking the information to existing nodes or by linking it to newly-formed dimension nodes. All other things equal, then, spending more time elaborating on information relevant to some object should yield more stored relations between pieces of information. Therefore, if attitude importance does, indeed, inspire deeper processing of relevant incoming information, it should also yield more elaborate organization of relevant knowledge stored in memory.

Assessing Knowledge Organization

In order to test this hypothesis, we needed to select some method(s) with which to assess the extent and patterns of knowledge organization. Previous researchers have generally adopted one of three approaches to doing so. The first examines how easily people are able to use stored knowledge (e.g., Hymes 1986; Pratkanis 1989). Presumably, when knowledge is stored in better-organized structures, tasks requiring use of that knowledge should be performed more quickly and consistently. This is so because organizational nodes in elaborate knowledge structures should direct memory searches to needed subsets of the individual's total knowledge. Thus, by enabling the individual to ignore other, irrelevant subsets of his or her total knowledge, this type of organization may enable more efficient and reliable searches. In contrast, unorganized knowledge structures offer no guides or clues indicating how to most efficiently find the desired information. Consequently, searching for a needed piece of knowledge in an unorganized structure is likely to take more time, and may well yield different conclusions on different occasions.

A second method used to assess knowledge organization focuses on the order in which pieces of information are retrieved from memory. This order is presumed to reflect how that knowledge is stored (see, e.g., Lusk and Judd 1988; McGraw and Pinney 1990; McGraw, Pinney, and Neumann 1991; McGraw and Steenbergen in this volume; Ostrom, Pryor, and Simpson 1981; Rahn in this volume). Items linked to a common dimensional node in a cognitive structure ought to be generated close to each other when people are asked to list all of their knowledge on a topic. One can therefore assess how organized stored items are by examining how closely related items are generated.

The third common method for assessing knowledge organization examines the way in which people classify pieces of stored knowledge. According to this approach, the manner in which a person sorts, groups, or otherwise structures pieces of information reflects relations that exist among them in memory (Conover and Feldman 1984; Scott, Osgood, and Peterson 1979; Tourangeau, Rasinski, and D'Andrade 1991). Individuals who report more independent sources of relations among knowledge bits presumably have more dimensional nodes organizing them in memory.

To evaluate the hypothesis regarding attitude importance outlined above, we used all three of these methods. Each one has its own shortcomings and alternative explanations that may account for its results. But when all three methods support a consistent and sensible set of conclusions about memory organization, one can have greater confidence in the validity of those conclusions. Our first three studies, therefore, used each of these methods to test the general proposition that attitude importance is associated with greater organization of attitude-relevant knowledge.

An Initial Test: Inference Speed and Consistency

Our first study explored the relation between political-attitude importance and knowledge organization by examining facility at making inferences. To illustrate our approach more graphically, suppose a person whose knowledge about abortion is unorganized (as in fig.1) is asked to infer how likely it is that an elderly person favors legalized abortion. In order to make this judgment, he or she may search through knowledge relevant to abortion for any information about elderly people. Given that this search is likely to begin at the abortion node, there are over a dozen different directions the person can search in, and there are no guides or clues indicating how to most efficiently find the desired information. Consequently, searching for a specific piece of knowledge in an unorganized structure may take a relatively large amount of time, and may well yield different conclusions on different occasions.

In contrast, suppose we ask a person whose knowledge is well organized (as in fig. 2) to make the same inference. The better organization is likely to help the person engage in a very efficient memory search. He or she may have previously observed that people with certain characteristics, such as women and poor people, tend to favor legalized abortion, while other people, with other characteristics, tend to oppose abortion. Having previously noted and stored these relations, the task of finding the desired piece of knowledge is significantly simplified. The search may be directed first to the "proabortionists" node, around which characteristics typical of those who favor abortion are stored. If the sought-after information is not found here, the search may be directed to the "antiabortionists" node. The ability of dimensional nodes to direct memory searches may, thus, enable an individual to ignore some areas of the knowledge structure, while focusing attention on others. Therefore, this type of organization may enable a more efficient search and therefore perhaps a more reliable one, as well.

In our first study, subjects made several inferences relevant to attitudes on political issues, and we viewed the speed and consistency with which these inferences were made as indicators of knowledge organization. If attitude importance is related to knowledge organization, then inferences involving important attitudes should be made more quickly and consistently than inferences involving unimportant attitudes.

Subjects made two visits to our laboratory to complete three tasks. During the first visit, subjects completed an inference task, in which they indicated the likelihood that various demographic characteristics or social-category memberships were associated with different attitudes on five political issues. Approximately twenty-four hours later, subjects completed the same inference task again, and filled out a questionnaire assessing the importance of their own attitudes on the five political issues.

For the inference tasks, subjects were seated in front of an IBM microcomputer in individual cubicles. Subjects read instructions explaining that phrases describing personal characteristics would appear on the computer screen. When the first characteristic (referred to as a "stimulus phrase") appeared, they were told to think about someone who possessed that characteristic. After the second characteristic (referred to as a "target phrase") appeared, they were instructed to decide whether it was likely or unlikely that a person who possessed the first characteristic would also possess the second one. Subjects were instructed to depress one of two labeled keyboard keys to indicate their responses. The computer recorded subjects' responses and their latencies (the length of time between a target phrase's appearance and a subject's response).

On half of the trials, the stimulus phrase indicated an attitude position (such as proabortion or anti-gun control), and the target phrase denoted membership in a social category (such as Republican or poor). On the other half of the trials, stimulus phrases denoted social category membership, and target phrases indicated attitude positions.

We used the response latency data from the inference task to compute measures of inference speed. Subjects made a total of four hundred inferences across the two inference tasks, eighty on each of five issues: legalized abortion, capital punishment, legalization of marijuana, gun control, and nuclear energy. The eighty response latencies for each issue were averaged and subjected to a logarithmic transformation to normalize their distributions (see Fazio 1990).

Measures of response consistency were also computed from the inference task data. Subjects saw forty unique attitude position-personal characteristic permutations for each issue (2 attitude positions × 10 personal characteristics × 2 target types). Each of those permutations was presented twice, once on the first day and once on the second day. A measure of inference consistency was computed by summing the number of times a subject made the same inference for the same permutation on each issue. Thus, a value of forty indicates that all forty inferences were made identically on the two days, whereas a value of zero indicates that none of the inferences were made identically.

Measures of attitude importance were computed for each issue by summing responses to two questionnaire items that asked how personally important each issue was to subjects, and how much they cared about the issue.

In order to test for associations between attitude importance and inference speed and consistency, we computed two regression equations. In these equations, the dependent variable (either inference speed or inference consistency) was regressed on attitude importance, while controlling for individual and issue differences. This was done by adding dummy variables representing the 134 subjects and the 5 issues to the equations. Thus, the coefficient for attitude importance indicates the association between importance and the target variable combining across the 5 issues.

As expected, subjects made inferences more quickly when they involved personally important attitudes than when they involved unimportant attitudes ($\beta = -.04$, $p < .05$, $N = 135$). Also as expected, subjects were more consistent in their inferences when the inferences involved personally important attitudes ($\beta = .09$, $p < .01$, $N = 135$). Quick and consistent inferences suggest that subjects were able to locate and access relevant knowledge more easily when the knowledge was relevant to an important attitude, a consequence that would be expected of greater organization. Therefore, these results support the hypothesis that knowledge relevant to important attitudes is better organized.

These findings resemble some of our previous evidence regarding the correlates of attitude importance. As we mentioned above, important attitudes are more stable over long periods of time during the course of daily life (Krosnick 1988b), and they are reported more quickly (Krosnick 1989). Our first study of organization goes a step further, by showing that inferences about others that are relevant to more important attitudes are also more stable and accessible.

A Second Test: Proximity of Related Knowledge Bits

Although the results of our first study are certainly consistent with this hypothesis, there are alternative explanations for the observed results. For example, the same associations between importance and inference speed would have been obtained if knowledge relevant to important attitudes was simply more accessible than knowledge relevant to unimportant attitudes. That is, it may be that the links between knowledge bits and the central object node are stronger, thereby making the individual bits more accessible. Or it is possible that subjects are simply more practiced at performing inferences relevant to important attitudes, and are therefore quicker and more efficient in doing so (see, e.g., Smith 1989; Smith and Lerner 1986).

Therefore, in order to further explore the relation between attitude importance and knowledge organization, we conducted a second study, using a different methodology. Specifically, we assessed how organized stored items are by examining how close to each other related items are generated in an undirected knowledge-listing task.

Subjects in our second study completed three tasks. First, they listed the first twelve pieces of knowledge that came to mind when thinking about either abortion, capital punishment, or gun control (determined randomly). Next, subjects identified up to twelve pairs of knowledge bits that they felt were similar in some important respects, and they wrote short phrases describing what each pair had in common. Finally, subjects completed a short questionnaire measuring the personal importance of their attitudes on all three issues.

We computed measures of attitude importance for each issue, as in the previous study, and we used data generated by the pairing task to compute measures of knowledge organization. These measures were computed by looking at what pieces of knowledge subjects indicated were similar, and when those pieces were generated during the listing task. If two pieces of knowledge were psychologically related, those pieces should have been written down near each other during the initial listing task. Consequently, we measured organization by computing the average number of pieces of information listed in between the two items in each pair of related knowledge bits. The fewer such in-between pieces of information, the more organized the knowledge presumably was.

In order to assess the relation between importance and knowledge organization, we again computed regression equations pooling across the various issues.[1] As expected, the combined association between importance and the average distance between paired items was negative and marginally significant ($\beta = -.20$, $p < .10$, $N = 86$). This indicates that subjects who considered an issue to be important listed psychologically related pieces of knowledge closer to each other than did subjects who considered an issue to be unimportant. Thus, this result is consistent with the hypothesis that knowledge relevant to important attitudes is better organized than knowledge relevant to unimportant attitudes.

A Third Test: Assessing Organizational Dimensions

Taken together, our first two experiments provide evidence that attitude importance is related to knowledge organization. Using markedly different methods for measuring knowledge organization, both studies indicated that knowledge relevant to important attitudes is more organized in memory. Our third study tested this hypothesis using yet another method for measuring knowledge organization: one that assesses the number of organizational dimensions underlying subjects' sorting of knowledge into groups.

In this study, subjects completed four tasks. First, subjects listed their knowledge about abortion or capital punishment (determined randomly). Second, subjects formed groups of pieces of knowledge that they felt were related to one another in some respect. For each group, subjects provided a short description of why those pieces of knowledge were related. Third, subjects rated how well all of the knowledge bits were described by each descriptor phrase. Thus, subjects generated a matrix of pieces of knowledge by number of groups in which an entry indicated the applicability of a descriptor to a piece of knowledge. Finally, subjects indicated the importance of their attitudes on both issues.

We assessed the number of independent dimensions necessary to account for subjects' grouping and rating of their knowledge, using the dimensionality measure developed by Scott, Osgood, and Peterson (1979).[2] To compute this measure, intrasubject correlation matrices were calculated from subjects' rating data. That is, for each subject, we computed a matrix of correlations between group descriptors. A large correlation between two descriptors indicated that, for that subject, those two descriptors were redundant. The sum of the squared intrasubject correlations is, thus, an indicator of the redundancy among groups formed by subjects. Our measure of independent dimensions used by a subject increased with the number of groups formed, and decreased with the amount of redundancy between these groups (as measured by the sum of the squared intrasubject correlations). When there is complete redundancy among all groups, our measure, D, equals 1, the minimum possible value. When there is no redundancy among groups, D equals the number of groups formed; thus D has no necessary maximum value.

As expected, more important attitudes were associated with more organizing dimensions. In a regression equation, pooling across the two issues, the combined association between importance and number of dimensions was significant and positive ($\beta = .24$, $p < .05$, $N = 117$).[3] This result again supports the hypothesis that the knowledge structures accompanying important attitudes are more elaborately organized than the structures accompanying unimportant attitudes.

Agreement-Based Knowledge Organization

Using three different methods, we have seen evidence supporting this hypothesis. However, these studies do not indicate precisely which organizing dimensions become more prominent under conditions of high importance. Of the many candidates, one that has received a great deal of attention is attitudinal agreement (Hymes 1986, Judd and Kulik 1980, McGraw and Pinney 1990; Pratkanis 1989). Knowledge organized in terms of attitudinal agreement is clustered into two groups: knowledge that agrees with one's attitude, and knowledge that disagrees with one's attitude. In the extreme, an individual may use only an agreement dimension for organizing his or her knowledge.

An agreement-based knowledge structure for someone who favors legalized abortion is illustrated in figure 3. Here, pieces of knowledge that agree with, or support, his or her attitude (such as "Women have rights to reproductive freedom," and "Unwanted children may suffer") are linked to the "agree" node, whereas bits of knowledge that disagree with, or challenge, his or her attitude (such as "Life begins at conception") are linked with the "disagree" node. Because information that neither agrees nor disagrees with the individual's attitude (such as "Abortions are easy to obtain") cannot be readily linked to one of these nodes, such information is linked directly to the attitude object.

A number of studies suggest that agreement-based organization may vary systematically across individuals. For example, political experts have been shown to be more likely than novices to exhibit agreement-based organization of knowledge about policy issues (McGraw and Pinney 1990) and knowledge about political actors (Lusk and Judd 1988). However, other research has found political expertise to be unrelated to agreement-based organization of knowledge about candidates (McGraw, Pinney, and Neumann 1991), even under conditions conducive to such organization (McGraw and Steenbergen in this volume). Agreement-based organization has also been shown to be positively associated with attitude extremity (Hymes 1986). However, because attitude importance is essentially independent of political expertise (Judd and Krosnick 1989), and only moderately associated with attitude extremity (Krosnick et al. 1993), it is difficult to use these findings to anticipate how attitude importance will be related to agreement-based clustering of knowledge.

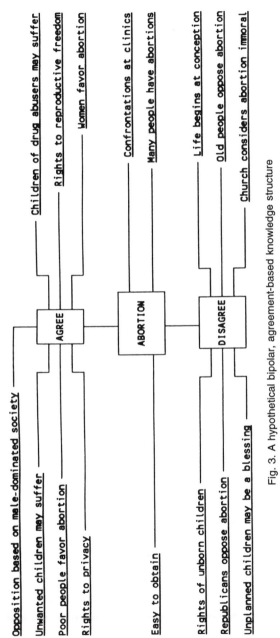

Fig. 3. A hypothetical bipolar, agreement-based knowledge structure

A Test of Agreement-Based Organization

In order to investigate the relation between importance and the organizational centrality of attitudinal agreement, we conducted a final study. As in our second study, we measured knowledge structure by examining the order in which knowledge is retrieved from memory in an undirected knowledge-listing task. In this study, subjects completed three tasks. First, they listed all of their knowledge on three issues: abortion, capital punishment, and U.S. military involvement in Kuwait.[4] Then, subjects indicated whether each piece of knowledge agreed with, disagreed with, or was neutral with respect to their own attitude positions. Finally, subjects reported the personal importance of their attitudes.

We used data from the knowledge-listing and rating tasks to compute measures of agreement-based organization. Specifically, we computed adjusted ratios of clustering, or ARC scores (see, e.g., McGraw and Steenbergen in this volume; Ostrom, Pryor, and Simpson 1981). In general, this measure gauges the frequency with which pieces of information are immediately followed by other pieces of information that are the same on some specified dimension. In the current study, larger ARC scores indicate a greater tendency to follow pieces of agreeable knowledge with other pieces of agreeable knowledge, disagreeable knowledge with disagreeable knowledge, and neutral knowledge with neutral knowledge. Consequently, larger scores indicate more agreement-based knowledge organization.

A regression analysis collapsing across the three issues and controlling for individual and issue differences indicated that agreement-based organization was *less* central in the knowledge structures accompanying *more* important attitudes ($\beta = -.20$, $p < .05$, $N = 106$).[5] This result suggests that knowledge relevant to unimportant attitudes is organized primarily in agreement-based structures, whereas knowledge relevant to important attitudes is organized in multidimensional structures, in which attitudinal agreement is less central. Thus, even among people whose attitudes on a political issue are unimportant, attitudinal agreement shapes reaction to and storage of attitude-relevant information, perhaps quite automatically and effortlessly. Perhaps only when individuals' attitudes are personally important do they think more extensively about relevant information, and come to see other types of relations between pieces of attitude-relevant knowledge.

Conclusion

In this chapter, we have described the results of four experiments that investigated the relation between attitude importance and knowledge organization. The results of these studies support two general conclusions. First, knowledge relevant to important attitudes is apparently more elaborately organized in memory than knowledge relevant to unimportant attitudes. Second, attitudinal agreement seems to be a more central organizing dimension in stored knowledge relevant to unimportant attitudes.

These findings suggest a possible explanation for various previously observed effects of attitude importance. For example, a number of studies have shown that important attitudes are more resistant to change than unimportant attitudes (Ewing 1942; Fine 1957; Knower 1936; Krosnick 1988a). Elaborate knowledge organization may provide individuals with the resources necessary for efficiently and effectively resisting the influence of attitude-challenging information. That is, organization around more dimensions may enable people to quickly locate information in memory needed to counterargue each new piece of challenging information, thus allowing them to resist any influence of this information, thus preserving the attitude.

Similarly, previous research has indicated that attitude importance is associated with better memory for attitude-relevant information (Berent 1990). A multidimensional organization of knowledge may provide individuals with a better cognitive framework for incorporating relevant information, which should make it easier to store, locate, and retrieve relevant information from memory. Consequently, information relevant to important attitudes may be better remembered than information relevant to unimportant attitudes, because of the efficient method of storage and retrieval afforded by the multidimensional organizations characteristic of important attitudes.

This reasoning has useful implications regarding evaluations of political candidates. During political campaigns, voters are exposed to information about where candidates stand on a variety of political issues. Voters presumably attend to such information and use it to form candidate preferences. However, the similarity between candidates' and voters' attitudes on political issues has more impact on candidate preferences when attitudes are important than when they are unimportant (Krosnick 1988b). This may occur because important attitudes are accompanied by multidimensional organizations that better equip voters to understand, remember, and use information about candidates' positions on those issues. This organizational structure may thereby be partly responsible for the greater accuracy in candidate perceptions associated with attitude importance (Krosnick 1991).

Before concluding that multidimensional organization plays the above mediating roles, a few caveats should be mentioned. First, the research described here has only documented a relation between importance and organization. Although the idea that importance causes organization fits in nicely with a large body of existing research (see, e.g., Boninger, Berent, Krosnick, and Fabrigar, n.d.), it is also possible that organization causes importance, or that some third factor causes both importance and organization. It is also possible that our subjects inferred the importance of their attitudes, based upon their performance on the organization-assessment tasks we administered to them. In order to fully understand the relation between importance and organization, future research should, therefore, explore the causal influence of importance on organization, and the causal influence of organization on these effects. This can be accomplished either through experimental manipulation of importance and organization, or by statistically disentangling the causes and effects, through multivariate analysis. Until the causal relation between importance and organization is more fully investigated, definitive statements about the mediating role of organization must remain tentative.

Second, our reliance on correlational analyses in these initial investigations does not enable us to rule out other factors that may influence either organization or the relation between importance and organization. A variety of factors could play such roles, including expertise (see, e.g., McGraw and Pinney 1990), prior thought (see, e.g., Linville 1982; Millar and Tesser 1986), and direct experience (see, e.g., Fazio and Zanna 1981). Because expertise is uncorrelated with attitude importance (Judd and Krosnick 1989), it seems unlikely to be able to account for the relation we observed. Consistent with this expectation, some of our studies controlled for all global individual differences, and observed the same importance-organization relation within individuals across attitudes. Therefore, we expect that this relation is due to specific attributes of important attitudes, not to artifactually confounded global individual differences.

Finally, because knowledge structures are not physical structures that are directly observable, the way in which knowledge is organized can only be inferred using indirect indicators. Furthermore, such measures of knowledge organization may be influenced to some degree by factors other than organization. For example, a measure of organization that relies on a person's knowledge listing may reflect that person's motivation to list knowledge and memory search strategies, as well as the way in which knowledge is organized. Whereas no method generates a pure measure of organization, the use of multiple methods that all reflect some degree of organization allow us to triangulate to the real relation. The fact that several disparate methodologies all suggest a relation between importance and organization, therefore, heightens our confidence that such a relation does exist.

It is useful to note that the work presented in this chapter addresses a growing concern among political scientists: that cognitive psychological constructs have done little to advance understanding of political behavior (see, e.g., Kuklinski, Luskin, and Bolland 1991; for an alternative view see Lodge, McGraw, Conover, Feldman, and Miller 1991). Previous investigations of political cognitive organization have rarely measured the features that define these organizations, such as constituent cognitions and the connections among them. This has led some critics to charge that little, if anything, new has been gained by the importing of concepts such as schemas (Kuklinski, Luskin, and Bolland 1991). Coupled with the work of Lusk and Judd (1988), McGraw and Steenbergen (in this volume), and others, the research presented in this chapter demonstrates how investigations of political knowledge can, indeed, benefit from direct measurement of cognitive organization. We look forward to future research adopting similar approaches to the study of political information processing.

NOTES

We wish to thank Lisa Frankenfeld, Lisa Hadding, Diane Helmick, Liz Mernick, Wendy Smith, and Seleesa Stover for their help in collecting and preparing the data. We also wish to thank Richard Petty, William von Hippel, Gifford Weary, and the students of the Ohio State University social psychology graduate program for their helpful comments and suggestions.

1. The regression analysis employed here was somewhat different than the analysis employed in the first study. Although subjects completed attitude-importance questions for all issues, they completed the knowledge listing and pairing tasks for only one political issue. Thus, they generated a measure of knowledge organization for only that issue. Consequently, dummy variables representing subjects would be completely redundant with dummy variables representing issues. In order to control for individual differences in this study, subjects' average importance rating across all three issues was entered into the regression equation. In addition, the importance of the target issue was entered as a predictor as well. The coefficient reported for this latter effect therefore represents the association between attitude importance for the target issue and organization for that issue, controlling for individual differences in average attitude importance and issue differences in average organization across all issues.

2. Our measure of the number of dimensions is conceptually similar to Scott's *H* measure, used by both Linville (1982) and Millar and Tesser (1986).

3. The measure of organization was simultaneously regressed on attitude importance, a dummy code representing issue, and subjects' average importance rating, as in our second study.

4. Data for this study were collected during the early part of 1991, during the period in which the United States was militarily involved in the conflict.

5. The measure of knowledge organization was simultaneously regressed on attitude importance and dummy codes representing individuals and issues, as in our first study.

CHAPTER 6

Toward a Procedural Model of
Candidate Evaluation

Milton Lodge

Until that happy day when physicists present us with a unified theory of everything, those of us trying to figure out how people form their impressions of political candidates and choose among them must make do with less-than-grand theories. In this chapter, I review the problems and prospects of one such intermediary theory, the information-processing approach, as it applies to the evaluation of political candidates. My characterization of the evaluation process relies heavily on the literatures of cognitive psychology, social psychology, behavioral decision theory, and last named but foremost in my concern, political science. My hope is to put forth in general terms what I see as the main architectural and procedural features of a psychologically realistic model of the candidate-evaluation process that is faithful to what is known about human cognition, and at the same time does not fly in the face of what political scientists know about how citizens go about forming their impressions of political candidates and making their vote choice.

The Blackbox Model Of Candidate Evaluation

Our focus on cognitive mechanisms runs counter to the dominant "black-box" perspective in political science, which, although silent about the processes that drive their explanations, nonetheless makes robust assumptions about what citizens know about parties, candidates, and issues, and how they use this knowledge to inform their judgments (Lodge, Stroh, and Wahlke 1990; Wahlke 1991). Virtually all contemporary models of individual electoral behavior are implicit information-processing models, in that they treat the evaluation of candidates as a direct function of the information voters remember about each candidate as they enter the voting booth or talk to a pollster. While the Columbia, Michigan, and Rochester approaches differ in what "considerations" they suppose the voter has available in memory, and disagree as to what transformations voters perform on these considerations, they share in common the most basic of black-box assumptions—what we call the "memory-based" assumption—that whatever campaign information citizens can remember about the candidates at the time they are asked for an assessment directly contributes to their evaluation of the candidate.

The presumption of memory-based processing proves to be one of those "givens" that theorists cherish, for if it were true that voters could more or less faithfully recount the factors that contributed to their preferences, there would be no need to model the ongoing psychological processes that transform campaign stimuli into evaluative responses. All we would need to do would be to correlate candidate preferences with the respondent's net recollections of likes and dislikes, as do Kelley and Mirer (1974), in their model of the "simple act of voting," or predict candidate evaluation from their recall of self- and candidate-proximities on the issue scales (Enelow and Hinich 1984). This, indeed, is normal operating procedure in electoral research: We ask respondents to recount their likes and dislikes of the parties and candidates, and what we typically find is exactly what memory-based models predict—a positive correlation between voter memory and candidate evaluation, with, for example, the mix of pros and cons recalled from the National Election Survey's open-ended questions routinely predicting vote choice with 95 percent accuracy (Kelley 1983). The obvious interpretation flows naturally from the basic assumption: voter recollections are driving candidate evaluations—the causal arrow goes from memory to judgment.

All well and good, were it not for a most troublesome incongruity; to wit: citizens do not measure up to model specifications. Here is the rub, in fact two related paradoxes that plague our very best studies of voting behavior, one within the survey research tradition, the other an inconsistency between survey and laboratory findings. When voters are asked about parties, candidates, and issues in the NES, they are found to be ill-informed, the majority of respondents unable, for example, to cite more than one or two likes or dislikes to the open-ended questions and probes, and for many of these good citizens, their responses are, to put it kindly, "diffuse" (Gant and Davis 1984). So it is that many of the very same citizens who are modeled as informed voters do not appear to have the factual or conceptual wherewithal to meet the minimal requirements of informed-voter models. It is as though the black box is taking in great quantities of information and putting out affect, but without the requisite mindstuff needed to transform campaign events into informed judgments. The problem, then, is not prediction, as the correlation from memory to judgment is strong, but our *explanations of when and how* citizens go about forming their impression of candidates. The paradox is this: How is it that such an ill-informed citizenry can make such reasonable judgments (Key 1966; Page and Shapiro 1992; Popkin 1991; Sniderman, Tetlock, and Brody 1991)?

Before turning to the large body of laboratory research in social and cognitive psychology that challenges the memory-causes-judgment interpretation of NES data and holds promise for an answer to this puzzle, take note of Graber's (1988) conclusion to her longitudinal study of the 1976 presidential campaign, in which she compared what respondents read and heard throughout the campaign (as reported in a daily log) to what they could later recollect about the candidates:

> The fact that so little specific information can be recalled from a [news] story does not mean that no learning has taken place. *The information base from which conclusions are drawn may be forgotten, while the conclusions are still retained.* This seems to happen routinely. Voting choices, for instance, often match approval of a candidate's positions even when voters cannot recall the candidate's positions or the specifics of the policy. In such cases, media facts apparently have been converted into politically significant feelings and attitudes and the facts themselves forgotten. (Graber, 1988, emphasis added)

This transmutation of media events into feelings, followed apparently by the forgetting of the facts that entered into the evaluation, captures in broad sweep an alternative to memory-based models, what we call the *on-line, impression-based model of candidate evaluation* (Lodge, McGraw, and Stroh 1989). Impression-based processing implies that although citizens generally cannot recount accurately the specific bits and pieces of evidence that originally led to their preferences, the considerations that actually entered into their evaluative tally were factored in *at the moment of exposure,* and not held in memory until some future date, when respondents would then be forced to construct an evaluation from whatever evidentiary residue still resided as memory traces.

The On-Line Model Of Candidate Evaluation

A schematic depiction of our expectations for on-line (OL) and memory-based (MB) processing is presented in figure 1. The OL model holds that people form evaluations immediately upon exposure to the "raw data" of the message (the solid arrow from Candidate Message to OL Tally depicting a strong, direct relationship), and then immediately integrate the affective charge of this raw material into a running evaluative tally (Lodge and Stroh 1993). Accordingly, when one's goal is to form an impression of some person, place, or thing, most people most of the time appear to simplify the judgmental process by spontaneously culling the affective value from the message *on the spot*, as the information is before their eyes, so to speak, and then and there integrate this affective value into a summary evaluation. This running tally—what Hastie and Park (1986) call a "judgment operator" and Wyer and Srull (1986) call an information "integrator"—is then immediately stored in long-term memory, and the considerations that contributed to the evaluation are quickly forgotten. If, later, an evaluation is called for, this cumulative tally is simply retrieved from memory and reported as the candidate evaluation (as depicted by the solid arrow from OL Tally to Evaluation).

Essentially, then, the OL model posits a direct effect of attention on judgment, hence, there is no necessary relationship between the pros and cons that actually enter into the evaluation and one's memory of these considerations (as shown in fig. 1 by the weak path from Recall to Evaluation). Thus it is that voters can oftentimes tell you how much they like one candidate or another but not be able to tell you many if any of their reasons why. *Or* (this is the reason we think for the strong correlation between recall and evaluation in the NES), having forgotten much if not all of the considerations that entered into their overall evaluation, when called on to report the whys and wherefores for their evaluation, respondents are prone to search memory for supporting "evidence," and dredge up commonsensical rationalizations for their preferences (Lau 1982; Nisbett and Ross 1980; Wilson and Schooler 1991), as depicted by the solid arrow leading from Evaluation to Recall in fig. 1. From this perspective, then, the evaluation process can be, and oftentimes is, separate from and independent of the information retrieval process (Anderson and Hubert 1963; Dreben, Fiske, and Hastie 1979; Reyes, Thompson, and Bower 1980).

Support for the on-line model, and a direct challenge to the memory-causes-judgment assumptions of contemporary political science models, is the demonstration in social and cognitive psychology of correlations in the direction and strength depicted in fig. 1 (cf. Hastie and Park 1986; Lichtenstein and Srull 1987; Sherman, Zehner, Johnson and Hirt 1983; Srull and Wyer 1988). Well-controlled experimental tests in which the researcher manipulates the amount and content of information the individual is exposed to (the message) show that what people can remember of what they read, saw, or heard about other people, places, and things provides a relatively poor account of their political evaluations. What citizens are likely to recollect about candidates is their global assessment of them, not the specific considerations that actually entered into the evaluation. *At best*, if the citizens' recollections will represent a biased sampling of the actual causal determinants of the candidate evaluation (e.g., Anderson and Hubert 1963).

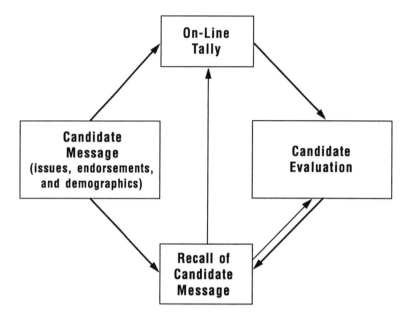

Fig. 1. A schematic representation of MB and OL processing

At worse (this, perhaps, the source of the difference between survey and experimental findings), the correlation between recall and judgment is spurious—controlling for message, the recall to judgment connection fails. Depending on various contextual factors, some, many, or all recollections are rationalizations (Brody and Page 1972; Lodge, McGraw, and Stroh 1989; Rahn, Krosnik, and Breuning 1992).

This on-line mode of information processing appears to operate whenever people see their task in terms of forming or updating an impression; this in contrast to those more demanding instances in which people set out consciously to learn and remember specifics about some person, place, or thing, as when, for instance, they expect to have their opinions challenged, in which case memory-based processing would be prudent (Cohen, 1981; Ostrom, et al. 1980). When an impression is being formed in "real-time," citizens can act naturally as "bounded rationalists" by simply storing this summary tally in memory, and then in good conscience forget the specific considerations that went into the evaluation. Unless the information is particularly important, vivid, or incongruous, people appear to exert little effort to remember each bit, once its affective value has been extracted and integrated into an impression.

Clearly, the choice between the impression-driven and memory-based models puts at stake how we model and explain the evaluation of political candidates (and, we suspect, policy preferences). At issue are the questions: "What information will be integrated into an overall candidate evaluation?" When?" How?" In this chapter, I describe the rudiments of a process model of candidate evaluation that—following the lead of Anderson (1983); Brewer (1988); Fiske and Pavelchak (1986); Hastie (1988); and Wyer and Srull (1986)—sets forth the basic components and mechanisms of a cognitively-informed model of candidate evaluation which I hope will deal effectively with the aforementioned informed voter paradox, as well as provide a persuasive account of how voters go about forming and updating their impressions of political candidates.

The argument throughout is that researchers must understand how campaign events are processed inside the "black box" if we are to understand how citizens evaluate political events and make political choices. I opt for the impression-driven model of candidate evaluation, in part because the empirical evidence points that way and also because the on-line impression-driven model appears to be more cognitively efficacious than are memory-based models, as the citizen need only retrieve the summary tally from long-term memory, not the bits and pieces of information that originally contributed to the evaluation. With this model, I hope to account for what are seen as some of the most robust findings of prior research on individual voting behavior, among them: (1) the perseverance of beliefs and prior evaluations in the face of new information, what are called "anchoring effects" on judgment; (2) its corollary, insufficient "adjustment" to new (short-term) information in the updating of evaluations, and, of course (3) I hope to provide an account for how campaign events impact on evaluations without necessarily leaving a trace in memory, an explanation, perhaps, for the paradox of informed voting.

The Information-Processing Approach

The basic premise of the cognitive approach is that thinking is information processing. The brain is seen as an information-processing system, in which data are stored, retrieved, and operated upon, metaphorically, much like a computer. The focus of this approach is on process, on the chain of mental events that take place throughout the decision-making process. Accordingly, to understand human behavior, researchers must look inside the "black box" and work with the mental representations people construct to understand and act upon the world (Lippmann 1922).

Within this perspective, human thinking and reasoning can be modeled in terms of "elementary information processes" operating in a small set of "functional components" (Sanford 1987). Contemporary models of human information processing typically assume two "functional components": (1) a very large permanent memory, called long-term memory (LTM), and (2) a small, temporary memory store, called working memory (WM), where information is consciously attended to and actively processed.

Long term memory. A basic finding of research on long-term memory—this evidence dating back millennia—is that much of the information in long-term memory is organized associatively, that is, meaningfully, in "packets" of conceptual knowledge and associations (Collins and Quillian 1968; Collins and Loftus 1975). These semantically bundled units of associations can be represented as *nodes* that are *linked* together into associational *networks* (Rumelhart and Norman 1983). Concept nodes are activated directly whenever a person sees, hears, reads, or thinks about that person, place, thing, or idea, or may be energized indirectly by the activation of attributes associatively linked to the nodes (Anderson 1983). In either case, what is retrieved and acted upon is the information in long-term memory made available to working memory. Links—the implicational relationships between nodes—are formed when different objects of thought are thought about simultaneously (Judd and Krosnik 1989).

Working memory is the metaphorical "place" inside the head where information is attended to and integrated into impressions. Working memory corresponds to that set of things we are actively attending to at any given moment (Anderson and Hubert 1963; Belmore 1987; Fiske 1980). Information in working memory is readily accessible for further processing, whereas information in long-term memory must first be activated (transferred to working memory) before it can be utilized.

Three characteristics of working memory make it the "bottleneck" of human information processing: First, working memory has a *limited capacity*, limited, perhaps, to 7 ± 2 chunks of meaningful information (Miller 1956). Thus, as new information is "moved" into working memory, information previously stored there must be pushed out. The retention of information in working memory requires constant, effortful attention. Because attention is such a limited resource, only the most strongly activated chunks of information can make their way into working memory, and thereupon become directly accessible to conscious thought.

A second characteristic of working memory, and a serious constraint on human information processing, is the *serial* nature of attention. Because attention is a one-bit-at-a-time sequential process, a person can consciously attend to but a small number of facts and dimensions at a time, here again limiting the depth and breadth of considerations that can be simultaneously taken into account when making judgments (Payne 1982).

A correlated limitation of human information processing is the *"slow fixation rate"* required to transfer information from WM to LTM. To create or revise a representation in long-term memory, that is, to learn, associations must first be encoded ("written to memory") and associatively linked to other nodes in the knowledge structure. Processing times on the order of 8–10 seconds are estimated to assemble the bits and pieces of information in WM and store them in LTM as a new "chuck," or connection (Simon 1979), thereby making it difficult to form new connections while simultaneously trying to keep abreast of fast-flowing information.

Taken together, the limited capacity, serial nature, and slow fixation rate of information transfer are the cornerstones of *"bounded rationality"*— the mind is a limited-capacity information processor.

What ties these cognitive elements and procedures into a coherent theory of evaluation is *the constructionist nature of human information processing* (Martin and Tesser 1992), essentially, the notion that

> preferences for and beliefs about objects and events of any complexity are often constructed—not merely revealed—in the generation of a response to a judgment or choice. (Payne, Bettman, and Johnson 1992, 89)

This idea, that preferences are constructed in real time, on the fly so to speak, from whatever considerations are in working memory at the time a judgment is being formed or updated, goes well beyond a mere denial that observed preferences result from reference to a "master list" of well-formed opinions in long-term memory. More to the point:

> In a very real sense . . . people do not know their own minds. Instead, they are continuously making them up. Knowledge and belief are not static memories but typically involve active, momentary cognitive processing. (Anderson 1991, 7)

From which it follows:

> Knowledge consists only in small part of stored data, or even of subroutines for retrieving from storage. More important are the dynamic judgmental processes, including the subroutines for evaluating and integrating the information. (Anderson 1991, 7)

The constructionist view of human information processing, in focusing on the mechanisms and processes people use to form their beliefs and integrate information into evaluations, goes beyond the way we traditionally analyze political attitudes and behavior in positing a dynamic model of the candidate evaluation process.

At this point in time—awaiting the conceptual big bang—there is a paradigmatic consensus among social and cognitive psychologists as to some of the basic mechanisms and procedures that drive human information processing and severely constrain how much of what kinds of information people can routinely integrate into their evaluation of people, places, and things (Lachman, Lachman, and Butterfield 1979; Fiske and Taylor 1991). From this base let me now set forth in broad strokes (with elaboration of key points in ensuing sections) what I see as the principle characteristics of an impression-based model of candidate evaluation:

1. For most citizens most of the time impression formation and belief updating is an *"on-line"* process in which each piece of campaign information is immediately evaluated and linked to the candidate node *in working memory at the time of exposure,* when the information is in the senses, so to speak, and not typically computed at a later date from memory traces (McGraw and Pinney 1990).

2. Because information processing (and political campaigns) are *sequential,* impressions are continuously evolving, as new information is first evaluated and then integrated into an overall, summary impression. In Norman Anderson's (1981) words:

> In everyday life, information integration is a sequential process. Information is received a piece at a time and integrated into a continuously evolving impression. Each such impression, be it a theoretical issue, another person, or a social organization, grows and changes over the course of time. An any point in time, therefore, the current impression looks both forward and back. (Anderson 1981, 144].

3. Affect in our model is central: *all social stimuli are thought to be affectively charged,* and what citizens do when evaluating candidates is to cull the affective value from each element of campaign messages to update their overall assessment of the candidates. From this perspective, affect and cognition are not independent, but are *"unitized,"* as an evaluative tag—summarizing the evaluation of all prior messages—is directly attached to the conceptual node itself (Fazio 1986; Pratkanis 1989; McGraw and Steenbergen in this volume). Beliefs are, in Abelson's (1968) apt phrase, *"hot cognitions";* hence, *beliefs and feelings cannot be disentangled,* for they travel together from LTM to WM and back again on the same node structure (Lodge and Stroh, 1993).

4. New information is encoded in terms of a *single, bipolar like-dislike dimension*—solely in terms of its *positivity or negativity*—perhaps along the "directional" lines proposed by Rabinowitz and Macdonald (1989) and Judd and Kulik (1980), or perhaps is evaluated on but one or two highly corre-

lated dimensions, such as "good-bad," "strong-weak," and "active-passive" (Osgood, Suci, and Tannenbaum 1957).

5. Once an impression is formed new information is then evaluated in terms of one's then-current on-line tally. In keeping with modern usage, we see this running evaluative tally as *"anchoring"* the processing of subsequent information (Anderson 1991; Hogarth and Einhorn 1992). Thus, our expectation is that sequential *anchoring and adjustment* models will prove superior to alternative models that ignore order effects and assume the equal weighing of information.

6. The strong expectation here is for *candidate-focused* information processing, whereby citizens update their tally of each candidate separately and only when explicitly called on to choose among candidates will they directly compare their respective tallies and vote for the most positive or against the candidate with the most negative tally. The implication here—this in direct contrast to Herstein (1981) and Lau (in this volume), but in line with Rahn, et al. (1990)—is that the candidate evaluation process is *compensatory, but not comparative,* compensatory in that citizens adjust their on-line tally of each candidate upward or downward in response to the perceived positivity or negativity of the message, but only compare candidates in terms of their OL tallies. Unlike the reasoning underlying spatial models of candidate evaluation, we posit that, typically—unless the voter is explicitly directed otherwise—there are no direct issue × issue comparisons across candidates: Vote choice and comparative candidate assessments are made from the direct comparison of the respective on-line tallies. If, indeed, this is a fair approximation of the process, voters can rely on this relatively simple within-candidate *compensatory heuristic* when revising their impressions, and are not compelled to make trade-offs across issues between candidates when updating their beliefs and preferences (see the Lau and Taber-Steenbergen chapters in this volume for specifics and alternatives).

In sum, the expectation is that human information processing may be fruitfully described as an *on-line, affect integration process characterized by a candidate-centered anchoring and adjustment process.* This characterization of the judgmental process raises important what-when-how questions—*What* information finds its way into the judgment? *When* is information integrated into an evaluation? And *how* is this information tallied up? The answers to these questions are important, for it is the content and structure of campaign messages "out there," in the world, as well as the information processes going on inside the head, that jointly determine the direction and strength of candidate evaluations (Ericcson and Simon 1984).

Having set forth the primary characteristics of this impression-driven model, let us now delve more deeply into the black box, to specify the manner in which the candidate-evaluation process might work. Our aim here is to develop a working model of the candidate-evaluation process that will incorporate the major findings of the political science literature on electoral behavior, while *not* violating the constraints imposed by psychological realism.

A Flowchart of the On-Line Tally Model of Candidate Evaluation

A basic premise of the information-processing approach is that information processing proceeds *in stages.* Taking our lead from Anderson (1983), Brewer (1988), Fiske and Ruscher (1989), and Hastie (1988), and relying heavily on the paper-and-pencil simulation of the evaluation process in Lodge and Stroh (1993) as well as the initial effort to build a computational model of the candidate-evaluation process in Boynton and Lodge (1992), we propose in figure 2 a flowchart model depicting in broad stokes our on-line impression-based model of the candidate-evaluation process.

Encountering Information

The impression-formation (and impression-updating) process starts with exposure to campaign information. The key assumption we make in this initial stage of the process is that *whatever information is attended to gets processed.* A simple example: assuming here a relatively knowledgeable citizen reading the newspaper headline "Clinton is Pro-Choice" would automatically activate their "Clinton" and "Pro-Choice" nodes in LTM and "deposit" them into working memory, along with their most strongly linked associations, up to the *combined total* of 7 ± 2 associations. In this sense, our model is "exposure driven," as whatever information is attended to— whether pictures, slogans, or policy statements, whether triggered by environmental stimulation or by simply thinking about political figures, campaign events, or issues—gets "popped" into WM, and is thereupon tallied into the evaluation.

Recognition/Comprehension/Categorization

Processing continues when a stimulus configuration (say, the headline "Perot Enters Race") activates a search through long-term memory for categories whose features match those of the stimulus. The question being asked is "does this instance or feature *fit* an existing category?" Here, the individual is essentially asking "Who is Perot?" "What is a race?" Recognition occurs automatically (that is, without conscious awareness of the matching process involved), and unless the stimulus is ambiguous, the categorization process

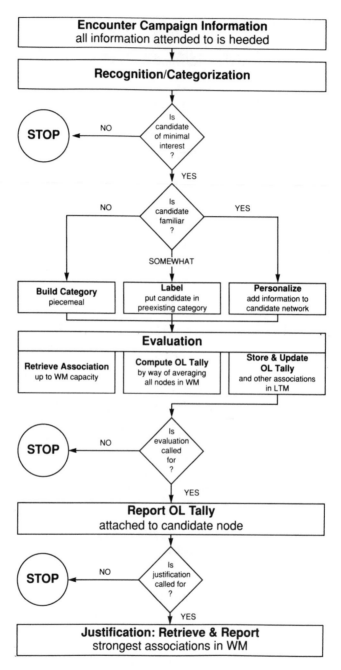

Fig. 2. Flowchart model of the candidate-evaluation process

occurs almost instantaneously (Neely 1977) So, given a modicum of political savvy, the headline would not be ambiguous but would automatically activate Perot-is-a-candidate and race-as-election memory structures, rather than a horse-race scenario.

Categorization is the central trust and basic act of information processing (Lakoff 1987; Rosch 1978; Rosch and Marvis 1975; Smith and Medin 1981). Categories "straddle the boundary between the mind and the world": they are socially developed "pictures in the head" that must fit the configuration of the "world out there" if they are to be useful (Neisser 1987). At this decision point in our model, the process branches, the route taken dependent on what category, if any, is activated in long-term memory. We posit three outcomes of the "fit-to-category" process, the choice a function of how one's existing memory structure for the candidate is organized in memory.

1. *Build a category*. If the candidate is an unknown figure, as was Perot to almost everyone in the early days of the 1992 primary, *and* if the citizen is interested enough to make the cognitive effort required to place Perot within some semantic framework, a new category will be pieced together from whatever associations are activated in LTM by the Perot headline. Creating a new category structure attribute-by-attribute is effortful and time-consuming, as the individual must try to create a new memory structure from bits and pieces that do not as yet have a well-defined node structure or firm links to other concepts. We suspect that for most citizens most of the time, such "bottom up" processing is relatively rare, as the political contexts in which candidate messages appear are likely to instantiate one or another initial characterizations of the information, here, given the link to elections, perhaps activating one or another party label. Given how arduous it is to build a category structure from scratch, such piecemeal processing is thought to be characteristic of the earliest stages of the political socialization process and is called into play thereafter only after initial attempts at categorization have failed to fit a new concept into the existing political lexicon or when new information is incongruent with the initial categorization, and only then if the individual is highly motivated to resolve the ambiguity (Fiske and Neuberg 1988).

2. *Labeling*. Called "category-based" processing by Brewer (1988) and "confirmatory categorization" by Fiske (1988). Labeling is activated when the candidate is a relatively ill-defined entity with few individuating characteristics, as was Perot in the early polls in the 1992 primary season when, apparently, he was known to many people as an instance of the category "Political Independent" or "Millionaire." The consequences of categorizing a candidate as a member of a group are formidable, as the instance "inherits" the attributes of that category. So it may be that Perot, on being categorized

a millionaire, would inherit the most stereotypic attributes of the label by default, perhaps "enriching" Perot with such attributes as his being "probusiness" or "antitaxes," or, if categorized as an "Independent," perhaps seen as "antiparty."

3. *Personalization/individuation.* Our impression-driven model posits a developmental process whereby those citizens with a smidgen of interest in politics will, over the course of the campaign, move from a label-based to a candidate-centered memory representation. Over time, given the media's focus on candidate-centered information, we expect that most citizens will develop a candidate-based knowledge structure in LTM in which the candidate becomes a distinct, relatively cental node in the network, instead of being configured as a mere instance of a superordinate category. Once individuated, the voter can treat the candidate as a particular personality, with distinct traits and policy positions that differentiate him from other members of the same category. Figure 3 depicts our understanding of the difference between category-based and candidate-centered memory structures.

In a category-based node-link representation, the candidate is seen as an instance of some superordinate category, typically as a member of one of the party concepts, "Republican" or "Democrat." In figure 3 we portray this superordinate category as having a name, what Wyer and Srull (1986) call a "header," here, for example, the label "Republican," with "slots" built into the "bin" to hold the category's most defining associations, the "D" to symbolize such prototypic *demographic* associations of the Republican label as "white," the "T" symbolizing the *trait* assessments thought by this individual to characterize the party's prototypical candidate (perhaps seeing Republican candidates as "responsible"), and "G"-type attributes signifying the *"gist"* meanings of the party's most representative issue positions (perhaps identifying the Republican party as probusiness or antiabortion), with all of these attributes popping into conscious memory whenever the party concept is activated. In figure 3a, the candidate is represented as a rather impoverished instance of the party category, with but two individuating "D" attributes, perhaps that he is white and male. Given this knowledge structure, any evaluation of the candidate would necessarily reflect the default characteristics of the category, a clear case of stereotyping.

Following along figure 3, over the course of a campaign the citizen develops a candidate-centered knowledge structure, in which the candidate is "personalized" by specific demographic information, traits, and issue positions (with "s" representing the *specific* issue positions and *specific* behavioral acts that individuate the candidate with distinct policy stands and personal attributes). Note throughout figure 3 that *affective tags,* depicted by plus and minus signs, are attached to each node in memory, this to represent the assumption that every social concept in LTM is affectively

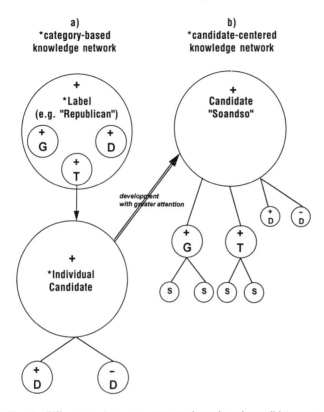

Fig. 3. Differences between category-based and candidate-centered memory structures: *a*, category-based knowledge network; *b*, candidate-centered knowledge network

charged. Given some prior exposure to and assessment of a candidate, people are thought to store their overall affective assessment (their OL Tally) in the name "header" of the candidate node.

Evaluation

We treat the candidate-evaluation process as a chained sequence of three steps that follow immediately upon the initial categorization of the campaign message.

First, the *retrieval* of *all* the activated associations linked to the candidate node, up to the 7 ± 2 chunk capacity of WM. However "rich" the representation of the candidate in LTM memory, the amount of categorical or individuating material that makes its way into WM, and thereupon get factored into the evaluation, is limited to the 7 or so strongest associations then in WM.

Next, the *computation* stage, where we assume that the OL tally is updated by averaging the affective weights of each association now "residing" in working memory to the pre-existing affective tag attached to the candidate node. Assuming as we do that *all* associations in LTM are affect-laden and enter WM with their affective tag attached, the evaluative value of each node in WM is directly available, and does not require additional search through memory for assemblage (Hastie, 1988). Following Anderson's (1991) lead, we think that the affective weight *of each associative node in WM*—first and foremost the candidate's preexisting summary tally—is now updated by averaging to generate a current evaluation that reflects the contribution of each association in WM (with more on the averaging process later).

Lastly, the *updating and storage* phase, where we hold that this newly updated OL tally is now rebonded to the candidate node and returned to LTM, as are the updated affective tags of each of the associations in WM. Further, each node and each associational link between nodes in WM is strengthened as a consequence of having been thought about, thereupon making it easier next time for these nodes and their connections to be activated from LTM and again contribute to the overall summary tally.

Reporting an Impression

In contrast to the evaluation process, we see the act of reporting one's evaluation to be a relatively *simple memory-based process,* whereby the respondent, when called on to express an evaluation, retrieves the candidate node directly from LTM and "reads" the on-line tally from the category "header" (if the candidate is a subordinant instance of a category) or (if the candidate is individuated) "reads" the tally directly from the candidate node, in either case without having to compute a value from the attributes of the category. From this perspective, given that one's evaluation is continuously being upgraded at the time of exposure, and not computed later from memory traces, we think it likely that one's summary evaluation will more accurately reflect the citizen's evaluation of *all* the information she was exposed to and thought about than would an evaluation based on whatever considerations she could later remember.

Justification

The final step in the process only takes place when citizens are called on to give reasons for their choices. As a memory-based process, the justification process is thought to be relatively *independent* of the evaluation process (Anderson and Hubert 1963). Whereas the evaluation process is thought to be on-line and the reporting of one's candidate evaluation is viewed as a simple memory-based act of retrieval, we see the recounting of recollections as a *reconstructive memory-based process* whereby whatever associations strong enough to enter WM (up to WM capacity) are "read" from WM and supplemented with rationalized "evidence" justifying one's evaluation.

A key point here is that the considerations cited as evidence are *not* likely to reflect the actual factors that entered into the evaluative tally, since: (1) some or many of the pieces of information that contributed to the tally are forgotten (about which, more later); (2) some of the factors that originally entered into the tally are no longer among the strongest associates in WM, and consequently do not now reach consciousness (this, too, undermining the causal path from recall to evaluation); and (3) because the comprehension process is constructive—its hallmark being the spontaneous drawing of inferences—when respondents are asked for their recollections, they have difficulty recalling the specific "raw material" of the message and are prone to fill in memory gaps with ad hoc rationalizations (Nisbett and Ross 1980; Wilson and Schooler 1991). What is noteworthy here is that, at best, one's recollections are those considerations *available at the time the question is asked, not the facts, figures, and considerations thought about at the time the evaluation was made.* So, it is our contention that the past is better reflected in the current evaluation than in the recollections of things past.

While we do not have many, if any, "laws" of political action that can stand as firm referents against which to test the adequacy of our proposal, we can and will now look at various plausible mechanisms of information processing that have been, or could be, tested empirically. This criterion test of plausibility is admittedly a problematic standard against which to evaluate theories and models, as many different architectures and processes may conceivably lead to the same response, but, until that happy day when physics, neurophysiology, and the social sciences become one, it appears to be the best we can do.[1]

The On-Line Model: Problems And Prospects

The distinction between on-line (OL) and memory-based (MB) processing is critical to our understanding of the evaluation of candidates (as well, perhaps, of parties, issues, and events), normatively important in how we evaluate the role of citizens, theoretically important in how we conceive of the evaluation process, substantively important in that the factors operating on the two judgmental processes are different and consequential, and methodologically important in terms of how we measure belief updating and attitude change. Generally speaking, OL processing is most likely when the person being evaluated is judged on such dimensions as likability, job suitability, blame or responsibility, when, in short, the decision maker sees the judgmental task as forming an overall impression. Conversely MB processing is more likely than OL processing when the decision maker is called on to actively consider the trade-off of costs and benefits, is motivated to think seriously about the perceived consequences of the decision, or is asked to recount or publically justify the considerations that entered into the evaluation.

Recall from our discussion of figure 1 that a strong, positive correlation between the mix of pros and cons recollected from memory and candidate evaluation is commonly seen as an indicator of memory-based processing (message to memory to evaluation), whereas a strong positive correlation between the evaluative weights of each piece of information the respondent was exposed to in a candidate message and the subsequent evaluation is treated as indicating on-line processing (message to evaluation). In short, controlling for message wipes out the recall-evaluation relationship.

Unfortunately, there are problems with this reliance on correlation as a criterion test for choosing between models (Hastie and Pennington 1989). Again, the problem stems from the constructive nature of human information processing. When testing for memory-based processing, is one's overall evaluation based on recall of the *specific* bits and bytes of campaign messages, or is the candidate evaluation computed from the *inferences* drawn from campaign messages? For example, when updating their impression of George Bush, do citizens store a facsimile of what George Bush actually said about, say, spotted owls, or do they rely on inferences they draw from his statement, perhaps that he cared more about jobs—his own or those of lumberjacks—than owls?

In general terms—this in line with the extensive literatures on trait inferencing in both psychology (Cantor and Mischel 1979; Hastie and Kumar 1979; Heider 1958; Wyer et al. 1992) and political science (Kinder 1986; Stroh in this volume)—we think it likely that citizens typically deal with campaign issues by "personalizing" them, that is, in seeing policy statements and campaign events as reflecting on the character of the candidate. This is in contrast to issue-voting theories of evaluation and choice, which commonly suppose that voters compare their own policy position to that of the candidates and assign a positive value to the candidate "closest" to them on the issues. Indirect support for trait-mediated reasoning comes from the experiments of Bargh and Thein 1985; Bassili and Smith 1986; Newman and Uleman (1989); Winter and Uleman 1984), who find that experimental subjects spontaneously draw trait inferences about other people "on-line," at the time of exposure, from the target's ongoing statements and behaviors.

This distinction between the *"raw material" of a message* and *inferences drawn from the message* cuts across the OL and MB modes of processing, as inferences could be made immediately at the time of exposure (as the OL model holds) or only be made later, at the time of recall from whatever memory traces are then available in memory (as MB processing would have it). From the MB perspective, if one's evaluation is not dependent on the recall of campaign specifics, but on inferences drawn from whatever recollections are currently in WM, then the correlation between memory-for-the-facts and judgment would be low, because inferences mediate the relationship. At this point in time, there is no clear-cut solution to the problem, leaving us with arguments of plausibility, with our interpretation favoring the OL Model on two counts:

1. A good deal of experimental evidence has accumulated over the past decade or so demonstrating that decision makers rarely store a veridical representation of the raw data of a message in long-term memory. Studies of reading comprehension, for example, show that inferences are drawn and elaborations made spontaneously and immediately *at the time of encoding* (Branford and Johnson 1972; Morrow, Greenspan, and Bower 1989; McKoon and Ratcliff 1992). It is inference making that allows subjects to make sense of the raw material of a message (Carpenter and Just 1975), and it is this constructed, inference-laden "picture in the head" that becomes the basis for judgment, not the raw material of the message (Bargh 1988; Harris 1981; Uleman and Bargh 1989).

2. As will be discussed in the next section, people appear to forget much of the information they are exposed to, but—this the key—the memory decay curves appear to be steeper for the facts in the message than for the inferences drawn from the facts, or one's summary evaluation of the candidate. If inferences are drawn on-line, then the "raw material" that originally entered the evaluation is very likely to be forgotten.

Memory Decay And Candidate Evaluation

Memory is the cornerstone of all models of candidate evaluation, as even the OL model makes minimal demands on memory, in its reliance on the voter's ability to recall the affective tally from candidate nodes. Critical as is the role of memory in our thinking about politics, there is little theoretical appreciation, and still less empirical work in the literature, on what may be the most critical aspect of memory; to wit: human memory is fallible. Memories fade over time. Thus it is that virtually all experimental studies of memory report a precipitous decay of veridical memory over time, even after short, 2–10 minute, interludes, especially of the specific details of a message. Consequently, over time, memory comes to reflect a mix of imagination and reality, as memories are increasingly made up of fuzzy recollections and schematic inferences.

Despite the importance of forgetfulness on the judgmental process, there have been few studies of memory decay in the political science literature, the most notable exceptions being Graber's (1988) analysis of diary entries, the Zaller and Price (1990) analysis of aggregate trends, and the Lodge, McGraw, and Stroh (1989) and McGraw, Pinney and Newman (1991) studies that follow the practice in psychology of looking at recall after a short distractor task. What is lacking is research on the functional forms of memory decay and of the relationship of judgment to memory after delays of a day, a week, or, ideally, the longer time spans of campaigns.

To this point in time, we have been looking at the relationship between evaluation and memory as if both recollections and judgment were stable things. Consider now the more realistic hypothesis that memories become increasingly irretrievable over time and that different types of information decay at different rates. The expected decay curves are depicted in figure 4. Here, the on-line tally tagged to the candidate node is predicted to decay most slowly over time, the gist meaning of issues somewhat faster, while the specifics of a candidate's policy positions are predicted to fade away quickly.

The reasoning underlying these expectations is fueled more by empirical results observed in our laboratory than by any clear theoretical rationale. The most straightforward line of reasoning looks at repetition and reinforcement effects: perhaps the affective tally attached to the candidate node is most resilient to decay over time because it is activated most often. In most newspaper and TV-news accounts of electoral events, the candidate's name and picture are presented many more times than are the candidate's general or specific policy positions. As the focal point of the evaluative process, the candidate node would be "popped" into memory most often and its node strength would thereby be strengthened with each iteration. (This is the mechanism written into the Boynton and Lodge (1992) computational model of candidate evaluation.)

Assuming for the moment that memory fades over time more or less along the lines depicted in figure 4, a critical set of hypotheses relating memory to judgment come to the fore.

First off, the potential contribution of recollections decreases over time, as fewer and fewer considerations are available as inputs to the evaluation. Conversely, the OL tally—being relatively stable over time—continues to reflect the citizen's prior assessments of *all* of the campaign information

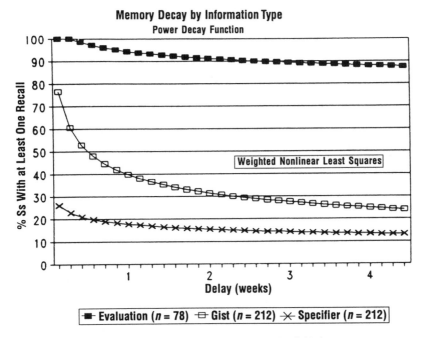

Fig. 4. Memory decay curves over twenty-eight days

(gists and specifics) she was exposed to. Studies are underway at Stony Brook to test the hypotheses depicted in figure 4 (Lodge, Steenbergen, and Brau 1992). Specifically, we expect the candidate evaluation at each lag time to be better predicted by the evaluation of each piece of information in the original message than is the mix of "evidence" then available in memory.

Relatedly, the OL model would predict that many of those citizens who cannot recollect *any* of the message would nonetheless be able to come up with an evaluative tally for the candidate, a tally that we would bet is in the same direction as and of similar magnitude to their initial OL evaluation. Hypothetically, this "judgment without memory for the facts" would hold even after offering respondents' incentives for recall, since the effect is thought to reflect cognitive-processing limitations that are not dramatically affected by motivation. And, this too untested, we would expect that the positive message to evaluation correlation after a delay is not a function of the citizen having actually voiced an impression at some prior time, since impressions are thought to be computed spontaneously and unconsciously whenever the candidate node is activated, and are not dependent on the individual having stated an opinion beforehand.

Assuming the researcher has obtained the respondent's evaluation of each bit of information in the message (and an evaluation of each inference drawn from the message) we would expect the correlation between memory and judgment to decline over time, as memory traces fade, unless, of course, the respondents were to rationalize a set of tally-consistent inferences to compensate for their embarrassment at not being able to think of good reasons for their preferences. Admittedly, given the constructive nature of the evaluation process, discriminating such judgment-causes-memory effects from simple MB processing is no mean feat.

The Sequential Nature Of Evaluations

Just as campaigns unfold over time, the process of belief updating is thought to be carried out in steps. Information processing is sequential—impressions are evolving continuously, as new information is first evaluated and then integrated into an overall summary impression. Once a judgment is formed (and retrieved, when reactivated) it contributes to the updating of subsequent information. This step-by-step sequential process can be treated as an *anchoring and adjustment process,* whereby (depending on various individual and contextual factors) information is turned into evidence on being evaluated in terms of its positive (consistent) or negative (inconsistent) relevance to one's current belief (McGraw, Lodge, and Stroh 1990). The adjusted belief then becomes the anchor for subsequent information processing.

Following Norman Anderson's (1990) lead we posit—this in contrast to virtually all political science models—that the revision of impressions is based on an *averaging,* rather than an additive, process. A characteristic of averaging models is that they show a curvilinear impact of new information on judgment, what may be called a "discount function," whereby information evaluated early in a sequence has greater impact on the evaluation than would the same information presented later in the sequence.

An illustration of averaging, this adapted from Lindsay and Norman's (1977) classic text on human information processing: A friend tells you that candidate Soandso "is a sincere person." "Sincere" is a highly positive trait, rated to be one of the most desirable of 585 personality traits scaled by Anderson (1968). Suppose you were to scale "sincere" as an 8, and, some time later, were to see the candidate in a TV soundbite from which you inferred he was "a good speaker" (valued as a +4). If positive evaluations were simply added, then because both characterizations are positive, the candidate would be judged better than earlier, when he was simply sincere $(8 + 4 = 12)$. If, on the other hand, impressions are updated by averaging, then one's overall evaluation of the candidate described as "sincere" *and* "a good speaker" would be $8 + 4 = 12 \div 2 = 6$. This outcomes defies common sense, in that two positives are evaluated less positively than was the case with but one positive, but such averaging models do, indeed, describe the impression-formation of people under many well-controlled experimental situations, clearly a non-Bayesian result.

Another example, this from Anderson (1974), looking at the assessment of U.S. Presidents. Experimental subjects were presented with two paragraphs of information portraying the statesmanship of presidents that had previously been rated as low, medium, or highly favorable or unfavorable. Specific to the question of how people integrate information into a summary evaluation, the striking result of this study—replicated many times over (Anderson 1973)—is that the ratings of presidents after people had read only one highly positive paragraph were essentially the same as after their reading of two highly positive pieces of information and were higher than after reading sets of information that were highly positive and moderately positive. This is what you would expect, if impressions are based on the averaging, rather than the adding up of information.

The consequences of averaging, as opposed to the additive revision of beliefs, is a curvilinear relationship between the *flow* of information and judgment: new information presented late in the flow counts less than would the same piece of evidence had it appeared early in the sequence. This curvilinear relationship—whether logarithmic or a power function—implies, psychologically, that first impressions count most, and will show up in the summary evaluation as a primacy effect. While the general form of the anchoring and adjustment model is curvilinear, the degree of curvature—the extent that positive and negative information is discounted—depends on various task and context effects. Looking at this question in terms of sensitivity to new information, it is important that people adjust their beliefs to reflect new evidence, yet not be so responsive to new information that they forgo their history of experience. A basic finding of the decision-making literature is that people are sometimes more and at other times less sensitive to new information than normative models would like, depending on context. For example, numerous studies detail serious biases in the judgmental process whereby people are overly responsive to deviations from expectations, unusual events and otherwise nonrepresentative information (Kahneman and Tversky 1972; Quattrone and Tversky 1988). Unchecked, this would be a prescription for disaster, in that unusual events and exceptional outcomes—while memorable—are atypical by definition, and would be maladaptive if relied upon. Survival requires a countervailing force that would be more responsive to statistical base rates.

Owing much to Hogarth and Einhorn's (1992) "belief adjustment model," the variable effects of information on judgment can be characterized as a conflict between adaptation and inertia, between the strength of one's

anchoring opinion and the impact of new evidence. Accordingly, beliefs, evaluations, and impressions tend toward inertia, as new information—whether negative or positive—counts less over the course of information flow, hence the oft-noted "perseverance of beliefs" in the face of new, incongruent information (Rothbart 1981). Here is an example of order effects on evaluations, first demonstrated by Solomon Asch (1946), and later elaborated upon by Tversky and Kahneman (1986) as a framing effect:
    On a scale that ranges from

— — — — — — — —
+4   +3   +2   +1   −1   −2   −3   −4

evaluate a person described thusly:

    smart, artistic, sentimental, cool, awkward, faultfinding

Now consider a different person described as:

    faultfinding, awkward, cool, sentimental, artistic, smart

    When Anderson and Barrios (1961) carried out this experiment, their subjects rated the first person positively, with an average score of 1.4, whereas the second person was evaluated slightly unfavorably, with a mean rating of −0.07, despite the only difference being the order in which the trait attributes were presented, from which we conclude, (this quite a stretch from the laboratory), *political campaigns matter*—the sequence of political events affects evaluations differentially, depending on the strength of initial impression. Thus, *when* citizens learn about candidates may count for as much as *what* they hear about them. This the case, more dynamic analyses of the unfolding of campaign events will be required to track the ebb and flow of evaluations.

Conclusion

While little is known about how people deal with the complexities, uncertainties, and ambiguities of political life, other than to say that they deviate wildly from rational expectations (Payne, Bettman, and Johnson 1992), it is now clear that judgment and choice are constructive and contingent processes by which people—bounded rationalists—employ various heuristic mechanisms to simplify the representation of alternatives and the evaluation of prospects (Sniderman, Brody, and Tetlock 1991). The information-processing approach provides a coherent perspective for analyzing and interpreting the evaluation process, while the OL model provides a plausible explanation for some of the more troubling paradoxes that plague contemporary electoral research.

Given the constructionist nature of human information processing, the key research questions are: How much of what kinds of information enter into the decision calculus? Where, when, and how will people look at (all, most, some, little, or none) of the available information, and, if attended to, how does this heeded information inform judgment and choice? The overarching question becomes: How, and under what conditions, do people bring their prior knowledge to bear in the evaluation of political candidates?

In broad terms, we hypothesize that information is tallied up in real time from the small set of information made available to working memory at the time of exposure, first among them the preexisting tally, with each of the 5–7 chunks of information that make their way into working memory contributing to an updated evaluation by a simple *averaging procedure* that weighs one's prior experience heavily. On each cycle through WM, each concept node, as well as its connections, is strengthened, and thereby made more easily activated later. Conversely, of course, memory traces weaken over time, if not reactivated. Hence, a plausible explanation for the failure of citizens to recall many, if any, campaign events is that most instances and policies are so seldom activated—as compared to the candidate's name, party label, and perhaps one or two of the major themes of a campaign—that they weaken with disuse and become decreasingly accessible.

While nodes and their connections can be popped into WM by thinking about the election, we think that most political information processing is *exposure driven*, by which we mean that any attention-getting stimulus is automatically deposited in WM, along with its associations, and thereupon contributes to the OL tally. Given the heavy reliance on candidate-centered information in newspapers and on television, the media strongly influences what information citizens see, hear, and thereby process. So, for example, the newspaper headline "Jesse Jackson Endorses Clinton" would deposit the "Clinton" and "Jackson" nodes in WM, along with their strongest associates, perhaps "President," "Democrat," "black leader," and "affirmative action," with each node carrying its own affective tag into WM. These are the strongest associations of the Clinton and Jackson nodes, and reach WM in competition with all the other associations in the network. Together, these bundles of associations establish the context for the interpretation of the campaign event. With every cycle of new and old information through Working Memory, the affective tag of each node is integrated into the OL tally for Clinton, and each of the associated affective tags is also adjusted. So if Jesse's endorsement of Clinton was thought to be positive, Jackson's tag would be boosted, as would be the affective tag of "black leader" and "affirmative action." On their return to LTM, each of the nodes would be strengthened, as would their connective links.

This OL model has significant substantive and methodological consequences for our understanding of how citizens evaluate candidates and choose among them. By way of conclusion, let me highlight what I see as the major substantive and methodological consequences of the OL model of candidate evaluation.

1. Affect is central in our model, as all social beliefs are *"hot cognitions."* Accordingly, what citizens do when updating their impression of candidates is first cull the affective weight from each element of a campaign message and then immediately integrate these values into their overall assessment of the candidate. From this perspective, affect and cognition are "unitized," a notion similar to Fazio's (1986) conception of attitude as an "object with affect attached." From this assumption, note that it would be difficult, if not impossible, for citizens to disentangle their beliefs from preferences, and for you or I to maintain that recollections are "causing" evaluations.

2. Beliefs and evaluations have been shown to change via a *sequential anchoring and adjustment process* (Hogarth and Einhorn 1992), whereby one's current position provides an anchoring opinion, and adjustments to the anchor are made on the basis of additional information. Consequently, information presented later in the campaign will have to be especially strong and distinctive to have a measurable impact on the evaluation. Once the anchor is adjusted, this updated position becomes the anchor for the assessment of new information, with the information-integration process progressing sequentially (McGraw, Lodge, and Stroh 1990).

3. Unless strongly motivated to process information accurately, carefully, and deeply (conditions not thought to be characteristic of electoral decision making for most citizens), the *construction of judgments* (from the associations then current in working memory) does not routinely reflect an unbiased search through LTM for a fair and representative sampling of considerations. Rather, once an evaluation is formed, *"expectancy-confirmation biases"* favor the encoding and retrieval of information that fits expectations (Lord, Ross, and Lepper 1979; Stephan 1989) and motivate a *"directed search"* for affectively congruent evidence (Kunda 1990). Together, the cognitive and affective mechanisms conspire to bolster one's priors.

4. The OL model sees the candidate-evaluation process as *compensatory, but not comparative.* Citizens are thought to update their tally of each candidate separately, and only when explicitly called on to choose among candidates do they directly compare their respective tallies and vote for the

most positive or against the candidate with the most negative tally. The implication here is that, whereas citizens adjust their on-line tally upward or downward in response to the perceived positivity or negativity of campaign messages, they do not (cannot?) follow the dictates of spatial models of candidate evaluation in making direct issue × issue comparisons across candidates (see Rahn 1990, for a comparison of within- versus between-candidate information processing). The key question is: At what point in the evaluation process are the candidates directly compared? The OL model implies that comparative candidate assessments are not made attribute-by-attribute, but are rendered only when a comparative judgment is required, whereupon a direct between-candidate evaluation is made of the respective on-line tallies. This relatively simple *compensatory process*—if confirmed—would allow citizens to revise their impressions easily, without having to make complex trade-offs across issues between candidates when updating their beliefs and preferences.

5. *People forget a lot*, hence the relationship between memory and judgment not only will change over time, but will predictably deteriorate. Our preliminary analyses, backing up the expectations in figure 4 (Lodge, Steenbergen, and Brau 1993), suggest that the decay curves for the specifics of a campaign are lost first, followed by the gist meanings of the candidate's issue positions, with the candidate's name and evaluative tally fading more slowly. Thus it is that recall (if relied on) would be a poor basis for evaluation.

6. Whereas the evaluation phase of the impression-formation process is hypothesized to be carried out in real time in the moments of exposure, the *justification phase is thought to be a separate, independent, memory-based process,* whereupon respondents are actively engaged in a motivated search of LTM for evidence. What people are likely to report as the reasons for their preferences—in addition to the one, two, but no more than a few associations in working memory—is "what seems plausible as a cause, what is easiest to verbalize, and what is most available in memory" at the time the question is asked (Wilson, Dunn, Kraft, and Lisle 1989, 335). In summing up their classic studies on rationalization, Nisbett and Wilson (1977) propose:

> that when people are asked to report how a particular stimulus influenced a particular response, they do so not by consulting a memory of the mediating process, but by applying or generating causal theories about the effects of that type of stimulus on that type of response. (1977, 248)

The key distinction here, between the considerations that enter into an evaluation and the reasons people give for their preferences, is important, in that the factors that entered into an evaluation on-line need not be (and in fact, are *un*likely to be) the same considerations that come to mind via a *post facto* memory search (Wilson and Hodges 1992). The citizen has the OL tally in mind; it need not be computed from scratch; and so we think it most likely that responses to recall questions, especially the "cued" like-dislike NES-type questions, will more likely reflect the search for supporting evidence than an unbiased sampling of pros and cons (Lau 1982). Our expectations (in line with the panel study of Rahn, Krosnick, and Breuning 1992, 16) is that "verbal reports of voters' likes and dislikes are mostly rationalizations of preexisting evaluations."

7. The key assumption of the information-processing approach is that process matters—explanation depends on being able to trace the mechanisms people use to form and update their impressions and apply their beliefs to action. To the extent that methodological questions can be separated from substantive concerns, the need to look at how information is represented and processed will demand new-to-political-science methods for determining the content and structure of people's knowledge structures, and new methods for tracing the evaluation process. These methods imply an *experimental focus*—whether manipulating the content and context of messages in the laboratory or incorporating experimental manipulations inside survey instruments—since evaluation is a *dynamic process.* Information-processing models, whether MB or OL, are all about learning, how one's prior knowledge determines how subsequent information will be comprehended, and how one's prior evaluations will influence the integration of new information. While cross-sectional studies can illuminate group differences, and a series of cross sections could allow us to trace the marginal patterns of learning, one or another *process-tracing method (perhaps of the type employed by Lau in this volume) will become indispensable as we turn our attention to the evolution of beliefs and learn to treat judgment and choice as conditional* on a chain of prior beliefs and impressions.

8. Finally, what may be the most important substantive consequence of our impression-driven model of candidate evaluation: the OL model posits and our preliminary analysis support, the hypothesis that experimental subjects (Boynton and Lodge 1992) and survey respondents (Lodge, Steenbergen, and Brau 1992) are sensitive to the candidates' message; to wit: we typically find that the summary tally derived from the respondents' evaluation of the gist meanings and specific policy planks in a candidate's message is moderately to strongly correlated with their overall evaluation of the candidate—even over extended time spans—whereas, of course, the correlation between recall and evaluation is but weakly correlated, and the coefficient drops precipitously over time.

This brings us full circle. We started out this essay with a paradox: how is it that such apparently knowledge-poor citizens appear to make reasonably informed candidate evaluations, or, the same point made along the lines depicted in Figures 1 and 4, how is it that our experimental subjects are responsive to the candidate message, but are unable to recount the reasons for their preferences? The OL answer to the puzzle ends on a positive note: our depiction of the voter is, if not sanguine, certainly not as pessimistic as normally portrayed in the empirical literature, since what little data as exists today on the message to OL tally relationship suggests that *citizens are responsive to the content of campaign messages,* but are just unable—for good reason—to reproduce the factors at a later date. I think a close reading of the empirical voting behavior literature would show that much of our discipline's pessimism is based on the respondents' inability to recall campaign information or answer recall-based questions. From our perspective, the long-suffering American voter—long thought to be a fool for not being able to recollect many, if any, facts about the campaign—might more rightly be considered an efficient information processor of the "bounded rationalist" school, who in "real time" routinely integrates the raw material of the campaign into an overarching impression and who is content to let the facts that originally contributed to this on-line tally slip from memory.

NOTES

Much of the original research on impression formation carried out at Stony Brook was funded by NSF Grant SES 8819974.
    1. Samuel C. Patterson, Personal Communication, Montecatini Alto, Italy, July 3, 1993.

CHAPTER 7

Computational Experiments in Electoral Behavior

Charles S. Taber and Marco R. Steenbergen

Behind every voting theory there is a metaphor or an analogy, either implicit or
explicit, about the process of choice.

—Samuel Popkin

Electoral research has shown many advances since early assessments of the
field (cf. Rossi 1956), most notably in the areas of data collection, statistical
modeling, and normative modeling. However, despite the progress, several
important paradoxes remain. One such paradox can be found in the vast gap
between *prediction* and *explanation* that exists in voting research. As a rule,
we can predict individual voting behavior rather accurately, but we still lack
a reliable understanding of the mental processes that underlie such behavior.[1] In other words, voting models remain very much "black-box" models
(Lodge, Stroh, and Wahlke 1990). A second paradox lies in the tension that
exists between *assumptions* and *evidence* in electoral research (Page 1977;
Wahlke 1991). That citizens possess enough knowledge about and interest
in politics to make informed vote choices is crucial in most research on
voting behavior. But an impressive array of evidence from electoral studies
belies this assumption (see Berelson 1952; Berelson, Lazarsfeld, and
McPhee 1954; Campbell et al. 1960; Campbell, Gurin, and Miller 1954;
Converse 1964, 1975; Lazarsfeld, Berelson, and Gaudet 1944; for recent
evidence see Delli Carpini and Keeter 1991; Page and Shapiro 1992; and
for reviews see Kinder and Sears 1985; Neuman 1986). Most electoral
research portrays the citizen as politically uninterested and unaware, on the
one hand, and highly motivated and capable of complex decision processes,
on the other. In short, the basic assumptions of most voting studies conflict
with several well-established findings about human behavior, both inside
and outside the voting booth.

1. People do not passively absorb information from their environment,
   but, rather, they *actively process* it (Newell and Simon 1972; Simon
   1957). In particular, human information processing is *sequential* in

nature, in that information is not processed in a vacuum (as if the mind were a tabula rasa), but on the basis of existing knowledge that affects the way people interpret and integrate incoming information (Hogarth and Einhorn 1992).

2. Limitations in human information-processing capacity place serious constraints on what people can do, in terms of judgment and choice. That is, the capacity to process information is limited, so that people are *boundedly rational,* at best (Markus and Zajonc 1985; Simon 1957, 1985).

3. Politics is not among citizens' most prominent life concerns (Lippmann 1992; Kinder and Sears 1985). Hence, we should not expect voters to make decisions through elaborate processes that require more motivational resources than may be available. As *cognitive "misers"* (Markus and Zajonc 1985), they may use highly simplified heuristics, avoiding more demanding decision processes.[2]

These findings call for voting models that focus on the *processes* involved in electoral choice. Indeed, some work has moved in this direction, resulting in more psychologically realistic views of electoral choice (Boynton and Lodge in this volume; Einhorn, Komorita, and Rosen 1972; Herstein 1981; Lodge, McGraw, and Stroh 1989; Lodge and Stroh, 1993; McGraw, Lodge, and Stroh 1990; Ottati and Wyer 1990; Rahn et al. 1990). However, given the subject matter of electoral research, namely judgment and choice, one analytic framework has been conspicuously absent in recent work on voting behavior: *behavioral decision theory.*[3] Behavioral decision theory takes into account the active, boundedly rational, and heuristic nature of human cognition, while concentrating explicitly on judgment and choice. In addition, behavioral-decision theorists have developed several methods for process tracing that provide a useful supplement to the standard survey approach of electoral research.

The theories and approaches of cognitive science, including computational methods, have also had little impact on electoral research (but see the prescient work of McPhee 1963, and McPhee and Smith 1962). Because of its long tradition of unconcern with assumptions and satisfaction with predictive success, electoral research has been largely unaffected by the cognitive revolution. This, too, is changing (e.g., see Boynton and Lodge in this volume; Wahlke 1991). Computational methods provide a powerful and flexible language for modeling the complex symbolic processes that cognitive science (and behavioral decision theory) posit for the information-processing black box (Ostrom 1988; Taber 1992; Taber and Timpone n.d.).

In this chapter, we apply many of the results and ideas of behavioral decision theory to the study of voting behavior. We also develop a new method for electoral research, rooted in some of the technical developments in behavioral decision theory and cognitive science. Combining survey data with computer simulations, making for what we call *computational experiments,* we compare and evaluate several process theories of candidate evaluation and electoral choice drawn from behavioral decision theory and electoral research.[4] Though we will present illustrative data from an initial study, our main emphasis in this chapter is on the development of the method of computational experimentation and on sketching the parallels between behavioral decision theory and models of electoral choice.

Behavioral Decision Theory

Over the past two decades, the decision-making literature has undergone a definitive change, that one might almost call paradigmatic. Early models of decision making—not unlike most current electoral research—were premised on an economic view of human behavior, which claims that people seek to maximize the benefits from their behavior, in terms of the goals they have. However, over the past two decades, the image of the economic actor has faced increasing competition from another image, that of human beings as psychological actors. The adoption of this psychological image has called into question the fundamental assumption of human rationality—that of optimizing behavior—in favor of the belief that human decision making is subject to important cognitive limitations. Behavioral decision theory has stood at the helm of many of these dramatic developments.

The image of suboptimal human decision making has been substantiated by a wide array of experimental data (Abelson and Levi 1985; Einhorn and Hogarth 1981; Elster 1991; Hogarth 1987; Schoemaker 1982; Simon 1985; Wright 1984). But behavioral-decision scientists have done more than just generate data that defy an easy explanation by normative theory. They have also developed their own theoretical models to explain the data, and with very few exceptions, these models emphasize the importance of process in decision making, focusing on the intervening mechanisms that transform decision inputs (for example, information) into outputs (judgment and choice), on the sequence of decision making, and on the cognitive limitations of the decision maker (Carroll and Johnson 1990).[5]

Process Tracing

If we want to engage in an in-depth analysis of the dynamic processes that underlie voting behavior, the standard methods of electoral research are of little use. In general, electoral studies focus on outcomes, such as vote intentions, vote choices, and candidate evaluations, and their determinants, connecting predictors and outputs through some statistical model. If one's goal is to trace down the mechanisms that transform inputs into outputs, however, explicit process data must be collected or postulated, and integrated in a dynamic theoretical framework.[6]

Behavioral process tracing. Empirical process-tracing methods are quite diverse (for overviews see Carroll and Johnson 1990; Einhorn, Kleinmuntz, and Kleinmuntz 1979; Ericsson and Simon 1984; Ford et al. 1989; Jacoby et al. 1987), but share several core characteristics. First, real-life decision makers are studied, either in natural decision settings or in laboratory settings, with experimental decision tasks. Second, the main objective of the methods is to infer the decision-making process that gives rise to the decisions that are made. This analytic inference rests on the information inputs, on the decision output, *and* on explicit process data.

Two major behavioral process-tracing methods have so far found application. In *verbal protocol analyses,* subjects are asked to provide verbal descriptions (either concurrently or retrospectively) of their decision-making processes (see Ericsson and Simon 1984; Lusk and Judd 1988; Newell and Simon 1972). Unfortunately, verbal protocols can only provide data on processes about which the decision maker is cognizant (see Jacoby et al. 1987; Nisbett and Wilson 1977). Moreover, the obtrusive nature of "think aloud" verbal protocols may well affect decision-making processes (Ericsson and Simon 1984). These weaknesses are important enough to consider alternative methods, like *information-search monitoring.* Here, the premise is that one can infer decision-making processes from the information-search patterns of the decision maker (Jacoby et al. 1987; Johnson and Payne 1985; Payne 1976; Payne, Bettman, and Johnson 1988; Wilkins 1967). Information search may be traced by monitoring the eye movements of subjects as they process visually displayed information (Russo and Rosen 1975) or by recording the search patterns of subjects who must physically manipulate an "information board" to access particular pieces of information (Herstein 1981, 1985; Lau 1989, in this volume).

Of course, information-search methods assume that search is indicative of choice. But the selection of information may be a separate decision that precedes the choice of an alternative and follows, in fact, a different process (Carroll and Johnson 1990). Information-search methods register the sequence and duration of access to information items; they do not trace the actual processing of the items (Jacoby et al. 1987).

Computational process tracing. Where behavioral process-tracing methods seek to infer information processes from a behavioral trace, computational methods *postulate* theoretical information processes and explore their implications through simulation. In their most useful form, these simulations are then validated with behavioral data (Abelson 1968; Hovland

1960; Ostrom 1988). Computational methods provide modeling languages with the necessary expressibility to represent the detailed theories of behavioral decision making (Ostrom 1988; Taber 1992). Since nearly all of these cognitive theories involve the complex processing of information, an adequate modeling language must flexibly deal with the manipulation of symbols, with uncertain and vague information, and with tremendous complexity, while maintaining analytic rigor. Computer simulation—the "third symbol system," to use Ostrom's (1988) apt phrase—can express the essential features of *homo symbolicus* as neither natural language nor mathematics can.

Working computational models "behave" in accordance with the predictions of a theoretical model (or set of models); they become "experimental animals" (Abelson 1968; Stasser 1988). In a very real sense, computational models may be used for the same purpose as "thought experiments" for simple verbal theories or formal analysis for relatively simple mathematical models—to draw out the implications of a theoretical system under novel or otherwise interesting conditions. The difference, of course, is in the complexity and flexibility of the models that may be explored. In the electoral context, for example, we can posit a number of complex process theories of electoral decision making and faithfully represent those theories as computer programs. We will then have a set of "electoral robots" with which to experiment, each robot behaving according to the theory on which it is based. It is then a simple matter to manipulate features of the decision task to explore the behavior of the theory. For most nontrivial process theories, this exercise would be near impossible, using thought experiments or mathematical analysis.

Though a variety of computational analyses have been reported recently for important topics in social psychology (Hastie 1988; Smith 1988; Stasser 1988), cognitive science (see Collins and Smith 1988), and political science (Carbonell 1978; Sylvan, Goel, and Chandrasekaran 1990; Spellman and Holyoak 1992; Taber 1992), we know of no current applications of computer simulations of decision-making processes in electoral research.[7] Payne and Johnson (Johnson and Payne 1985; Payne, Bettman, and Johnson 1988, 1990), however, have simulated a variety of decision problems and decision rules in other contexts. In particular, they explored the impact of task variations—the number of alternatives, the number of outcomes, the probabilities of outcomes, and the presence or absence of dominant alternatives—on the accuracy of and effort required by different choice rules from the behavioral-decision literature.[8]

The major problem with the computational approach—as well as its strength—stems from its purely theoretical nature. In general, no positive statements can be made about the type of decision-making process that actually takes place in a given decision context. The empirical value of a simulation is limited by the validity of the theoretical models on which it is based, and this validity cannot be assessed without collecting behavioral process and outcome data to validate the predictions.

Process tracing through computational experiments. Behavioral process tracing and computational process tracing each have significant strengths, though they suffer from serious defects. But it is important to emphasize that they do not *share* strengths and weaknesses. In fact, we suggest combining elements of these methods, to minimize the limitations of the approaches when used separately. Behavioral methods provide process data, while computational methods generate theoretical predictions.

We propose a method in which actual decision makers provide information that constrains computational process tracing in two important ways. First, the inputs for the simulation are elicited from real people, instead of being generated randomly. As in behavioral process-tracing methods, we can derive from experimental subjects the information they use in making a decision, (i.e., the inputs). This might be done through verbal protocols or information-search monitoring as described above. Or, as in the study reported below, a survey may be constructed to elicit this information. Second, the subjects make actual choices, against which we can gauge the performance of the simulation. Instead of relying on purely normative criteria of performance (which may not exist), we can assess the process models in terms of real inputs and outputs.

In addition, computational experimentation retains the most important benefit of simulation-based process tracing. We can still postulate decision rules and examine their performance rigorously. Empirical process-tracing methods must find (sometimes rather clever) ways of inferring an unobservable process. Computationally, we can simulate that process. We can directly and unambiguously trace the processing of information, according to the theories embodied in the simulation. The method is quite flexible, allowing a direct interplay between empirical-process data and computational models based on behavioral decision theory. If we have some result (or even simply a hunch) that suggests a different integration or decision rule, we can program the new rule and explore its performance. This opens the door to rather detailed computational thought experiments.

Moreover, the method allows more sophisticated simulations than those reported here. We can use Monte Carlo techniques to vary features of the decision rules, or even combine features of several rules into new models, thereby exploring a much larger sample of possible theoretical processes.[9] Similarly, we can vary features of the decision task—complexity, for example. This would enable us to explore a variety of "what if" situations.

Counterfactual simulation techniques like this have rapidly become one of the main features of simulation analyses (Taber 1992).

The following sections describe an example of computational experimentation in electoral behavior, beginning with a discussion of a variety of theoretical voting models. These voting models are then computationally instantiated; in essence, they become our "electoral robots."

Decision Rules and Voting Behavior

Decision rules can be defined as explicit models or algorithms that specify how decision inputs (information about attributes or alternatives) are transformed into decision outputs (judgment and choice). By now, behavioral decision theory has produced a rather lengthy catalog of such rules, which cannot be discussed extensively within the confines of a single chapter (for reviews, see Hogarth 1987; Wright 1984). Instead, we will focus on a limited number of rules that appear to be particularly relevant for the domain of voting behavior, either because these rules have clear counterparts in existing theoretical models of electoral choice or because they have proven to be important in previous empirical work on candidate evaluation.

Weighted-Additive Rule

First, we consider the weighted-additive model, which expresses the evaluations of alternatives as the weighted sum of their attribute values:

$$Y_i = \sum_{j=1}^{m} w_{ij} e_{ij} \qquad (1)$$

Here Y_i is the evaluation of alternative i ($i = 1, \ldots, k$; $k \geq 2$), w_{ij} is the weight of the jth attribute of alternative i ($j = 1, \ldots, m$), and e_{ij} is the value of the jth attribute. Following convention for similar decision problems (cf. Kahn and Meyer 1991), we assume that the attribute weights will be invariant over the alternatives ($w_{ij} = w_{.j}$).[10] The attribute values can be any ordinal or cardinal numbers that rate the attributes along a given dimension (for example, likability). The aggregate of these values, weighted by the w_{ij}, gives the overall impression or evaluation of an alternative. The weighted-additive rule assumes that decision makers will choose the alternative with the highest overall evaluation. Hence, the rule captures a maximization principle.

Clearly the weighted additive model belongs to the class of general linear decision models (see Dawes 1979). The rule's distinctive feature is that it integrates decision inputs across attributes, within alternatives, unlike other linear models that integrate across alternatives, within attributes (Hogarth 1987). The weighted-additive model, itself, can be further divided into two subgroups: alternative-based and attribute-based models (Carroll and Johnson 1990). The former work backward from the evaluation of a given alternative to the contributions of the component attributes. The logic here is that of a regression analysis, where the overall impression of an alternative is regressed on the attribute values for that alternative and the w_{ij} can be viewed as regression weights (Dawes 1979). The attribute-based model works from the attribute values to the evaluation of the alternatives. In this case, the statistical logic is that of linear composites, and the w_{ij} can be interpreted as decision weights or alternatively, as we will do in this chapter, as importance ratings of the different attributes of the alternatives (Carroll and Johnson 1990).[11]

Here we will only consider the attribute-based version of the weighted-additive model. In terms of decision theory, this model can be viewed as a specific parameterization of (expected) utility theory, provided that the attributes are interpreted as possible decision outcomes for a given choice, the e_{ij} as the utilities of those outcomes, and the w_{ij} as the (subjective) probabilities of the outcome (cf. Savage 1954; Von Neumann and Morgenstern 1944). The weighted-additive model, however, is also related to several expectancy value theories of attitudes (Ajzen 1991; Anderson 1971; Fishbein 1963; McGuire 1989). As such, this model specifies a principle of information integration, as well as a decision rule.

In terms of electoral behavior, the weighted-additive model is perhaps the most universal formulation of *normative* (rational choice) models of the vote choice.[12] The hallmark of these models, as Ottati (1990, 159) states, is that "the voter makes a deliberate assessment of politically substantive criteria prior to forming an opinion and uses this information in a relatively logical or reasonable manner when forming a political judgment."[13] Because the weighted-additive model, as we use it, is attribute-based rather than alternative-based, and because information is integrated in an ostensibly reasonable way (no information is neglected, for example), it appears that normative models of voting behavior can, indeed, be accommodated rather well in the framework of the weighted-additive decision rule.[14]

Several theories of voting behavior can be cited as special cases of the decision calculus of the weighted-additive model. First, *spatial theories* of voting behavior express the evaluation of a candidate in terms of the distances between a voter's ideal points and a candidate's perceived stands on the issues (Davis, Hinich, and Ordeshook 1970; Enelow and Hinich 1984; Enelow, Hinich, and Mendell 1986; Shapiro 1969; cf. Downs 1957). This logic can be captured by the weighted-additive model, by defining the e_{ij} as the (Euclidian) distance between the voter and a candidate on an issue.

Second, *directional theories* of voting behavior claim that issue distances do not matter as much as the direction of a voter's and the candidates' positions on the issues: voters will vote for a candidate who tends to be on the same side of the issues as the voter (MacDonald, Listhaug, and Rabinowitz 1991; Rabinowitz and MacDonald 1989). To present this line of reasoning in terms of the weighted-additive model, we could simply define

$$e_{ij} = \text{(candidate location} - \text{neutral point)} \times \text{(voter location} - \text{neutral point)}$$

(*cf.* Rabinowitz and MacDonald 1989, 97). Finally, *retrospective* voting models define the components of candidate evaluation and vote choice not in terms of prospective policies that the candidates may pursue, but rather, in terms of retrospective evaluations of the candidates. This emphasis was already visible in *The American Voter* (Campbell et al. 1960), but is especially pronounced in the work of Key (1966) and Fiorina (1981). The literature on congressional elections, in particular that concerning the "midterm puzzle," also abounds with analyses of retrospective voting (see Abramowitz, Cover, and Norpoth 1986; Bloom and Price 1975; Born 1990; Kramer 1971; Mueller 1970; Tufte 1975). These analyses can be captured in the weighted-additive model by specifying the e_{ij} as retrospective judgments (for example, approval ratings) about candidates along several dimensions (for example, the economy, foreign policy, and crime).

Although the parallels between the aforementioned voting models and the weighted-additive decision rule are striking, it must be emphasized that they tend to become weaker at the level of empirical tests. For one, the empirical tests have typically taken the form of a regression analysis, and are, hence, more in keeping with the logic of alternative-based models than attribute-based models. Furthermore, there has been a tendency to aggregate the attributes of alternatives into linear composites that use equal weights. By doing this, the w_{ij} have lost much of their importance. Finally, it should also be noted that all of the aforementioned voting models have been narrowly concerned with political issues: they are *issue-voting models*. Hence, only a narrow subset of applications of the weighted-additive model has been studied.[15] However, because this subset has been so prevalent in political research, much of our concern in the present chapter will be with issue voting, even if the decision rules and our research methodology are more general in nature.

Our conceptualization of issue voting is prospective (we do not look at incumbent officials), and operationalizes the e_{ij} as the likability of issue positions that candidates take. (Note that this, in fact, simplifies the weighted-additive rule considerably, in terms of cognitive operations.) For example, given a domestic- and a foreign-policy issue, an issue-evaluation scale that ranges from −2 (strongly dislike) to +2 (strongly like), and an issue-importance scale that ranges from 0 (not at all important) to 2 (very important), a candidate is rated neutrally if the issue evaluations are −2 and 1, respectively, and the importance ratings are 1 and 2, respectively: $1 \times (-2) + 2 \times 1 = 0$ (see table 1).

Equal-Weighting Model

The weighted-additive model can be simplified by eliminating the w_{ij}, resulting in an equal-weighting model. This model is also capable of describing the aforementioned voting models, and also rests on a maximization principle, but it no longer allows the issues to be weighted by their importance. In this respect, the equal-weighting model is in line with much empirical research on voting behavior, which has often used unweighted additive scales to sum up candidate attributes. From the perspective of bounded rationality, the equal-weighting model seems more plausible than the weighted-additive model, because the consideration of importance ratings complicates the decision calculus considerably (cf. Carroll and Johnson 1990). Perhaps because of this complexity, empirical comparisons of the weighted-additive and equal-weighting models have often failed to demonstrate any superior performance of the former, despite its use of more decision-relevant information (see Dawes 1979).[16]

Table 1 presents an application of the equal-weighting decision calculus, using the same issue evaluations as in the illustration of the weighted-additive model but ignoring the importance ratings. As the choice outcome in the hypothetical example shows, neglecting issue importance can result in different election outcomes, although this is not necessarily the case (Dawes 1979).

Kelley-Mirer Voting Model

We also obtain a special case of the weighted-additive model if the e_{ij} are rescaled to binary variables that take on the value +1 if an attribute is liked and −1 if the attribute is disliked. This model coincides with Fishbein's (1963; also Ajzen 1991) expectancy value theory of attitudes, if the w_{ij} are interpreted as belief strengths. If the w_{ij} are left out of consideration, as in the equal-weighting model, then a decision rule is obtained equivalent to Kelley and Mirer's (1974) theory of "the simple act of voting."[17] According to the Kelley-Mirer model, voters count their likes and dislikes for each candidate, compare the liking and disliking counts, and then vote for the candidate with the largest number of *net* likes.[18] In terms of our notation, the likes and dislikes are given by the binary e_{ij} (or binary transformations of nonbinary attribute values), whereas the net liking scores are given by the Y_i. Since Kelley and Mirer assume that voters choose the candidate with the highest net liking, a maximization principle is again involved (see table 1 for an example). It should be noted that, in the original model, party identification (PID) was considered only as a tiebreaker, when two candidates had the same net liking scores. Reformulations of the Kelley-Mirer model, however, make the more realistic assumption that PID is another candidate attribute that enters the calculation of Y_i (Garand and Ruiz 1987). We use the reformulated specification of the Kelley-Mirer (1974) model in this chapter.

Prospect Theory

All of the voting models and decision rules that we have considered up to this point can be reduced to a simple linear model (equation 1). One of the main characteristics of linear models is that the weight of attribute values does not depend on the direction of these values. That is, ceteris paribus,

TABLE 1. Examples of Decision Calculi

	Parameter Values		
		Evaluations of Candidates	
Issue	Importance	A	B
Domestic	1	−2	1
Foreign	2	1	−1
	Decision Calculi		
Rule	Y for A	Y for B	Choice
Weighted-additive	$1 \times (-2) + 2 \times (1) = 0$	$1 \times (1) + 2 \times (-1) = -1$	A
Equal-weighting	$-2 + 1 = -1$	$1 + (-1) = 0$	B
Kelley and Mirer[a]	$-1 + 1 = 0$	$1 + (-1) = 0$	—
Prospect theory[b]	$0.269 \times (-4.14) +$	$0.269 \times 1 +$	
	$0.465 \times 1 = -0.84$	$0.465 \times (-2.25) = -0.78$	B
Minimax regret[c]	-2	1	B
Lexicographic[d]	1	-1	A
Recency:			
Domestic then foreign	$0.5 \times (-2 + 1) = -0.5$	$0.5 \times (1 + (-1)) = 0$	B
Foreign then domestic	$0.5 \times (1 + (-2)) = -0.5$	$0.5 \times (-1 + 1) = 0$	B
Primacy:			
Domestic then foreign	$-2 + 0.5 \times (1 + (-2)) = -2.5$	$1 + 0.5 \times (-1 + 1) = 1$	B
Foreign then Domestic	$1 + 0.5 \times (-2 + 1) = 0.5$	$-1 + 0.5 \times (1 + (-1)) = -1$	A

[a]Attribute values have been rescaled to −1 and 1.
[b]Value function and weight function estimates.
[c]Most negative issue is domestic.
[d]Most important issue is foreign.

likes and dislikes of attributes of equal intensity receive equal weight in judgment and choice. Over the past three decades, however, heavy criticisms of this symmetric property of linear models have been offered. An impressive body of evidence in decision research suggests that the intensity with which people experience losses is greater than the intensity with which they experience gains, so that losses weigh more heavily in decision making than gains, despite ostensive equalities in expected utility levels (Fischoff 1983; Kahneman and Tversky 1979; Kanouse and Hanson 1986; Lopes 1987; Puto 1987; Thaler 1985; Tversky and Kahneman 1986). Furthermore, these findings comport with the literature on *negativity* biases in information integration (Fiske 1980; Hodges 1974; Jordan 1969; Kanouse and Hanson 1986; Lau 1985; Oden and Anderson 1971; Skowronski and Carlson 1987, 1989; Warr 1974), which in the context of voting behavior have received the label *negative voting* (Kernell 1977; for a recent discussion see Lau 1991).[19]

Kahneman and Tversky (1979; Tversky and Kahneman 1990) have proposed a particularly powerful framework for dealing with the asymmetric impact of gains and losses: prospect theory. The key premises of this framework are (1) that final outcomes matter less than how the outcomes compare with the judgmental standard that the decision maker uses, and (2) that the asymmetry in costs and benefits lies in the values people attach to each. Though derived from experimental work in nonelectoral decision making, these assumptions are quite consistent with two of the three explanations of negativity effects that electoral research has so far offered.[20]

Prospect theory provides a two-part model of decision making. The first part, the so-called editing phase, concerns the organization and reformulation of decision options and inputs so that they are amenable to judgment and choice (Kahneman and Tversky 1979; Tversky and Kahneman 1990). Although these operations are of great importance to decision making, we will not consider them in this chapter because the methodology that we employ is rather ill-suited for analyzing the consequences of editing. What we will consider, however, and what our methodology is extremely well suited for, is the second part of prospect theory, the evaluative stage. Here the information on the alternatives is integrated and a choice is made.

On the face of it, the evaluative stage of prospect theory looks very similar to the weighted-additive model. In our notation:

$$Y_i = \sum_{j=1}^{m} \pi_{ij} v(e_{ij}), \qquad (2)$$

where the attributes are rank-ordered in accordance with their value. The major difference from the weighted-additive model is that both π_{ij} and $v(e_{ij})$ are nonlinear functions. The value function, $v(e_{ij})$, maps the attribute values in a way that captures the asymmetry of losses and gains, or negative and positive attribute information. Specifically, $v(e_{ij})$ is such that losses relative to some reference point are weighted more heavily than gains, and losses and gains close to the reference point receive more weight than losses and gains further removed (Kahneman and Tversky 1979; Tversky and Kahneman 1990). A form suggested and empirically estimated by Tversky and Kahneman (1990) for the value function is

$$v(e_{ij}^{*}) = \begin{cases} (e_{ij}^{*})^{\alpha} & , \quad e_{ij}^{*} \geq 0 \\ -\lambda \, (-(e_{ij}^{*}))^{\beta} & , \quad e_{ij}^{*} < 0 \end{cases} \tag{3}$$

where the median empirical parameter estimates are: $\hat{\alpha} = \hat{\beta} = .88$; $\hat{\lambda} = 2.25$. The e_{ij}^{*} in equation 3 are rescaled attribute values: $e_{ij}^{*} = e_{ij} - r$, where r is the reference point. By rescaling the attribute values, we can distinguish losses and gains, the former being attribute values lower than the value of the reference point (resulting in negative e_{ij}^{*}) and the latter being attribute values at least as good as the reference point (resulting in nonnegative e_{ij}^{*}). Usually, the reference point is the status quo (Hogarth 1987; Quattrone and Tversky 1988), but other reference points are possible. In our analyses, the neutral point of an attribute-evaluation scale is the reference point, a choice in keeping with some empirical work on negativity (Jordan 1969).

The π_{ij} in equation 2 are decision weights that are a function of the risk levels associated with each of the attributes. The function is convex, in order to capture the empirical result that low probability attributes (outcomes) tend to be overweighted, while high probability attributes tend to be underweighted (Kahneman and Tversky 1979; Tversky and Kahneman 1990). Although the emphasis in this chapter is not on risk levels, but, rather, on attribute importance, there is reason to consider the decision-weight function. One reason, specific to our sample, is that many of our subjects gave low importance ratings to candidate attributes that are generally considered important, such as party affiliation and race. Since these attributes probably play a bigger role in the decision calculus than our importance ratings suggest, a correction through a decision-weight function may be appropriate. There is also a more theoretical reason to consider decision weights. Recent work on attribute importance has demonstrated that importance ratings sometimes behave similarly to probabilities, at least if they are rescaled so that the axioms of probability theory apply. For instance, Kahn and Meyer (1991) find that uncertainty about attribute importance closely resembles the phenomenon of risk ambiguity (see Einhorn and Hogarth 1985). This being the case, one may expect the importance ratings to be subject to the same under- and overweighting biases as risk measures, although caution is warranted because of the lack of empirical data on this matter.

To implement the decision-weight function, the importance ratings need to be rescaled so that they behave like probabilities. That is, the ratings must be nonnegative and must sum to 1. The transformed importance ratings, w_{ij}^*, should then be mapped into decision weights through an appropriate functional form. At present, functional forms have been offered by Tversky and Kahneman (1990) and Frank and Taber (1991). Because of a number of problems with the Tversky-Kahneman (1990) function (see Taber, Lin, and Frank 1990), we will use the alternative functional form by Frank and Taber (1991).[21]

Like the previous models, prospect theory assumes that the voter maximizes Y_i. For example, using the issues in table 1 we can calculate the value function for candidate A on the domestic issue as: $-2.25(2)^{(.88)} = -4.14$. The weight of the domestic issue is calculated as: $.116 + .318 \times (.33) + .423 \times (.33)^2 = .267$, rescaling the importance ratings so that they sum to 1. Similar calculations can be performed for the foreign policy issue and the other candidate, resulting in the decision outcome reported in table 1.

Minimax Regret Rule

Negativity effects do not only occur when negative information receives larger weight than positive information. They may also occur when a voter evaluates all candidates in an election negatively.[22] If, under these circumstances, the voter decides to choose the candidate that appears to be "the lesser of evils," one could speak of *negative voting* (Lau 1991).

The choice of the least disliked alternative substitutes a minimization principle for the maximization principle that dominates in the aforementioned decision rules. A typical minimization strategy can be found in the minimax regret decision rule, which states that decision makers pick the alternative that minimizes their maximum regret. This rule has long been recognized in normative models of decision making (see Von Neumann and Morgenstern 1944), but is not restricted to this theoretical framework. Normative versions of the minimax regret decision rule rely on the assumption that voters consider all attributes in a given choice situation. However, a strong minimax regret model can be formulated in terms of only the least liked issue. That is, if maximum regret is defined as the least liked policy intention that candidates may act upon, minimization should consist of choosing the candidate who has the least objectionable stance on that issue. If candidates score equally poorly, then the voter moves to the next-most disliked issue, to make a similar comparison.

For example, in table 1, the lowest e_{ij} is that for the domestic issue. On this issue candidate A is evaluated more negatively than B, so that the latter is chosen. Note that B's position is actually rated positively, so that no real negative-voting scenario is present. This indicates that the minimax regret rule is broader than just the case of negative voting, although that case is the clearest counterpart of the rule that is available in electoral research.

Lexicographic Rule

Rather than focusing on the worst issue in an election, voters may make the most important issue the basis of their vote choice. This results in what behavioral decision theorists have called the lexicographic decision rule (Hogarth 1987). The rule requires a rank-ordering of attributes (for instance, issues) by importance, followed by a comparative judgment of the alternatives (for instance, candidates) on the most important issue. The alternative with the highest attribute value for the most important issue is chosen, unless a tie occurs. In that case, the decision maker will move to the next-most important attribute, a process that continues until a single alternative stands out as the "best" choice (see table 1 for an example). Given the nature of this process, it is clearly driven by a maximization principle.

The lexicographic rule, as applied to electoral choice, corresponds with the idea of *single issue* voting—that is, the selection of a candidate on the basis of a single issue that is particularly important to the voter (see Krosnick 1989, 1990b). This may be a particularly good model of political behavior—although it is rather ill-documented—because survey evidence indicates that few citizens are opinionated and informed about all issues, but many hold opinions on at least a couple of issues (cf. Converse's [1964] notion of "issue publics").

Sequential Decision Rules

The decision rules that we have discussed up to this point do not explicitly consider the sequential nature of human information processing. For each of the rules, we could present the attribute information in any random order without affecting the outcome. In light of our earlier discussion of sequential information processing, this assumption is hard to sustain (Anderson 1974; Hogarth 1987; Nisbett and Ross 1980).

One can think of two sequence effects on judgment and choice. In one, the most recent pieces of information receive a disproportionate weight relative to earlier information. This resembles the neglect of base-rate information, a well-documented phenomenon in behavioral decision research (Nisbett and Ross 1980; Tversky and Kahneman 1974). On the other hand, recent information may also be underweighted relative to older information (Edwards 1968), resulting in primacy effects. Both primacy and recency effects have been observed in studies of candidate evaluation, although the effects appear to be contingent on individual-difference variables like political sophistication (McGraw, Lodge, and Stroh 1990).

Recency model. We consider the following recency model:

$$Y_{i,t} = \begin{cases} e_{i,t} & , \quad t = 1 \\ 0.5\,(e_{i,t} + Y_{i,t-1}) & , \quad t > 1 \end{cases} \tag{4}$$

That is, the evaluation of the ith alternative at time t ($t = 1, \ldots, p$) is equal to the arithmetic mean of the evaluation at time $t - 1$ and the value of the attribute information that is presented at time t. (For simplicity, we assume that only one piece of attribute information is received at any given point in time.) To see that this model discounts prior information about attributes as the decision maker progresses in time, consider the evaluation of a political candidate at the time that, for example, the third information item is presented ($t = 3$). By our model, $Y_{i,3} = 0.5(e_{i,3} + Y_{i,2})$. However, $Y_{i,2}$ itself, is a function of $Y_{i,1}$: $Y_{i,2} = 0.5(e_{i,2} + Y_{i,1})$. Substitution gives: $Y_{i,3} = 0.5e_{i,3} + 0.25e_{i,2} + 0.25Y_{i,1}$. Since $Y_{i,1}$ solely depends on $e_{i,1}$, the final result is: $Y_{i,3} = 0.5e_{i,3} + 0.25e_{i,2} + 0.25e_{i,1}$. Thus, information that is presented at time $t = 3$ is weighted twice as much as information that was presented earlier (for another illustration, see table 1). It can be easily demonstrated that the weight of an information item over time is given by the expansion of the following series: $\delta_0(.5)^q$, where q is the number of time units between the current evaluation period and the time when information about an attribute value was first introduced, and δ_0 is a parameter giving the initial weight of a piece of information—that is, the weight of information when it was first introduced.[23]

The recency model, as we present it, requires that voters make *on-line* judgments about candidates: they establish a running tally for each candidate, which is sequentially updated as new information is received (Hastie and Park 1986; Hastie and Pennington 1989; Lodge, McGraw, and Stroh 1989; McGraw, Lodge, and Stroh 1990). To make a vote choice, voters simply retrieve their tallies for the candidates and vote for the candidate with the highest overall evaluation. To these general features of the on-line model the recency model adds two more components. First, the importance of candidate information is not part of the decision calculus, an assumption in keeping with existing empirical tests of the on-line model (see Lodge, McGraw, and Stroh 1989; McGraw, Lodge, and Stroh 1990). Second, the effect of candidate-attribute information is assumed to be very short-lived: eventually, information about a candidate, whether positive or negative, will lose influence on the impression-formation process. It will do so automatically, without voters having to keep track of the number of information items that they receive, because the recency model is a simple averaging model (cf. Anderson 1974). Given the simplicity of the model, we believe that it is entirely in keeping with the notions of bounded and "low-information" (Popkin 1991) rationality.

Primacy model. Unlike recency models, primacy models give a disproportionate weight to information that was introduced early in the decision-making process. That is, early information serves as an anchor that is minimally adjusted by subsequent data (Edwards 1968; Tversky and Kahneman 1974). The idea of anchoring and adjustment underlies several models of belief updating (Anderson 1974; Hogarth and Einhorn 1992), and is another possible parameterization of on-line models of candidate evaluation (Lodge, McGraw, and Stroh 1989; McGraw, Lodge, and Stroh 1990).

In our analyses, we use our own version of anchoring and adjustment, which requires minimal assumptions about the information-processing capacity and motivation of decision makers. Mathematically, the model can be written as:

$$Y_{i,t} = \begin{cases} e_{i,t} & , \ t = 1 \\ Y_{i,t-1} + 0.5(e_{i,t} + Y_{i,t-1}) \ , & t > 1 \end{cases} \tag{5}$$

According to this equation, the evaluation of an alternative at a given point in time takes the previous evaluation as an anchor. This anchor is adjusted by newly presented information about the attributes of an alternative, but this information is processed against the background of a very strong reference point (cf. Hogarth and Einhorn 1992), that is, the previous evaluation. Thus, new information is averaged with the prior evaluation, and this average is then latched to the prior evaluation (see table 1 for an example).

One consequence of this specification is that there is no decay in the effect of information (there is, in fact, bolstering): positive or negative attribute information that is processed early in the decision-making process continues to exert a strong influence, and it may take many strong negatives (or positives) to neutralize the initial impression. Consider, for instance, the determinants of candidate evaluation at the time of presentation of the second piece of information about a candidate. By our model, $Y_{i,2} = 1.5Y_{i,1} + 0.5e_{i,2}$. Since $Y_{i,1} = e_{i,1}$, this implies that $Y_{i,2} = 1.5e_{i,1} + 0.5e_{i,1}$. In other words, by the time a voter receives the second piece of information, it receives three times less weight than the information immediately preceding it. In general, the weight of a decision input $e_{i,t}$ over time is found through the expansion of the following series: $(\delta_o^{1-q}(1.5\delta_o)^q = \delta_o(1.5)^q$, where δ_o and q have the same meaning as in the recency model. Note that the weight of information goes to positive infinity as q goes to infinity, clearly demonstrating the bolstering effect for information.

As a final note concerning the primacy model, it should be realized that our model, again, is based on a maximization principle and does not require decision makers to keep track of the amount of candidate information that they process. In this respect, our model is much less effortful than Anderson's (1974) averaging model and similar in difficulty to the models developed by Hogarth and Einhorn (1992). This makes it reasonable to assume that voters may actually use the primacy model in real-world candidate evaluation processes.

Party Identification

The final decision rule we consider is party identification. According to this rule, Democrats will vote for a Democratic candidate, while Republicans will vote for the Republican candidate. Barring bandwagon effects, independents are assumed to have a 0.5 probability of voting for the Republican candidate and an equal probability of voting for a Democrat. Our party identification rule is a very crude implementation of the Michigan model of voting behavior (Campbell et al. 1960; Campbell, Gurin, and Miller 1954; Markus and Converse 1979), which specifies many more indirect pathways between PID and the vote choice. In fact, our party-identification rule describes the case where voters have absolutely no knowledge about either the issues or the candidates, the only case in which the Michigan school allows PID to have a direct effect on the vote (see Campbell et al. 1960). Since so little information is required to employ the party-identification rule, it serves as a useful standard of comparison.

A Comparison of the Rules

Throughout the preceding discussion, we have alluded to several dimensions along which the decision rules can be distinguished. A more rigid comparison, however, may serve our understanding of the rules and the subsequent analyses. The behavioral-decision literature offers several standards for such comparisons: (1) the general choice principle that is involved; (2) the comparison mechanism of alternatives; (3) the possibility or impossibility of trade-offs between decision inputs; (4) the informational requirements of the rules; (5) the information-integration properties of the rules; and (6) the cognitive effort required by each rule.

Two general choice principles can be distinguished: maximization and minimization. The first principle dictates that decision makers choose the alternative that produces the maximum gains, however those are measured. The essence of the minimization principle, on the other hand, is to minimize the losses that may accrue from a decision (cf. Bell 1982). These principles are likely to be used under different circumstances. The maximization principle is reasonable whenever at least a subset of the alternatives is palatable to the voter. However, if it appears that none of the alternatives is attractive, a minimization strategy is more likely. The only rule that we consider that invokes a minimization principle is the minimax regret rule.

A second question concerns whether decision makers compare the alternatives for each attribute separately, or only in the end, after overall evaluations of the candidates have been obtained. Herstein (1985) makes a strong argument that within-attribute comparisons are psychologically more compelling than overall comparisons, though few of the existing voting models take this into consideration. In fact, only two of the decision rules that we discussed are based on within-attribute comparisons: the lexicographic rule and minimax regret. (For PID, the distinction between within-attribute comparisons and overall comparisons is trivial, since only one attribute is considered.) There is also some doubt as to whether Herstein's argument is factually correct. For instance, Rahn (1991) presents evidence that a presentation of candidate issue stands by issue (i.e., within attributes) creates considerable problems for voters, particularly if they are politically unsophisticated.

Trade-offs among decision inputs occur if negative attribute values can be compensated for (in principle) by positive values or vice versa (Fischer and Johnson 1986; Hogarth 1987). Not all decision rules allow for such compensation, so that it is useful to distinguish between compensatory and noncompensatory rules. Hogarth (1987) calls compensatory rules conflict-confronting, as the tension between positive and negative decision inputs is not shunted, but, instead, explicitly dealt with. On the other hand, noncompensatory rules tend to avoid conflicts (Hogarth 1987), often by preventing positive or negative information from entering the decision calculus. This can be done, for instance, by just considering one attribute in the entire decision-making process, as is usually the case with the lexicographic and minimax regret rules. In our study, these are the only two instances of noncompensatory decision rules besides the party identification rule.

The distinction between compensatory and noncompensatory rules partially gets at the amount of information that is taken into consideration in the decision-making process. But a more detailed picture may be obtained by explicitly looking at the informational requirements of the decision rules. Some rules postulate a fixed number of decision inputs, whereas others postulate variable inputs (Fischer and Johnson 1986; Hogarth 1987). Decision rules with a fixed input tend to be more information-intensive, as they usually require all of the available data on the attributes of an alternative to be considered. This is not the case with variable inputs, like minimax regret and the lexicographic rule. However, within the group of fixed input rules, there is some variation in the detail with which the information is processed.

For some rules, like the weighted-additive model, detailed information about the attributes is required (continuous measures of issue evaluation, for instance, may be needed). Other rules, like the Kelley-Mirer voting model, require only crude attribute evaluations in the form of binary judgments.

Once the decision inputs enter the decision calculus, the rules differ in the ways they combine the information. Most rules that we consider employ a linear operator to produce decision outputs. In a few cases, however, nonlinear operators are at work. This is most evident in prospect theory, where both attribute values and importance ratings are transformed through nonlinear functions. However, nonlinear processes also operate in the sequential decision models. Although our specification of these models is linear in time, tracking them over the duration of a decision process reveals that the weights of the decision inputs change through a power, rather than a linear, function.

Finally, these decision rules vary in the amount of effort they require of decision makers. We can estimate cognitive effort by decomposing the decision rules into elementary information processes (EIPs). Any serially represented decision process can, in principle, be broken down into a sequence of more primitive operations (Johnson and Payne 1985; Payne, Bettman, and Johnson 1988, 1990). Processes involving large numbers of EIPs are assumed, with some empirical support (Bettman, Johnson, and Payne 1990), to be relatively effortful. Consider the flowchart for the weighted-additive rule in figure 1. Seven subprocesses are distinguished, including READ, EVALUATE, RETRIEVE, and WEIGHT. Since processing must advance through each of these EIPs for every dimension and for every candidate, a rough measure of the computational effort involved in applying the weighted additive rule to evaluating a single candidate would be $7x$, where x denotes the number of dimensions over which the candidate is evaluated.[24] Table 2 gives crude estimates of the cognitive effort required for each decision rule, based on a count of EIPs.

A Computational Experiment in Electoral Behavior

Method

To show the logic of computational experiments and to assess the performance of the aforementioned behavioral decision rules, we designed a study in three parts: two experimental phases followed by a computational phase. The general research design is straightforward. The first experimental stage elicits from real-life subjects in a controlled setting a variety of possible inputs into the electoral decision. The second empirical phase draws electoral-decision outputs from the same subjects, as in a panel study. The

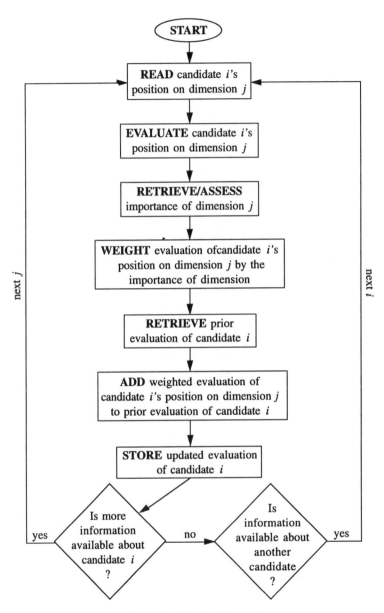

Fig. 1. Weighted-additive rule

computational phase explores a number of decision processes that may have converted the observed inputs into the observed outputs.

Subjects

One hundred and forty-five Stony Brook undergraduates took part in both experimental phases of the study, for which they received extra credit in an introductory international relations course. Missing data eliminated 40 of these, leaving 105 valid cases.

Experimental Phase 1

A survey was designed to extract three broad categories of information that may serve as inputs to a voter's decision in a congressional election: first, *information about the subject,* including demographics, party identification, ideological self-placement, knowledge about politics, political interest, and political participation; second, *information about general candidate characteristics,* including a candidate's demographics, party affiliation, ideological position, and political experience; and third, *information about issues.* For the second and third categories, subjects were asked to rate the *importance* of each piece of information in evaluating a potential candidate, and *the degree to which they liked or disliked* particular positions.

For example, the subjects rated, on a continuous scale, the importance of a candidate's age in deciding for which candidate to vote.[25] In a later section of the survey, the subjects rated, on a continuous scale, how much they would like or dislike a candidate who was sixty-six years old. (They also rated a thirty-six year-old candidate in a later part of the survey.)

TABLE 2.   Cognitive Effort in the Decision Rules

Rule	EIP Formula
Prospect theory (PT)	$7x$
Weighted-additive (WA)	$7x$
Primacy (PRM)	$6x$
Lexicographic (LEX)	$5x + 3$
Equal weight (EW)	$5x$
Minimax regret (MR)	$5x$
Recency (REC)	$5x$
Kelley-Mirer (KM)	$4x + 2$
Party ID (PID)	3

Note: The variable x denotes the number of considerations available for each candidate. The effort involved for LEX and MR is probably overestimated, because the process of discovering the most important or least liked consideration is included here; very likely, decision makers establish these at an earlier decision point.

Similarly, they were asked how important a candidate's position on abortion would be, and later were asked how much they would like a candidate who "is a pro-choice advocate" (they were later asked how much they would like a candidate who "is a pro-life advocate").

This survey produced importance ratings for 9 general candidate characteristics, 29 domestic issues, and 7 foreign policy issues. For each of these 45 information dimensions, liking scores were obtained for two contrasting positions.[26] The 45 information dimensions were selected on the basis of earlier studies and pretests, to provide a wide range of possible inputs into the electoral decision.

Experimental Phase 2

One week after phase 1, the same subjects completed a second survey. Under cover of a fictitious congressional race from upstate New York, the subjects were given two candidate profiles, one for Republican John Williams and one for Democrat Robert Johnson. After seeing a "fact sheet" on the first candidate, the subjects gave their "overall impression" of the candidate on a continuous scale. They then read a fact sheet about the second candidate and evaluated him. These profiles, purportedly compiled by a citizen's interest group, identified the candidate by name and party and listed the candidate's positions on a subset of the issues presented in phase 1.

The survey next asked for whom they would vote, if eligible (on a continuous scale) and how confident they felt about their decision. After intervening material about renting an apartment, they were asked to evaluate the candidates on a series of traits (for example, hard working, fair, power hungry).[27] Following the trait evaluations, they were asked again to evaluate each candidate, to choose between the two candidates, and to state a level of confidence in their choice. Finally, they were asked to recall information about the candidates.

We manipulated two factors: the amount of information presented in the fact sheets and the form of the recall task. Half of the subjects (by random assignment) read about stands on 9 issues, plus the candidate's party. Half read about 27 issue positions, plus party. Some subjects performed a free-recall task, while others received a cued-recall task. However, since we do not analyze recall data in this paper, we can ignore the manipulation.

By counterbalancing the order of presentation of the two candidates, we controlled for order effects. In addition, we constructed "mirror candidates" to facilitate comparisons. John Williams and Robert Johnson take opposite positions on the same 9 or 27 issues. Two-thirds of the issue positions for each candidate were consistent with the party's position on the issue, while one-third were inconsistent (where consistency was determined by a pretest). The first 9 issue positions of each candidate in the 27-issue condition were the same as the positions of the candidates in the 9-issue condition.

Computational Phase

We are interested in the processes by which the decisions in phase 2 were made. In particular, we want to explore the ability of behavioral decision models to predict the choices and evaluations of our subjects. We have a set of decision inputs—the importance and liking ratings for the ten or twenty-eight pieces of candidate information that we can draw from the much larger set collected in the first experimental stage. We have a set of decision outputs, collected in the second experimental stage. We now wish to explore various ways of attending to, ignoring, and combining these inputs that might account for the observed outputs.

Earlier, we described 9 decision rules (which may also be interpreted as information-integration rules) drawn from the behavioral decision literature. In the computational phase of the study, we constructed a computer program—the Candidate Evaluator (CANDI)—that instantiates each of these rules.[28] CANDI takes all of the information collected at stage 1 as input, processes the relevant pieces of that information according to each of the decision rules, and produces an evaluation of each candidate for each rule. CANDI thus makes 9 predictions of each subject's candidate evaluations for Williams and Johnson, which are based on the information collected from each subject in experimental phase 1, as processed according to the decision models.

Results

Our general research question may be rather crudely stated: do the predictions of the behavioral decision rules "match" the subjects' actual candidate evaluations and choices, collected in experimental phase 2? In addition, do certain rules perform better than others, in general or contingent on the decision task or on characteristics of the decision maker? Specific hypotheses will be presented as we turn to the different contingencies.

General performance of the rules. In terms of choice, the rules perform rather well. Table 3 gives the relative improvement over chance (RIOC) scores for each rule, and their significance levels.[29] According to the RIOC scores, the party identification rule gives rise to the greatest relative improvement over chance, namely 54 percent over all subjects. But all of the rules produce significantly accurate predictions. We do find that the full-information linear compensatory rules (WA, EW, and KM) perform better than other rules: M = 44.14, versus M = 39.02 for the full-information nonlinear compensatory rules (PT, REC, and PRM), and M = 37.47 for the remaining rules (MR, LEX, and PID). Despite these differences, the similarities among the rules are striking. Although none of the rules come close to reaching the upper bound of RIOC (100 percent), all of the rules significantly improve over chance prediction. That is, none of the rules perform particularly poorly.

The same pattern emerges when we analyze candidate evaluation. Table 4 gives the zero-order correlations of the evaluations produced by the decision rules with the evaluations of Johnson (D) and Williams (R), respectively. These correlations are indicative of weak to moderate relationships, with few of the decision rules having insignificant correlations. Contrast analyses were used to test the equivalence of different configurations of the decision rules (see Meng, Rosenthal, and Rubin 1992). These tests reveal that the compensatory rules (WA, EW, KM, PT, REC, and PRM) perform much better than the noncompensatory rules (MR, LEX, and PID) (z = 6.127, p = .000 for Williams; z = 4.694, p = .000 for Johnson) and that weighted decision rules (WA and PT) perform better than unweighted rules (z = 3.866, p = .000 for Williams; z = 3.286, p = .000 for Johnson). There is no significant difference between linear (WA, EW, KM, MR, LEX, and PID) and nonlinear (PT, REC, and PRM) decision rules (z = −1.173, *ns,* for Williams; z = 1.060, *ns,* for Johnson) and rules that are based on maximization, versus the rule based on minimization (MR) (z = .314, *ns,* for Williams; z = 1.408, *ns,* for Johnson).

In the final analysis, then, the decision rules that we discussed all

TABLE 3. Relative Improvement Over Chance (RIOC)

Decision Rule	All N = 105	Non-Soph. N = 52	Soph. N = 53	Low Info. N = 56	High Info. N = 49
Weighted-additive	45.95*	27.78	64.01*	53.18*	41.67*
Equal-weighting	45.95*	25.45	65.13*	53.18*	41.67*
Kelley-Mirer	44.17*	27.78	61.53*	53.18*	30.00*
Prospect theory	48.40*	32.03*	65.13*	58.02*	41.67*
Minimax regret	32.66*	27.78	35.63	41.23*	18.33
Lexicographic	25.78*	6.81	42.57*	21.46	25.76
Recency	39.62*	37.20	41.89*	35.93	37.50
Primacy	29.05*	20.31	37.01*	36.48	18.33
PID	53.98*	45.83	60.15	42.71	65.00*

Note: Test statistics were calculated on the basis of large sample properties in the first column and on the basis of small sample properties for the remaining columns.

* $p < .05$.

seemed to produce reasonable predictions of judgment and choice. In general, linear compensatory rules that use all presented information performed better than other rules, as far as choice is concerned. In terms of candidate evaluation, the distinction between linear and nonlinear rules seems less important, but compensatory rules clearly outperform noncompensatory rules. It should be noted, however, that these are general patterns in the behavior of the decision rules. Since these patterns may change, once task conditions and individual differences are considered, we will now turn to a discussion of these contingencies.

Task conditions and performance. Because of cognitive or motivational limitations in decision making, we expect that the more information-intensive and effortful choice rules will perform worse when many decision inputs must be processed (cf. Johnson and Payne 1985; Payne, Bettman and Johnson 1988, 1990). In the cognitive limitations explanation, subjects try, but fail, in using complex rules, while the motivational explanation suggests that subjects forgo the complex rules and use simpler heuristic rules in the high-information condition.

TABLE 4. Correlations with Candidate Evaluation

Decision Rule	All $N = 105$	Non-Soph. $N = 52$	Soph. $N = 53$	Low Info. $N = 56$	High Info. $N = 49$
Candidate Johnson					
Weighted-additive	.538**	.374**	.654**	.587**	.461**
Equal-weighting	.560**	.405**	.673**	.612**	.481**
Kelley-Mirer	.487**	.357**	.643**	.533**	.412**
Prospect theory	.522**	.439**	.571**	.607**	.466**
Minimax regret	.178	.122	.221	.244	.126
Lexicographic	.173	.047	.279*	.281*	.018
Recency	.162	.139	.182	.265*	.067
Primacy	.334**	.209	.429**	.496**	.122
PID	.350**	.192	.463**	.337*	.362*
Candidate Williams					
Weighted-additive	.560**	.391**	.692**	.698**	.370**
Equal-weighting	.549**	.399**	.681**	.688**	.352*
Kelley-Mirer	.332**	.091	.595**	.498**	.092
Prospect theory	.494**	.372**	.604**	.639**	.277
Minimax regret	.281**	.207	.358**	.393**	.012
Lexicographic	.448**	.383**	.515**	.505**	.363*
Recency	.192*	.083	.261	.337*	.035
Primacy	.396**	.258	.494**	.588**	.160
PID	−.401**	−.315*	−.464**	−.431**	−.370**

* $p < .05$.
** $p < .01$.

As the last two columns in table 3 show, it does seem that information-intensive rules perform worse under the high information condition than under the low information condition. The weighted-additive model, the primacy model, and prospect theory all perform worse under the high-information-load condition. On the other hand, the party-identification rule, which is the simplest of all rules, appears to perform better when the number of decision inputs is large.

A better picture of the differences may be obtained if statistical tests on the RIOC score differences are performed. The difference between the low- and high-information RIOC scores never turns out to be significant, except in the case of PID ($z = -2.081$, $p < .05$). The lack of significance for the decision rules partly reflects the small sample sizes in the different information-load conditions. The insignificance, however, is also due to the fact that the differences in RIOC scores in the low- and high-information conditions tend to be rather small. Thus, while the differences are in the correct direction, we should be careful not to exaggerate them.[30]

The same conclusion holds for the correlations of the decision rules with candidate evaluation. Although the three most information-intensive rules tend to outperform the two least intensive rules, regardless of the amount of information that needs to be processed, the differences are much bigger in the low-information condition than they are in the high-information condition. For candidate Williams, the average correlation between the information-intensive rules (WA, PT, and PRM) is .642 in the low-information condition, and only .269 in the high-information condition. The corresponding figures for candidate Johnson are .563 (low information) and .350 (high information). On the other hand, the two least intensive rules (PID and KM) show a change in correlation from .034 to −.139 for Williams, and from .435 to .387 for Johnson, as one moves from the low- to the high-information condition. These differences are substantially less than the differences for the information-intensive rules, corroborating our hypothesis that information-intensive rules may be particularly sensitive to changes in task demands.

In sum, there is modest evidence that information load has an impact on the performance of decision rules, with complex (i.e., information-intensive) rules being affected more than simpler rules. The effects, however, are not very strong. It may well be that this is due to the fact that even our high-information condition did not provide much of a problem to the subjects. There are two reasons to believe this. First, since the candidate's party identification was given, subjects may have extensively relied on PID to evaluate the candidates, an effect that was probably most pronounced as the information load grew. Party identification, however, also figures strongly in most of the decision rules, so that these rules should be able to recover candidate evaluation, even if the information load is high. The corollary of this explanation is that an increase in decision inputs from ten to twenty-eight, as in our study, may be much harder on decision makers if there is no heuristic like PID. A second reason to expect less pronounced differences due to information load is that the two candidates were mirror images. This may have reduced the true increase in information load. Rather than having to process 2×18 additional decision inputs in the high-information load conditions, there was, in fact, only an increase of 18 inputs, because the additional inputs for one candidate could be inferred from the other.

The role of political sophistication. We expect complex rules to be less effortful for sophisticates than for nonsophisticates (Fiske and Kinder 1981; Fiske, Lau, and Smith 1990; McGraw and Pinney 1990). On the other hand, political sophisticates may develop efficient strategies for information processing; they may be particularly good with less complex decision rules that do not use all of the information that is available (Fiske and Kinder 1981; McGraw and Pinney 1990). Thus, our hypothesis concerning sophistication is that across the board political sophisticates should perform better in the prediction of judgment and choice than nonsophisticates. This expectation is particularly plausible for the more complex and effortful choice rules, such as the weighted-additive rule and prospect theory.

Indeed, on all of the rules, the RIOC scores for the nonsophisticates fall short of those of the sophisticates. These differences are significant, in particular, for the most effortful rules: equal weighting ($z = -2.157, p < .01$); lexicographic ($z = -1.879, p < .10$); prospect theory ($z = -1.675, p < .10$); and weighted-additive model ($z = -1.944, p < .10$). No sophistication effects are found for the primacy model, despite its rather effortful nature. On the other hand, the relatively effortless Kelley-Mirer model shows a sophistication effect ($z = -1.862, p < .10$). This rule, however, is the only exception to the pattern that simple rules tend to work equally well for sophisticates and nonsophisticates.

For candidate evaluation, similar results are obtained. With very few exceptions, the correlations between the decision rules and candidate evaluation are higher for sophisticates than for nonsophisticates. Moreover, these differences are especially pronounced for the effortful rules. There are two major exceptions to this pattern. First, the sophistication effect for prospect theory is much more pronounced for candidate Williams than it is for candidate Johnson. Second, party identification performs very poorly for the nonsophisticates in the case of candidate Johnson, generating one of the biggest sophistication differences in the sample. Although the explanation of these results has to await further research, our suspicion is that it may be due to the distribution of party identification among sophisticates and nonsophisticates. In future work, we will follow up on this conjecture.

In sum, there are rather strong sophistication effects for the predictive performance of the decision rules. These effects indicate that sophisticates have a less troublesome time in piecing together the political world than nonsophisticates. Of course, this result is not surprising: much evidence has already been presented on this matter (see Fiske, Lau, and Smith 1990; Krosnick and Milburn 1990; McGraw and Pinney 1990). What is new is that we have demonstrated a sophistication effect at the level of information integration that shows that, in particular, with complex rules, sophisticates perform better. The term "better," however, should be taken relatively, for, despite all their differences, both sophisticates and nonsophisticates perform quite well in judgment and choice.

Effort and accuracy in choice. As we indicated earlier, none of the rules seem to perform particularly poorly in predicting judgment and choice. This simple fact should not be overlooked, for the quest to distinguish the rules may too easily exaggerate the differences. To emphasize this point, we looked at the correlations between candidate evaluation and the different decision rules, ranked by the amount of effort they take. Specifically, we compared the three most effortful rules (PT, WA, and PRM) with the two least effortful rules (PID and KM). A contrast analysis failed to show significant differences between these rules, except in one case. For sophisticates, the simpler rules perform better than the complex rules when it comes to predicting the evaluation of candidate Johnson ($z = -7.214$, $p = .000$). An explanation of this result is not readily available.

If supported by further work, these findings have important implications for democratic theory. There has been a tendency to expect that the democratic citizen invests quite some time in making political choices, even if some theorists doubted the rationality of such investments (see Downs 1957). Of course, this emphasis on the importance of the time and effort spent by citizens followed from the assumption that complex decision calculi would produce better choices. In this study, we have found evidence suggesting a somewhat different argument. Although effortful choice processes do, indeed, perform better overall, even the least effortful of rules seem to produce reasonable choices. If this surprising result survives further empirical testing, we may need to revise some of our normative thinking on democracy. The democratic citizen may not have to spend much time on electoral decision making. Citizens may be able to cast reasonable votes, despite their well-known lack of interest in politics.

Computational Experimentation: An Assessment

At a methodological level, we have suggested that computational experimentation can overcome several of the drawbacks of other methods. In particular, we argue, computational experimentation presents a viable alternative to experimental and survey approaches to electoral research, which usually do not permit a close tracking of the processes that underlie electoral choice.

Computational experimentation, however, is no panacea. Indeed, it has several important limitations. The most obvious and troublesome problem is that computational experimentation does not permit determinate statements about actual decision behavior. Because decision processes or algorithms are postulated, rather than inferred from process data, we lack the necessary information to make a positive statement about the actual decision rules that were employed to arrive at a given choice. Since we are concerned with process, this poses a problem. Though a given decision rule may perform well in predicting electoral choice, we cannot definitively attribute this to the fact that decision makers (at least in majority) actually used the rule. Another decision calculus may, in fact, have generated the choice data, but for some reason (perhaps mere coincidence) the postulated decision rule may also be capable of predicting those data (cf. Lau in this volume; Wahlke 1991).

It should be kept in mind, however, that this problem is rather general, extending to other methods as well. The verification of theories through data analysis poses great logical problems (see Popper 1968), and is hardly ever pursued in statistical science. Instead, empirical studies of almost any phenomenon are premised on the notion of the *modus tollens*. Rather than trying to verify a theory, one tries to disprove it: to the extent that one is successful in doing so, the theory is rejected; otherwise its validity is upheld until future tests and data may falsify it. The real problem with computational experimentation is that this logic is only of limited applicability. For instance, if a decision rule fits the behavioral choice data poorly, this could be interpreted as evidence that the rule was not used; hence, one could falsify the theory that the rule had produced the choice outcome, just as one would do in significance testing. However, it could also be the case that the decision makers did use the postulated decision rule, but were just not very successful at it. The lack of fit between a decision rule and decision data cannot discriminate between these possibilities. Additional information is required to disentangle the unsuccessful use of a decision rule and the lack of use of that rule.

Thus, computational experimentation does leave one in a somewhat awkward position, as far as empirical statements about decision behavior go: it is neither capable of verifying rules, nor of unequivocally falsifying them. But, in our view, this weakness is more than compensated for by the fact that computational experiments allow for *theoretically*-based counterfactual analysis. Not knowing the actual decision behavior of voters leaves open the possibility of postulating a wide array of decision rules, manipulating them, and tracing their predictive performance. We can trace the implications (i.e., predictions) of theoretical process rules through simulation under many conditions. Computational experimentation provides an experimental environment for generating conflicting predictions from decision rules. This possibility is generally not open to standard survey and experimental approaches.

It should also be emphasized that computational experimentation may be the only systematic way to study the decision rules that we have described. Many of these rules, like prospect theory, depend on rather intricate calculi, that involve many parameters. To infer those rules from process data may easily result in problems of empirical underidentification: the process data are simply not rich enough to shed light on the exact parameter values of the decision rules. How is one, for instance, to say what prospect theory's value function parameters are without having microscopically detailed information about decision making. Yet, knowing the parameter values may be the only way of distinguishing prospect theory from, for example, regret theories (Bell 1982). Computational experiments do not allow the estimation of parameter values, but they can look at the consequences of using different sets of parameter values. This information can shed light on the behavior of decision rules, which may then be used to interpret empirical decision data.

A second major criticism that could be made against computational experiments is their preoccupation with prediction. A critic might argue that this method does not allow tests of process validity, but rather—like most electoral research—relies on predictive accuracy to evaluate the rules. However, the status of prediction is very different in computational experiments. Rather than being a goal, as in many voting studies, prediction is used as a tool to ascertain process models. This tool is admittedly crude, but it is perhaps the best that is presently available.

Several other potential caveats of computational experimentation need to be addressed. Wahlke (1991) has recently called attention to the problem that a specification of decision calculi, as in this chapter, leaves too many questions unanswered. For instance, the assumption that voters incorporate their likes and dislikes for issues in their decision calculus leaves open the question of where issue preferences come from. The bottom line, according to Wahlke, is that the black-box character of voting models remains largely intact.

There are several responses to this argument. First, although we agree that a focus on decision calculi leaves out many aspects of the candidate-evaluation process, we believe that it at least partly unveils the processes underlying electoral choice. At a very minimum, the analysis of decision calculi sheds light on processes of information integration, which are not without consequence (Ottati and Wyer 1990), and which are difficult (or impossible) to trace, using information-search methods. Other aspects of political information processing, however, admittedly remain underspecified. But to some extent, this problem can be solved within the framework of computational experiments, and herein lies our second response.

So far, our approach has only dealt with the processing of information as it was presented and the assumption of fixed attitudes. However, we know that voters go beyond the information that they receive and engage in (schematic) inferencing (Conover and Feldman 1986; Lau 1986; Popkin 1991). We can incorporate these inferences in computational experiments by developing inference models and collecting inference data (see Stroh in this volume). Likewise, our treatment of attitudes as fixed mental constructs could and should be modified. We could, for example, use empirical measures of issue evaluation as the mean of a distribution of opinions (cf. Feldman in this volume) from which we could sample using Monte Carlo techniques. This would allow us to trace the impact of changes in decision inputs on the performance of the decision rules. Indeed, an emphasis on the sensitivity of rules to changes in inputs has been missing from decision research, though sensitivity analyses are an important part of most computational analyses in cognitive science (Taber 1992).

There are then several ways of addressing the limitations of computational experimentation. Although none of these poses a complete solution to the methodological problems that were raised, they can go a long way in alleviating those problems. Future research should make an attempt at doing this.

Computational Experimentation: A Research Agenda

Let us briefly outline the directions that future research on and with computational experimentation could take. For candidate evaluation and electoral behavior, we should obviously look at a larger number of decision contexts than we have done so far. First, in addition to the study of general elections, analyses of primary elections should be performed. This would not only eliminate party identification as a diagnostic decision input, it would also permit the study of decisions involving more than two candidates. Second, instead of being narrowly concerned with political issues, we should explore political inferencing processes. What processes underlie trait inferencing, for example? Also, instead of presenting mirror-image candidates, we should consider candidates that deviate from each other in less obvious ways. For instance, we could have the candidates address nonoverlapping sets of issues.

Methodologically, we see three developments in computational experiments. First, we will develop the logic of counterfactual experimentation more fully. Second, we will add Monte Carlo simulation as a component to computational experimentation. Finally, we will use computational experimentation as a stepping-stone to the development of computational models. Of course, these added complexities will not alter the basic nature of computational experimentation; we will still combine the simulation of theoretical models with empirically derived process data to explore human decision processes. But each addition will go a long way toward shoring up an important weakness of computational experimentation.

APPENDIX: THE CALCULATION OF RIOC

Given a dichotomous predictor variable X and a dichotomous criterion (outcome) variable Y, the following cross-tabulation can be obtained:

Pred	Outcome		
	1	0	
1	a	b	e
0	c	d	$n-e$
	f	$n-f$	n

In this table, a value of 1 on the predictor variable means that, according to his or her decision calculus, a voter should vote for candidate z. A value of 1 on the outcome variable means that a voter actually voted for candidate z. Cell 1, 1 is the cell that is of primary interest to us here, as it gives the number of voters who are predicted to vote for z and who actually do it. This is one of the cells with correct predictions; the other cell (0,0) follows automatically, from knowing the frequencies a, n, e, and f.

The problem in assessing the quality of prediction is that the number of people that can be a member of cell 1,1 is a function of the marginal frequencies e and f. As long as the ratios e/n and f/n are rather similar (i.e., if the marginal distributions of predictions and outcomes are comparable), no special problems occur. For instance, assume that out of 1,000 voters, 20 percent are predicted to vote for candidate z and 20 percent actually vote for the candidate. In this case, cell 1,1 can contain 200 cases maximally and cell 0,0 can contain 800 cases. Thus, the maximum on correct predictions equals 200 + 800, which exactly corresponds to the sample size. Consider now a somewhat different case: 40 percent are predicted to vote for z but z's vote share is only 20 percent. In this case, cell 1,1 can maximally contain 200 cases, whereas cell 0,0 can only contain 600 cases at maximum. Thus, the maximum number of cases that can be correctly predicted is 200 + 600 = 800, which is considerably less than the sample size.

To take this problem into consideration, as well as the problem that frequency a may not exceed what one would expect by chance, Copas and Loeber (1990) suggest the *relative improvement over chance* (RIOC) index, which is given by

$$\text{RIOC} = \frac{\text{Total Correct} - \text{Chance Correct}}{\text{Maximum Correct} - \text{Chance Correct}} \times 100\%$$

This generic formula is estimate by the following expression:

$$\text{RIOC} = \frac{na - ef}{n.\min(e,f) - ef} \times 100\%$$

The asymptomatic and small sample properties of this estimator are discussed in Copas and Loeber (1990).

NOTES

We are grateful to Milton Lodge, our collaborator. This research was supported by NSF Grants SES9106311 and SES9102901.

1. Electoral research has generally been concerned with *outcome validity*, not with *process validity*. In this work, we make a strong pitch for the importance of process, but this should not obscure the necessity for outcome validation. Explanation requires accurate prediction of decision outcomes, along with explication of the processes that led to those outcomes.

2. Although there is a tendency in the political and psychological literatures to use the notions of bounded rationality and cognitive miser interchangeably, it is useful to keep these terms distinct. Bounded rationality does not depend on a motivational explanation; it can be explained entirely in terms of the neurological structure of the mind. However, to speak of cognitive misers is to imply a motivational underpinning of subrational behavior: the cognitive miser actively shuns away from effortful information processing, because of a limited interest in the decision or judgmental task at hand (Markus and Zajonc 1985; Fiske and Ruscher 1989).

3. For partial exceptions see Fischer and Johnson (1986), Herstein (1981), Frank and Taber (1991), and Lau (in this volume).

4. For a similar, but noncomputational study, see Einhorn, Komorita, and Rosen (1972).

5. In this literature, however, there has not been much attention paid to the motivational reasons for nonoptimizing behavior (i.e., the cognitive miser).

6. Although the necessity of process data seems rather obvious, several problems immediately arise. First, in a process model, any given predictor may be connected to a given outcome in myriad ways. Cognitive psychology has produced many competing models of mental processes, each receiving empirical support and each capable of explaining observed outcomes (see Anderson 1990). We need detailed process data to sort out these competing theories. But this raises a second problem. Though our theories of mental processes are microscopic in detail, our best measures of these processes remain relatively crude, relying on observable behavior to indicate unobservable characteristics of the human mind (cf. Conover and Feldman 1991). This being the case, empirical-process measures often require elaborate theoretical assumptions, to make them acceptable indicators of any hypothesized mental process.

7. The closest approximation of simulation methods that exists is the work of Boynton and Lodge (e.g., Boynton in this volume). However, in this work, decision rules are of less importance than models of memory organization and spreading-activation. See also the early work of McPhee (McPhee and Smith 1962).

8. Many decision contexts involve trade-offs between the accuracy of choice mechanisms and the cognitive (or motivational) effort they require. And it is not at all obvious that these trade-offs must be decided in favor of accuracy. In fact, if Simon's (1955) notion of satisficing holds true, then decision makers may forgo accuracy in favor of reduced effort. In electoral research, an explicit consideration of effort is of rather recent date (see Lodge, McGraw, and Stroh 1989; Lodge and Stroh, 1993), and has not yet been clearly linked to accuracy considerations.

Recent studies in behavioral-decision science have examined the effort/accuracy trade-off using a cost-benefit approach (reviewed in Payne, Bettman, and Johnson 1992). This work claims that the nature of information processing is contingent on the costs and benefits involved in a particular decision task.

9. To jump ahead, we could, for example, vary some parameter controlling the degree of importance a piece of information must have before it is processed. Such a parameter might have rather profound effects on the behavior of several of the decision rules.

10. This assumption could be relaxed in Monte Carlo fashion to allow the importance of some dimensions to vary across candidates. For example, one might expect the importance of age to vary as a function of candidate age and health.

11. Technically, importance ratings are only one possible component of decision weights. They measure the relevance of an attribute if it is known that an alternative possesses the attribute. In other words, importance ratings are conditional measures. The question of whether an alternative does or does not possess an attribute is of a different nature: it involves a probabilistic statement, not unlike the notion of belief strengths in the attitude literature (Ajzen 1991; Fishbein 1963), that decision theorists often refer to as risk (see Kahn and Meyer 1991). Although risk levels contribute to decision weights, the distinction between the latter notion and importance ratings loses its merits under two conditions: (1) when all risk levels are unity; or (2) when risk levels are constant across attributes and alternatives. In the latter case, merely paying attention to importance ratings underestimates the amount

of uncertainty that is involved in the choice process, but it does so equally for all alternatives and attributes. Of course, it is unlikely that conditions 1 and 2 will normally be fulfilled, in the case of elections. For instance, in a race between an incumbent and a challenger, behavioral data for the former are available, but not for the latter. Consequently, risk levels for the incumbent may be lower than those for the challenger. As of yet, we have not incorporated risk in our analyses. However, in future work we will use Monte Carlo simulations to trace the impact of risk on the performance of various decision rules.

12. It should be noted that some rational choice theorists have moved away from mathematical formulations, replacing them with verbal schemes (Budge, Farlie, and Laver 1983). However, this seems to be a minority position among normative theorists.

13. For similar definitions, see Berelson 1952; Berelson, Lazarsfeld, and McPhee 1954; McKelvey and Ordeshook 1986.

14. One potential mismatch lies in the requirement of normative voting theories that politically substantive judgmental criteria are employed. The weighted additive model is agnostic about the nature of the attributes that enter the decision calculus, and may thus cast its nets too broadly for normative theories. However, to the extent that normative voting models define "rationality" in terms of means rather than ends (see Downs 1957) the mismatch can be solved. In that case, any criterion or attribute can enter the voting calculus, as long as it has an instrumental value to the goals that the voter pursues. For instance, a candidate's physical appearance, which at first glance seems to be highly irrelevant to democratic politics, may be a substantive attribute for the voter who values the election of an attractive president.

15. This does not mean, however, that all issue-voting models are equally well represented through the weighted-additive decision rule. In particular, dynamic models with an issue-voting component (Markus and Converse 1979; Page and Jones 1979) contain a time variable that is ill-suited to the static nature of the weighted-additive model. It should also be noted that several spatial theories have started to consider factors other than issues in their models, including partisanship and group identifications (see Enelow, Hinich, and Mendell 1986; McKelvey and Ordeshook 1986).

16. This, of course, by no means implies that importance per se is irrelevant. The work by Krosnick (1988a, 1988b, 1989, 1990b) provides sufficient evidence to believe that issue importance does matter. However, the mechanisms that are responsible for this relevance are related to the encoding and retrieval stages of information processing and not to the information-integration stage. Moreover, the encoding and retrieval effects of issue importance do not seem to require much effort.

17. The Kelley-Mirer (1974) model resembles another decision rule as well, namely, the majority of confirming-dimensions rule (Russo and Dosher 1983). However, the latter rule relies on comparative judgments of the alternatives on the attributes, whereas the Kelley-Mirer (1974) model assumes a separate evaluation of the alternatives on the attributes, with a comparative judgment only being made after all attributes have been considered.

18. Kelley and Mirer (1974) depict these steps as essentially memory-based

operations (Lodge, McGraw, and Stroh 1989), but at this stage of our research we have not yet taken this into account.

19. Already, in *The American Voter* (Campbell et al. 1960), it was observed that the incumbent party is punished for its mistakes, but rarely rewarded for its successes. Bloom and Price (1975) established a similar asymmetry in reward and punishment, later labeled *negative voting* by Kernell (1977) and negativity by Lau (1982, 1985, 1991). Evidence for *negativity* effects has continued to amass (see Born 1990; Cover 1986; Klein 1991; but see the critical assessment by Fiorina and Shepsle 1989), establishing a clear need to postulate electoral decision rules that can take the phenomenon into account.

20. In one of these theories, negativity is explained as a perceptual phenomenon: because people expect positive behaviors from politicians, negative candidate attributes stand out and are, hence, more informative (Lau 1985). Another theory explains negativity in motivational terms, as cost-avoidance: people are assumed to be more motivated to avoid costs than to seek out gains (Lau 1985). These explanations both look at negativity in terms of attribute values based on a comparison to some reference point. This is not true of a third explanation of negativity in electoral behavior, rooted in economic theory (Fiorina and Shepsle 1990).

21. The Frank-Taber (1991) decision-weight function can be approximated by a 3-parameter quadratic form that behaves as prospect theory describes (Taber, Lin, and Frank 1990):

$$\pi_{ij} = \pi(w_{ij}^*) = \sigma + \gamma_1 w_{ij}^* + \gamma_2 (w_{ij}^*)^2$$

The least squares parameter estimates that best fit the data reported by Tversky and Kahneman (1990) are: $\hat{\sigma} = .116$; $\hat{\gamma}_1 = .318$; $\gamma_2 = .423$ (Frank and Taber 1991; Taber, Lin, and Frank 1990).

22. A third form of negativity occurs if a decision maker uses negative attributes to eliminate certain alternatives. This is what Tversky (1972) has labeled elimination-by-aspects. We will not consider this choice principle in this chapter, since we concentrate on a 2-candidate election in which elimination-by-aspects is unlikely to occur. Moreoever, with only two alternatives, elimination-by-aspects and minimax regret may become very difficult to distinguish.

23. The weight is 1 for the first information item, since $Y_{i,1}$ solely depends on $e_{i,1}$. The weight is 0.5 for any subsequent piece of information, because subsequent values of $Y_{i,t}$ only weigh concurrent pieces of information by 0.5. Note that the item weight approaches 0 as q goes to infinity.

24. Unfortunately, several ambiguities arise when using EIP counts to measure cognitive effort. First, it seems extremely unlikely that each of these subprocesses is equally effortful. What reason do we have to expect an input operation like READ to consume the same amount of cognitive resources as EVALUATE? Furthermore, each of these EIPs could, itself, be logically subdivided. EVALUATE, for example, may require several smaller steps to perform. From a cognitive-science perspective, the unanswered question asks at what level processes are *compiled* in human information processing.

25. The importance ratings were explicitly related to the act of making a vote choice, thus providing a close match to decision-making processes.

26. In general, for each candidate attribute or issue two questions were asked, referring to different attribute values. It should be noted that the issues that were presented were exact mirror images in most cases. However, we were reluctant to assume that there is a symmetry in evaluations of such issues. That is, issue positions that are mirror images do not necessarily produce evaluations that are mirror images. This was the reason that separate evaluations were asked for the two sides of an issue.

27. We do not analyze the trait responses here.

28. CANDI was programmed in C on a Dell System 310 personal computer, using Microsoft C 5.1.

29. The RIOC score corrects for ceiling effects, as well as for floor effects, in analyzing chance levels of correct predictions in contingency tables. Certain configurations of marginal distributions produce ceilings on correct predictions, thereby biasing statistical tests that only correct for lower bounds on predictive performance (see Copas and Loeber 1990; Loeber and Dishion 1983; and the appendix to this chapter).

30. Of course, the differences are likely to be more pronounced for nonsophisticates. However, we have not pursued the analysis of an interaction effect between information load and sophistication, because we lack the statistical power to do so.

CHAPTER 8

Information Search during an Election Campaign: Introducing a Processing-Tracing Methodology for Political Scientists

Richard R. Lau

Anyone studying political behavior is—or ought to be—interested in the information people use to make political decisions. Whether we are concerned with how people acquire (or change) opinions on public policy issues, how they form impressions of candidates running for office, how they decide whether to participate in the political process, or so on, we are interested in basic (political) information processing. Indeed, *any* theory of public opinion or candidate evaluation could be called, at least implicitly, an information-processing theory (Lodge, Stroh, and Wahlke 1990).

Virtually all models of political behavior fail to look carefully at how people *acquire* the information they ultimately use in making decisions, however, and fail to seriously consider the *decision rules* or *choice strategies* by which people utilize the information they acquire to choose among alternative courses of action. Instead, various models of political behavior have focused almost exclusively on the *type* of information that influences political decisions—social background characteristics and the opinions of primary group members (Lazarsfeld, Berelson, and Gaudet 1944; Berelson, Lazarsfeld, and McPhee 1954), party identification (Campbell et al. 1960), "rational" calculations, like issue voting (Nie, Verba, and Petrocik 1976) or economic self-interest (Kinder and Kiewiet 1979; Lau and Sears 1981; Sears et al. 1980), candidate assessments (Kinder 1986; Miller, Wattenberg, and Malanchuk 1986), and so on.

While these questions are all quite important, by ignoring information-acquisition and choice strategies, political-behavior models often make information-processing assumptions that are psychologically unrealistic. Put simply, while a few studies of voting behavior pay nominal heed to the role of information in political behavior (e.g., Downs 1957), the way political information is actually gathered and transformed into some decision (e.g., whether, and if so, how, to vote) is a neglected aspect of the whole process.[1]

This has serious consequences for how we model political judgments. Even models that posit psychologically realistic choice strategies implicitly make assumptions about how information should be acquired to implement those choice strategies, and those information acquisition assumptions, in turn, may be unrealistic.

Political Science Models of the Vote Decision

As an example of the information-processing assumptions implicitly made by different theories in political behavior, consider one of the most popular models of the vote decision, Kelley and Mirer's (1974) "simple act of voting." According to Kelley and Mirer,

> the voter canvasses his likes and dislikes of the leading candidates and major parties involved in an election. Weighing each like and dislike equally, he votes for the candidate toward whom he has the greatest net number of favorable attitudes. (1974, 574)

Apparently, voters search through memory for all of the reasons they like and dislike a candidate and, treating each like and each dislike equally, form a simple summary evaluation of that candidate. Voters repeat this procedure for each candidate, and ultimately vote for the candidate with the most favorable evaluation.[2]

At first glance, this model does, indeed, appear to be quite simple: only one candidate is considered at a time, and the only "mental arithmetic" required is addition and subtraction. The ultimate decision rule is also simple: after going through this process for each candidate, vote for the one with the highest total. But if we grant the reasonable assumption that people will gather the information they need to make a decision (i.e., follow a decision rule) *and no more,* we can nevertheless make several inferences about information acquisition, even from models as simple as this one. Since the information comes from memory, and memory—at least "short-term" or "working" memory—is limited (e.g., see Anderson 1983; Hastie 1986; Simon 1979a), there is no reason for voters to go out of their way to learn much about any candidate, because they cannot "operate" on much information in working memory at any given time.[3] Since all likes and dislikes are treated equally, neither is there any reason to expect voters to go out of their way to find *specific* types of information about any candidate; one bit of information is as good as any other. Thus, according to Kelley and Mirer's model, information search should be limited and, with one possible exception, random or haphazard. This possible exception concerns the order in which information might be sought. To the extent that voters actively seek out information in a manner that will facilitate their subsequent retrieval of that information from memory—and again, Kelley and Mirer (like all political-science models) are silent on this point, but it would be a reasonable inference—they should prefer to receive information about the candidates one at a time. These inferences—let me call them predictions—of limited and fairly random information search, are certainly consistent with decades of survey research exploring political knowledge and/or ideological consistency in the mass public (Converse 1975; Kinder and Sears 1985).

As a second example, consider the apparently much more complicated "spatial" or "rational choice" models of candidate evaluation (e.g., Davis, Hinich, and Ordeshook 1970; Enelow and Hinich 1984; Riker and Ordeshook 1973; Shapiro 1969). According to these models, voters compare a candidate's "stands" on a set of issues or attributes to a vector of "ideal points." Squaring the distance between where the candidate is perceived to stand on these attributes and the voters' own ideal points, and weighing these squared distances by the importance of each attribute, voters compute a summary evaluation or "subjective expected loss" associated with each candidate. Voters prefer (vote for) the candidate with the smallest expected loss.

Now, the mental arithmetic is definitely more complicated here, although the "decision rule" is, in fact, quite similar to that assumed by Kelley and Mirer's model: form a summary evaluation of each candidate, and vote for the one with the most favorable (or least unfavorable) evaluation. Both models are clearly *memory-based, moment-of-decision* models, in which all relevant information must be brought from long-term memory into working memory for some decision to be reached. But what does this model suggest about information search? First, unlike the random or haphazard search assumed by Kelley and Mirer's model, spatial models predict a "guided" or "intentional" (or "rational?") search process, because voters should be motivated to search for the most important or heavily weighed attributes in their vector of ideal points. Although spatial models have no way of telling us which attributes are, in fact, most important to any individual voter, they clearly predict that voters should be motivated to search for the *same* (important) information about all candidates in the decision set, so that the "expected losses" associated with all candidates will be comparable. Second, we can infer that information search will be at least as limited—if not more limited—than is the case with Kelley and Mirer's model, because people are working with the same cognitive limits, but in this model every bit of information about a candidate that is considered must be accompanied by the voter's own "ideal point" on that attribute, when brought into working memory, thus "using up" some of the available space. Third, to the extent that information is actively sought in a manner that will facilitate its retrieval from memory, voters should try to learn all of the information they consider important about each candidate one-at-a-time. To introduce a term I will develop more thoroughly below, both Kelley and Mirer (1974) and spatial models therefore predict a preference for *intracandidate* search.

As a third example, consider what is probably the best-known model of the vote decision, that of *The American Voter* (Campbell et al. 1960), although the revision by Markus and Converse (1979) is more precise. In this revision, differential candidate evaluations are modeled as a function of a comparison of the candidates' personalities, a comparison of the losses associated with their issue stands, and a comparison of their parties. Party is given predominant theoretical status, because it affects the vote choice directly, and also works indirectly through perceived candidate personalities and candidate evaluations.

Like the two models already discussed, this model is memory-based, moment-of-decision. But there are two important differences in the information-acquisition patterns implicitly assumed by Markus and Converse that distinguish it from two models already discussed: (1) party affiliation should be considered very early in the search process; and (2) search should be *intraattribute,* rather than intracandidate. That is, all candidates' party affiliations are examined first, then all candidates' personalities (or issue stands, or whatever) are compared, and so on. So the information-acquisition assumptions built into Markus and Converse's model—assumptions not just about the *type* of information considered, but also about the *order* in which it is considered, distinguish it from the first two models of the vote decision.

My own model of the vote decision (Lau 1986, 1989a) is, for present purposes, a variation on the *American Voter's* model. Although based on very different theoretical perspectives, it too is memory-based, and it too predicts a preference for intra-attribute search. The major difference between my model and that of Markus and Converse (1979) is that my model does not predict a universal preference for party information. Instead, my model predicts that people actively seek out information that "fits" with their "chronically accessible political constructs," or their political *schemata* (see also Lau 1989b). Thus, an advantage my model has over spatial models is the ability to predict what general types of information voters consider important.

As yet another variant, Fiorina's *Retrospective Voting* model (1981) involves a combination of intracandidate search processes (in calculating the subjective expected loss associated with each candidate) and intra-attribute search (where the attributes are the broad categories of retrospective and prospective considerations). Fiorina's model also assumes a memory-based, moment-of-decision choice strategy, but Fiorina predicts that voters should have a preference for retrospective evaluations of past performance (compared to prospective policy promises), because of the much greater reliability of the former type of information.

Let us consider one final example that is, in many ways, dramatically different from our other examples. In contrast to various memory-based, moment-of-decision models, Lodge, McGraw, and Stroh (1989) propose that people keep a "running tally" summary evaluation of each candidate. As new information about a candidate is encountered, it is used "on-line" to update the running tally, but then the information itself can be (and often is) discarded. Although Lodge, McGraw, and Stroh have never extended this model to the vote decision, presumably people would utilize the same process for forming evaluations of all candidates, and then vote for the one with the highest evaluation.

The advantage of this "on-line" model is that it allows people to take much more information into account when making their decision. In essence, the Lodge, McGraw, and Stroh model is Kelley and Mirer, with an important twist. Like Kelley and Mirer, Lodge's model says nothing about any information being more important than any other type of information, so it cannot predict anything other than random or haphazard information searching. It can predict (or at least accept without contradiction) much more information seeking, however, because the running-tally device allows much more information to be taken into account in the decision process. To the extent that information search is at all guided, it should be intracandidate, to facilitate the updating of the running tally.

Figure 1 summarizes the differences between these six models. How could we choose between them, if our goal was to come up with the "best," or most accurate, model of the vote choice? The first criterion that comes to my mind—and, I suspect, the only criterion that would matter to many political scientists—is how well they predict the vote. Unfortunately (or fortunately, depending on how you look at it), in practice we cannot choose between models on predictive accuracy, because they all do an excellent job of predicting the vote—better than 90 percent correct vote predictions. But predictive accuracy does not necessarily mean *descriptive* accuracy. These models all get to the same place in the end, but by somewhat (and in several cases, *very*) different routes.

We need some other mechanism for choosing between these models, and the way that people actually acquire information and make decisions are two additional criteria that could be used. In the next section, I will briefly describe a field of research that has explicitly studied these two criteria.

Model	Content of Search	Depth of Search	Sequence of Search	Decision Strategy
"Simple Act of Voting" (Kelly & Mirer 1974)	Random, haphazard	Shallow (memory-based)	Intracandidate	Compensatory
Spatial Models (e.g., Enelow & Hinich 1984)	Nonrandom: More, and earlier, search for information voters consider important	Shallow (memory-based)	Intracandidate	Compensatory
Michigan Model (e.g., Markus & Converse 1979)	Party early	Shallow (memory-based)	Intra-attribute	Compensatory
Schematic Model (e.g., Lau 1986, 1989)	Nonrandom: Guided by political chronicities	Shallow (memory-based)	Intra-attribute	Compensatory
Retrospective Voting (Fiorina 1981)	Nonrandom: Preference for retrospective information	Shallow (memory-based)	Intra-attribute and Intracandidate	Compensatory
On-Line Model (Lodge, McGraw, & Stroh 1989)	Random, haphazard	Deeper (on-line)	Intracandidate	Compensatory

Fig. 1. Information search and decision strategy assumptions of political science models of the vote decision

Behavioral Decision Theory

Behavioral decision theory is the field that studies how decisions are actually made (see Dawes 1988 and Lau and Levy 1993 for recent reviews). It usually takes as a starting point the normative model of decision making, which argues that decision makers should gather all possible information about every conceivable alternative course of action, carefully consider the consequences associated with each alternative, evaluate those consequences, and choose among the alternatives according to some value-maximizing decision rule (e.g., von Neumann and Morgenstern 1944). With this normative model in the background, scores of studies in the diverse fields of decision making have recognized that most decisions are based on much less information and less "rational" decision rules than normative choice theories expect (e.g., Allison 1971; Ebbesen and Konecni 1975; Einhorn 1974).

Although decision makers tend to be selective, and hardly use all of the available information, the information-search process is not random (Jacoby et al. 1987). On the contrary, people select information about alternatives in but a few systematic ways (c.f. Hogarth 1981; Payne 1976, 1982; Payne and Braunstein 1978; Russo and Dosher 1983; Svenson 1979). The behavioral decision theory approach considers people to be active in seeking out and extracting information from the environment. More importantly, research has shown that *different patterns of information acquisition clearly reflect distinguishable choice strategies.* Thus, according to this approach, a key to understanding any decision lies in observing how people acquire information, because this, in turn, sheds light on the choice strategies or decision rules that people use to make the decision. This has led behavioral-decision theorists to develop techniques for studying information acquisition, which fall under the general rubric of "process-tracing models" (Carroll and Johnson 1990).

Process-Tracing Models of Decision Making

Information-search or process tracing models start with the basic assumption that decision making is best studied by collecting data while the decision is being made (Ford et al. 1989; Jacoby et al. 1987). Two major techniques have been developed to study this process, verbal protocols (Ericsson and Simon 1980) and information boards (Payne 1976).[4] With verbal protocols, decision makers are asked to "think aloud" while they are making a decision. A recording is made of the protocols, which can later be transcribed and coded. This is a somewhat intrusive data-gathering technique, and it forces people to perform a natural activity (making a decision) in an unnatural way (talking aloud while making the decision), although many subjects can, with practice, provide quite useful protocols. A big advantage of this technique is its ability to provide a record of the information from memory that a subject brings to bear on a decision, along with any information provided by the experimenter. A big disadvantage of this technique is how labor-intensive it is: protocols must be recorded, transcribed, and coded before they are ready to be analyzed.

   "Information board" techniques present subjects with an $m \times n$ matrix of information. They usually require a subject to choose among several alternatives (the columns of the matrix), differing in one or more attributes (the rows). This technique has been widely used in marketing research, and it provides a good analog to a consumer choosing among different brands of a product—varying in price, effectiveness, attractiveness of packaging, and so on—on a supermarket shelf. In a political context, subjects could be asked to choose between two or more candidates (alternatives) differing in their policy stands, backgrounds, personalities, and so on (i.e., the attributes; see Herstein 1981). Subjects do not initially see the content of this information (i.e., do not see where each candidate actually stands on an issue); they see only the attribute labels, and must physically "access" the information (by turning over a file card or manipulating a computer screen) to read the information. Thus, the actual information that is accessed and the order in which it is accessed can easily be recorded and used to distinguish between alternative decision-making strategies.

Process-tracing techniques that allow the monitoring of information acquisition during an election campaign should lead to a better understanding of the processes and strategies that voters actually use to evaluate candidates and make vote choices. Before describing such a technique, I must be more precise about "different choice strategies" and "different patterns of information acquisition."

Choice Strategies

No matter what procedure is used to acquire information, at some point it must be combined and analyzed to produce some choice between the available alternatives. Two major types of "choice strategies," or "decision rules," have been identified.

1. *Compensatory* strategies are fairly complex, involving trade-offs in which a low value on one dimension of judgment can be compensated for by a high value on another dimension (e.g., when a candidate's lack of experience in foreign affairs is balanced against her expertise on economic matters). The two most straightforward variants of the compensatory decision strategy are the "linear" and the "additive-difference" models, where the former assumes intra-alternative search, and the latter assumes intraattribute search.[5]

2. *Noncompensatory* strategies are conflict-avoidance strategies that do not allow trade-offs (Hogarth 1987). That is, a low value on one dimension of judgment is not compensated for by a high value on another dimension (Billings and Marcus 1983). Noncompensatory decision processes cover a wide range of decision rules, all of which are designed to simplify the complexity of a decision problem. For example, the *conjunctive* rule assumes that people set a cut-off point on all relevant dimensions of judgment, and reject all alternatives that fall below any criterion value. The *elimination-by-aspect* rule

(EBA), on the other hand, is a decision-making strategy, in which alternatives that do not exceed a certain criterion on the most important attribute are eliminated from consideration. If too many alternatives remain, the next-most important attribute is considered, and so on.

It is easy to imagine situations in which a voter, utilizing a noncompensatory decision rule, would select a candidate that is, on the whole, clearly inferior to one or more rejected candidates, because the candidate is inferior on attributes that were never examined (Plott and Levine 1978; Tversky and Sattath 1979; Wright and Barbour 1977). From a normative point of view, this is a serious drawback of noncompensatory decision rules: potentially suboptimal decisions. In theory, compensatory choice strategies, which dictate that some weight must be given to all relevant attributes, produce more optimal decisions. However, there is some question about how frequently noncompensatory choice strategies actually lead to inferior decisions (Russo and Dosher 1980; Thorngate 1980). According to Abelson and Levi (1985), noncompensatory decision rules might represent true cognitive "bargains," in that they produce large savings of cognitive effort at little cost of decision quality.

Information-Acquisition Patterns

If behavioral decision theory research more generally has focused on the choice strategies people use to make decisions, process-tracing studies have usually focused on the search strategies that people employ in gathering information. Three broad categories of variables are considered: (1) content of search, (2) depth of search, and (3) the sequence of search. Each of these variables reveals important aspects of information-acquisition and search strategies.

Content of search. Content refers to the specific information acquired during search. For example, political scientists are interested in the voter's reliance on such candidate attributes as trait characteristics and issue positions. Content measures can inform researchers about the type of information people seek out about candidates under varying conditions of information load and degree of complexity. Among the more useful measures is the proportion of times a given attribute or class of attributes (such as personality traits) is accessed and the priority of accessing different types of information. Content measures can be used to distinguish between, say, *The American Voter*'s model (Campbell et al. 1960), that would expect a heavy emphasis on party identification, and any issue-voting model, that would expect heavier emphasis on candidates' policy stands.

Depth of search. There are a variety of important measures of depth of search, including (1) the proportion of all the available information that was accessed; (2) the number of different alternatives considered; (3) the number of different attributes considered; (4) the proportion of acquired items devoted to the alternative chosen; and (5) the variance of the number of attributes considered per alternative. Depth measures can be used to distinguish between memory-based models, which (because of cognitive limitations) posit relatively shallow search, and on-line models, which can handle more in-depth search.

Sequence of search. Sequence refers to the temporal order in which information is acquired. One or another variant of "transition analysis" is employed to detect search patterns (Payne 1976; Jacoby et al. 1987). Although four different types of transitions are possible,[6] the primary question in the literature is whether the transitions are intra-alternative or intra-attribute.

All of these measures can help political scientists determine the descriptive accuracy of different models of the vote decision. For example, any model that expects intracandidate search would predict a high proportion of same-candidate, different-attribute transitions (e.g., Kelley and Mirer 1974; spatial models; Lodge, McGraw, and Stroh 1989), while models expecting intra-attribute search would predict a high proportion of different-candidate, same-attribute transitions (e.g., Lau 1986, 1989a; Markus and Converse 1979). Similarly, seeking out a high proportion of the total available information about the competing candidates would indicate very deep information processing, whereas attending to relatively little of the available information would indicate shallow information processing. Searching the same *proportion* of information for each candidate (low variability of search) indicates the use of a compensatory strategy, while high intercandidate *variability* indicates noncompensatory decision rules. Even more directly, a high proportion of all attributes searched that are examined for all candidates indicates a compensatory decision strategy.

What Do People Actually Do When They Make Complex Decisions?

One of the major findings of contemporary decision-theory research is that people can, and frequently do, use different choice strategies—and, thus, different information-acquisition patterns—in different situations (Johnson and Payne 1985; Russo and Dosher 1983; Svenson 1979). The choice among decision strategies is largely a function of what psychologists call "task demands." Generally speaking, the more complex the decision task, the more likely people are to use noncompensatory decision rules to simplify that task. In fact, strong evidence now exists demonstrating that people can, and oftentimes do, use a combination of strategies in the course of making a difficult choice (Beach and Mitchell 1978; Johnson and Payne 1985; Russo and Dosher 1980; Thorngate 1980).

The problem for political science is that if anything characterizes political decisions, it is their complexity; yet *every political science model of the vote decision that I am aware of* (including my own) assumes some compensatory decision rule. Look back at figure 1. The six models represented differ in their assumptions about the content, depth, and sequence of search, but all of them assume a compensatory strategy for combining information and reaching a vote decision. In other words, our models of how people decide how to vote fly in the face of scores of studies on how people actually make other types of complex decisions. Either the vote decision is different in crucial ways from the other types of decisions that have been studied, or we political scientists have gotten our models wrong.

In light of the evidence from behavioral decision theory, then, it would seem that voters will, in general, rely on noncompensatory strategies in making their vote decisions, particularly when the number of candidates is large, and/or when the issues are complex, ambiguous, or numerous. This is certainly the case in the early stages of presidential primaries in the United States, when voters are often faced with an unusually large number of candidates (there were five Democrats and three Republicans at the outset of the 1992 campaign), or in any parliamentary election where the number of parties is large. Using noncompensatory decision rules, voters can quickly screen out some candidates or parties, and then, conceivably, move to more compensatory strategies on a reduced set of alternatives (Olshavsky 1979; Payne 1976; Hogarth 1987).

Gathering Data on Political Decision Making

To begin gathering data on the descriptive accuracy of any model of the vote, we must have information about how voters make their decisions. Process-tracing methodologies have been developed for just this task. But there is a problem with the standard methodologies: none of them are well suited for analyzing choices in a protracted, dynamic decision context, like an election campaign. Consider the standard information board: all of the information (attributes) about every alternative is available all of the time, whenever a subject wants to access it; furthermore, all of the information is equally difficult (or, rather, easy) to acquire.

Nothing could be further from the truth in an actual election campaign, where "hoopla and horserace" information seem to dominate the airways, where detailed policy positions from any candidate are extremely hard to come by and where campaign managers and media moguls have almost complete control over what information is available, and when it is available. Moreover, candidates differ in the resources they have to advertise or otherwise make available their positions, differ in the themes or issues they wish to stress in their campaigns, and differ in the clarity with which they take stands (with most candidates, most of the time, making very ambiguous statements about their positions; see Downs 1957; Page 1978). In other words, a standard information board represents an "ideal world" that is close to existing for choosing breakfast cereals off a supermarket shelf, but clearly does not exist for choosing political candidates.[7]

A Dynamic Process-Tracing Methodology

I have developed a new process-tracing technique that retains the most essential features of the standard information board, while making it a better analog of an actual political campaign. My guiding principle was to devise a methodology that would mimic an actual election campaign, while still providing a detailed record of the actual search process employed by subjects.

> If a standard information board is too artificial because it is static and therefore too "manageable," I wanted to overwhelm subjects with information.
> If the standard information board is too artificial because it makes all information available whenever a subject wants it, I wanted to mimic the ongoing flow of information during a campaign, where information available today might be much harder to find tomorrow.
> If the standard information board is too artificial because all different types of information are equally available, I wanted to model, in a realistic way, the relative ease (or difficulty) of finding different types of information during a campaign.

I accomplished these goals by designing a radically revised information board, in which the information (the attribute labels), rather than being in a fixed location, "scrolled" down a computer screen. There were six attribute labels visible at any one time. The rate of scrolling was such that most people could read two or three labels before they moved. Subjects could "access" the information behind the label by clicking a mouse. The scrolling continued while subjects processed the detailed information they had accessed, however, so that there was a new screen when subjects returned to the scrolling.

I created a scenario for a mock 1992 election involving three Democratic and three Republican candidates.[8] The six candidates were all designed to be very realistic, although I was careful to avoid making any of them appear too much like some actual individual. Creating mock candidates provides crucial control over differences between subjects in prior knowledge of actual politicians. No one had any knowledge of any "candidate" before the campaign began.

The dynamic scrolling format of the information presentation accomplished two of my goals, by making only a subset of the information available at any one time, and by making the entire information-processing task much less "manageable." I also wanted to make some types of information "harder" to get than others, and I did this by varying the probabilities that specific types of information would appear on the screen. To make these probabilities realistic, I first conducted an elaborate study of the prevalence of different types of information in newspapers during the 1988 presidential campaign (Lau 1992), and modeled my probabilities after the actual prevalence of those types of information during the 1988 campaign.[9]

Subjects and Procedure

I have now run two experiments with this new process-tracing technique. The first was run as a class project for a political science seminar at Carnegie Mellon University in the spring of 1990. A convenience sample of subjects was recruited, with the only restriction on selection being that a subject had to be an eligible voter in U.S. elections (i.e., an adult citizen of the United States.). Three-quarters of the subjects were students; there was a definite Republican bias in their political leanings. Subjects in the first experiment were paid five dollars.

The second experiment was run in central New Jersey during the 1992 primary season. I explicitly recruited two types of subjects: political "experts"—colleagues in the Political Science Department at Rutgers University[10]—and "novices," defined a priori as everyone else in the study. None of our novices were college students, although virtually all had a college degree. There was a definite Democratic bias in the political leanings of subjects in the second experiment. Novices were paid ten dollars for their time; our experts worked gratis.

Subjects in both experiments were told the study involved political decision making. They first filled out a fairly standard political questionnaire, in which their political attitudes and general knowledge of American politics were measured. Then subjects were asked to imagine that it was shortly before the Pennsylvania[11] primary in 1992, and that six candidates— three Democrats and three Republicans—were all competing for their party's nomination. The experiment was trying to simulate the flow of information during a presidential campaign—both during the primaries and the general election that follows in the fall—and while none of the candidates actually existed, subjects were assured that the candidates were all very much like the type of people who have actually run for president over the past few elections. The general scrolling procedure was described, and subjects were given practice using a mouse to stop the scrolling. Subjects were also informed that information about the three Democrats would appear on one side of the screen, while information about the three Republicans would appear on the other side, but that the computer would randomly determine the location. This grouping of information by party was used because, during actual primaries, information about the candidates and the separate races is usually grouped by party. Subjects were also informed of the existence of certain types of information (group endorsements and poll results) relevant to *multiple* candidates, that was distinguishable from the candidate-specific information because its labels were written in all-capital letters.[12]

Subjects were told that the "primary campaign" would last ten minutes (twelve minutes in the second experiment), after which they would have to "vote" for one of the candidates in their party. As in the actual primaries in Pennsylvania and New Jersey (where the experiments were run), subjects had to "register" to vote in either the Democratic or Republican primary before the campaign actually began, although they were free to look at any information about any candidate from either party. Subjects could "exit" the campaign and vote at any time they wanted, but most subjects used all of the time available to them. After the primary campaign was over (or subjects had chosen to "exit" from it), subjects were asked to evaluate all six candidates on "feeling thermometers," and to "vote" for one of the three in their party.

After a short delay, the general election "campaign" began. It was much like the primary, except that only information about the two remaining candidates was available. At the end of the allotted time (or when subjects elected to "exit" the campaign), subjects were asked to evaluate the two finalists, and to "vote" for one of them.

After voting in the general election campaign, subjects received an unexpected memory task, in which they were asked to recall as much as they could about each of the six candidates.[13] Subjects were also asked to place the six candidates on each of the political-attitude questions on which they had expressed their own opinion on the preexperiment questionnaire.

Finally, subjects were thanked for their participation and debriefed. During debriefing, subjects were shown the "log" of the information they had sought out during the two campaigns. They were asked to look through the log and try to explain why they had chosen to look at each type of information. The debriefing was recorded on audiotape, and while they have not yet been transcribed for analysis, I view the information collected during the debriefing as a vital part of the overall technique. I think of it as a "retrospective protocol analysis." Because the debriefing was conducted immediately after the campaign was completed, and subjects had the log of their actual information search as a memory guide, I believe they were able to remember and report many of their internal deliberations, as they were going through the campaigns, and, thus, provided valuable insights into the decision-making process.

Experimental manipulations can be built into this general procedure at different points in the campaign. In the two experiments run so far, I have manipulated "task demands"—the difficulty of the decision task—in three different ways: whether the candidate in the general election from the subject's party was the person the subject voted for in the primary election (Experiments 1 and 2: a decision involving a most-preferred alternative is easier than one with less-preferred alternatives); how ideologically distinctive the two candidates running in the general election campaign were (Experiment 1 only: the more distinctive the candidates, the easier the decision); and whether information during both campaigns was presented in the dynamic scrolling format described above, or presented in the static format of a standard information board (Experiment 2 only: the static format is much more "manageable"). I decided to manipulate the format through which information was presented by including a standard information-board version of the campaign—which I have criticized as too unrealistic—for two major reasons. First, by utilizing a format similar to that of all previous process-tracing studies, I can more closely compare my results to prior research in the field. Second, the static information board represents the "ideal" situation for gathering information and making a decision. All of the available information about every alternative is laid out in a coherent fashion; it is always available, it can be accessed whenever the decision maker wants to look at it, in any order and for any amount of time. Although such a condition never exists in any real political campaign, the results here can be used as a "what if" baseline against which to judge the results from the more realistic presentation formats.

The primary dependent variables generated from this experiment are an ordered list of candidate attributes that were accessed during the two "campaigns," and the evaluations of the candidates and consequential vote choices. Combined with the standard political questionnaire that all subjects filled out prior to the experiment, I can begin to determine the decision rules that subjects actually used in making their vote choices in my mock campaign, the "rationality" of the choices made, and the descriptive accuracy of the different vote-choice models to predict how subjects would go about choosing. In the remainder of this chapter, I will focus on that latter point, the descriptive accuracy of different political-science models of the vote choice. I have begun to address the first two points elsewhere (Lau and Redlawsk 1992).

Although it should go without saying, let me explicitly state at the outset that the data which follows must be taken provisionally. Any experiment simplifies reality, and any new experimental paradigm should start relatively simply, before building in obvious complexities. I will discuss at the end of this chapter some of the more obvious (over?) simplifications of my use of this research paradigm to date, most of which have probably already occurred to the reader. The findings reported here are only the first in what, hopefully, will be a long line of research applying this basic paradigm. Their contribution to political science will rest in the cumulative record, not the results of any one or two experiments.

Results

Content of Search

What sort of information do voters search for during the course of a political campaign? Tables 1 and 2 report the *content* of search during the primary and general-election phases of the two experiments. For simplicity, I have grouped the information into broad categories that, with the exception of party affiliation, summarize across many individual attributes.[14] The first column of each table reports the percentage of all individual attributes accessed that fell into each broad category. The second column reports the percentage of each type of information that was available (i.e., the odds that each type of information would appear on the screen for potential access). If voters are *actively seeking out* specific types of information to help them make their vote decisions, and if the political environment does not provide the ideal mix of that information, the observed frequencies in column 1 should differ from the "expected" frequencies in column 2. In twenty-two of the thirty possible comparisons, the observed frequency does, in fact, differ significantly from what would be expected by chance.

Here we have our first opportunity to evaluate the political-science models of the vote decision listed in figure 1 above. These results provide a mild strike against Kelly and Mirer's "Simple Act of Voting" and Lodge, McGraw, and Stroh's "on-line" model, which give us no reason to expect anything but random information search (although neither model actively predicts any type of information search, including random search).

The remaining models are more explicit in predicting the content of information search. Consider first the *American Voter model* (Campbell et al. 1960), which predicts that voters will show a preference for party infor-

TABLE 1. Content of Information Search, by Categories (Experiment 1)

	Mean Percentage Accessed (observed)	Percentage Expected (if random)	Percentage of subjects Accessing Category	Mean Priority of Those Who Accessed	Robust Estimate of Priority
Primaries					
Party affiliation	13*	24	96	2.6	2.0
Issue stands	22	20	98	7.3	6.8
Group endorsements	15*	4	90	6.5	7.0
Retrospective evaluations	16*	23	98	4.7	4.1
Candidate information					
Candidate backgrounds	8*	6	54	9.1	14.3
Candidate personalities	15*	19	96	6.1	5.6
Hoopla and horserace					
Poll results	11*	4	92	7.8	6.7
General Election					
Party affiliation	6*	21	65	7.9	10.2
Issue stands	46*	29	100	2.4	1.9
Group endorsements	7*	5	75	11.5	11.3
Retrospective evaluations	10*	14	81	5.6	5.4
Candidate information					
Candidate backgrounds	8*	6	58	7.1	10.1
Candidate personalities	12*	15	83	5.3	5.9
Hoopla and horserace					
Poll results	10	10	79	9.7	10.2

Note: $N = 52$. "Percentage Expected" is based on the actual prevalence of the various categories of information during the primary and general election campaigns. "Priority of Access" refers to the priority of the first item within each category to be accessed. The "Robust Estimate of Priority" assumes everyone would eventually access information within each category.

* indicate the observed frequency differs from the expected frequency, $p < .05$.

TABLE 2. Content of Information Search, by Categories (Experiment 2, Dynamic Scrolling Condition)

	Mean Percentage Accessed (observed)	Percentage Expected (if random)	Percentage of subjects Accessing Category	Mean Priority of Those Who Accessed	Robust Estimate of Priority
Primaries					
Party affiliation	13	16	90	5.1	4.4
Issue stands	11	15	80	12.8	13.0
Group endorsements	18*	6	95	7.2	5.3
Retrospective evaluations	26*	32	100	2.9	2.7
Candidate information					
Candidate backgrounds	5	4	65	11.9	13.9
Candidate personalities	7*	10	75	14.5	13.0
Hoopla and horserace					
Poll results	14*	8	95	7.8	5.8
Campaign slogans	3	4	65	23.8	20.6
Candidate pictures	3*	5	65	20.1	20.3
General Election					
Party affiliation	7*	10	80	8.8	11.7
Issue stands	44*	27	100	2.9	2.0
Group endorsements[a]					
Retrospective evaluations	24*	29	100	3.5	2.9
Candidate information					
Candidate backgrounds	5*	11	70	17.4	15.7
Candidate personalities	12	13	80	8.6	7.4
Hoopla and horserace					
Poll results[a]					
Campaign slogans	5	5	70	15.8	15.1
Candidate pictures	3*	6	55	14.1	17.0

Note: $N = 52$.
* indicate the observed frequency differs from the expected frequency, $p < .05$.
[a] Information was never available during the general election, due to a computer bug.

mation, and Fiorina's *Retrospective Voting model* (1981), which predicts a preference for retrospective evaluations. In fact, although virtually everyone accessed *some information from these two categories, voters accessed significantly less information from both categories than would be expected by chance.*

But let us reconsider our dependent measure, particularly with respect to party information. Because the information about the candidates was grouped by party, there was no logical reason for anyone to access party more than once, because that one access provided all the party information about every candidate. And if party affiliation were accessed for one of the candidates during the primary, there was no reason to access it again during the general election, assuming that it could be recalled. An alternative measure of the importance is the *priority* of accessing information within each category. Thus, column four of tables 1 and 2 reports the average priority of seeking the *first* item within each broad category of information for those subjects who accessed some information from that category, and column 5 reports what I consider a more robust estimate of priority, valid across all subjects (granted certain reasonable assumptions).[15] Whichever figure you use, party and retrospective evaluations are, on average, the first items people look at. Thus, here we have some supportive evidence for the predictions of *The American Voter*'s model (Campbell et al. 1960) and the *Retrospective Voting* model (Fiorina 1981).

It is instructive to compare the data in tables 1 and 2 to table 3, where comparable information is presented from the static information board "ideal world" condition of experiment 2. Here all information is equally available, and the priority scores unambiguously represent importance, rather than availability. Party still has a relatively low priority score, although it is exceeded, on average, by both issue information and candidate-background information. But the priority of accessing retrospective evaluations of the candidate's past performance falls back to the middle of the pack.

The two remaining models in figure 1 make the most specific predictions about content of search. Spatial models assume that voters weigh each candidate attribute according to a vector of importance scores. It would only be rational, when time and resources are limited, to seek the most important information sooner, and to seek more of it. My own schematic model predicts that people will weigh certain types of "chronically accessible" information more heavily in their candidate evaluations, because they will be more likely to have noticed it or actively sought it out, in the first place, and more likely to remember it when they are forming evaluations. Again, it is reasonable to assume that people will seek more of the chronically accessible categories of information, and to seek it sooner.

Although I have devised a reasonable means of measuring the strength

TABLE 3. Content of Information Search, by Categories (Experiment 2, Static Information Board)

	Mean Percentage Accessed (observed)	Percentage Expected (if random)	Percentage of subjects Accessing Category	Mean Priority of Those Who Accessed	Robust Estimate of Priority
Primaries					
Party affiliation	8*	2	90	11.7	9.1
Issue stands	51	51	100	10.1	4.5
Group endorsements	5	3	60	49.3	36.6
Retrospective evaluations	7*	4	90	24.3	22.3
Candidate information					
Candidate backgrounds	15*	20	85	9.5	5.5
Candidate personalities	6*	12	75	27.4	25.2
Hoopla and horserace					
Poll results	1*	5	40	56.4	47.9
Campaign slogans	2	2	70	30.2	30.2
Candidate pictures	5*	2	60	31.3	32.3
General Election					
Party affiliation	3	2	19	3.7	11.4
Issue stands	48	42	100	4.5	2.3
Group endorsements	6*	15	19	4.3	N.A.[a]
Retrospective evaluations	5	3	31	10.6	8.1
Candidate information					
Candidate backgrounds	15	17	63	5.1	4.3
Candidate personalities	4*	10	31	10.0	9.2
Hoopla and horserace					
Poll results	10	8	38	7.5	10.1
Campaign slogans	3	2	38	10.3	9.8
Candidate pictures	7*	2	38	4.4	6.3

Note: $N = 20$ for the primary election; $N = 16$ for the general election.
* indicate the observed frequency differs from the expected frequency, $p < .05$.
[a] Not applicable

of different chronically accessible political constructs (see Fiske, Lau, and Smith 1990; Lau and Redlawsk 1992), there is no good way of measuring the spatial model's more detailed "importance" vector. In Experiment 1, in addition to measuring chronically accessible political constructs from open-ended questions about Bush, Dukakis, Jackson, and Reagan in the preexperimental questionnaire, I asked subjects in the postexperimental questionnaire to rate the general importance of the different categories of information in making their vote decisions. The problem with this direct method is that it could be confounded with subjects thinking back to the types of information they had, in fact, accessed during the experiment, and answering accordingly.[16] The measure of the chronically accessible constructs avoids this problem, because it is much more indirect. As a plausible measure of importance, I combined the direct ratings of category importance with the indirect measures of the political constructs.

Table 4 shows the simple correlation between these measures of importance and the measures of content of search from table 1. For simplicity, I average together the correlation from the primary and general elections. The correlations are generally what we would expect: positive between importance and the amount of a certain type of information, negative between importance and priority of accessing that information. Moreover, with the exception of the amount of person information accessed, the highest correlations appear where they should—on the main diagonal of the table. These correlations are not strikingly large, but that is undoubtedly due, in part, to measurement error. At the very least, we have some mild support for predictions of spatial models and my own schematic model vis-a-vis the content of information accessed. If you are keeping score, the field as a whole is not doing too badly: 3, and perhaps 4, of the models have found some support in the data.

These models, as a group, start doing less well when we turn to the remaining criteria, however. Table 5 displays some important measures of *depth* of search: the time subjects spent searching for information, the number of individual items considered, the number of distinct attributes considered, and the number of alternatives (candidates) considered. With a limit in short-term memory of about 5–9 "bits" of information, there is no reason for subjects to seek more information than that, unless they are using an "on-line," rather than a "memory-based" evaluation process. In both of my experiments, subjects chose to access far more information than they could ever keep in active memory, providing a serious strike against the five models that assume a memory-based process, and providing solid support for a prediction of Lodge, McGraw, and Stroh's on-line model.[17]

The vote-decision models also make predictions about transitions from one item of information to the next, some hypothesizing mostly intracandidate search, others predicting mostly intra-attribute search. Without even looking at the data, we can reject on logical grounds any model assuming intra-attribute search, at least in most situations, because there simply will not be many situations in which intra-attribute search is even possible. Information is usually presented with a person, rather than an attribute, focus or organization, thus making intracandidate search much more feasible. Data from the two experiments confirm this reasoning. Roughly half of all the transitions in the two experiments involved intracandidate search, while less than 10 percent involved intra-attribute search. Only in the "ideal world" situation created for one condition in experiment 2 did intra-attribute search constitute a reasonable proportion of all transitions, and even in this condition, intracandidate transitions exceeded intra-attribute transitions.

Finally, the data on search processes can be used to infer the type of decision or choice strategy employed by subjects. A compensatory choice strategy requires that the same information be gathered about each alternative. Table 5 includes the most direct measure I could devise—the proportion of all information accessed that was gathered for all relevant candidates.[18] The denominator of this variable is the number of distinct attributes examined (candidate-specific plus multicandidate items), while the numerator is the number of distinct group endorsements and poll results examined, plus the number of candidate-specific items that were accessed for all relevant candidates.

TABLE 4. Correlations between Importance and Information Search

| | Importance of: | | | |
	Party Information	Group Information	Issue Information	Person Information
Amount of party information accessed	.26	.00	.21	−.12
Priority accessing party information	−.14	−.07	−.05	.01
Amount of group endorsements accessed	.22	.24	.12	−.04
Priority accessing group endorsements	−.11	−.26	−.22	.00
Amount issue stands accessed	−.11	.03	.07	−.02
Priority accessing issue stands	.07	−.07	−.12	.06
Amount person information accessed	.01	−.27	−.05	.13
Priority accessing person information	−.10	.30	.02	−.05

Note: Table entries are the average correlation from the primary and general elections.

The data, shown in table 5, do not provide much evidence for the use of compensatory decision strategies. In the more realistic scrolling condition, about one third of all information gathered is gathered about all relevant candidates—a number far less than would be expected of a decision maker utilizing a compensatory decision rule.[19] Only in the ideal world of the static information board condition did this crucial indicator exceed 0.5, and then just barely. One is hard pressed to see any support in these experiments for the use of compensatory decision rules as a primary means of making the vote choice.

TABLE 5. Depth and Sequence Measures

| | | Experiment 2 | |
	Experiment 1	Scrolling Condition	Static Condition
Primary Election			
Total time searching	7.9 min.	8.6 min.	18.9 min.
Number of items examined	25.9	33.2	52.5
Number attributes examined	22.6	18.4	21.2
Number candidates examined	4.7	5.0	4.9
Number relevant candidates examined[a]	3.0	2.7	2.9
% intracandidate, interattribute transitions	44.9%[b]	7.8%	46.1%
% intra-attribute, intercandidate transitions	(<5%)	9.6%	39.0%
% of all attributes examined, considered for all relevant candidates	38.0%	45.6%	53.5%
General Election			
Total time searching	6.8 min.	7.9 min.	4.2 min.
Number of items examined	22.0	28.4	14.2
Number attributes examined	20.3	18.0	10.5
Number candidates examined	2.0	2.0	1.9
% intracandidate, interattributes transitions	66.6%[b]	49.8%	40.0%
% intra-attribute, intercandidate transitions	(<5%)	5.1%	37.1%
% of all attributes examined, considered for both candidates	27.5%	27.7%	58.9%

[a]"Relevant Candidates" are candidates in the primary in which the subject registered to vote. One subject did not look at all three relevant candidates.

[b]"Intracandidate transitions" were defined more leniently in Experiment 1 than in Experiment 2. The ambiguity comes in the treatment of group endorsement and poll information, which contain information about multiple candidates, but arguably could be part of an intracandidate search sequence. In any case, the mean in Column 1 is not comparable to the means in Columns 2 and 3.

Summary and Conclusions

This chapter began with a description of the assumptions about information search that are implicit in several of the leading models of the vote decision. I went on to describe a set of process-tracing techniques that have been developed in other disciplines for exploring information-search patterns.[20] A new, more dynamic process-tracing technique aimed specifically at exploring information search during political campaigns was then presented. My focus has been on describing the type of dependent variables that can be gathered via process-tracing techniques and the types of inferences that can be based on them.[21]

Let me briefly review the major findings as they reflect on the relative veracity of different models of the vote decision. First, there is no doubt that information search during political campaigns is guided. Voters are constrained by their own cognitive limits and by what information is available at any point in time, but within those constraints (or perhaps because of those constraints) people seek out highly diagnostic information (e.g., party identification) and other types of information they think is important. People willingly seek out far more information than they could possibly hold in working memory, which points to the importance of some on-line, running-tally method of forming evaluations of the different candidates. Most information search proceeds along intra-candidate (rather than intra-attribute) lines, and the vote decision is based on some noncompensatory choice strategy.

These results, if they hold up to future research, should present a strong theoretical challenge to political science research on voting behavior. If one were to "grade" each of the political science models listed in figure 1 according to the descriptive accuracy of the four criteria considered in the table, two of the models would get D's and the other four models would fail.[22] In fairness to the authors of these models, none of them were trying to pass the test I am forcing them to take. But my point is that if we want to develop descriptively accurate models of the vote decision, than we must begin taking these criteria into consideration when offering our models.

Like any new research technique, this one has some bugs that must be worked out. With each iteration I have learned of new ways of presenting the campaign stimuli, new content that ought to be available, new dependent variables that should, and could, be gathered. For simplicity, in the designs utilized so far, all candidates have been given the same "resources" (i.e., the same type and proportion of information was available about all candidates), but that would be easy to vary in future experiments. Likewise, I have forced subjects to actively "choose" to expose themselves to any information about the campaign, where in actual campaigns it is almost impossible to avoid inadvertent exposure to unsolicited information about the candidates and campaign, but again, such a change could easily be built into the basic experimental paradigm. These and other obvious complications can be added to future iterations of the mock election campaign.

Consequently, the experiments described herein could be considered almost pilot studies, and again, their conclusions must be accepted provisionally. I doubt that any of the authors of the models I "grade" with this data will lose sleep over the poor grades they receive. As a new technique for exploring political campaigns, however, the experimental simulation described here—and process-tracing techniques more generally—offer an exciting new avenue for research, with almost limitless possibilities. If political decisions are based on the information at hand when the decision is made— and what type of decision is not?—then it is time for political scientists to begin studying explicitly how information is gathered, and how it is combined into a decision.

NOTES

1. Various chapters in Ferejohn and Kuklinski (1990) are beginning to correct this neglect.

2. If there is such a candidate; otherwise voters fall back on party identification (if they have one) as a tiebreaker.

3. Most models of memory include an unlimited "long-term memory" store and a much more limited "short-term" or "working" memory (Anderson 1983). More precisely, the limits of short-term or working memory appear to be about 5–9 distinct "bits" of information.

4. A third technique has been developed and used by a few researchers— monitoring eye movements as subjects scan some visual display.

5. A major shortcoming of compensatory decision rules that might not be immediately obvious is the necessity that all dimensions of judgment be *commensurable*. That is, a voter must be able to compare and trade off a candidate's stand on national defense, say, against her general integrity or support for minorities or whatever other attributes the voter cares about.

6. The different types of transitions possible include:
   a. Intra-attribute, intra-alternative (i.e., immediately re-accessing the same item);
   b. Intra-attribute, inter-alternative (i.e., seeking the same information about different candidates, which we will call more simply *intra-attribute* search);
   c. Intra-alternative, interattribute (i.e., seeking different information about the same alternative, which we will call *intracandidate* search); and
   d. Interattribute, interalternative (i.e., seeking different information about different candidates).

Note that if information search is random, interattribute, interalternative transitions should predominate.

7. In fact, the only study that I am aware of that has explored information search in a political campaign (Herstein 1981) used a standard information board, and reached some peculiar conclusions, the most glaring of which was that party identification is not very important in the vote decision of most people. Party identification *is* very important, for at least two reasons: (1) it is widely available; and (2) it is a heuristic that summarizes (or allows reasonable inferences to be made about) much issue-and group-based information. Herstein's conclusions were misguided, I would argue, in large part because the standard information board is a poor representation of an actual political campaign.

8. Because I did not want incumbency to be a confounding factor in the experiment, the scenario stated that neither President Bush, who had developed serious health problems, nor Vice President Quayle, who had been tragically killed in a golfing accident, were running for reelection.

9. To gather this information, my students and I selected eleven weeks during the 1988 campaign for study. These weeks were not selected randomly, but rather were intended to capture the main events of the 1988 campaign, when people would be paying the most attention to the campaign. We intentionally selected for study, then, the week of the New Hampshire Primary, the Pennsylvania Primary, the two party's conventions, the week of the debates, and so on. During each week, we selected two newspapers for study (one local Pittsburgh paper, one national paper) and coded information from every article about the campaign that appeared in the newspaper that week. Each article was broken into different "units" (essentially paragraphs), and each unit was coded for the presence of ten different types of information (party, issues, groups supporting the candidate, candidate personalities, candidate-background information, performance evaluations, campaign strategies, polls, horserace and hoopla, and a residual "other" category). The eleven weeks were broken into five distinct periods (early primaries, late primaries, conventions, early general election, and late general election) and the proportion of each type of information appearing in each period was calculated. These proportions were each based on information from four different newspapers, from two to three weeks of the campaign. The proportions were then used to calculate the relative odds of the different types of information appearing at different times during my mock election campaign.

10. All of whom had at least a master's degree in political science.

11. Because New Jersey's primary comes on the last day of primary elections, when the race is typically already decided, we asked subjects in the second experiment to imagine they were living in New Hampshire, and could vote in the first primary of the year.

12. In the second experiment, all attribute labels scrolled down the center of the computer screen. The attribute labels for the Democratic candidates were in one (randomly assigned) color, while those for the Republican candidates were in a second color.

13. The order in which the six candidates were presented for evaluation at the

end of the primary campaign varied randomly. Subjects were asked to recall information about the candidates in the same order in which they earlier had been asked to evaluate them.

14. Candidates took stands on twenty-five distinct policy issues; eighteen different groups made endorsements; there were retrospective evaluations of three distinct aspects of each candidate's political career; there were ten different bits of background information provided about each candidate, and six distinct evaluations of their personalities; and reports from nine different election polls were available. In Experiment 2, pictures of the candidates and campaign slogans were added as possible attributes for access, but, like party affiliation, there was only one slogan and one picture per candidate.

15. For the primary election, I assumed that subjects who never accessed any information from a category would have accessed information from that category if they had accessed one more item. Thus, they were give a priority score for all categories they never accessed equal to one more than the total number of items accessed during the primary. I made a similar assumption during the general election. This procedure does result in a rather skewed distribution, so I then computed several "robust" maximum likelihood estimates of central tendency that give less weight to extreme values of a distribution. The data reported in the last column of tables 1 and 2 is the average of Andrew's, Hampel's, Huber's, and Tukey's estimates.

16. Asking these questions before the experiment would only reverse the problem: then we could not know whether subjects' information choices were guided, in part, by what they had said was important to them.

17. That is one reason Lodge and McGraw are editing this book, rather than me.

18. There are three relevant candidates in the primary election (the three competing in the party's primary in which the subject registered to vote), and two in the general election.

19. And a number that is as high as it is only because group endorsements, polls, and party information were included in the calculations.

20. For anyone wishing to learn more about process-tracing techniques, I recommend Abelson and Levi 1985; Carroll and Johnson 1990; Ford et al. 1989; and Jacoby et al. 1987.

21. See Redlawsk 1992 for a description of the computer program.

22. Even when I grade on a curve, I cannot give a passing grade to any student who does not score more than 50 percent on the various tests in a class. Keeping those same standards here, spatial models and the on-line model (strange bedfellows indeed) receive D's for being correct on 2 of the 4 criteria presented in figure 1. The rest of us all get F's, for only being right on 1 of the 4 criteria.

CHAPTER 9

Voters as Pragmatic Cognitive Misers: The Accuracy-Effort Trade-off in the Candidate Evaluation Process

Patrick K. Stroh

Models describing voting behavior often portray citizens as "cognitive-misers"; that is, voters continually behave as if cognitive limitations influence when and how they form candidate evaluations. These cognitive limitations presumably underlie the voter's desire to minimize the amount of time and mental effort demanded by an evaluative strategy, while also maximizing feelings of decision "accuracy." In other words, voters behave pragmatically, weighing (or at least subconsciously learning) the costs and benefits of using particular considerations in the candidate-evaluation process. Using this reasoning, many researchers argue that simple decision-making criteria, such as party identification and character (personality) impressions, reflect an "optimal" effort-accuracy trade-off, from the standpoint of most voters. The logic frequently goes as follows. First, the quantity of partisan and character-oriented information broadcast by the mass media causes voters to learn about and use these decision criteria. Practice, in turn, lowers the necessary expenditure of cognitive effort, and therefore increases the future likelihood that the voter will use the criteria in the candidate-choice process. Next, party identification and character assessments represent reliable predictors of candidate activities and performance. Putting the pieces together, voters use the partisan and character attributes of the candidates, because they represent cheap and useful considerations in the voting process (e.g., Shively 1979, 1040–42; Fiorina 1981, 198–99).

The causal logic of the pragmatic cognitive-miser framework rests on general principles of cognitive psychology and economics, namely the minimization of cognitive costs and maximization of choice accuracy (e.g., Downs 1957; Shugan 1980). But what many researchers fail to do is to incorporate an explicit trade-off between cognitive effort and criterion usefulness in the candidate evaluation process (see Shively 1979, for one such effort). No doubt, this empirical gap results from the inability of survey methodologies to adequately measure cognitive effort. Instead, researchers assume that issues consume more cognitive effort than either partisan, character, or perhaps, ideological considerations (Downs 1957; Nie, Verba, and Petrocik 1976; Kinder and Fiske 1986). Alternatively, Shively (1979) argues that less educated voters necessarily experience higher decision costs than more educated voters, and higher decision-making costs force voters to rely on simple decision rules, such as party identification. However, demonstrating that character assessments, party identification, ideology, or issues represent an optimal balance between effort and anticipated accuracy requires a comparison of the impact of considerations on candidate evaluations "per unit of cognitive effort"; and few (if any) researchers claim to do so. Therefore, we cannot determine the source of the decision weight—accuracy maximization or effort minimization—given to any particular consideration in the candidate evaluation process (see Shively 1979 and Fiorina 1981, for similar points).

This chapter describes and then empirically tests a "pragmatic cognitive-miser" model of the candidate evaluation process. Here, voters consider candidate attributes—e.g., group membership, ideology, policy positions, character (personality) traits—on the basis of processing effort. More specifically, the chapter examines the hypothesis that partisanship and character assessments represent an optimal trade-off (from the voter's standpoint) between decision-making simplicity and usefulness (perceived accuracy). Using reaction times to measure cognitive effort, statistical analyses then examine the impact of partisanship, ideological, and character attributions on candidate evaluations per unit of cognitive effort. The chapter concludes by presenting an extended character-oriented model of candidate evaluation, wherein developments and changes in the evaluation and popularity of public figures result from a problem-to-candidate (traits) matching process.

Literature Review

A major strand of reasoning in political science centers on the effects of cognitive limitations on voter decision making (e.g., Herstein 1981). In this framework, voters necessarily trade off the cognitive effort consumed by considering candidate attributes against each consideration's perceived ability to forecast the performance of the candidate. (A "consideration" refers to the active use of a candidate attribute, such as character trait, partisanship, or issue position, for the purpose of evaluating the candidate; Kelley 1983; Zaller and Feldman 1992, 585.) Presumably, well-practiced considerations, such as partisanship, prior voting behavior, and character impressions, represent such an optimal or pragmatic effort-accuracy trade-off. To date, however, no model of the candidate-evaluation process proves the "pragmatic cognitive-miser" model of decision making. At best, the voter's reason for using particular considerations is supported by theoretical conjecture and anecdotal evidence alone.

The following literature review examines the proposition that character impressions, ideology, and partisanship represent effective, but simple, criteria for evaluating political candidates. Then, the chapter presents one methodology capable of measuring cognitive effort, namely reaction-time measures.

Effort Minimization

Among the different considerations used by voters in the candidate-evaluation process, impressions of candidate character or personality traits represent one of the classic examples of the cognitive-miser framework (e.g., Kinder and Fiske 1986). In this literature, the cognitive effort consumed by character considerations flows directly from the continual use of character-related concepts in everyday social and political life. For instance, character impressions, as opposed to physical characteristics or attitudes and beliefs, represent the most common medium for describing individuals during our everyday lives (Fiske and Cox 1979; Park 1986). References to character traits also figure prominently in public discourse about politicians on television and in newspapers (Patterson 1980; Graber 1988). Consequently, as voters practice forming impressions, the cognitive resources necessary to construct and use the impressions diminish, thereby freeing an individual's attention for other concerns.

Given the continual use of character-related concepts, the formation of character impressions becomes spontaneous, effortless, and occasionally unconscious in social situations (Ostrom 1984; Winter and Uleman 1984; Newman and Uleman 1989). Indeed, the potential exists for using character concepts as the key interpretative framework as an individual forms impressions from various signals, including policy statements. As Graber (1988, 304) writes: "Stories discussing issues may underlie the conclusion that a candidate is capable or compassionate or smart or likable" (also see Kinder 1986). Presumably, the individual then retrieves and uses these preformed impressions as an exogenous template for describing an individual, perceiving and processing additional information, predicting the individual's future behavior, and for constructing behavioral responses to an individual (Park 1986).

Given the prevalence of character impressions in everyday and political life, many researchers suggests that there is little individual variation in the use of character attributions when people think about political candidates.

Here, the tendency to form and use impressions is invariant across expertise and interest levels because everybody forms trait impressions in their day-to-day lives and encounters the character-saturated reporting of political events (Rahn et al. 1990; Reed 1990; Miller, Wattenburg, and Malanchuk 1986). As such, the routine and effortless nature of trait impression formation contributes to the prevalence of character attributes in the open-ended like-dislike reports about candidates (usually accounting for 30 to 40 percent of all such reports; see Kessel 1984; Lau 1986). Hence, it appears that voters use the character impressions of candidates in the same fashion as they do for more common folk during everyday social life.

A similar effort-minimization logic runs through research on partisan, ideological and "easy issue" voting (Downs 1957; Goldberg 1969; Reynolds 1974; Popkin et al. 1976; Shively 1979; Helm 1979/1980; Carmines and Stimson 1980). For example, Campbell et al. (1960, 126–27, 128) write: "having the party symbol stamped on certain candidates . . . is a psychological convenience [because] the complexities of politics and government increase the importance of having relatively simple cues to evaluate what cannot be matters of personal knowledge." Downs (1957, chap. 12) outlines a similar argument, wherein party or ideological labels cut the "information costs" associated with choosing candidates.

As with character considerations, the use of partisan shortcuts develops with practice and repetition; and the "corollary notion is that the absence of those experiences might well result in one's 'forgetting—his original party attachment" (Campbell et al. 1960, 93–95; also see Howell 1981; Jennings and Markus 1984). In this framework, partisan identification represents the product of learning habitual responses toward candidate attributes, such as party affiliation. Hence, several authors attribute the decline of partisan voting (e.g., party references in the open-ended candidate likes and dislikes) to changes in the availability of clear partisan information and cleavages (for one review, see Campbell et al. 1986). (Indeed, the decline of partisan voting parallels the rise of personality-oriented references in the same open-ended remarks; Miller and Miller 1976.)

Finally, the relationship between the public agenda, use/practice and cognitive simplicity also explains the effect of "easy issues," such as racial integration, on voter decision making (Carmines and Stimson 1980). In this case, "easy issue" voting "occurs when a particular issue becomes so ingrained, over a long period, that it structures voters' "gut responses" to candidates and political parties" (Carmines and Stimson 1980, 165). "Hard issues," however, consume too many cognitive resources (because of their novelty and concern with complex policy-means) for persons unable or unwilling to think about the issues. As such, easy issues influence the decision making of all voters, while hard issues only influence the choices of "sophisticated" voters (Carmines and Stimson 1980; Bowen and Bacot 1991).

In brief, research on character impressions, party identification, and easy issues strongly suggests that cognitive effort at least partially underlies the voter's use of any consideration used to evaluate or choose candidates.

Accuracy

In tandem with research addressing the routine nature of candidate character impressions, as well as partisan and issue considerations in voter cognitions, many studies specifically assign choice criteria the role of accuracy maximization. Here, simple considerations serve an evaluative function, aside from being well practiced and effortless, namely, the maximization of one's subjective (expected) satisfaction with candidates. From the standpoint of normative decision theory, an accurate or optimal choice "maximizes" "some explicit and measurable criterion . . . conditional on certain environmental assumptions and specified time horizon" (Einhorn and Hogarth 1982). Subjective accuracy, of course, does not involve any normative "reality test." Indeed, we simply do not know the voter's goals, the optimal set of choice criteria used for achieving the goals (e.g., issues versus character impressions), or the voter's "time horizon." Therefore, researchers developed an alternative measure of criterion accuracy.

In place of an objective accuracy standard and an ability to ascertain an "accuracy maximizing" set of choice criteria, researchers simply "back-solve" for an attribute's usefulness in the choice process. Large regression weights or open-ended attributions of criterion importance indicate those considerations that maximize the voter's subjective sense of choice accuracy. For example, mentions of character traits, such as honesty and competence, consistently rank near the top in frequency among voters asked to describe their ideal political candidate (Sigel 1966; Blumer and McQuail 1969; Nimmo and Savage 1976). Empirical studies also reinforce the self-reports of voters; character impressions exert an important influence over voter decision-making (Campbell et al. 1960; Nimmo and Savage 1976; Fenno 1976; Markus and Converse 1979; Page and Jones 1979; Kelley 1983; Miller and Wattenberg 1985; Lau 1986). By inference, the candidates' character traits contribute to the voter's sense of choosing the "correct" candidate for the office; hence, character considerations help maximize the subjective accuracy of the choice. (Of course, the voter's subjective sense of criterion accuracy could be wrong, in terms of reality; hence, Kinder's (1986) association of the phrase "fundamental political attribution error" with character-oriented choice criteria.)

In this scheme, character assessments do not just dominate the thoughts of the simple-minded and naive (as portrayed by Campbell et. al. 1960, 223; Converse 1964). Indeed, the evidence points in the opposite direction, as the more educated and more attentive segments of the population refer to and use candidate character impressions in larger proportions than less educated and attentive citizens (Miller, Wattenberg, and Malanchuk 1986; Lau 1986; McGraw and Steenbergen in this volume). This implies that character impressions serve an accuracy-maximization function; (sophisticated) voters use character assessments because of their forecasting ability (e.g., Kinder and Fiske 1986, 194–95). Fiorina (1981) states this view clearly: Since voters choose candidates on the basis of anticipated performance, "the electorate's collective perception of the candidates focuses heavily on instrumental qualities that enhance or detract from an office-holder's ability to govern" and not on "idiosyncratic physical or personality traits" (Fiorina 1981, 150; citing Miller and Miller 1976). Here, "Judgments of competence, integrity and personal characteristics are reasonable things to carry over from the past" (Fiorina 1981) when predicting future candidate performance. Or, as Page (1978: 262) puts it:

> Experience and competence surely have something to do with whether a candidate will be able to solve unforeseen problems and realize voters' values.... Warmth and activity are related to the general direction which policy is likely to take.... In short, these matters bear upon the utility income or benefits which voters expect to get from alternative electoral outcomes.

Therefore, voters use character impressions as part of an accuracy-maximization process, and perhaps as a surrogate for more complex issue considerations.

Researchers less often portray partisan and ideological voting as possessing an accuracy component, because their *direct effect* on candidate evaluations and choice is usually lower than character considerations (e.g., Markus and Converse 1979), except for cases of choice between candidates possessing equal evaluations (i.e., for indifferent voters, see Markus and Converse 1979, 148; Kelley and Mirer 1974). At best, partisanship and ideological labels enable voters to predict the policies advocated by candidate (e.g., Hamill, Lodge, and Blake 1985; Conover and Feldman 1986). In this vein, issues rank higher than partisanship, in terms of direct regression weights or open-ended importance ratings (Markus and Converse 1979; RePass 1979; Herstein 1981). Indeed, researchers almost unanimously represent specific issues as being the most accurate (or desirable) manner for choosing candidates, because they involve more information about the *means* used to achieve particular goals (e.g., peace and prosperity, see Enelow and Hinich 1984; Chapman and Palda 1983).

The Accuracy-Effort Trade-off

Despite an extensive amount of research documenting the pivotal role played by various considerations in the candidate-evaluation process, prior empirical research does not clearly distinguish between the components of the accuracy-effort trade-off, namely, accuracy maximization and cognitive-cost minimization.[1] Accuracy maximization refers to the evaluative implications of candidate attributes for the judgment process, while cognitive-cost minimization refers to the amount of "mental effort" consumed by using the candidate attributes in the judgment process. Since voters want to be pragmatic (i.e., make accurate decisions within the parameters of their cognitive limitations), the two factors—accuracy maximization and cost minimization—must be simultaneously integrated into the judgment process. After all, the consideration of complex and resource-consuming attributes, albeit useful for determining the "best candidate," breeds indecision and mental agony. On the other hand, the mindless consideration of simple candidate attributes, while minimizing the time and effort consumed in the judgment process, frequently leads to evaluation errors, wrong decisions, and feelings of regret. Therefore, voters continually seek to resolve the problem of maximizing their choice accuracy (by considering "accuracy maximizing" candidate attributes), while simultaneously consuming as few cognitive resources as possible.

The empirical gap between the demonstration of accuracy maximization and cost minimization no doubt results from an inability of traditional methodologies (especially surveys) to adequately control for cognitive effort. To demonstrate that character impressions or party identification represent the simultaneous balance of effort and accuracy requires an examination of the impact of considerations "per unit of cognitive effort," as compared to other candidate attributes (e.g., character impressions versus ideology). If equally effortless considerations exert the same influence over candidate evaluations, then each consideration does not possess any unique role in the evaluation process, due to accuracy considerations. (In essence, the decision-making model becomes "contentless," once the researcher controls for cognitive effort.) If, however, particular considerations exert more influence over candidate evaluations than alternative considerations per unit of cognitive effort, then voters clearly use the consideration, because they represent the "most useful" among equally simple considerations.

My empirical exploration of a pragmatic cognitive-miser model of the candidate-evaluation process combines work on cognition limitations and adaptive decision making (Payne, Bettman, and Johnson 1990; Herstein 1981) with research on candidate character impressions, ideology, and partisanship. Following the mainstream literature on the candidate-evaluation process, the accuracy of various considerations is ascertained by comparing regression slope coefficients across different considerations about candidates. The steeper the slope coefficients for particular considerations, the greater the evaluation change per consideration unit. In this way, researchers attribute more or less importance to party identification, issue considerations, or candidate character impressions in standard treatments of the candidate-evaluation process. But how do researchers measure the cognitive effort demanded by the utilization of particular considerations?

Measures of cognitive effort usually incorporate an implicit calculation of the information-processing stages necessary to evaluate the candidate. In this framework, candidate evaluation involves the retrieval of candidate attributes and affective reactions from long-term memory, and the integration of the information into an overall evaluation. To do this, the individual first searches for and selects the considerations most relevant to the decision, including character impressions, partisanship, and issue positions. Next, the voter considers the evaluative implications of the considerations. Finally, the voter integrates the considerations into an overall evaluation or choice. These cognitive steps, or "elementary information processes," can be measured in several ways, including the number of implicit steps involved in the calculations, or self-reports of overall decision making difficulty (Payne, Bettman, and Johnson 1990, 132).

Paralleling the characterization of "cognitive steps" as being equivalent to cognitive effort, several researchers also claim that candidate descriptions reported in open-ended interviews represent the easiest and most accessible information from long-term memory. For example, Lau (1986) argues that open-ended like-dislike questions measure the relative ease and accessibility of candidate attributes, because individuals report the most accessible information from long-term memory (i.e., the first attribute mention is easier than subsequent mentions). As such, the most accessible considerations also dominate individual decision making, because of their presence in short-term or working memory (Lau 1986; Kelley and Mirer 1974).

Assuming that open-ended "first mentions" always consume the same amount of cognitive effort, the pragmatic cognitive-miser framework suggests an examination of the impact of particular considerations on candidate choice at each level of mention order. In other words, we could compare the impact of character, partisanship, ideology, and issue considerations on candidate choices at the "first mention" level, then at the "second mention" level, and so on, down the ladder of cognitive difficulty. If the considerations did not differ significantly from one another at each level, we would say the minimization of cognitive costs drives candidate choice (i.e., the considerations are equally "accurate" predicators, given an equal amount of cognitive effort). If the considerations differ from one another at each level of cognitive effort, we would attribute the differences to variations in the subjective accuracy of the considerations. Thus, controls for cognitive effort enable tests of the pragmatic cognitive-miser hypothesis, by separating the two portions of the accuracy-effort calculation.

Methodologically, however, the use of open-ended questions to measure cognitive effort possesses several weaknesses. First, it assumes an equal amount of cognitive effort for each order of mention; "first mentions" always consume the same amount of cognitive resources, and so on. Presumably, the cognitive effort associated with any open-ended remark varies across individuals. By not controlling for or measuring the amount of deliberation that produces an open-ended remark, the procedure undercuts an examination of the pragmatic cognitive-miser hypothesis. Second, Park (1986) demonstrates that individuals often do not report the most accessible (or most easily retrieved) concepts in their open-ended descriptions of other people. In light of these two problems, any examination of the pragmatic cognitive-miser hypothesis requires an alternative measure of cognitive effort.

A more direct technique for assessing cognitive effort sees the individual's response latency, or reaction time, as being equivalent to the amount of mental resources necessary to perform an information process. In this framework, the time taken for an individual to express an attitude or judgment measures the accessibility of attitudes and choice considerations from long-term memory. The faster an individual's response, the more spontaneous, simple, and effortless the consideration; the slower an individual's response, the more deliberative, complex, and demanding the consideration (Hogarth 1987). Thus, *reaction time measures cognitive effort*—the more accessible and faster the judgment, the less the cognitive effort (Payne, Bettman, and Johnson 1990, 141).

In this framework, several authors report associations between reaction time and choice behavior in several task situations (e.g., Jamieson and Petrusic, 1977; Petrusic and Jamieson 1978). Fazio and Williams (1986), for example, demonstrate that candidate choice covaries with the speed of one's attitude responses toward the candidates. Presumably, accessible considerations also exert an important influence over candidate evaluations, for at least two reasons. First, as measured by reaction times, accessible concepts dominate an individual's thinking or working memory about social objects (for social cognition examples, see Hastie and Kumar 1979; Higgins and King 1981; Cohen 1981; Hastie and Park 1986; Fazio 1986; Lichtenstein and Srull 1987; Bassili 1989). Second, information that occupies working memory exerts an important influence over the judgments and behavior of individuals (e.g., framing; Quattrone and Tversky 1988). Together, these two lines of research suggest that reaction-time measures represent an effective tool for addressing the pragmatic cognitive-miser hypothesis.

All together, this chapter examines the trade-off between cognitive effort and accuracy maximization in the candidate-evaluation process, concentrating primarily on candidate character impressions, ideology, and partisanship. Presumably, the use of simple, but effective, considerations overcomes the voter's cognitive limitations and maximizes choice accuracy. However, no prior research measures the cognitive effort associated with particular considerations used in the candidate-evaluation process; hence, researchers must assume that character, ideological, and partisan considerations require less cognitive effort than alternative considerations. The following experimental design and statistical analyses present a more appropriate test of the accuracy-effort trade-off—an examination of the impact of evaluative considerations per unit of cognitive effort, as measured with reaction times.

Research Design

The experiment consists of three stages: (1) measures examining the interrelationships between partisan labels, policy proposals, personality traits, and individual preferences; (2) exposure of the subjects to information about a fictitious Democratic presidential candidate; and (3) posttest measures of the subject's description and evaluation of the fictitious Democrat and George Bush. The actual measurements use a reaction-time paradigm. Here, the concepts appear on a computer screen in an "[x] describes [y]" fashion, and the subject confirms or disconfirms the proposition as quickly as possible. The speed of the judgments measures the cognitive effort associated with any particular response (i.e., the ease of the response).

Experimental Subjects

The experiment was performed under the auspices of the Department of Social and Decision Sciences at Carnegie Mellon University during the Fall Semester of 1991. The student and nonstudent subjects (numbering 42; and recruited through on-campus advertisements and a $7 participation fee) represent a nonprobability sample of the campus community. Overall, the sample is young (median age = 22 years), male (68 percent) and highly interested in politics. Furthermore, the sample consists of 39 percent Strong, Weak, and Leaning Democrats, 24 percent Independents, and 36 percent Strong, Weak, and Independent Republicans. Furthermore, it leans toward the liberal end of the ideological spectrum (53 percent Very or Somewhat Liberal, 20 percent Middle-of-the-Road, and 27 percent Somewhat or Very Conservative).

Experimental Procedures and Materials

Upon completing an informed consent form, subjects were introduced to the experimental equipment and materials. In the introduction, subjects practiced using the equipment by responding either "Yes" or "No" to various unpaired and paired concepts, such as *good, bad, helpful, harmful, intelligent, unintelligent, caring, uncaring, honest, dishonest, inspiring, uninspiring, liberal, conservative, Democrat, Republican, blacks, whites, poor people,* and *rich people.* (See below for the instructions; these practice responses are not used in the data analyses.) Here, as well as during all subsequent reaction-time tasks, the subjects were encouraged to "answer as quickly as possible without making any mistakes." The computer automatically recorded the subject's response time (in milliseconds), and erased the word before continuing on. If the subject did not respond within 3 seconds, the computer erased the screen and presented the next target word, after a 2-second pause (see Fazio 1990, for an introduction to the reaction-time methodology).

After completing the practice tasks, the subjects completed a brief demographic questionnaire, and then received an "information brochure" about a political candidate. The instructions read:

> Now we're going to present the views and background of an actual or potential Democratic candidate for the office of U.S. President. Although we've changed the name and background of the candidate, the information we've written down corresponds to the actual views of the candidate. Please think about the candidate as if an election were being held today between George Bush and the Democrat described on the next page.

The subjects then read about the fictitious candidate *Tom Messinger,* as portrayed in the Appendix. (The sequence of the statements was varied slightly to control for order effects in the judgment process). After reading about the candidate, the laboratory assistant said:

> In the next part, we're going to repeat the same part you did at the very beginning. A single word will appear on the screen; if your reaction is positive to the term, person or group, then press the YES button; if your reaction is negative, then press the NO button. *Please answer as quickly as possible without making any mistakes.*

For example, the computer screen would present a fixation point (*****) for 2 seconds, followed immediately by the target word *Democrat* (for up to 3 seconds, or until the subject responded to the concept). These responses represent the subject's evaluation of the terms and groups (to be) associated with Tom Messinger and George Bush.

Next, the laboratory assistant instructed the subject that:

> In the next part of the experiment, one of two candidate names will appear on the screen—George Bush or Tom Messinger. It will be followed by the terms you've been seeing throughout the experiment. If you associate the term or group with the candidate, then press the YES button. If you do not associate the term or group with the candidate, then press the NO button. Please answer as quickly as possible without making any mistakes.

For example, the screen would present a fixation point (*****) for 2 seconds, then *George Bush* for 3 seconds. *George Bush* would then be replaced by another concept, such as the target word *Democrat,* for up to 3 seconds, or until the subject confirmed or disconfirmed the association of *George Bush* with *Democrat.* In doing so, the subject's reaction time to the association measures their "description" of the candidate (e.g., "Is George Bush a Democrat? Yes or No?"). At this point, I assume the speed of the candidate description measures the cognitive effort consumed by the consideration; that is, faster responses represent the considerations that easily and effortlessly enter the subject's mind, as they think about the candidate. In turn, these considerations drive the decision-making process, as the subject integrates the considerations—affective values into an evaluation.

Finally, subjects completed a short, self-administered questionnaire, including an overall evaluation of George Bush and Tom Messinger (5-point scale; ranging from "Very Positive" to "Very Negative"). After completing these questions, the laboratory assistant debriefed the subject, especially about the fictitious nature of the candidate Tom Messinger, and paid the subject's participation fee.

In summary, the experiment consisted of three groups of measures after the subject read about the fictitious candidate Tom Messinger: (1) the subject's evaluations of partisanship, ideological, and personality-oriented concepts, (2) the subject's association of the concepts with the candidates Tom Messinger and George Bush, and (3) the subject's evaluations of Tom Messinger and George Bush. All together, the experiment usually lasted one hour.

Data Analysis

The purpose of the data analysis is to examine the influence of character traits, partisanship, and ideology on candidate evaluations, while simultaneously controlling for the amount of cognitive effort consumed by each consideration. By examining only three potential considerations (character, partisanship, and ideology), the data analyses do not represent an entirely adequate representation of voter decision making. However, the theoretical logic and empirical strategy used here (1) provides a preliminary framework for examining the effort-accuracy trade-off, as suggested by the pragmatic cognitive-miser framework, and (2) suggests avenues for future research that incorporate controls for cognitive effort.

Measures and Data Transformations

The model described below uses the subjects' (1) discrete positive or negative attitude toward potential attributes of the candidates and (2) continuous reaction-time measures of the association of the candidates (George Bush and Tom Messinger) with particular attributes (i.e., the "candidate attributes"). Together, the unpaired attitude and candidate attribute measures constitute the "considerations" used by the subjects to evaluate the candidates. In order to continue, however, the candidate-attribute measures are transformed in the following way: First, each measure is normalized on the basis of each subject's overall speed on the reaction-time tasks. Accordingly,

$$z_{ij} = [(\frac{x_{ij} - \bar{x}_i}{\sigma_i}) + 10] \qquad (1)$$

Here, the subject's normalized reaction time score to each candidate attribute (z_{ij}) is equal to the subject's raw reaction time toward that attribute (x_{ij}) minus the subject's mean reaction-time across all judgments ($x_{i\cdot}$) (excluding the practice items in Part 1 of the experiment) divided by the standard deviation of the subject's response times, plus an arbitrary constant of 10 (thereby ensuring nonnegative scores). This normalization procedure controls for individual differences in task performance and the accessibility of candidate attributes from memory. Although theoretically unlimited in range, the calculated values at this point range from 7.25 (i.e., 2.75 standard deviations below the mean response for that particular subject) to 13.25 (i.e., 3.25 standard deviations above the mean response for that particular subject). Presumably, the faster responses (or lower values) consume less cognitive effort than slower responses.

Next, the normalized score is multiplied by the direction of the subject's response (+1 for "Yes" responses and −1 for "No" responses) and the subject's discrete attitude toward the concept, as measured in Part 5 of the experiment (negative reactions toward the concepts are scored as −1 and positive responses as +1). Finally, the reciprocal is taken for the resulting normalized, positive-negative scores, thereby producing an overall attitude accessibility or "consideration effort" score that ranges from fast negative responses, through slow responses to fast positive responses, (i.e., it incorporates evaluative implications, as well as effort). The complete four-step transformation appears as follows:

$$\frac{1}{(z_{ij})(d_{ij})(a_{ij})} \tag{2}$$

where the normalized, candidate-attribute reaction-time score (z_{ij}) is conditioned by the direction of the subject's response to the candidate attribute (d_{ij}), as well as their attitude toward the attribute (a_{ij}). Here, (z_{ij}) measures the subject's cognitive effort associated with each consideration (i.e., the product of d_{ij} and a_{ij}). For example, imagine a hypothetical subject attributing the concept *honest* $(x_{i,honest})$ to George Bush after 700 milliseconds (here, $d_{ihonest}$ equals +1). For this example, assume the subject's mean response time across all measurements equals 1000 milliseconds, and the standard deviation across the measurements equals 300 milliseconds. The normalized score $(z_{ihonest})$ equals (700 − 1000)/300, or −1 standard deviations below the mean response time. To ensure the score is positive, the arbitrary constant of 10 is then added to the score, thereby producing the result of 9.00. At this point, relatively fast responses fall below the normalized mean (10), while relatively slow responses fall above the normalized mean.

The transformed reaction-time score (9.00) is then multiplied by $d_{ihonest}$, or +1 in this case, because the subject confirmed the association between the concept *honest* and the candidate. The result is multiplied by the subject's evaluation of the concept (+1 in this case). The reciprocal is then taken for the result, thereby producing 1/9.00 units of "consideration effort" on the positive-evaluation side. Note: the longer the subject's reaction time to the candidate attribution, the smaller the score; hence, the transformed score ranges from fast, positive attributes of the candidate at the uppermost extreme (as in our example) to fast, negative attributes at the lowermost extreme of the scale. Therefore, the relationship between the accessibility measurements and candidate evaluation should be positive; positive feelings toward the candidate result from (1) confirmations of positive attributes, and (2) disconfirmations of negative attributes, while negative feelings toward the candidate result from (1) disconfirmations of positive attributes, and (2) confirmations of negative attributes.

All together, the "consideration effort" score includes three parts: (1) the normalized reaction time score, which measures the speed of the association judgment between an attribute, such as Democrat, and the candidate; (2) the direction of the attribute-candidate association as being either confirming or disconfirming; and (3) the subject's attitude toward the attribute, as being either positive or negative. The total score's reciprocal indicates the amount of cognitive effort associated with each consideration about the candidate.

One final step remains, prior to the model specification—researchers usually distinguish between several stable, underlying character dimensions that produce the specific adjectives used to describe political candidates. An examination of a close-ended battery of trait adjectives by Kinder and his colleagues (Kinder 1986; Kinder and Fiske 1986) reveals four dimensions of candidate appraisal—competence, leadership, integrity, and empathy. Miller, Wattenburg, and Malanchuk's (1986) examination of the open-ended likes and dislikes about candidates uncovers similar dimensions— competence, integrity, reliability, charisma, and appearance. More recently, Reed (1990) examined the "accessibility" of trait cognitions by using a reaction-time paradigm [pairing candidates with Kinder's (1986) trait adjectives and measuring response latencies] and uncovered dimensions similar to those of other researchers (but especially competence and integrity). In light of these findings, the following analysis incorporates scale measures of four character impressions—integrity, empathy, leadership, and competence. These scales represent the average transformed measure for the positive instances of the trait adjectives used by Kinder (1986):

$$integrity = (z_{ihonest} + z_{imoral})/2$$
$$empathy = (z_{icaring} + z_{ifair})/2$$
$$leadership = (z_{iinspiring} + z_{istrong})/2$$
$$competence = (z_{iintelligent} + z_{ieffective})/2$$

Each scale exceeds the reliability criteria used by most researchers (Cronbach alphas > 0.65). The other exogenous variables simply represent the normalized concepts of *Democrats, Republicans, liberals,* and *conservatives,* as evaluated and attributed to the two candidates.

The Causal Model

The research hypothesis states that experimental subjects rely heavily upon particular considerations (controlling for their cognitive costs) for the purpose of evaluating candidates (i.e., the slope coefficients for each consideration differ significantly from one another). The null hypothesis states that experimental subjects rely equally upon considerations that consume the same amount of cognitive effort (i.e., the slope coefficients for each consideration do not differ significantly from one another). As such, the hypothesis test involves the joint distribution, or relationship, between the transformed reaction-time, "consideration effort" scores and the candidate evaluations. (The research and null hypotheses say nothing about the average speed of the various considerations; and the nonprobability sample discourages any hypothesis-testing using the central tendencies of the measures.)

Using the close-ended evaluations of Tom Messinger and George Bush as the endogenous variables, the statistical analyses estimate the following ordinary least-squares equation for each candidate:

$$\text{Eval}_{candidate} = \alpha + \beta_1 \ (liberal,\ conservative)$$
$$+ \ \beta_2(Democrat,\ Republican) + \beta_3(leadership) + \beta_4(integrity\ ) \qquad (3)$$
$$+ \ \beta_5(empathy) + \beta_6(competence\ ) + \varepsilon$$

Here, the concepts *liberal* and *Democrat* are seen as being relevant only to the Democrat Tom Messinger, while the concepts *conservative* and *Republican* are relevant only to the Republican, George Bush.

All of the parameter estimates should be positive; the more accessible the positive consideration, the more positive the candidate evaluation. More importantly, the model incorporates "cognitive effort" into the subjects— decision making, because the reaction-time measures range from "effortless and negative" considerations, through "difficult" or time-consuming considerations (negative and positive), to "effortless and positive" considerations. Any differences in the magnitude of the slope coefficients, in turn, indicate variations in the "accuracy-maximizing" function of particular considerations. Previous researchers, as discussed earlier, suggest that character considerations epitomize the cognitive-miser's trade-off between cognitive effort and decision accuracy (e.g., Kinder and Fiske 1986). Partisanship and ideology, however, simplify the choice either too much or not enough; so, the coefficient magnitude of these nonoptimal considerations should be small, compared to the character-related coefficients.

Results

Since the reaction-time measures operationalize cognitive effort, it remains to be seen whether the slope coefficients for the character traits exceed the slope coefficients for the partisan and ideological considerations. The steeper the slope, the more "accurate," or important, the consideration per unit of cognitive effort. If, however, the slope coefficients do not differ significantly, the considerations are equally valuable, given the same amount of cognitive effort. The results of the ordinary least-squares (OLS) estimation appear in tables 1 and 2.

Table 1 displays the results for George Bush. As readily seen, three variables exceed an acceptable level of statistical significance (critical *t*-value = 1.65, 1-tailed alpha = 0.05). For every unit of consideration effort associated with *integrity*, the candidate evaluation measure increases by 4.923 units ($t = 1.847$, $p < 0.05$). (Recall, the consideration effort scores possess an absolute-value mean of 0.10 and standard deviation of 0.10.) The remaining independent variables do not reach an acceptable level of statistical significance.

Table 2 shows the results for the fictitious Democrat Tom Messinger. The consideration effort associated with *liberal* contributes to evaluations of the candidate, albeit marginally ($t = 1.766$, $p < 0.05$). Attributions of *leadership* also exert an influential role over candidate evaluations, adjusting the candidate evaluation by 3.753 per unit increase in consideration effort ($t = 1.797$, $p < 0.05$). Thus, the close association of ideological, leadership, and integrity concepts to the candidates represents an important consideration in the minds of subjects.

All together, the results reported in tables 1 and 2 provide minimal support for a character-oriented model of candidate evaluation. Leadership and integrity considerations do outweigh rival attributes of the candidates. However, the coefficients do not meet standard levels of statistical significance, in several cases, and the magnitude of the differences across the slope coefficients does not differ significantly. Therefore, among the subjects in this experiment, leadership, and integrity considerations serve an important "accuracy-maximization" function, aside from the purpose of effort minimization.

TABLE 1. Reaction-Time Model of Evaluation of Bush

	OLS Estimate	Standard Error	*t*-value
Intercept	3.491	2.418	1.444
Conservative	2.783	1.824	1.525
Republican	1.578	2.276	0.693
Leadership	4.489	2.896	1.550
Integrity	4.923	2.665	1.847*
Empathy	0.580	1.243	0.643
Competence	1.084	2.937	0.369

$F (6,34) = 2.736$, $p < 0.05$. $R^2 = 0.325$, Adjusted $R^2 = 0.206$.

* $p < .05$, one-tailed.

Put briefly, the experimental analyses examine the assumption that an effort-accuracy trade-off underlies the use of particular considerations in the candidate-evaluation process. In this scheme, many researchers argue that voters focus on candidate character impressions for two reasons: cognitive simplicity and accuracy maximization. Character considerations consume little effort, because of their prevalence in everyday life and political discussion; additionally, they also enable voters to—accurately—project the future performance of political candidates. In this experiment, the proposition is partially confirmed; there is a tendency for integrity and leadership considerations to exert a strong influence over candidate evaluations. However, the strength of these effects does not reliably exceed the impact of ideological or partisan considerations.

Discussion and Conclusion

Researchers often represent voters as pragmatic cognitive-misers; as such, they consider only the most simple and effective means for anticipating the candidate's future performance. Using an experimental design and reaction-time measures, this chapter explicitly controls for the amount of cognitive effort consumed by character, ideological, and partisan considerations, and then examines the impact of those candidate attributes on candidate evaluations. The results provide weak support for the proposition that character impressions represent an efficient and powerful mechanism for evaluating candidates.

The experimental design and analyses leave open several avenues of future investigation. These include methodological improvements, such as probability sampling (e.g., Bassili and Fletcher 1991) and the inclusion of additional candidate attributes. Indeed, the experimental stimuli did not present the candidate's policies as one-word "sound bites" or "hot buttons,"

TABLE 2.   Reaction-Time Model of Evaluation of Messinger

	OLS Estimate	Standard Error	t-value
Intercept	2.881	0.163	17.618
Liberal	0.267	0.151	1.766*
Democrat	1.531	1.654	0.926
Leadership	3.753	2.089	1.797*
Integrity	3.741	2.282	1.639
Empathy	0.790	0.785	1.007
Competence	0.161	2.147	0.941

$F(6,34) = 3.797$, $p < 0.05$. $R^2 = 0.401$, Adjusted $R^2 = 0.295$.

* $p < .05$, one-tailed.

but rather, as complete sentences and short paragraphs. Because these policy statements took time to read, the subject's reaction time (or "reading time") represented an inaccurate measure of the cognitive effort associated with issue considerations in the evaluation process. Therefore, future research should explore techniques for measuring the cognitive costs consumed by issue considerations in the candidate-evaluation process.

An additional methodological limitation centers on the subjects' evaluations of particular considerations. In particular, the causal model does not incorporate the extremity of the subjects' evaluative responses to the candidate attributes (only their discrete positive-negative reactions). This procedure avoids an increase in model complexity (an untenable proposition, given the number of experimental subjects), but limits any broader inferences drawn from the statistical results. Therefore, future work should incorporate measures of evaluative extremity into the accuracy-driven portion of the causal model.

Overall, the model presents an exploratory and tentative empirical test of the accuracy-effort framework. Future research should address its methodological limitations and improve its overall predictive level. At this point, the new model does not provide accurate predictions (note the low R-squares for tables 1 and 2), nor provide definitive inferences about voting behavior. However, estimates of the causal model do provide the only empirical, albeit tentative, test of the accuracy-effort trade-off hypothesis in the context of candidate-evaluation research.

Several substantive elaborations of the pragmatic cognitive-miser framework could also be explored in the future, including the spontaneous construction of character impressions from candidate information. If character traits represent an easy organizational format and (presumably) predict the performance of candidates, then voters should think about candidate information continually in terms of character—spontaneously calculating impressions from campaign information (e.g., Rapoport, Metcalf, and Hartman 1989), and then translating these general impressions into choices (e.g., Lodge, McGraw, and Stroh 1989). In this expanded model, character impressions (as well as partisan and issue considerations) would become endogenous variables in a comprehensive model of the candidate-evaluation process (e.g., Markus and Converse 1979; Page and Jones 1979; Rahn et al. 1990).

Additionally, if voters continually focus on just a few national problems due to mass-media agenda setting (Iyengar 1979; Behr and Iyengar 1985), then perhaps voters use particular considerations in differing circumstances. Here, voters could see certain character traits as more or less relevant to particular national problems, just as voters view political parties as being more or less desirable, given economic or international conditions

(Budge 1982). In this speculative model, using character traits as the key determinant of an evaluation could represent the most "fundamental political attribution error" (a term used by Kinder and Fiske 1986; see Campbell et al. 1960, 240), because voters represent and evaluate politicians chiefly in terms of their character. But perhaps character impressions do represent the most efficient predictor of future candidate performance for the mental resources needed in their use during the choice process. Proof of such an optimal and contextual trade-off between cognitive effort and accuracy maximization would lend further and more elaborate support to the pragmatic cognitive-miser framework so often espoused in voting-behavior studies. Furthermore, extensions of the framework would necessarily address the question of why character assessments represent an optimal solution to the accuracy-effort trade-off.

APPENDIX A: DESCRIPTION OF THE DEMOCRATIC CANDIDATE

In this section, we're going to present the views and background of an *actual or potential* Democratic candidate for the office of U.S. President. Although we've changed the name and background of the candidate, the information we've written down corresponds to the actual views of the candidate.

Please think about the candidate *as if an election were taking place today* between George Bush and the Democrat described on the next page.

After reading about the candidate, turn to the next part of the questionnaire. (Please!—do not turn back to previous parts of the questionnaire.)

Tom Messinger, Democrat	
Background	Born: March 4, 1943, Hometown: Greensburg, Pennsylvania. Education: B.A., M.B.A. Slippery Rock School of Business. Career Highlights: U.S. AirForce (1962–65), County Commissioner (1968–74), State Assemblyman (1976–84) and State Secretary of Commerce (1986–present). Married to Gladys, three children—Frank, Beth, and Peter.
The former Soviet Union	The United States ought to help the Soviet Union continue its democratic and economic reforms. This includes food shipments and low-interest loan guarantees.
Health Care	Tom supports the establishment of a federal health-insurance program by requiring businesses to insure their workers or contribute to a government health-insurance fund. The program would include prenatal and infant check-ups, screening for common cancers, and regular physical examinations.
Abortion	Tom supports the abortion rights of women. He also supports the prevention of unwanted pregnancies, counseling pregnant women on their medical options, including abortion, and rules allowing Medicaid to pay for abortions for poor women who are victims of rape and incest.
Budget Deficit	To meet the deficit-reduction targets, the government should improve its efficiency and eliminate nonessential programs. Under no circumstances should the government raise taxes to balance the budget.
Education	Tom favors an expansion of federal education programs. This includes the establishment of nationwide testing for high-school student competency, giving parents the right to choose the best school for their children, and the creation of federally-financed "magnet-schools."
Crime and Drugs	Tom supports federal laws which crack down on drugs and crime. He favors the death penalty for murderers, mandatory sentences for drug kingpins, and a mandatory waiting period and background check to purchase a firearm.
Space Program	Tom favors the reordering of our priorities in outer space. He wants to cut the space station budget, and use unmanned rockets to lift satellites into orbit.

NOTES

A previous version of this chapter was delivered at the 1992 Annual Meeting of the Midwest Political Science Association, Chicago, Illinois, April 9–13. Research supported by National Science Foundation Grant SES-9106311 and the Carnegie Mellon Research Initiative. The author would like to thank Milton Lodge, Kathleen McGraw, and an anonymous reviewer for comments on an earlier draft, and Paul Welding and Iliya Rybchinsky for their assistance in conducting research.

1. Helm (1979/80, footnote 39) concurs, "The SRC [i.e., Campbell et al. 1960] gives no evidence to substantiate the claim that the voter is concerned to preserve psychological energy."

CHAPTER 10

Computational Modeling: A Computational Model of a Survey Respondent

G. R. Boynton

Contemporary cognitive science traces its roots to two research traditions. One is the post-World War II research and theorizing of Newell and Simon, Minsky, Papert, and others that is artificial intelligence (McCorduck 1979). The other, and much older, research tradition is psychology, which was busy with stimulus-response when artificial intelligence was being founded in the 1950s. But by 1979, it could be claimed that the study of cognition had taken over psychology (Lachman, Lachman, and Butterfield 1979). Since the 1960s, the two research traditions have explored cognition, bringing to bear and sharing their rather different insights and technologies. Very roughly, the two traditions can be identified by their preferred research tools: artificial-intelligence research using production systems, and psychological research using analyses of variance. The tools both reflect and produce the different modes of thinking in the two traditions. Analysis of variance is object-property thinking. Production systems involve action thinking.

There are two reasons for recounting these distinctions in a paper on computational modeling. The first is the general admonition to know thyself. Social scientists, especially, should be self-conscious about the basic cultural categories structuring our thinking about human beings, social relations, and society. We are engaged in the reflexive act of using categories drawn from a culture to explore and explain the culture, and the only escape from this reflexivity is self-consciousness.

The second reason is much more specific. As political scientists begin to explore cognition and politics, we bring with us our own research traditions. Regression analysis, our preferred research tool, is strongly object-property oriented, as we use it. An object (a person, for example) with property 1 (a value on variable 1) is likely to have property 2 (a value on variable 2). A social category, an attitude, other measurements—even an affective tag—may be treated as a property of the individual, in this style of analysis. In our history, you find this conceptualization of "property space analysis" articulated most explicitly by Paul Lazarsfeld (Barton 1955). We are currently less self-conscious about this framing of explanations, but it is no less present in our analysis. The point is not that there is something wrong with this tradition. Instead, the point is that, as we shift our focus to studying cognition, we are likely to find one of the cognitive-science traditions to be familiar and to be puzzled by the other. Object-property thinking with analysis of variance is closely related to object-property thinking with regression; they are both specifications of the general linear model. Production systems, on the other hand, may seem strange constructions that do not connect to our tradition of research.

This chapter introduces computational modeling, which is the standard mode of operation in the artificial-intelligence tradition of cognitive science, by describing a computational model of a survey respondent.

Anomalies in Our Understanding of Question Answering

We say we have opinions, attitudes or preferences,[1] and with that metaphorical twist we construct opinions as objects—something we can have. Memory is the repository of the objects, and survey research is the technology for extracting the opinions from memory, so they may be observed and aggregated.

"Having" is one insight into our ability to speak with ease about a wide range of subjects. But it is an insight that leads to puzzles, when the implications are traced out with some care, as Zaller and Feldman (1992) have done. Some of the puzzles are illustrated by the two survey questions most frequently used to investigate public opinion about going to war in the Persian Gulf.

As you may know, the United Nations Security Council has authorized the use of force against Iraq if it doesn't withdraw from Kuwait by Jan. 15. If Iraq does not withdraw from Kuwait, should the United States go to war against Iraq to force it out of Kuwait at some point after Jan. 15 or not?

The United Nations has passed a resolution authorizing the use of military force against Iraq if they do not withdraw their troops from Kuwait by Jan. 15. If Iraq does not withdraw from Kuwait by then, do you think the United States should start military actions against Iraq, or should the United States wait longer to see if the trade embargo and other economic sanctions work?

Both questions remind, or inform, respondents about the United Nations resolution authorizing the use of force against Iraq. Both incorporate the deadline of January 15. The first question is: go to war, yes or no? The second question is: go to war, or wait to see if sanctions work before going to war?

They are not the same question, but they are not very different. And that leads to a puzzle. If respondents "have" opinions, do we understand them to have many opinions about going to war in the Persian Gulf, two opinions (one for each question), or one opinion? And if only one opinion, how is it matched to the two questions to produce a response?

In this case, the question asked made a difference in the responses. In a split-half survey—half of the respondents were asked one question and the other half were asked the other question—62 percent answered "yes," when asked the yes/no question, and 49 percent answered "go to war" when asked the go-to-war/give-sanctions-longer question (Morin 1991). Were 62 percent of us in favor of going to war, or only 49 percent? Would other questions have produced a different result?

The questions produced a readily detectable difference in the aggregated results. But the puzzle would have remained, even if the answers of the two groups had been equal. The possibility of going to war in the Persian Gulf was a matter of widespread concern. It is plausible that most respondents had opinions about going to war. It is implausible that most respondents had two opinions that exactly matched the wording of the two questions. If they did not have ready-made opinions, how did they answer the questions?

To push the puzzle a little further, before August, 1990, the date of the Iraqi invasion of Kuwait, persons in the United States could not have had an opinion about going to war to expel Iraq from Kuwait; the invasion, had not occurred. An opinion had to be constructed after the invasion. Any theory of answering questions should be able to account for how respondents might have answered the question immediately after the invasion, as well as after the respondents had had four and one-half months to learn how to think about it.

Zaller and Feldman (1992) review a number of studies of public opinion that produce similar puzzles, and they come to the conclusion that, in many cases, constructing opinions *on the spot* is a better way to understand respondents' question answering than is extracting an already-established opinion. Payne, Bettman, and Johnson (1992) review a large research literature on decision making and conclude that persons must often construct preferences on the spot in decision-making situations. The evidence that opinions-attitudes-preferences often must be constructed is substantial. But it is only *often;* there are occasions and questions when we *have* an opinion. The theory of question answering should be able to incorporate the differences that we mark off by "having an opinion" and "constructing an opinion."

Our standard practice is to assume that persons have opinions, and we ask them questions to discover what their opinions are. We assume the process of answering questions is consistent across questions and across persons—hence, unimportant. When there is reason to doubt that "having" opinions is a safe assumption, then the processes of answering questions become important for our research. One cannot tell whether the answer is created on the spot or has been a consistent answer over time, by examining the answer. Because our standard assumptions about question answering are now challenged by what we know, we must understand the processes by which questions are answered.

A Theory of Question Answering

The strength of computational models is explicit in theorizing about and modeling how a political process works; the computer program is a model of the theory. The model of a survey respondent developed in this paper illustrates the construction of a computational model for the actions of a person—a person answering survey questions. This section outlines the theory; the next section describes the computational model of the theory. "Information processing" is the founding metaphor of artificial intelligence as cognitive science (Simon 1979a). Human beings are understood as information processors. But information only becomes information in the processing; hence, understanding the processes by which humans interact with their world is the science. How sounds or alphabetic characters become questions and answers is one of many human information-processing activities that can be investigated. The starting point for theorizing about cognitive processes, such as asking and answering questions, is the organization of memory, understood as operations.

The standard way of thinking about memory in cognitive science is as a semantic, associative network. In the Boynton-Lodge research, a semantic, associative network can be pictured as in figure 1. The person whose answers are pictured in figure 1 was given nine statements about a fictitious candidate, John Williams. As each statement was read, the person was asked to write what came to mind when they read this statement about the congressional candidate. The responses to these questions are our procedure for constructing the associative network of each respondent. In the figure, candidate Williams is the central node in the network. The nine statements are the inner circle of nodes around the Williams node; they are what the respondents learned about the candidate. What came-to-mind are the nodes associated with (linked by arrows to) the nine nodes on the inner circle. There is redundancy in the figure; Republican and George Bush appear, as nodes several times in the figure. The figure can be redrawn, as in figure 2, with Republican and George Bush as the central nodes, with the same associations as in figure 1. The network is reorganized in figure 2 as a partial network for Republican and George Bush for this person. Redrawing the figure illustrates one feature of associative networks: the apparent organization of the network being investigated will vary, depending on where you tap into it; there is no unique solution for picturing a network (Roberts 1976).

A network is not a process, and some conception of the process of answering a question is required. One way to think about the process might be: step 1: understand the question; step 2: devise an answer; and step 3: speak the answer. Research in two fields of cognitive science suggest a less differentiated process. Dyer (1983) presents evidence for and argues for an integrated parser. With an integrated parser—not a separate step for understanding the question—the information needed to answer the question is available as the question is being parsed, or understood. But parsing only works on words and sentences. Rachael Reichman (1985) argues for integration, when theorizing about conversation. She argues that the process of listening in a conversation is the same process as speaking in a conversation; that the necessity of keeping track of the flow of the conversation is the same for listening and speaking. Research on cognition at two rather different levels of granularity suggest strongly integrated processing, rather than a differentiated step-by-step process.

One memory organization that will support integrated processing that has been widely investigated is "spreading activation." Nodes, as pictured in figures 1 and 2, are conceptualized as activity. With stimulation from the external environment, or in production processing, some nodes will be activated, and that activation will spread to other nodes associated with the nodes activated first. A very simple account of parsing is: activation of the node for the Bush who is president, rather than the node for the bush in my backyard. When respondents learn that Williams is in favor of a strong defense, that activates the nodes for candidate Williams and strong defense and spreads activation to the nodes that come to mind. If the respondent had learned that Williams was supported by environmental groups, the nodes activated by "Williams" would have been the same, but the nodes activated by "environmental groups" would have been different than those activated by strong defense. Quillian (1969) and Collins and Quillian (1969, 1972) were important in the contemporary articulation of this conception of memory. John Anderson (1983) has been one of the most important researchers developing the idea, and his model of spreading activation is used in this research. While "spreading activation" is not as widely shared in cognitive science as is the "semantic, associative network," it is the dominant view of memory, and many hundreds of experiments have been conducted investigating and using this conception of memory.[2]

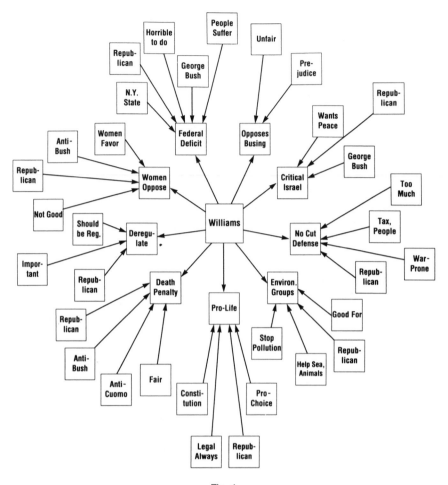

Fig. 1

Spreading activation is motion in an associative network, and thus provides a dynamics by which one associative network can interact with another: the question and the answer. Spreading activation leads to its own puzzle, however: when to stop? If the spreading activation that is understanding the question activates nodes that are an answer, then it can stop to speak, but there is no guarantee that the spread will stop before going past the answer. Human beings have a parallel problem. Powell (1989), using careful statistical analysis of survey data, and McGraw, Lodge, and Stroh (1990), using experimental design to control the information provided to the subjects, both found a great deal of stereotyping in answering survey ques-

Fig. 2

tions. It is particularly clear in the experimental studies that the subjects were describing candidates based on what they know about politicians in general, as well as based on what they learned about the specific candidate they were asked about. When remembering, people do not easily differentiate the information presented to them from what they know in general. Another way to phrase it is that they do not know when to stop searching. The politically sophisticated, with a more fully developed political network, give more stereotypical answers than do the less politically sophisticated. Spreading activation through a semantic, associative network is a theoretical construct that can develop answers *on the spot,* with some of the same foibles humans bring to the task.

Learning is three-fold in the theory. First, there is the learning that is reinforcing what we already know. Memory fades, and that feature of human cognition is captured in the theory with "node strength." When a node is activated, its strength is augmented; when a node is not activated, its strength decays. Repetition, practice, and redundancy in communication are all important in the theorizing, since they contribute to maintaining the strength of the nodes in the network. Node strength is particularly important in making sense of puzzles in research on communication about what can and cannot be remembered (Boynton 1990b).

Second, learning is adding nodes to the network. For example, between August, 1990, and January, 1991, Saddam Hussein became a node in the network of many U.S. citizens who had never before had reason to know about him. Activation and the learning that is establishing a new node in a network operate on different time scales. Activation is measured in milliseconds (Anderson 1983). Learning, establishing new nodes, is measured in seconds (Simon, 1979b). Communication can be attended to more rapidly than it can be learned. The experience of reading, watching or hearing and understanding all of the details, but then not being able to remember all of the details after the communication is completed is quite general, and it can be accounted for by the difference in the timing of activation and encoding a node in a network. Simple exposure is not enough to account for this type of learning; either repetition or a goal of learning Saddam Hussein's name, for example, is required.

Third, learning is changing the associations between nodes in the network. Activation spreads between nodes that are associated. Some associations are stronger than others, and more activation spreads through the stronger associations. The associations are not constants, but change through time, as the pattern of communication changes. Associations grow stronger when nodes are regularly conjoined in communication. When Saddam Hussein and the invasion of Kuwait are the daily news, the association between the two grows stronger. When "civil rights" are regularly conjoined with "quotas" in the various media and in conversation, the association between the two grows stronger. Strength (including zero) of association between nodes is the structure of the network. It is what controls what comes to mind as we process information. Changes in the structure are changes in the way we process information.

The theory is spreading activation through a semantic, associative network. How learning is involved in constructing and reconstructing the network has been described. But I have not yet discussed the affective character of our involvement in politics. Here is what came to mind for one of the subjects, on learning that candidate Williams supported the pro-life position.

Absolutely wrong
Who is he to make such decisions for other people?

How many adopted children does he have?
Will he ever have to give birth? (of course not)
That alone is a very bad position for him

The language is affect-laden. There is no mistaking the impression of Williams's position; Williams is "absolutely wrong." You can almost hear the sneer in "Will he ever have to give birth? (of course not)." The person knows and uses the arguments against the pro-life position: reproductive rights is a private sphere that government should not enter; adoption is an alternative in argument, rather than in practice; males should not be setting the rules for females, who must bear the child. But to notice only what the person knows is to miss the affect in which this knowledge is embedded. The impression of Williams is an affect-loaded impression. Nor is there any mistaking the affective character of the impressions of Williams in the one-thousand or so answers not quoted. What "comes to mind" is as affective as it is cognitive.

Social scientists, especially cognitive scientists, normally distinguish cognition and affect—what you know and what you like—and they conceptualize and study them separately. But the language of the responses to "what comes to mind" does not fit this bifurcation. It is both cognitive and affective. Lodge and I follow Abelson (1968) in calling it "hot cognition," as a way of uniting cognition and affect.

There are three points to make about affect in this theory. First, affect is located in the node; it is the affective tag/integrator referred to in the introduction. The evidence supporting this point is two-fold. Affect is accessible more quickly than would be true if it involved a search process. And affect is remembered longer than is the information that led to the affect. Just as a network may be thought of as a pattern of activation and node strength, so may it be thought of as a pattern of affect.

Second, affect spreads through the network in parallel to spreading activation. The best evidence for this point is the large body of research conducted by social psychologists on forming impressions of persons. The theory of impression formation has its roots in the work of Norman Anderson and Stephen Hubert (1963), and has become a large subfield of research. A standard procedure is to collect information about a subject's feelings toward persons with certain characteristics. Some time later, the subject is given information on a person and asked to make an assessment of the person. The prior information is then used to predict the assessment. Implicit in this procedure is *spread* of affect from the traits to the person being assessed; the affect for the traits spreads to become affect for the person.

Third, affect is cumulative. Norman Anderson (1989) has repeatedly demonstrated that this takes a form he calls anchor and averaging. The first information learned about a person contributes more to the final score than information learned later, and this is true even when the information is presented in varying patterns of first and last.

The final piece of the theory is providing the program with language to use in responding to questions. Survey researchers use questions with many different formats. Almost all of them share the characteristic that they ask the respondent to tell how he or she feels about some subject. How are you going to vote? Do you approve of the job being done by the president? Do you think...? Do you support...? It is the language of approval or disapproval, of support or opposition.

Survey respondents are not able to translate their approval or support into numbers very well. Krosnick (1991) reviewed the reliability of a number of answer formats and found that the thermometer scale, a scale from 0 to 100, and seven-point scales, with only the extreme values identified linguistically, are substantially less reliable than response formats that linguistically identify all of the possible responses. We have quite a lot of practice using the language of support, but very little practice specifying our feeling of support by numbers.

Lodge, Cross, Tursky, and Tanenhaus (1975) did a series of studies to determine the consistency in the use of approval or support language. The research demonstrated that known relationships between physical responses to physical stimuli applied equally well when the stimuli were words drawn from the language of approval or support. So-so was used as the point of reference between approval and disapproval, and they were able to show that the relationship between so-so and words of approval and disapproval stayed the same when the object of approval and disapproval shifted from the U.S. Senate to the Suffolk County Police, to the Supreme Court's decision on abortion, to support for Nixon's handling of domestic affairs. A simple illustration of the consistency is the use of "very." "Very good" is 1.39 times more supportive than "good," and "very bad" is 1.39 times worse than "bad." One of the physical responses used in the research was line length. Subjects were instructed to draw a line that reflected the support or disapproval in the statements. Line length was related to the other physical responses in the expected manner. In the Boynton-Lodge research, an approximation of line length was used. The subjects were asked to mark their choice of the candidates on a line immediately after learning about the candidates. Then they answered a series of questions not related to voting. After this interlude, they were asked to mark their choice again. The means of the two, when the marks were converted to a zero to one hundred scale by coders, were sixty-three and sixty-two, the correlation between the two was 0.96, the intercept was 1.3, and the slope was 0.97. There is remarkable consistency in the responses at the two points in time.

The Model of Question Answering

The theory is:
Spreading activation through
an associative network of *meaning*
an associative network of *affect*
Learning is
reaffirming by using what is already known
adding new nodes to the network
changing connectivity in the network
Answering a question is articulating the result of this activity

The computational model is a set of equations, plus the loop structures that iterate the computations; it is a mathematical articulation of the theory. Each node is three equations: an equation for activation, an equation for affect, and an equation for node strength. *Hot cognition* is produced by conjoining the equations for activation and affect for each node.

The equations for activation combine an input term, terms for each of the other nodes in the network, a term for activation of the previous time period (or iteration) and a term for current activation. A three-node activation network would have the following equations.

$$\text{act}_1(t) = c_{11}\text{act}_1(t-1) + c_{12}\text{act}_2(t-1) + c_{13}\text{act}_3(t-1) + u_1(t)$$
$$\text{act}_2(t) = c_{21}\text{act}_1(t-1) + c_{22}\text{act}_2(t-1) + c_{23}\text{act}_3(t-1) + u_2(t)$$
$$\text{act}_3(t) = c_{31}\text{act}_1(t-1) + c_{32}\text{act}_2(t-1) + c_{33}\text{act}_3(t-1) + u_3(t)$$

It is an n by n matrix with an input, $u_n(t)$. The coefficients—c_{11} through c_{nn}—control the flow of activation between nodes. It is a matrix of nonlinear first-order difference equations; nonlinear because the coefficients are time varying.

There is a parallel matrix for affect. It is also an n by n matrix. The coefficients for the affect matrix are the same as the coefficients for the activation matrix. By using the same coefficients in the two matrices, affect and activation spread in parallel throughout the network. The equations in the affect matrix do not have input terms. The input to the activation matrix is sufficient.

The equations for node strength are simpler. The three node-strength equations for the above matrix would be:

$$\text{nodestr}_1(t) = c_1\text{nodestr}_1(t-1) + u_1(t)$$
$$\text{nodestr}_2(t) = c_2\text{nodestr}_2(t-1) + u_2(t)$$
$$\text{nodestr}_3(t) = c_3\text{nodestr}_3(t-1) + u_3(t)$$

They are linear first-order difference equations. The mathematical analysis of first-order difference equations is complete, which means that it is possible to determine what the output will be, analytically, by knowing the initial conditions and the pattern of inputs. The input term for the node-strength equations is the same as the input for the activation equations.

The procedure for setting the coefficients is the most unusual feature of the matrices. There are three sets of coefficients. The coefficients for the self-referential term in the activation and affect matrices—$c_{11}\text{act}_1(t - 1)$ and $c_{11}\text{aff}_1(t - 1)$, for example—were estimated in experiments. Attention changes very rapidly in human cognition, so this number is quite small. Anderson (1983) says it should be set at .01. Affect changes much more slowly; hence, the number should be substantially greater. We follow Hastie (1988) and set it at .5 for affect. Forgetting is relatively slow, on the time scale of the coefficients in the equations, hence, the coefficients for node strength are set at .9.

The other coefficients—the coefficients off the diagonal—are either zero or a number greater than zero and less than one. The coefficients change from zero to greater than zero when there is an input to the two nodes in the same communication. There will be many more zeros than not-zeros in a typical matrix. "Dog" and the Newtonian equations of motion are not often spoken together, for example, and that would put a zero as the coefficient linking the two. Since this is a switch, or logical operator, it is another nonlinearity in the matrix. When the coefficients are not zero they are the relative strength of the node. Each coefficient—$c_{12}\text{act}_2(t - 1)$, for example—is computed by summing the node strengths of all variables with a not-zero coefficient for $\text{act}_1(t)$ and dividing that into the node strength for $\text{act}_2(t)$. Because the not zero variables for $\text{act}_1(t)$ and $\text{act}_2(t)$ will often not be the same, the matrix of coefficients will ordinarily not be symmetric; c_{12} and c_{21} might well be different, for example.

The dynamics of the model are: input; activation spreads through the activation network, giving a new value for activation for each node; affect spreads, giving a new value for affect for each node; a new value for node strength is computed for each node; and the coefficients of the activation and affect matrices are recomputed. Then another iteration. With each iteration, some node strengths will decay and others will increase. Since the coefficients are relative node strength, the changes in the strength of the various nodes will lead to changes in the matrix of coefficients. Because the coefficients change with each iteration, a full analytic solution is not possible. There are, however, two properties of the matrix, which are not at all obvious from this description, that yield theorems of considerable cognitive importance.

The first theorem is important for categorization. Categorization is an important element of cognition and language. "Dog" starts as the furry creature that is always around. "Dog" becomes lots of furry creatures that are all called by the same name. "Dog" becomes differentiated by breed: collie, wolfhound, and others. Any theory of cognition must have some provision for categorization; specifically, a theory of cognition needs a mechanism for producing the process of categorization. The matrix of equations, as specified, gives a spreading activation version of the process of categorization. Understanding how this is the case begins with a theorem.

THEOREM 1. *For any two nodes, if their node strength is equal and the not-zero coefficients are with the same nodes, then the coefficients between the two nodes will be equal.*

Earlier, I said that c_{12} would not normally be equal to c_{21}. Theorem 1 states a condition when they will be equal; it is the only condition in which the two coefficients must be equal. The importance of this theorem is in what it does not say. In all other conditions, the coefficients may or may not be equal, and for many conditions they will not be equal. The asymmetry in the matrix produces a form of spreading activation that facilitates categorization. Categorization proceeds as follows: this furry creature: dog. These furry creatures: dog. Collie: dog. Wolfhound: dog. Every time we think about dog, we do not think about wolfhound, but every time we think about wolfhound, we think about dog. Spreading activation achieves this result with an asymmetric flow of activation, which is what the asymmetric coefficients produce. More activation will spread from the more narrowly defined node (a node with few connections to other nodes) to the more broadly defined node than will spread the other way. Assuming, for most persons "wolfhound" has fewer connections than "dog," then the asymmetric spread of activation gives just the results that we call categorization: wolfhound and dog are connected; wolfhound recalls dog more than dog recalls wolfhound.

The second important cognitive process for which the network provides an unexpected mechanism is remembering a bundle of closely linked ideas. An example: A person was well-known at some time in the past; the person is encountered for the first time in a long time; a whole host of what was known about the person comes flooding back. In 1992, George Bush compared his campaign for reelection to that of Harry Truman. Harry Truman had not been on the tongue of many observers of American politics for some time. How did what was known about Harry Truman become active when President Bush reminded us of the 1948 campaign of Harry Truman? The puzzle: Why don't the connections between the diverse pieces of information about a person decay, so that they have to be recalled individually, rather than being remembered as a collection? How does what was closely linked stay closely linked? This theory of spreading activation specifies decay in node strength if the node is not activated. This permits forgetting or, more precisely, not being able to activate a node as easily as when the node was stronger. Since there is decay in node strength, it is not clear why the connections between the nodes might remain the same. Theorem 2 states the conditions where the connections, or coefficients, will not change.

> THEOREM 2. *For any two nodes, if both the nodes and those nodes they are connected to are not activated for a period of time, then the coefficients between the two nodes will not change.*

The theorem is about a bundle of nodes; two nodes, and the nodes for which they have not-zero coefficients. How this happens in this version of spreading activation is determined by the constant rate of decay of node strength and the procedure for computing the coefficients. The strength of each node decays at the same rate; therefore, the relative sizes of the strengths of the nodes do not change. Since the coefficients are relative node strengths, which do not change, the coefficients do not change, even though each node is decaying. When we are reminded of Harry Truman, much of what we knew about him is activated through the network of connections, or the coefficients, which have not changed while we were not thinking about Harry Truman.

We have so far presented a mathematical articulation of the theory, and two properties of the theory that provide a spreading-activation version of two important cognitive processes. We have not yet arrived at a model of answering questions.

How This Is a Model of a Survey Respondent

There are two sets of questions for which we systematically examined the ability of the model to produce the same answers as the subjects in the experiments. One set was nine questions that asked the subjects: What comes to mind when you learn that a candidate ... ? The other question was the choice of one of the two candidates.

The computational experiments with the model require initial conditions for the values of the three variables that constitute each node. Two weeks before the experiments, the people who participated in the experiments filled out a questionnaire that included two batteries of items to be used in the experiments. One set of more than forty questions asked what they would think about a candidate who .... For each question, the respondent marked a spot on a line, indicating what they would think of such a candidate. A second battery of questions asked how important it was to the respondent that a candidate had this characteristic. The same line-drawing procedure was used to obtain responses to the important questions. The lines were measured on a scale from zero to one hundred, and the spot marked on the line was given the appropriate value. The answers to these questions serve as the initial conditions for affect and node strength. The initial conditions for activation can be set at zero, or they can be systematically varied, to study priming effects in the model. In the experiment, the subjects were given nine statements for each of two candidates. The statements were drawn from the larger battery of questions in the initial survey. The statements were balanced in three ways. The candidates opposed each other. If one candidate favored a strong defense, the other wanted to reduce the defense budget. They were also balanced so that one candidate had six statements generally associated with Republicans and three statements generally associated with Democrats, and the other candidate had statements that were the reverse. They were also balanced so that some subjects learned about one candidate first and other subjects learned about the other candidate first. After reading the nine statements about the candidates, the subjects were asked, "What comes to mind when you learn that a candidate has this characteristic?" for each of the nine characteristics. The average number of responses to these questions was 3.7. Then they were asked what they thought about a candidate who had each of the characteristics they mentioned, to obtain affect, and how important this was, to obtain node strength. For each subject, we had initial conditions for affect and node strength on the nine statements made by the candidates, taken from the initial questionnaire. We had also initial conditions for affect and node strength for the what-comes-to-mind items obtained during the experiment. Using all of the values of node strength, an initial matrix of coefficients was computed for each subject. Because the number of nodes in the matrix varies between subjects, there is a separate model/computer program for each subject, that has the equations for each node they identified and that starts with the values of the initial conditions for that subject. With the initial conditions for the model for each subject, we were able to conduct experiments in which the model answered questions.

After reading the nine statements about one candidate, the subjects were asked to provide the "first five associations that came to mind" when they read each of the statements. The theory accounts for the answers as resulting from spreading activation. The ideas most closely associated with each statement should become most active, and the answers should be the most active ideas. The model version is: an input for the candidate node, an input for the statement node, and iteration to permit activation to spread through the network. The most active nodes after activation are the answers of the model. The model was successful at producing the same answers as the respondents (Boynton and Lodge 1993). It should be noted that this was a modest test of the model. The only nodes in the network were those provided in the questionnaire, and the coefficients were derived from information provided by the subjects. It would have been quite disappointing if the model had not been successful, but the information reproduced was the information used in setting up the experiment.

After reading the nine statements about the two candidates, the subjects were asked to choose one. The theoretical account is: establishing a node in memory for each of the candidates; spreading affect, depending on both the statements read and the spread of affect through the what-comes-to-mind nodes; generating an affect for each candidate; and finally, choosing the candidate with the greatest affect. In the experiment, establishing a node for the previously unknown candidates was facilitated by the repetition of the candidates' names while reading the statements about them; the subjects read the candidates' names more than twenty times in reading the materials about the candidates. Choosing a candidate involved marking a spot on a line with one candidate's name at one end and the other candidate's name at the other end.

Since the candidates were unknown to the subjects, it is possible that their answers contained a considerable random element. The information that we have on their choices suggests this was not the case. Immediately after reading the nine statements about the candidates, the subjects were asked to make a choice. They were asked to give their impressions of the candidates again after they had completed several other parts of the experiment. Not only is the correlation between the two measures almost 1.0 ($r = .96$), but the slope was very close to 1.0 ($b = .97$) and the intercept was very close to 0 ($a = 1.3$, on a scale of 0 to 100), as would be the case if the answers were exactly the same. The ability of the subjects to reproduce their original responses was quite impressive.

The question that the model was used to answer was the choice of candidates. Running the model involved two inputs for each iteration: an input to one candidate node and for the nine nodes, in sequence, for that candidate and then an input for the other candidate, and the nine nodes for that candidate. At the end of the 18 iterations, the candidate with the greatest affect was the choice of candidates. When the model was run using only the nine nodes for the statements read about the candidates, the answers that the model produced were only about as good as a variety of other models were able to do, using the same data (Taber and Steenbergen 1992). When the model was run using the what-comes-to-mind nodes as well as the eighteen nodes for statements read, there was a marked improvement, with very few differences between the answers of the model and the answers of the subjects (Boynton and Lodge, 1993). How a respondent will answer a question depends, according to the theory, on prior information processing. If the question asks about one's preference between two candidates and the respondent knows nothing about the candidates, then some respondents will mentally flip a coin and others will answer "I don't know."

Survey-research organizations are not paid to report that most people answer "I don't know." So they generally include enough information in questions to permit respondents to construct an answer on the spot, if they had not previously thought about the question. The questions about going to war with Iraq, for example, included information about the U.N. Security Council resolution. The information in the question and what comes to mind when processing that information is what the respondent has to use to devise an answer. This point can be illustrated with an electoral example. A question asks about two candidates who are unknown to the respondent, and it includes information about the party of each of the candidates. The respondent has no node—hence no affect—for the candidates. But there will be nodes for the parties and other nodes that are connected to the nodes for the parties. The affect connected with these nodes becomes the answer of the respondent. Without having thought about the candidates before the question was asked, the respondent is able to construct an answer on the spot. The respondent may (or may not) learn the name of the candidates, which would include beginning to establish affect for the candidates. A question about going to war with Iraq, asked immediately after the Iraqi invasion of Kuwait, would work much the same way. Even if the person had not thought about going to war with Iraq, he or she is likely to have thought about going to war and to have feelings about that, and those feelings might be conditioned by apparent ease of victory. If you have never heard of Iraq, a reasonable surmise is that it is not a militarily powerful country. Hence, the U.S. military might well be able to defeat Iraq with little loss of life.

Again, the respondent is able to construct an answer on the spot, based on prior cognitive processing. In either of these examples, the response will be quite sensitive to the information in the question. If the question includes information on the candidates' positions on a policy issue, that may well produce different responses than would the question that included information on party. If the question says that the Iraqi army is the fourth-largest in the world, that may change the answer to the question about going to war. The theory does not suggest that respondents always have to construct an answer on the spot. On-line processing is an ongoing activity. During an election campaign, people receive hundreds, or even thousands, of communications about the candidates. For each communication, the person is learning, as specified earlier, and in the process forming an impression of the candidates. At the end of the campaign, when asked about the preferred candidate, the respondent does not have to review what he or she knows about the candidate. The respondent can simply compare the impressions formed of the candidates and select the one for whom the impression is most favorable. The respondent cannot know all of the communications that led to the impressions. There are too many. As Milton Lodge (in this volume) emphasizes, much of that information was not learned. In on-line processing, the communication contributes to the affect toward the candidate and the information is thrown away.

It is important to note that a question about candidate choice is a rather special case. The choices are fixed, both for those who write the questions and for the respondent. Question writers have more latitude when asking about policies—going to war with Iraq, for example. When "continuing economic sanctions" is included in the question, it is a different question than one that does not include " continuing economic sanctions."

Did the respondents have one opinion about going to war with Iraq? As many opinions as there were questions? Or did they have even more than that? What I have tried to show, in developing this computational model, is that having an opinion is not a very satisfactory way to understand answering questions. It is the language of "having" that leads to the puzzle. All of our opinions are constructed. Some are constructed on the spot when we have not thought about the subject very much. The theory of answering questions and the model of the theory are one way of understanding how we can construct opinions on the spot. But answering questions with which we have much practice, that we have been considering for a lifetime—and hence, have immediate and firm answers ready for the question—are equally understood as a process accounted for by the theory. The flexibility in the responses is as much the result of the what-comes-to-mind as it is of the information in the question. The more we know—the more fully developed the network for a subject—the more flexibly we can address a subject. A person well informed about a subject will be able to answer an indefinite number of questions about the subject. Once you begin to think about the process of answering questions, the urge to think about a well-informed person as having an indefinite number of opinions fades.

Conclusion

The theory of *hot cognition* that Milton Lodge and I have developed has been put to work as a theory and computational model of a survey respondent answering questions. It is a theory and model of the process of answering questions. We are driven to a process model to account for anomalies increasingly apparent in our understanding of survey responses. In the limited domain in which we have put it to work, it performs rather well. But some of the limits of the theory should be noted.

The theory and model developed here cannot perform as simple a cognitive task as adding two and two. It is limited to spreading activation and affect. This is not a necessary restriction on the theory. In this version, the nodes have been limited to what would ordinarily be called declarative knowledge; though our version incorporates affect, which is not ordinarily included in declarative knowledge. One extension of the theory would include nodes that permitted more elaborate reasoning than involved in spreading activation—rules for adding, for example. In research on congressional committees, I have constructed computational models that do more elaborate information processing than this model can perform (Boynton 1990a, for example). These models can also answer questions, but the nodes are if-then statements or "productions" in the language of cognitive science. For well-informed survey respondents, a model more elaborate than spreading activation probably should be devised. After all, a professor of political science might be called upon to answer questions, and we are pretty sure that our reasoning is not limited to spreading activation through a network of declarative knowledge—though that will be an important facet of the process by which we answer questions.

Computational models need not be limited to models of cognition. Most of the computational models constructed by political scientists have been theories of international relations. The Alker and Christensen (1972) model of U.N. peace keeping was one of the first—self-consciously—computational models in political science. More recently, Alker, Duffy, Hurwitz, and Mallery (1991) have developed a computational model of language processing. Sanjoy Banerjee (1991) theorizes about the reproduction of perceptions during a period of the Cold War. Valerie Hudson (1991) has produced a model of the interaction of nations as comparative foreign policy. And Philip Schrodt (1987) has been developing models of pattern matching and categorization, using events data from international interactions as the database.

What these models have in common is not cognition, though many of the researchers have been influenced by artificial-intelligence programming. What they have in common is process. Each is theorizing and modeling process. We theorize about process quite often in studying politics, but our models are frequently not appropriate to the theorizing. There is no process in property-space analysis. Computational modeling is one way to bring our models into line with our theorizing.

NOTES

1. I will use "opinions" in the rest of the paper, instead of shifting between the different locutions.

2. Current research on brain activity also supports this conception of memory. See Philip J. Hilts, "Photos Show Mind Recalling a Word X-Ray Data Yield Surprises on Workings on Memory," *New York Times,* 11 November 1991, A1, A6.

CHAPTER 11

Answering Survey Questions: The Measurement and Meaning of Public Opinion

Stanley Feldman

When Thurstone (1927) began his pathbreaking work on the measurement of attitudes, he proceeded from an explicit model of how survey responses are generated from the attitudes people hold. Drawing upon research in psychophysics, Thurstone argued that reactions to a stimulus (attitude statement) elicit a discriminal process on some psychological dimension. His assumptions about the nature of this discriminal process allowed him to develop his law of comparative judgment, which permits a series of attitude statements to be located (scaled) along a single dimension. Thurstone, thus, produced a measurement model in which psychological reactions to attitude statements were explicitly linked to responses to the attitude question.

With confidence that attitudes could be measured, and the survey questionnaire as a perfect vehicle for reaching large numbers of respondents, researchers quickly devised survey questions to measure almost every imaginable mental entity, in almost every conceivable subject area. More recently, increasingly sophisticated methodological tools have been used in the analysis of survey responses: models for unidimensional and multidimensional scaling, factor models, latent trait models, and covariance structure models, to name just some of the most prominent. However, as survey research gained in popularity, the initial concern in Thurstone's work with modeling the processes generating survey responses diminished greatly.[1] Researchers have generally been content to use survey responses as direct indicators of unobserved psychological constructs, recognizing that survey questions may be affected by random and systematic measurement error, but only occasionally attempting to explicitly deal with the consequences of these errors for statistical estimation.

The Fragility of Survey Responses

Fairly early in the history of survey research, practitioners recognized that responses to attitude and opinion questions are subject to the influence of

249

relatively minor changes in wording, question order, and response options (see Rugg 1941). These findings have motivated a great deal of research using experimental designs to study the effects of questionnaire structure on survey responses (see, for example, Schuman and Presser 1981). Although many of these "response effects" result in small changes in marginal distributions, the effects can sometimes be substantial. Perhaps the best-documented case comes from a pair of questions on Communist and American newspaper reporters (Schuman and Presser 1981). When asked "Do you think the United States should let Communist newspaper reporters from other countries come in here and send back to their papers the news as they see it?" 37 percent (in 1948) said yes. When this question was preceded by one asking if American reporters should be allowed to report the news from communist countries, like Russia, yes responses to the Communist reporters question increased to 73 percent. Response effects are almost never this large, but they are frequently observed.

Many careful studies have illustrated the consequences of question wording, question placement, numbers of response categories, and other such factors on marginal and multivariate distributions. This research has produced valuable results on the susceptibility of certain survey questions to various context effects. But, thus far, this literature has failed to develop general principles that can be used to predict when such effects will occur. Often context effects seem to be question-specific, and sometimes even reliable effects fail to replicate from one experiment to another (Schuman and Presser 1981, 317–24). Converse and Presser (1986, 41) note that "Even small changes in wording can shift the answers of many respondents, but it is frequently difficult to predict in advance whether a wording change will have such an effect." There is no question that this experimental research has contributed to our understanding of survey questions and public opinion. However, after having examined "several hundred experiments in 344 surveys," Schuman and Presser (1981, 307) conclude: "Experiments do not always produce interpretable results, nor always cumulate to yield general conclusions, nor always even replicate well." What is lacking is a general understanding of when these effects will occur, and how large they will be.

A second well-known problem (embarrassment?) with answers to survey questions is response instability. Although Converse (1964) was not the first to discover that responses to survey questions often show a great deal of inconsistency across waves of panel data (see Kendall 1954), social scientists have been acutely aware of this issue since his 1964 paper on mass belief systems. How are we to interpret the large random component to most political issue questions? The phenomenon of response inconsistency is perhaps the best example of the inability to settle key problems with survey data in the absence of a model of underlying process. The basic characteristics of the data are largely agreed upon. From several sets of data, we know that there is little or no systematic attitude change on most issues (but see Smith 1984b). There is, however, a stochastic component that is as large as 60 percent of the observed variance of some questions (Achen 1975; Erikson 1979).

The problem is that different sets of (untested) assumptions lead to alternative statistical models that yield very different conclusions. Two interpretations are prominent in the literature: nonattitudes (attitude crystallization) and measurement error. Each interpretation generates a statistical model that appears to fit the data well (see, for example, Converse 1970; Erikson 1979; Brody 1986; Feldman 1989). Yet neither model is derived from a theoretical understanding of the survey-response process. The nonattitudes model simply assumes that people with real attitudes will give error-free responses to survey questions. Any temporal inconsistency can, thus, be attributed to other people providing interviewers with nonattitudes. The measurement-error model assumes that the stochastic component of the responses, i.e., that part of the temporal variation that deviates from a simple model of true attitude change, is random measurement error, as defined in the test theory literature: normally distributed response error around the true score.[2]

At the same time that both models appear to fit the data extremely well, there is empirical evidence that contradicts both accounts.[3] Contrary to the assumptions of the measurement-error model, response inconsistency *is* related to measures of political information and sophistication (Zaller 1990; Feldman 1989; Norpoth and Lodge 1985).[4] Contrary to the nonattitudes model, response inconsistency is not directly predicted by attitude centrality or salience (Feldman 1989). And response error is still substantial, even among those highest in political information (Zaller 1990; Feldman 1989; Norpoth and Lodge 1985). In this case, goodness-of-fit statistics do not appear to be of much assistance. Not only do two very different models fit the same data well, but *neither* appears to survive straightforward tests of key predictions.

The nonattitudes (or attitude crystallization) model now seems to fail in another important respect: it does not successfully predict susceptibility to response effects in surveys. Despite obvious predictions that context effects in surveys ought to be much less pronounced among those with crystallized attitudes than among those likely to hold nonattitudes, two re-analyses of many experiments have failed to find substantial evidence for the hypothesis (Krosnick and Schuman 1988; Bishop 1990).[5] The measurement-error model is of no help at all in understanding response effects. If the model makes any prediction at all, it is that there should be no systematic response effects, since variations from true attitudes are simply random. With estimates of almost perfectly stable true scores over four-year intervals, how can properties of the measurement instrument produce significant changes in responses? Even if one of these models were to successfully explain response instability, we would apparently need at least one other model to account for the other sources of variability in survey responses.

True Scores and Errors

The development of a model of response error requires a criterion for the observation of "error." This typically starts with a definition of the hypothetical variable to be measured. What is the nature of the mental entity that we are trying to observe with survey questions? Implicit or explicit in most accounts and models of measurement error in survey data is the concept of a *true score*. From the perspective of true-score models, what we are trying to measure with our question(s) is a stable attribute of the individual that exists independent of the measurement instrument. Thus, party identification, attitude toward Bill Clinton, evaluations of personal financial well-being, and opinion on increases in taxes all exist somewhere in memory, waiting to be measured. Both the nonattitudes and measurement-error models assume that true scores really exist. That is, people (all or some) really have fixed opinions on these issues.

The concept of a true score has a very fuzzy history in the psychometric and survey literature. Some assume that Platonic true scores really exist. However, there is almost never a psychological interpretation of the true score. In most cases, the assumption is justified on the basis of the utility of true scores for defining and estimating measurement error. Given a true score, measurement error is simply the difference between the true score and obtained response. The difficulties with this position are sometimes recognized, but quickly dismissed, as can be seen in the following introduction to a discussion on measurement error in surveys:

> Let us assume that for each individual covered by the survey there is an individual true value (ITV). This value is quite independent of the survey, of the way the question is asked and by whom. If we ask the respondent how old he is, there is one unique correct answer; if we ask him how much he spent on chocolate last week there is again a unique correct answer. It is true that many questions are not so simple and— for instance with opinion questions—it would often be difficult to define the ITV. However, this difficulty is beside the point here. (Moser and Kalton 1972, 378)

Others define true scores statistically (Lord and Novick 1968). The true score for an item (or series of items) is the expectation of an infinite number of responses to that question. The statistical definition avoids the question of exactly what the mental representation of a true score is (if there is one). It is easy, however, to slip into the trap of believing that the statistical concept is a real one. Moreover, if the true score is the mean of the distribution of responses obtained from repeated responses, what is the proper interpretation of the variance of this distribution? If it were simply due to imperfections in the measurement instrument, then the mean is, in fact, estimating a Platonic true score, and we are back to the previous position.

Another basis for establishing true scores is to posit a set of survey procedures and then define measurement error as the difference between the observed response and the response that would have been obtained if the survey procedures were carried out "correctly" (see Lessler 1984). Although this strategy seemingly avoids the need to conceptually define true scores, it is not apparent how measurement error of this sort can be operationally estimated for subjective phenomena like attitudes and opinions. How do we know if survey conditions are really carried out correctly?

The problem with applying the true-score concept to attitude and opinion measurement is not simply that it is difficult to operationalize. The lack of a psychological understanding or justification of true scores means that measurement models for surveys based on true scores start from a precarious position. Despite the problems of defining true scores for subjective phenomena, the common understanding of attitudes and opinions is that true scores really do exist. This is clear in both the nonattitudes and measurement-error models. The nonattitudes model assumes that there are real opinions and that they are reported without error when they exist. The noise appears when those without real opinions attempt to give substantive responses. The measurement-error model more closely follows a true-score model, and assumes that survey questions are fallible measures of true opinions. Real opinions are widespread, and the noise is in the survey questions. The key question for both models is: To what extent is it reasonable to assume that true scores exist independently of the measurement instrument?

Without a better understanding of this problem, it is difficult to know how to justify the choice of measurement models for survey data. Suppose you were interested in studying response stability and response error in panel data. One option would be to use a single-indicator model, like that in Wiley and Wiley (1970). Observed responses for each question are modeled as a function of a true score *for that question* and random measurement error (see Erikson 1979; Achen 1983; Feldman 1989). The true scores are then assumed to be related across the panel waves in a simple autoregressive manner: the true score at time t is a linear function of the true score at $t - 1$ plus a random disturbance term. An alternative to this single-indicator approach would be to assume that several questions measure the same construct and use a factor analytic approach. In this case, there is *one true score* for all of the questions (at each point in time) and a residual factor for each question that includes random error and unique item variance. Although the same questions often can be analyzed in both ways, the assumptions are very different. There is also no guarantee that similar conclusions will result (Saris and Van Den Putte 1988). The problem is that there is currently no theoretical basis for choosing among competing statistical models of survey responses; this would require an understanding of the relationship between the "true scores" and the survey responses.

Much statistical firepower has been directed at the response-instability issue, and hundreds of experiments have been designed to shed light on the problem of response effects. Is it likely that more work of this type will provide the understanding of responses to survey questions that has not yet emerged from all this research? The answer seems to be no. In the conclusion of their analysis of experimental work on response effects, Schuman and Presser (1981, 313) argue: "What is needed most is theoretically directed research, but exactly what this means is not so clear." Although Schuman and Presser were skeptical of the utility of theories in cognitive and social psychology for directing research on the nature of the survey response, an impressive body of research has developed in the ten years since Schuman and Presser's book that draws directly on those theories. This research provides a very different understanding of the survey response than the implicit model that underlies much of the empirical work that uses survey data. In the end, it may also require that we alter our view of the nature of public opinion.

A New View of the Survey Response

The standard view of the survey response is that when a respondent is asked a question, she simply recalls the "true score" required by the question (assuming that it does exist; i.e., that there is an attitude, rather than a nonattitude) and reports that value. Should we believe this to be an accurate representation of the process of answering survey questions? It would mean that people carry around in their heads preformed answers to virtually all of the types of questions that survey researchers are capable of constructing. Every time a survey question is asked, the respondent would have a response to the question already stored in memory. Even if this were true, we also have to believe that respondents are able to quickly recall all of these preexisting responses under the time pressure and low relevance of a survey. This does not seem very plausible.

If the face validity of this "model" appears suspect, it is also challenged by recent attempts to construct cognitive models of the survey response (see Tourangeau 1984; Tourangeau and Rasinski 1988; Hippler, Schwarz, and Sudman 1987; Zaller and Feldman 1992). These models start by assuming that answering a survey question is, in principle, no different from answering any other type of question. Thus, responding to a question about Bill Clinton's handling of the economy is structurally no different than answering a question on a final exam in a political science course or responding to a question on who the best pitcher in baseball is. This approach forces us to consider exactly what respondents are doing when we ask them to answer our survey questions. This process cannot yet be specified precisely. Moreover, as will be seen, there is still a substantial gap between understanding the structure of the response process and having sufficient information to predict responses to particular questions. However, enough is known of the cognitive processes involved in question answering to suggest what a cognitive model of the survey response should look like, and to guide future research on this subject.

It has become the norm in discussions of the cognitive models of the survey response to divide the response process into four steps: interpreting the question, searching for information, formulating the answer, and reporting the response. In practice, it is not at all clear that these are discrete steps. For example, interpretation may determine the information that is recalled, and the resulting answer may be strictly determined by that information. It is nonetheless useful to maintain these distinctions for analytic purposes. Several detailed discussions of these new models of the survey response are available (see Tourangeau 1984; Hippler, Schwarz, and Sudman 1987). The following discussion will focus on those aspects of the process of question answering that are most central to understanding the statistical properties of the survey response and the interpretation of public opinion. In particular, I will give the greatest attention to interpretation and information retrieval, since they are the most distinctive aspects of this approach and are particularly relevant for understanding response effects and attitude instability.

Interpretation

As a general proposition, it seems perfectly straightforward to assume that interpretation is a necessary first condition for answering a question. It is difficult to give a reasoned answer to a question that is not understood (although Converse might argue that responses are frequently given to survey questions that are not fully comprehended). It is also easy to imagine how variations in interpretations of a question can lead to very different responses. The importance of interpretation to responses to survey questions can be appreciated by considering research on reading comprehension. A large body of work shows how broad interpretative frameworks—often labeled frames, scripts, or schemata—strongly influence the way people understand the meaning of a text. In one such demonstration (Anderson et al. 1977), two groups of students were presented with two passages to read. Each passage could be given at least two different interpretations. The first could be interpreted as either a prisoner planning a prison escape or a wrestler attempting to break the hold of an opponent. The second could be seen as a description of either a group of friends getting together to play cards or a rehearsal of a woodwind ensemble. The subjects were male students from weight-lifting classes and female students who were working toward a degree in music education. As expected, interpretations of the two passages were strongly related to the backgrounds of the students. The study also found that the subjects usually gave each passage one distinct interpretation. There was little evidence that the subjects were simultaneously able to see each passage from both perspectives. Having located one interpretation, there is apparently no desire (or ability) to generate alternative perspectives.

It may not be so surprising that these results hold for reading ambiguous text; their applicability to survey questions may be more doubtful. It is a common (and commonsensical) recommendation in most texts on survey methods to make questions as clear and unambiguous as possible. Assuming that researchers strive to do just that, is there reason to believe that variations in interpretation will be substantial? The answer seems to be yes. The best (and most disturbing) evidence comes from a series of studies reported by Belson (1981). Using postinterview intensive debriefing, Belson found that people *commonly* misunderstood and misinterpreted seemingly straightforward survey questions. In fact, relatively few respondents seemed to interpret the questions in exactly the way they were intended. These results are especially disconcerting, since many of the items Belson examined were fairly simple recall questions regarding media use. A priori, most researchers would believe that these questions are less subject to multiple interpretations than attitude or opinion questions.

The existence of ambiguity in survey questions is probably a fact of life. Language is simply not capable of communicating a single unambiguous message. Consider the following survey question: How difficult is it to obtain drugs in this neighborhood? (With appropriate fixed response categories.) Embedded in a survey on crime, it will likely be interpreted to ask about the ease of buying crack in a nearby alley. In a health survey, the same question would generate responses about the location of the nearest pharmacy (Strack and Martin 1987).

Research by Fee (1981) provides a nice example of the sources of ambiguity in opinion questions. She focused on multiple word meanings, specifically the case of "big government." Using a combination of open-ended questions followed by specially constructed closed-ended questions, Fee found that there were at least four different interpretations of big government. Each of these interpretations had a distinct pattern of relationships with demographic and political variables. As Fee (1981, 72) notes, "words, like 'big business,' 'liberal,' or 'Democrat,' evoke different reactions from different respondents; yet they are the interesting stuff of politics and life in general." It is difficult to imagine constructing valid opinion questions without using the symbols common to political rhetoric. Yet, those symbols are inherently ambiguous (Edelman 1964; Graber 1976). So, too, must be the survey questions.

Fee's findings show that interpretations of words like *government* can vary substantially from person to person. Zaller and Feldman (1992) show that multiple interpretations of a survey question can appear in repeated responses of a single individual. Using open-ended probes of standard National Election Studies issue questions obtained from a two-wave panel study, Zaller and Feldman found changes in reported thoughts about the issues indicative of different interpretations of the issue questions. Response stability across the two waves of the panel was then correlated with a measure of ambivalence—the extent to which respondents reported thoughts supporting both sides of the issue. Two versions of the ambivalence measure were constructed: one that measured ambivalence across the two waves and another that only took into account responses on the first wave. Response instability was strongly related to the global measure of ambivalence, and not at all related to the first wave measure. Ambivalence due to changes in considerations from wave 1 to wave 2 accounted for all of the correlation between response instability and total ambivalence. These findings indicate that response instability in panel data derives, to a great extent, from the activation of different interpretations across repeated interviews. (Zaller and Feldman found apparent variations in interpretations in panel waves spaced only one month apart.)

These results suggest that when respondents are presented with a survey question, the first thing they do (most likely automatically) is to activate an interpretative framework (script, frame, schema) to make sense of the question. Most respondents are able to draw from multiple (but not unlimited) interpretations, but only one is activated at any point in time. Once an interpretation is activated, much of the variation in information search may be eliminated. Information consistent with the interpretation is considered, inconsistent information is never examined.

Information Search

Given an interpretation of the question, how does the respondent go about finding an answer? An obvious strategy is to search for the preexisting judgment specified in the question (as interpreted). That is, to directly recall the opinion or attitude required. It was previously argued—on the basis of face validity—that this is an unrealistic model to apply to most respondents on many survey questions. A more direct treatment of mechanisms of memory and recall reinforces this conclusion.

Most models of memory distinguish between long-term and short-term (or working) memory. Long-term memory has almost unlimited capacity to store information. Only a very small portion of the contents of long-term memory can be accessed at any point in time. Short-term memory contains that small portion of long-term memory that we are consciously aware of at any given moment. Information in long-term memory is typically represented as a "node" on a graph, with links, or associations, indicating relationships among the nodes. (For good introductions to associative memory models, see Hastie 1986, 1987.) Information is accessed by the principle of spreading activation: once a particular node (piece of information) is activated by some cue, activation spreads along the links to other nearby nodes. The stronger the connection (association), the more likely that one node will be activated by another.

There are two key points about memory retrieval that are central to understanding survey responses. First, since long-term memory is very capacious, it can be difficult to quickly locate any specific bit of information, unless the connection between the cue and the correct node is very strong. Second, retrieval from long-term memory is probabilistic (Raaijmakers and Shiffrin 1980). For any particular cue, there is a set of probabilities that define the likelihood of retrieving information associated with that cue. If these characteristics of memory retrieval are accepted, they lead to a conclusion that is contrary to an assumption of direct recall of responses to survey questions. As Reeder (1982, 252) argues, "fact retrieval (trying to find an assertion in memory) is often less efficient than computing plausibility (or inferring) and . . . it is not always the first strategy employed in sentence verification." Reeder further asserts that:

> In everyday life it is unlikely that all facts or even the majority of facts on which people are queried are directly stored in memory. Further, memory is a rich, highly redundant store of information. Searching for

any specific proposition may not be much easier than searching for a needle in a haystack. Therefore, it is often faster to select the first few relevant facts found in memory (and compute the answer) than to continue to search until an exact match can be found (1982, 252).

The nature of the survey process almost certainly exacerbates the tendency to limit the memory search process. Whether interviewed in person or over the phone, most respondents are probably quite intent on finishing the interview as quickly as possible. Short of ejecting the interviewer from the house or hanging up the phone, the best way to rapidly conclude the interview is to provide responses to the questions as quickly as possible. This decreases the likelihood that long memory searches will take place, and suggests that respondents will probably answer survey questions on the basis of the first thing or things that they recall (see Zaller and Feldman 1992).[6]

This leads to the conclusion that survey questions are *inherently* noisy measures. Stochastic variation is introduced, first through the availability of multiple interpretations of the question and then through an incomplete and probabilistic memory search. It is not clear that "better questions" would ever be able to eliminate this variability. It is possible, however, that variability at the retrieval stage can be reduced by encouraging a more systematic memory search.

A strategy to do this was developed and tested by Zaller and Feldman (1992). One half of the respondents in a split-half survey design were presented with three standard NES issue questions asked in the normal manner. The other half of the respondents were asked the same questions but, *before they were allowed to answer,* were required to "stop and think" about the question. Specifically, they were asked to report what came to their mind as they thought about each component of the issue questions. Analysis showed that the relationship between responses to the issue questions and location on a general measure of political ideology was twice as large for the stop-and-think group than for those who gave "top of the head" responses; but only for those in the top 40 percent of a measure of political information. If memory search was already extensive, or if people directly recalled their opinions, there should have been little or no effect of the stop-and-think manipulation.

It is also significant that the effect of the stop-and-think manipulation was evident for the most informed in the sample. It is generally assumed that these are the people most likely to have "true attitudes." Converse's nonattitudes model assumes that these opinions are reported to interviewers with little or no error. If that were true, the stop-and-think manipulation should have the *least* affect on these people. However, we observe just the opposite. Letting the most informed people think a bit more about their response before answering the question substantially increased the relationship between the expressed issue position and the respondent's overall ideological position. If we believe that this relationship will be strong for those with high levels of political information, we must, therefore, conclude that the standard operating conditions of surveys result in noisy responses, even for the most politically sophisticated. The stop-and-think manipulation should have reduced the noise in the responses only if these people were engaging in a memory-search process that could be improved by additional retrieval time.

Retrieval of information from long-term memory may be probabilistic, but that does not mean that it is random. To the contrary, information is assumed to vary in its *accessibility* to recall. Accessibility is believed to be a function of factors, including recency, frequency, and salience (see Bargh et al. 1986; Higgins and King 1981; Bodenhausen and Wyer 1987; Krosnick 1989). Thus, even if a person has absorbed no new information over a period of time, responses to survey questions—-and, therefore, our observation of public opinion—may change because of systematic alterations of the accessibility of information relevant to answering those questions.

The phenomenon of *priming* derives from the effect of recency of activation on the accessibility of information. Categories or information that have been recently used are more likely to be retrieved in response to a new question. Therefore, the previous retrieval of information increases the likelihood that it will influence subsequent questions. Priming is an important component of a model of the survey response, because it helps to explain context effects in surveys. These context effects may occur when items preceding a survey question alter the interpretation of the question and/or the considerations that are retrieved in response to that question. Experimental studies of question-order effects (Tourangeau and Rasinski 1988; Tourangeau et al. 1989a) have found evidence consistent with the priming hypothesis. It is important to keep in mind, however, that priming cannot generate any desired response. If a particular piece of information is not at all available in memory, attempting to prime it will have no effect on the response. Priming can only increase the likelihood that an already-existing node in memory will be activated.

Formulating the Answer

Having recalled information relevant to the question, the respondent must then use it to compute a response to the question. This is an issue, first, of how the information that has been recalled is combined to produce a single implication, and then of how that judgment is translated into the desired response.

Any problems of combining information will be conveniently eliminated if the memory search ends very quickly—after the first relevant consideration has been recalled. Zaller and Feldman (1992) speculate that, under
the pressure of quickly responding to each question, it is distinctly possible
that people may use the first thing that comes to mind to construct a response. However, while the limitations of working memory suggest that
respondents will probably not recall more than 7 (plus or minus 2) discrete
bits of information in response to a question, it also seems likely that a
memory search may result in the activation of more than one piece of
information. Although crudely measured, Zaller and Feldman (1992) find
that people report, on average, about 3 or 4 distinct thoughts after responding to an NES issue question. This suggests that people must frequently
combine recalled information in order to arrive at a single judgment. There
is no substantial empirical evidence on how survey respondents do this.
However there are at least two bodies of theory and research that provide a
basis for thinking about this.

Information-integration theory (Anderson 1974) argues that people
combine multiple pieces of information into a single judgment, through the
use of simple algebraic rules. In particular, it appears as if social information
is combined according to a simple averaging model (see Lodge in this
volume). Although these rules for information integration appear to be
widely applicable, they are most easily applied in situations that require a
simple affective judgment. Some survey questions do require nothing more
than a statement of overall affect—for example, feeling thermometer and
good-bad semantic differential type questions. However, many other questions ask for more complicated judgments, opinions, probabilities, and so
on. Simple algebraic rules may not suffice.

Another body of research that may be useful in understanding how
respondents combine discrepant information into particular survey responses
is the literature on cognitive heuristics and biases (Kahneman, Slovic, and
Tversky 1982; Nisbett and Ross 1980). Heuristics like availability, representativeness, and anchoring and adjustment may come into play as respondents
answer different types of survey questions (Tourangeau 1984; Strube 1987).
There is no shortage of research documenting the existence of these heuristics and cognitive biases. What is lacking are studies of what role these play
in answering survey questions.

Choosing a Response

The respondent's task does not end with the mental formulation of a judgment. The response must be given to the interviewer, or at least written
down on paper. For the common closed-ended questions, the respondent

must choose a specific response category from the alternatives presented. It is at this point that two traditional categories of survey "error" likely emerge: random-measurement (instrument) error and social-desirability bias.

In the case of open-ended questions, respondents can simply report their answers to the survey questions to interviewers verbatim. Since most survey questions are of the fixed-choice variety, respondents must select one of the presented options. Even if the respondent knows what her evaluation of the question is, she must still figure out which response category is most appropriate. To the extent that the meaning of the response alternatives is hazy, the choice of a response will be probabilistic. Achen's (1975) model of measurement error in survey responses is based on the response categories being perceived as distributions, rather than fixed points. Over repeated presentations, perfectly stable evaluations will exhibit instability, due to variability in perceptions of the response categories.

There is a body of experimental research that has examined the effects of using open-ended versus fixed-choice response formats and of varying the nature of the response alternatives. This work has been largely exploratory—there are few, if any, explicit hypotheses being tested—but the results indicate that response format can have an effect on the distribution of responses (Schuman and Presser 1981). Researchers are now beginning to consider the effects of response formats from a cognitive perspective: what information do the response alternatives provide the respondent and how do the presented alternatives structure the response process (see Ostrom 1987; Strack and Martin 1987; Schwarz and Hippler 1987)?

Two different types of evidence show that the structure of response alternatives have an effect on measurement error. Using a large data base of survey questions with alternative formats and response options, Andrews (1984) concludes that error variance is, in part, a function of the nature and number of response alternatives. His design does not permit an estimate of the error inherent in the ambiguity of the response options. Belson (1981) examined this problem using in-depth follow-up interviews with survey respondents. He found a substantial amount of "misunderstanding" of the meaning of the response options. It is clear from his data that respondents' perceptions of the response options (as well as other components of the question) would likely vary considerably in repeated administrations.

Social-desirability problems arise when respondents begin to edit their choice of a response option. If this editing is a function of the characteristics of the interviewer, it is often called an interviewer bias instead. The effect of social desirability has been studied and debated in the survey literature for well over thirty years. There is not sufficient space here to even summarize the research and conclusions.[7] The major point to keep in mind is that however automatic interpretation and retrieval may be, respondents have full control over the response they give to the interviewer. Evidence of social desirability and interviewer effects are prevalent enough to remind researchers that respondents can be influenced—sometimes to a substantial degree—by perceived reactions to their responses.

Types of Survey Questions

To this point, the discussion has given the possibly misleading impression that a single process governs responses to all survey questions. Having specified a memory-search model of question answering, it is now necessary to consider its applicability to various types of questions. As a starting point, we can distinguish three "types" of survey questions: questions of fact (i.e., age, education, income, retrospective vote reports), simple affective evaluations (affect toward candidates, parties, groups; "feeling thermometers"), and questions of "judgment" or belief (opinions, issue positions, perceptions of candidates or of the state of the economy). This categorization of types of survey questions is obviously quite loose, but it is a useful starting point for organizing our thinking about survey responses.

A sizable literature is developing on inaccuracies in the measurement of facts, and ways to improve survey measures of such variables (see Loftus, Fienberg, and Tanur 1985; Strube 1987). This type of response does fall into the general domain of the memory-search model just discussed. Sometimes these questions require access to very simple information (what was the last year of schooling you completed?) or single events (who did you vote for in the last presidential election?). In other cases, recall of multiple events is required (how many times in the past year have you attended a political rally?). Although there is a great deal of interesting work being done on questions like these, I will not pursue this any further in this paper. Questions of fact are generally not where political scientists are most worried about response error (although error in vote reports is a topic of great interest). The sorts of issues that arise with these types of questions are typically very different from those associated with questions of evaluations and judgments.[8]

Evaluations and judgments (beliefs) are distinguished because of recent research that examines the on-line processing of attitudes (Hastie and Park 1986; Lodge, McGraw, and Stroh 1989; Lodge in this volume). This research shows that evaluations are often uncorrelated with recall of the information that initially determined the evaluation. In order to account for this, it has been hypothesized that new information about a person or object is used to update a "judgment operator" that keeps a running tally of the evaluation—on-line. When an individual is called upon to make an evaluation of the person or object, the judgment operator is recalled, rather than the original information.

This model is very different from the memory-search model that has been discussed here. If the on-line processing model describes the way in which survey responses are generated, it would be a case in which the concept of a true score had a real psychological foundation. Survey measures of evaluations would therefore be quite reliable, since the vagaries of a probabilistic memory search would not be present. It is important to recognize, however, that these two models may not be making competing predictions. The on-line model is applicable to cases in which a simple *affective evaluation* is being constantly updated. Moreover, as Hastie and Park (1986) note, this updating will occur when the information is salient to people, and when they expect that they will have to offer an evaluation of the object.

This situation is likely to occur in politics primarily for salient political figures. Responses to survey questions that ask for purely affective judgments about politicians—like feeling thermometers—may be generated by directly accessing the on-line operator. This process would closely resemble the "true attitude" models. Even for evaluations of political figures, however, there may be limits to responses generated on-line. Following Hastie and Pennington (1989), the judgment operator may not be constantly updated for political figures that are not very salient to the respondent, or in cases in which the respondent does not expect to have to make a judgment about that person (if, for example, that person never votes or engages in political discussions). In addition, McGraw, Lodge, and Stroh (1990) have found that political sophistication increases the efficiency of on-line processing, while those low in sophistication appear to rely more on memory-based evaluations.

Many of the survey questions used by social scientists are not simple evaluations, but rather opinion or judgment questions. For political issues like guaranteed jobs, or the state of the economy, or even evaluations of government performance in many areas, there may not be a constantly updated judgment operator to recall. The "object" of these questions is often vague, abstract, or multidimensional, and it is unlikely that these issues will be salient enough to most people to generate such highly specific evaluations. Indeed, given recent discussions of the conditions for on-line processing (Hastie and Pennington 1989), it would be surprising if it applied to most opinion or judgment questions.

This discussion suggests that it may be misleading to assume that a single model of the survey response can account for responses to all survey questions. The single-minded application of *any* measurement or statistical model to all survey questions ignores the likelihood that there may be substantial differences in response processes. Thus, to the extent that the on-line processing model accounts for evaluations or simple affective judgments, true score models, like the Wiley and Wiley (1970) model for panel data, can be effectively used to estimate error variance and attitude change. In the absence of a similar understanding of true scores, the application of the same model to issue preferences may lead to uninterpretable parameter estimates.

For example, Feldman (1989)—using five-wave panel data from the 1976 election—found that the Wiley and Wiley measurement model fit responses to candidate evaluations very well. The error variances across a number of candidates were quite low, and did not vary much from candidate to candidate. Substantial amounts of true attitude change were also observed, as might be expected in the midst of a presidential election campaign. Application of the same model to issue preferences also resulted in statistically good fits, but estimates of the error variances were much higher and, more importantly, varied greatly across the issues. Overall, the results of the simple measurement model—which assumes true scores for each response—appeared much more "plausible" for candidate evaluations than for issue preferences.

Since it is not necessarily the case that responses based upon specific information and on-line evaluations are highly correlated (Hastie and Park 1986; Lodge, McGraw, and Stroh 1989; Pavelchak 1989) the response process that is used may have a significant effect on the observed survey response. For example, consider a survey question on welfare spending. Assume a respondent has a very negative attitude toward the category of welfare recipient. That respondent will almost certainly have negative beliefs about welfare and welfare recipients, but may very well also possess some sympathetic beliefs as well (the children of welfare recipients are being disadvantaged; people on welfare do not have sufficient education). Suppose we were to ask this respondent the same question on welfare spending many times (conveniently erasing the memory of having responded each time). If the survey question is answered directly from the general evaluation of welfare recipients, then the response will always be that welfare spending should be reduced. On the other hand, if the judgment is based on the attribute information, it is possible that some of the positive beliefs about welfare recipients may be recalled and influence the response in a positive direction (at least some of the time).

The nature of the response process should, therefore, influence the observed stability of responses. Answers to survey questions drawn from general (on-line) evaluations should be more stable over time than those constructed piecemeal from specific information. Since the information is likely to be at least somewhat heterogeneous (see Feldman and Zaller 1992; Zaller and Feldman 1992), sampling that information will produce a noisier response than invoking a single evaluation. We should thus find substantially less response instability for questions that elicit on-line responses than for those questions that are based on information-retrieval processes.

The Nature and Measurement of Public Opinion

The models and hypotheses discussed in this paper have formed the basis for a growing experimental literature on context effects (Tourangeau and Rasinski 1988; Tourangeau et al. 1989a; Bishop, Oldendick, and Tuchfarber 1982), response instability (Zaller and Feldman 1992), and responses to questions requiring factual recall (Strube 1987; Croyle and Loftus 1992; Abelson, Loftus, and Greenwald 1992). The results to date provide encouraging evidence that useful models of the survey response can be based on an examination of the cognitive processes of responding to questions. Many more studies are still needed to examine the complex interactions predicted by these models and, especially, to begin to estimate some of the basic parameters governing the response process. However, what has been missing in all of this is an appreciation of the larger implications of this approach for survey measurement and our understanding of the nature of public opinion.

There are several important conclusions that emerge if the cognitive response framework is taken seriously. The most obvious implication is that survey questions are inherently noisy measures. Stochastic variation is introduced, first through the availability of multiple interpretations of the question and then through an incomplete and probabilistic memory search. "Better questions" will never eliminate this variability.

This stochastic variation is not simply a problem for opinion measurement; it reshapes our basic understanding of the nature of opinions. Respondents do not answer opinion questions by directly recalling their opinion. Indeed, in this understanding of the survey response, opinions exist not as individual mental representations, but as *distributions of considerations—* the attitudes, beliefs, values, and information that can be retrieved in response to a question. Thus, typical survey methods that estimate the central tendency of this distribution tell only part of the story. It is also necessary to estimate the shape of the distribution: is this pool of potentially retrievable considerations homogeneous with respect to the final response (small variance), or do the considerations suggest ambivalence (large variance)? There is as much or more information in the shape of the distribution of considerations as in the central tendency. Yet, when we do obtain information about the shape (variance) of the opinion distribution, it is typically labeled error variance and considered nothing more than a threat to proper parameter estimation.

The concept of a distribution of considerations generating survey responses provides a new understanding of apparent attitude fluctuations in panel data. This response instability should derive in large part from the probabilistic nature of the response process—interpretation and then retrieval. Answers to an opinion question will vary across administrations except under two conditions: if the respondent does have a fixed opinion on an issue that can be consistently retrieved under survey conditions or if all of the considerations relevant to the survey question have identical implications. Instead of a dichotomous distinction between attitudes and nonattitudes, it is probably more useful to consider the variance of considerations with respect to an issue. As the considerations become more homogeneous, responses to survey questions will look like Converse's conception of real attitudes. The opinions of some activists on the abortion issue, for example, may approximate this condition. At the other extreme, very heterogeneous considerations will behave like nonattitudes. It is likely that most people's opinions on most issues will fall between these two extremes. Yet, even when opinions look most like nonattitudes, this framework suggests that the nonattitudes label may be something of a misnomer. Opinions based upon heterogeneous considerations may behave in capricious ways, but the underlying considerations can be quite real.

I have previously noted that priming—the effect of recency of activation on accessibility—provides an explanation for question-order effects in surveys. For the most part, these order effects, and other response effects, have been treated as methodological nuisances. The hope is that they do not appear in the experimental studies designed to detect them or that they can be eliminated by some aspect of survey construction. Given the model of the survey response developed here, it appears that response effects are inherent in the response process. However, it is possible to see this as more than just a methodological problem. If opinions are not fixed, then their expression—in a survey or some other interpersonal situation, or in the context of voting—will depend on the retrieval of particular considerations. Therefore, *anything* that affects accessibility will potentially influence the expression of opinion, whether on a survey or in "real life."

For example, Kinder and Sanders (1990) argue that the effects of changes in question wording can mimic the consequences of political debate for public opinion by altering the considerations that respondents use to generate an opinion. Their argument builds on the work of Gamson (Gamson and Lasch 1983; Gamson and Modigliani 1987) on the framing effects of political discussion—particularly in the media. Frames focus attention on specific dimensions (explanations) for understanding issues. In our terms, frames highlight connections between issues and particular considerations, increasing the likelihood that these considerations will be retrieved when thinking about the issue. Gamson shows how these frames develop and are transmitted through the media. Kinder and Sanders demonstrate that manipulating question wording to reflect alternative frames produces patterns of relationships in survey data consistent with the set of considerations elicited by those frames (wording).

Context effects in surveys that typically get labeled methodological artifacts are, thus, similar in structure to the priming of opinions by politicians and the mass media. In an important substantive example, Iyengar and Kinder (1987) show that even small changes in news coverage can alter the likelihood that certain considerations will be retrieved when people are asked to evaluate the president. Priming alters evaluations of the president, even though "beliefs" about the president may be unaffected by the media. Many context effects in surveys may work the same way.

It is important to recognize, however, that this perspective on public opinion does not imply that any response to a survey question is possible or that question wording or order can dramatically change the expressed opinions of all people. A distribution of considerations relevant to a survey question has an implied variance that can range from zero to infinity. Although there is evidence that many people have conflicting considerations underlying their opinions, the range of such conflict does not necessarily support any imaginable response. In the U.S. context, for example, we would not expect a person who is highly conflicted over social-welfare policy to endorse communism. In general, a set of considerations will generate a *range* of possible responses to questions on that topic. As the considerations become more heterogeneous, that range should increase.

Although developed from a very different perspective, this model of opinions closely resembles the social-judgment theory of Sherif and Hovland (1961). As in their attitude model, it may be useful to think of opinions as having a latitude of acceptance, a region of indifference, and a latitude of rejection. Policy positions that fall within the first region will be endorsed (perhaps depending on the framing of the question), while those that are encompassed by the later region will likely be opposed. The existence of the latitude of rejection indicates that not all policy options can be framed to obtain positive responses from a given individual. A critical issue in public-opinion research should therefore be the assessment of the width of the latitude of acceptance. What is the typical variance of considerations for people on different types of issues, and how much does it vary across people?

The distribution of considerations that generates opinion responses is also important from the perspective of politics and the shaping of public opinion. It is much easier to understand how "opinions" may change when seen from the perspective of the retrieval of heterogeneous considerations than by assuming that issue preferences are single-fixed values. The connection between priming in surveys and the political world suggests that response effects in surveys are important *opportunities* to study public opinion. Once we recognize that an "opinion" on an issue is generally a range of possible reactions, rather than a single point, multiple questions and question orders can be important tools in examining the entire distribution of opinion on an issue. These results can help us to better understand "opinion changes" in the real world as well. It is time to recognize that experimental studies of question wording and question-order effects can be substantive tools for understanding public opinion.

Further theory development is necessary to better specify the processes sketched out here. Much more empirical work is also necessary to determine the ability of these cognitive models to account for the properties of survey responses. Regardless of the outcome of future research, a major virtue of this approach is that it finally forces us to consider explicitly what a model of the survey response might look like. And, as I've tried to suggest here, these models may have major implications, not only for the measurement of public opinion and political attitudes, but also for the way we understand the phenomena themselves.

NOTES

An earlier version of this chapter was presented at the 1990 meeting of the American Political Science Association, San Francisco, August 30 to September 2. I would like to thank Kathleen Knight, Milton Lodge, Kathleen McGraw and Marco Steenbergen for their helpful comments.

1. These trends appear to be the result of a lack of concern with the theory of attitude measurement, an increased interest in the substance of public attitudes and opinions, and the conclusions of Likert and others that simple summated scales work as well as the more complex Thurstone techniques. For an excellent discussion of the early years of attitude measurement and survey research, see Converse (1987).

2. Achen (1975) did motivate his model of response instability from analyses of individual choice behavior and perceptual error. He began by partitioning response error into two sources: respondent inconsistency with respect to true preferences (nonattitudes) and vague questions; that is, problems in consistently understanding the scalar values of the response alternatives. Operationally, both sources of error are jointly estimated, and inferences about the two components are made indirectly, through a regression analysis on the residuals of the measurement model (estimated response error).

3. Until recently, it was not actually known how well these two models fit the

data, despite claims of excellent fits. Early applications of the measurement-error model relied on three-wave panel data which provides no excess degrees of freedom for evaluating goodness-of-fit (see Achen 1983). Feldman (1989) estimated the measurement-error model with five waves of data and found excellent fits across a wide range of issues. Applications of the nonattitudes (black/white) model have still been restricted to three-wave panel data. Final judgments of fit for this model should, thus, be reserved until more evidence comes in.

4. The first studies that examined the relationship between response instability and sophistication found no connection at all (Achen 1975; Erikson 1979). These null results appear to stem from the failure to adequately operationalize sophistication. Significant relationships are obtained when sophistication is measured directly, by levels of political information.

5. The one apparent exception to the pattern of null results is that the effect of providing a middle alternative is larger for those with less crystallized attitudes.

6. If responses to survey questions are ever directly recalled, they must be clearly formulated and very strongly associated with the cues used in the questions. Frequent rehearsal of the response is probably required. This is most likely to be found among some elites and political activists.

7. See DeMaio (1984) for a critical discussion of the effect of social desirability on survey responses.

8. For interesting discussions of what constitute "facts," and the problems of measuring "quasi facts," see Smith (1984a) and Bailar and Rothwell (1984).

Bibliography

Abelson, Robert P. 1968. Simulation of Social Behavior. In *The Handbook of Social Psychology.* 2d ed. Vol. 2, ed. Gardner Lindzey and Elliot Aronson. ed. Reading, Mass.: Addison-Wesley.

Abelson, Robert P., and Milton Rosenberg. 1958. Symbolic Psychologic: A Model of Attitude Cognition. *Behavioral Science* 3:1–13.

Abelson, Robert P., and Ariel Levi. 1985. Decision Making and Decision Theory. In *The Handbook of Social Psychology.* 3d ed. Vol. 1, ed. Gardner Lindzey and Elliot Aronson. New York: Random House.

Abelson, Robert P., Elizabeth Loftus, and Anthony G. Greenwald. 1992. Attempts to Improve the Accuracy of Self-Reports of Voting. In *Questions about Questions,* ed. Judith M. Tanur. New York, N.Y.: Russell Sage Foundation.

Abramowitz, Alan I., Albert D. Cover, and Helmut Norpoth. 1986. The President's Party in Midterm Elections: Going from Bad to Worse. *American Journal of Political Science* 30:562–76.

Achen, Christopher H. 1975. Mass Political Attitudes and the Survey Response. *American Political Science Review* 69:1218–23.

———. 1983. Towards Theories of Data. In *Political Science: The State of the Discipline,* ed. Ada W. Finifter. Washington, D.C.: American Political Science Association.

Ajzen, Icek. 1991. Attitudes and Thought Systems. In *Advances in Social Cognition.* Vol. 4, ed.Robert S. Wyer and Thomas K. Srull. Hillsdale, N.J.: Lawrence Erlbaum Associates.

Alba, Joseph W. and L. Hasher. 1983. Is Memory Schematic? *Psychological Bulletin* 93:203–31.

Aldrich, John. 1977. Electoral Choice in 1972: A Test of Some Theorems of the Spatial Model of Electoral Competition. *Journal of Mathematical Sociology* 5:215–37.

Aldrich, John H., and Richard D. McKelvey. 1977. A Method of Scaling with Applications to the 1968 and 1972 Presidential Elections. *American Political Science Review* 71:111–30.

Alker, Hayward R., Jr., and Cheryl Christensen. 1972. From Causal Modelling to Artificial Intelligence: the Evolution of a UN Peace-Making Simulation. In *Experimentation and Simulation in Political Science,* ed. J. Laponce and Paul Smoker. Toronto: The University of Toronto Press.

Alker, Hayward R., Jr, Gavan Duffy, Roger Hurwitz, and John Mallery. 1991. Text Modeling for International Politics: a Tourist's Guide to RELATUS. In *Artificial Intelligence and International Relations,* ed. Valerie Hudson. Boulder, Colo.: Westview Press.

Allison, Graham T. 1971. *Essence of Decision: Explaining the Cuban Missile Crisis.* Boston, Mass.: Little, Brown.

Allport, Gordon W. 1958. *The Nature of Prejudice*. Garden City, N.Y.: Doubleday and Company.

Anderson, John R. 1983. *The Architecture of Cognition*. Cambridge, Mass.: Harvard University Press.

———. 1990. *The Adaptive Character of Thought*. Hillsdale, N.J.: Lawrence Erlbaum Associates.

Anderson, John R., and Gordon H. Bower. 1973. *Human Associative Memory*. Washington, D.C.: Winston.

Anderson, Norman H. 1971. Integration Theory and Attitude Change. *Psychological Review* 78:171–206.

———. Information Integration Theory Applied to Attitudes About U.S. Presidents. *Journal of Educational Psychology* 64:1–8.

———. 1974. Information Integration Theory: A Brief Survey. In *Contemporary Developments in Mathematical Psychology: Vol. 2:Measurement, Psychophysics and Neural Information Processing*. Vol. 2, ed. David H. Krantz, Richard C. Atkinson, R. Duncan Luce and Patrick Suppes. San Francisco: Freeman.

———. 1981. *Foundations of Information Integration Theory*. New York: Academic Press

———. 1982. *Methods of Information Integration Theory*. New York: Academic Press.

———. 1988. A Functional Approach to Person Cognition. In *Advances in Social Cognition*, ed. Thomas Srull and Robert Wyer. Hillsdale, N.J.: Lawrence Erlbaum Associates.

———. 1989. Functional Memory and On-Line Attribution. In *On-Line Cognition in Person Perception*, ed. John N. Bassili. Hillsdale, N.J.: Lawrence Erlbaum Associates.

———. 1991. *Contributions to Information Integration Theory*. Vol. 1 and 2. Hillsdale, N.J.: Lawrence Erlbaum Associates.

Anderson, Norman H., and A. Barrios. 1961. Primacy Effects in Personality Impression Formation. *Journal of Abnormal and Social Psychology* 63:346–50.

Anderson, Norman H., and Stephen Hubert. 1963. Effects of Concomitant Recall on Order Effects in Personality Impression Formation. *Journal of Verbal Learning and Verbal Behavior* 2:379–91.

Anderson, Richard C., Ralph E. Reynolds, Diane L. Schallert, and Ernest T. Goetz. 1977. Frameworks for Understanding Discourse. *American Educational Research Journal* 14:367– 81.

Andrews, Frank M. 1984. Construct Validity and Error Components of Survey Measures. *Public Opinion Quarterly* 48:409–42.

Asch, Solomon. 1946. Forming Impressions of Personality. *Journal of Abnormal and Social Psychology* 41:258–90.

Axelrod, Robert. 1973. Schema Theory: An Information Processing Model of Perception and Cognition. *American Political Science Review* 67:1248–73.

Bailar, Barbara A., and Naomi D. Rothwell. 1984. Measuring Employment and Unemployment. In *Surveying Subjective Phenomena*, ed. Charles F. Turner and Elizabeth Martin. New York, N.Y.: Russell Sage Foundation.

Banerjee, Sanjoy. 1991. Reproduction of Perception and Decision in the Early Cold War. In *Artificial Intelligence in International Relations*, ed.Valerie Hudson. Boulder, Colo.: Westview Press.

Bargh, John. 1984. Automatic and Conscious Processing of Social Information. In *Handbook Of Social Cognition*. Vol. 3, ed. Robert S. Wyer and Thomas Srull. Hillsdale, N.J.: Lawrence Erlbaum Associates.

Bargh, John, R. N. Bond, W. J. Lombardy, and M. E. Tofa. 1986. The Additive Nature of Chronic and Temporary Construct Accessibility. *Journal of Personality and Social Psychology* 50:869–78.

Bargh, John, J. E. Litt, Felicia Pratto, and L. A. Spielman. 1988. On the Preconscious Evaluation of Social Stimuli. In *Proceedings of the XXIV International Congress of Psychology.* Vol. 3, ed. K. McConkey and A. Bennet, 1–57. Amsterdam: Elsevier/North-Holland.

———. 1988. Automatic Information Processing: Implications for Communication and Affect. In *Communication, Social Cognition, and Affect,* ed. Lewis Donohew, Howard E. Sypher, and E. Torry Higgins. Hillsdale, N.J.: Lawrence Erlbaum Associates.

Bargh, John, and Roman D. Thein. 1985. Individual Construct Accessibility, Person-Memory, and the Recall-Judgment Link. *Journal of Personality and Social Psychology* 49:1129–46.

Barsalou, Lawrence W. 1992. *Cognitive Psychology: An Overview for Cognitive Psychologists.* Hillsdale, N.J.: Lawrence Erlbaum Associates.

Bartlett, Frederick. 1932. *Remembering.* Cambridge: Cambridge University Press.

Barton, Allen H. 1955. The Concept of Property-space in Social Research. In *The Language of Social Research,* ed. Paul F. Lazarsfeld and Morris Rosenberg. Eds. New York: The Free Press.

Bassili, John N. 1989. *On-line Cognition in Person Perception.* Hillsdale, N.J.: Lawrence Erlbaum Associates.

Bassili, John N., and Joseph Fletcher. 1991. Response Time Measurement in Survey Research: A Method for CATI and a New Look at Nonattitudes. *Public Opinion Quarterly* 55:331–46.

Bassili, John N., and Marilyn C. Smith. 1986. On the Spontaneity of Trait Attribution: Converging Evidence for the Role of Cognitive Strategy. *Journal of Personality and Social Psychology* 50:239–45.

Beach, Lee R., and T. R. Mitchell. 1978. A Contingency Model for the Selection of Decision Strategies. *Academy of Management Review* 3:439–49.

Behr, Roy L., and Shanto Iyengar. 1985. Television News, Real-world Cues and Changes in the Public Agenda. *Public Opinion Quarterly* 49:38–57.

Bell, David E. 1982. Regret in Decision Making Under Uncertainty. *Operations Research* 30:961–81.

Belmore, Susan. 1987. Determinants of Attention During Impression Formation. *Journal of Experimental Psychology: Learning, Memory and Cognition* 13:480–89.

Belson, William A. 1981. *The Design and Understanding of Survey Questions.* London: Gower.

Bennett, W. Lance, and Bart Salisbury. 1987. Rational Choice: An Emerging Paradigm in Election Studies. *Research in Micropolitics* 2:1–30.

Berelson, Bernard. 1952. Democratic Theory and Public Opinion. *Public Opinion Quarterly* 16:313–30.

Berelson, Bernard, Paul Lazarsfeld, and William McPhee. 1954. *Voting: A Study of Opinion Formation in a Presidential Election.* Chicago: University of Chicago Press.

Berent, Matthew K. 1990. Attitude Importance and the Recall of Attitude Relevant Information. Master's Thesis, Ohio State University, Columbus.

Berns, Walter. 1954. Voting Studies. In *Essays on the Scientific Study of Politics,* ed. Herbert Storing. New York: Holt, Rinehart and Wilson.

Bettman, James R., Eric J. Johnson, and John W. Payne. 1990. A Componential Analysis of Cognitive Effort in Choice. *Organizational Behavior and Human Decision Processing* 45:111–39.

Bettman, James R., and Pradeep Kakkar. 1977. Effects of Information Presentation Format on Consumer Information Acquisition Strategies. *Journal of Consumer Research* 3:233–40.

Bettman, James R., and C. Whan Park. 1980. Effects of Prior Knowledge and Experience and Phase of the Choice Process on Consumer Decision Processes: A Protocol Analysis. *Journal of Consumer Research* 7:234–48.

Billings, R. S., and S. A. Marcus. 1983. Measures of Compensatory and Noncompensatory Decision Making Strategies: Judgment Versus Choice. *Organizational Behavior and Human Performance* 31:331–52.

Bishop, George. 1990. Issue Involvement and Response Effects in Public Opinion Surveys. *Public Opinion Quarterly* 54:209– 18.

Bishop, George, Robert Oldendick, and Alfred Tuchfarber. 1982. Political Information Processing: Question Order and Context Effect. *Political Behavior* 4:177–200.

Bloom, Howard S., and H. Douglas Price. 1975. Voter Response to Short-run Economic Conditions: The Asymmetric Effect of Prosperity and Recession. *American Political Science Review* 69:1240–54.

Blumer, Jay G., and Denis McQuail. 1969. *Television in Politics: Its Uses and Influence.* Chicago: University of Chicago Press.

Bockenholt, Ulf, Dietrich Albert, Michael Aschenbrenner, and Franz Schmalhofer. 1991. The Effects of Attractiveness, Dominance, and Attribute Differences in Information Acquisition in Multiattribute Binary Choice. *Organizational Behavior and Human Decision Processes* 49:258–81.

Bodenhausen, Galen V., and Robert S. Wyer. 1987. Social Cognition and Social Reality: Information Acquisition and Use in the Laboratory and the Real World. In *Social Information Processing and Survey Methodology,* ed. Hans J. Hippler, Norbert Schwarz and Seymour Sudman. New York, N.Y.: Springer-Verlag.

Boninger, David S., Matthew K. Berent, Jon A. Krosnick, and Leandre R. Fabrigar. n.d. Recent Research on Attitude Importance. In *Attitude Strength: Antecedents and Consequences: The Ohio State University Series on Attitudes and Persuasion.* Vol. 4, ed. Richard E. Petty and Jon A. Krosnick. Hillsdale, N.J.: Lawrence Erlbaum Associates.

Borgida, Eugene, and Beth Howard-Pitney. 1983. Personal Involvement and the Robustness of Perceptual Salience Effects. *Journal of Personality and Social Psychology* 45:560–70.

Born, Richard. 1990. Surge and Decline, Negative Voting, and the Midterm Loss Phenomenon: A Simultaneous Choice Analysis. *American Journal of Political Science* 34:615–45.

Bowen, Terry, and Hunter Bacot. 1991. The Two Faces of Issue Voting Revisited. Paper presented at the Annual Meeting of the Midwest Political Science Association, Chicago.

Bower, Gordon. 1981. Emotion, Mood and Memory. *American Psychologist* 36:129–48.

Boynton, G. Robert. 1990a. Ideas and Action: A Cognitive Model of the Senate Agriculture Committee. *Political Behavior* 12:181–213.

———. 1990b. Our Conversations about Governing. Paper presented at the Annual Meeting of the American Political Science Association.

Boynton, G. Robert, and Milton Lodge. 1992. A Cognitive Model of Forming Impressions of Candidates. Paper presented at the 1992 Annual Meeting of the Midwest Political Science Association, Chicago, April, 1992.

———. 1993. Voters' Images of Candidates. In *Presidential Campaigning and America's Self Images,* ed. Bruce Gronbeck and Arthur Miller. Boulder, Colo.: Westview Press.

Brady, Henry. 1990. Traits Versus Issues: Factor Versus Ideal-point Analysis of Candidate Thermometer Ratings. In *Political Analysis.* Vol. 2, ed. James A. Stimson. Ann Arbor, Mich.: University of Michigan Press.

Brady, Henry E., and Paul M. Sniderman. 1985. Attitude Attribution: A Group Basis for Political Reasoning. *American Political Science Review* 79:1061–78.

Branford, J., and Marcia Johnson. 1972. Contextual Prerequisites for Understanding: Some Investigations of Comprehension and Recall. *Journal of Verbal Learning and Behavior* 11:717–26.

Brent, Edward, and Donald Granberg. 1982. Subjective Agreement with the Presidential Candidates of 1976 and 1980. *Journal of Personality and Social Psychology* 42:393–403.

Brewer, Marilyn. 1979. Ingroup Bias in the Minimal Intergroup Situation: A Cognitive-Motivational Analysis. *Psychological Bulletin* 86:307–24.

———. 1988. A Dual Process Model Of Impression Formation. In *Advances in Social Cognition: A Dual Process Model of Impression Formation,* ed. Thomas Srull and Robert Wyer. Hillsdale, N.J.: Lawrence Erlbaum Associates.

Brewer, Marilyn, and Layton Lui. 1984. Categorization of the Elderly by the Elderly: Effects of Perceiver's Category Membership. *Personality and Social Psychology Bulletin* 10:585–95.

Brody, Charles A. 1986. Things are Rarely Black and White: Admitting Gray into the Converse Model of Attitude Stability. *American Journal of Sociology* 92:657–77.

Brody, Richard. 1986. Candidate Evaluations and the Vote: Some Considerations Affecting the Application of Cognitive Psychology to Voting Behavior. In *Political Cognition,* ed. Richard R. Lau and David O. Sears. Hillsdale, N.J.: Lawrence Erlbaum Associates.

Brody, Richard, and Benjamin Page. 1972. Comment: The Assessment of Issue Voting. *American Political Science Review* 66:450–58.

Brown, Steven R., ed. 1980. *Political Subjectivity: Applications of Q methodology in Political Science.* New Haven, Conn.: Yale University Press.

Budd, Richard J. 1986. Predicting Cigarette Use: The Need to Incorporate Measures of Salience in the Theory of Reasoned Action. *Journal of Applied Social Psychology* 16:663–85.

Budd, Richard J., and Christopher Spencer. 1984. Latitude of Rejection, Centrality, and Certainty: Variables Affecting the Relationship Between Attitudes, Norms, and Behavioral Intentions. *British Journal of Social Psychology* 23:1–8.

Budge, Ian. 1982. Strategies, Issues and Votes:British General Elections, 1950–1979. *Comparative Political Studies* 15:171–96.

Budge, Ian, Dennis Farlie, and Michael Laver. 1983. What is a "Rational" Choice? Shifts of Meaning Within Explanations of Voting and Party Competition. *Electoral Studies* 2:23–38.

Campbell, Angus, Phillip Converse, Warren Miller, and Donald Stokes. 1960. *The American Voter.* New York: Wiley.

Campbell, Angus, Gerald Gurin, and Warren E. Miller. 1954. *The Voter Decides.* Evanston, Ill.: Row, Peterson.

Campbell, James, Mary Munro, John Alford, and Bruce Campbell. 1986. Partisanship and Voting. *Research in Micropolitics* 1:99–126.

Cantor, Nancy, and Walter Mischel. 1979. Prototypes in Person Perception. In *Advances in Experimental Social Psychology.* Vol. 12, ed. Leonard Berkowitz. New York: Academic Press.

Cantril, Hadley. 1944. *Gauging Public Opinion.* Princeton, N.J.: Princeton University Press.

———. 1946. The Intensity of Attitudes. *Journal of Abnormal and Social Psychology* 41:1–12.

Carbonell, Jamie G., Jr. 1978. Politics: Automated Ideological Reasoning. *Cognitive Science* 2:27–51.

Carmines, Edward, and James Stimson. 1980. The Two Faces of Issue Voting. *American Political Science Review* 74:78–91.

Carpenter, Patricia A., and Marcel Just. 1975. Sentence Comprehension: A Psycholinguistic Model of Verification. *Psychological Review* 82:45–73.

Carroll, John S., and Eric J. Johnson. 1990. *Decision Research: A Field Guide.* Newbury Park, Calif.: Sage.

Chaiken, Shelly, and Suzanne Yates. 1985. Affective-Cognitive Consistency and Thought-Induced Attitude Polarization. *Journal of Personality and Social Psychology* 49:1470–81.

Chapman, Randall, and Kristian Palda. 1983. Electoral Turnout in Rational Voting and Consumption Perspectives. *Advances in Consumer Research* 9:337–46.

Chattopadhyay, Amitava, and Joseph Alba. 1988. The Situational Importance of Recall and Inference in Consumer Decision-Making. *Journal of Consumer Research* 15:1–12.

Clore, Gerald L., and Barbara Baldridge. 1968. Interpersonal Attraction: The Role of Agreement and Topic Interest. *Journal of Personality and Social Psychology* 9:340–46.

Cohen, Claudia E. 1981a. Goals and Schemata in Person Perception: Making Sense from the Stream of Behavior. In *Personality, Cognition and Social Interaction,* ed. Nancy Cantor and John Kihlstrom. Hillsdale, N.J.: Lawrence Erlbaum Associates.

———. 1981b. Person Categories and Social Perception: Testing Some Boundaries of the Processing Effects of Prior Knowledge. *Journal of Personality and Social Psychology* 40:441–52.

Collins, Allen, and Elizabeth Loftus. 1975. A Spreading-Activation Theory of Semantic Memory. *Psychological Review* 82:407–28.

Collins, Allen M. and M. Ross Quillian. 1969. Retrieval Time From Schematic Memory. *Journal of Verbal Learning and Verbal Behavior* 8:240–47.

———. 1972. Experiments on Semantic Memory and Language Comprehension. In *Cognition and Learning,* ed. L. Gregg. New York: Wiley.

Collins, Allen, and Edward E. Smith, eds. 1988. *Readings in Cognitive Science: A Perspective from Psychology and Artificial Intelligence.* San Mateo, Calif.: Morgan Kaufmann.

Conover, Pamela J., and Stanley Feldman. 1982. Projection and Perceptions of Candidates' Issue Positions. *Western Political Quarterly* 35:228–44.

———. 1984. How People Organize the Political World: A Schematic Model. *American Journal of Political Science* 28:95–126.

———. 1986. The Role of Inference in the Perception of Political Candidates. In *Political Cognition,* ed. Richard R. Lau and David O. Sears. Hillsdale, N.J.: Lawrence Erlbaum Associates.

———. 1991. Where is the Schema? Critiques. *American Political Science Review* 85:1364–69.

Converse, Jean M. 1987. *Survey Research in the United States.* Berkeley, Calif.: University of California Press.

Coverse, Jean M., and Stanley Presser. 1986 *Survey Questions: Handcrafting the Standardized Questionnaire.* Beverly Hills, Calif.: Sage Publications.

Converse, Philip E. 1964. The Nature of Belief Systems in Mass Publics. In *Ideology and Discontent*, ed. David E. Apter. London: Collier-Macmillan.

———. 1970. Attitudes and Nonattitudes: Continuation of a Dialogue. In *The Quantitative Analysis of Social Problems*, ed. Edward Tufte. Reading, Mass.: Addison-Wesley.

———. 1975. Public Opinion and Voting Behavior. In *Handbook of Political Science*. Vol. 4, ed. Fred Greenstein and Nelson Polsby. Reading, Mass.: Addison-Wesley.

Copas, John B., and Rolf Loeber. 1990. Relative Improvement Over Chance (RIOC) for 2×2 tables. *British Journal of Mathematical and Statistical Psychology* 43:293–307.

Cover, Albert D. 1986. Presidential Evaluations and Voting for Congress. *American Journal of Political Science* 30:786– 801.

Craik, Fergus I. M., and Endel Tulving. 1975. Depth of Processing and the Retention of Words in Episodic Memory. *Journal of Experimental Psychology: General* 104:268–94.

Creyer, Elizabeth H., James R. Bettman, and John W. Payne. 1990. The Impact of Accuracy and Effort Feedback and Goals on Adaptive Decision Behavior. *Journal of Behavioral Decision Making* 3:1–16.

Cronbach, Lee J. 1955. Processes Affecting Scores on "Understanding of Other" and "Assumed Similarity". *Psychological Bulletin* 52:177–93.

Croyle, Robert T., and Elizabeth F. Loftus. 1992. Improving Episodic Memory Performance of Survey Respondents. In *Surveying Subjective Phenomena*, ed. Charles F. Turner and Elizabeth Martin. New York, N.Y.: Russell Sage Foundation.

Davidson, Andrew R., Steven Yantis, Marel Norwood, and Daniel E. Montano. 1985. Amount of Information About the Attitude Object and Attitude-Behavior Consistency. *Journal of Personality and Social Psychology* 49:1184–98.

Davis, Otto A., Melvin J. Hinich, and Peter C. Ordeshook. 1970. An Expository Development of a Mathematical Model of the Electoral Process. *American Political Science Review* 64:426–48.

Dawes, Robyn M. 1979. The Robust Beauty of Improper Linear Models in Decision Making. *American Psychologist* 34:571–82.

———. 1988. *Rational Choice in an Uncertain World*. New York: Hartcourt Brace Jovanovich.

Dawes, Robyn M., D. Singer, and F. Lemons. 1972. An Experimental Analysis of the Contrast Effect and its Implications for Intergroup Communication and the Indirect Assessment of Attitude. *Journal of Personality and Social Psychology* 21:281–9.

Delli Carpini, Michael X., and Scott Keeter. 1991. Stability and Change in the U.S. Public's Knowledge of Politics. *Public Opinion Quarterly* 55:583–612.

DeMaio, Theresa J. 1984. Social Desirability and Survey Measurement: A Review. In *Surveying Subjective Phenomena*, ed. Charles F. Turner and Elizabeth Martin. New York: Russell Sage Foundation.

Dennett, Daniel. 1992. Filling in versus Finding Out: A Ubiquitous Confusion in Cognitive Science. In *Cognition: Conceptual and Methodological Issues*, ed. Herbert L. Pick, Paulus Van den Broek, and David C. Knill. Washington, D.C.: American Psychological Association.

Devine, Patricia G., and Thomas R. Ostrom. 1985. Cognitive Mediation of Inconsistency Discounting. *Journal of Personality and Social Psychology* 49:5–21.

Downing, James W. 1991. An Experimental Examination of Factors Influencing Political Impressions and their Accuracy. Ph.D. Diss. University of Colorado, Boulder.

Downs, Anthony. 1957. *An Economic Theory of Democracy*. New York: Harper and Row.

Dreben, Elizabeth, Susan T. Fiske, and Reid Hastie. 1979. The Independence of Item and

Evaluative Information: Impression and Recall Order Effects in Behavior Based Impression Formation. *Journal of Personality and Social Psychology* 37:1758–68.

Dyer, Michael George. 1983. *In-depth Understanding: A Computer Model of Integrated Processing for Narrative Comprehension.* Cambridge, Mass.: MIT Press.

Ebbesen, Ebbe B., and Vladimir J. Konecni. 1975. Decision Making and Information Integration in the Courts: The Setting of Bail. *Journal of Personality and Social Psychology* 32:805– 21.

Ebbinghaus, Hans. [1885] 1964. *Memory: A Contribution to Experimental Psychology.* New York: Dover.

Edelman, Murray. 1964. *The Symbolic Uses of Politics.* Urbana, Ill.: University of Illinois Press.

Edwards, Ward. 1968. Conservatism in Human Information Processing. In *Formal Representation of Human Judgment,* ed. Benjamin Kleinmuntz. New York: Wiley.

Einhorn, Hillel J. 1974. Expert Judgment: Some Necessary Conditions and an Example. *Journal of Applied Psychology* 59:562–71.

Einhorn, Hillel J., and Robin M. Hogarth. 1981. Behavioral Decision Theory: Processes of Judgment and Choice. *Annual Review of Psychology* 32:53–88.

———. 1985. Ambiguity and Uncertainty in Probabilistic Inference. *Psychological Review* 93:433–61.

Einhorn, Hillel J., Don N. Kleinmuntz, and Benjamin Kleinmuntz. 1979. Linear Regression and Process Tracing Models of Judgement. *Psychological Review* 86:465–85.

Einhorn, Hillel J., Stephen S. Komorita, and Benson Rosen. 1972. Multidimensional Models for the Evaluation of Political Candidates. *Journal of Experimental Social Psychology* 8:58–73.

Elster, Jon. 1991. When Rationality Fails. In *The Limits of Rationality,* ed. Karen Schweers Cook and Margaret Levi. Chicago, Ill.: University of Chicago Press.

Enelow, James M., and Melvin Hinich. 1984. *The Spatial Theory of Voting: An Introduction.* New York: Cambridge University Press.

Enelow, James M., Melvin H. Hinich, and Nancy R. Mendell. 1986. An Empirical Evaluation of Alternative Spatial Models of Elections. *Journal of Politics* 48:675–93.

Ericsson, K. Andres, and Herbert Simon. 1980. Verbal Reports as Data. *Psychological Review* 87:215–51.

———. 1984. *Protocol Analysis: Verbal Reports as Data.* Cambridge, Mass.: MIT Press.

Erikson, Robert S. 1979. The SRC Panel Data and Mass Political Attitudes. *British Journal of Political Science* 9:89–114.

Ewing, Thomas N. 1942. A Study of Certain Factors Involved in Changes of Opinion. *Journal of Social Psychology* 16:63–88.

Fazio, Russell H. 1986. How do Attitudes Guide Behavior? In *The Handbook of Motivation and Cognition,* ed. Richard Sorrentino and E. Tory Higgins. New York: Guilford Press.

———1989. On the Power and Functionality of Attitudes: The Role of Attitude Accessibility. In *Attitude Structure and Function,* ed. Anthony R. Pratkanis, Steven J. Brecker, and Anthony G. Greenwald. Hillsdale, N.J.: Lawrence Erlbaum Associates.

———. 1990. A Practical Guide to the Use of Response Latency in Social Psychological Research. In *Research Methods in Personality and Social Psychology,* ed. Clyde Hendrick and Margaret S. Clark. London: Sage.

Fazio, Russell H., Martha C. Powell, and Paul M. Herr. 1983. Toward a Process Model of the Attitude-Behavior Relation: Accessing One's Attitude Upon Mere Observation of the Attitude Object. *Journal of Personality and Social Psychology* 44:723–35.

Fazio, Russell H., David M. Sanbonmatsu, Martha C. Powell, and Frank R. Kardes. 1986. On the Automatic Activation of Attitudes. *Journal of Personality and Social Psychology* 50:229–38.

Fazio, Russell H., and Carol Williams. 1986. Attitude Accessibility as a Moderator of the Attitude-Perception and Attitude-Behavior Relations: An Investigation of the 1984 Presidential Election. *Journal of Personality and Social Psychology* 51(1): 505–14.

Fazio, Russell H., and Mark P. Zanna. 1981. Direct Experience and Attitude-behavior Consistency. In *Advances in Experimental Social Psychology.* Vol. 14, ed. Leonard Berkowitz. New York: Academic Press.

Fee, Joan F. 1981. Symbols in Survey Questions: Solving the Problem of Multiple Word Meanings. *Political Methodology* 7:71–95.

Feldman, Stanley. 1989. Measuring Issue Preferences: The Problem of Response Instability. *Political Analysis* 1:25–60.

Feldman, Stanley, and John R. Zaller. 1992. The Political Culture of Ambivalence: Ideological Responses to the Welfare State. *American Journal of Political Science* 36:268–307.

Fenno, Richard E. 1976. *Home Style: House Members in Their Districts.* Boston: Little, Brown and Co.

Ferejohn, John A., and James H. Kuklinski. eds. 1990. *Information and Democratic Processes.* Urbana, Ill.: University of Illinois Press.

Festinger, Leon. 1957. *A Theory of Cognitive Dissonance.* Stanford, Calif.: Stanford University Press.

Fine, Bernard J. 1957. Conclusion-Drawing, Communicator Credibility, and Anxiety as Factors in Opinion Change. *Journal of Abnormal and Social Psychology* 5:369–74.

Fiorina, Morris P. 1981. *Retrospective Voting in American National Elections.* New Haven, Conn.: Yale University Press.

Fiorina, Morris P., and Charles Plott. 1978. Committee Decisions Under Majority Rule. *American Political Science Review* 72:575–98.

Fiorina, Morris P., and Kenneth A. Shepsle. 1989. Is Negative Voting an Artifact? *American Journal of Political Science* 33:423–39.

———. 1990. A Positive Theory of Negative Voting. In *Information and Democratic Process,* ed. John A. Ferejohn and James H. Kuklinski. Urbana, Ill.: University of Illinois Press.

Fischer, Gregory., and Eric J. Johnson. 1986 Behavioral Decision Theory and Political Decision Making. In *Political Cognition,* Richard R. Lau and David O. Sears, ed. Hillsdale, N.J.: Lawrence Erlbaum Associates.

Fischoff, Baruch. 1983. Predicting Frames. *Journal of Experimental Psychology: Learning, Memory and Cognition* 9:103–16.

Fishbein, Martin. 1963. An Investigation of the Relationships Between Beliefs about an Object and the Attitude toward that Object. *Human Relations* 16:233–9.

Fishbein, Martin, and Icek Ajzen. 1974. Basis for Decision: An Attitudinal Analysis of Voting Behavior. *Journal of Applied Social Psychology* 4:95–124.

———. 1975. *Belief, Attitude, Intention and Behavior: An Introduction to Theory and Research.* Reading, Mass.: Addison-Wesley.

Fiske, Susan T. 1980. Attention and Weight in Person Perception: The Impact of Negative and Extreme Behavior. *Journal of Personality and Social Psychology* 38:889–906.

———. 1986. Schema-based versus Piecemeal Politics: A Patchwork Quilt, but Not a Blanket, of Evidence. In *Political Cognition,* ed. Richard R. Lau and David O. Sears. Hillsdale, N.J.: Lawrence Erlbaum Associates.

————. 1988. Compare and Contrast: Brewer's Dual Process Model and Fiske et al.'s Continuum Model. In *Advances in Social Cognition,* ed. Thomas K. Srull and Robert S. Wyer. Hillsdale, NJ: Lawrence Erlbaum Associates.

Fiske, Susan T., and Martha Cox. 1979. Person Concepts: The Effects of Target Familiarity and Descriptive Purpose on the Process of Describing Others. *Journal of Personality* 47:136–61.

Fiske, Susan T., and Donald R. Kinder. 1981. Involvement, Expertise, and Schema Use: Evidence from Political Cognition. In *Personality, Cognition, and Social Interaction,* ed. Nancy Cantor and John F. Kihlstrom. Hillsdale, N.J.: Lawrence Erlbaum Associates.

Fiske, Susan T., Richard R. Lau, and Richard A. Smith. 1990. On the Varieties and Utilities of Political Expertise. *Social Cognition* 8:31–48.

Fiske, Susan T., and Patricia Linville. 1980. What Does the Schema Concept Buy Us? *Personality and Social Psychology Bulletin* 6:543–51.

Fiske, Susan T., and Steven Neuberg. 1988. A Continuum Model of Impression Formation From Category-Based to Individuating Responses: Influences of Information and Motivation on Attention and Interpretation. In *Advances in Experimental Social Psychology.* Vol. 23, ed. Mark Zanna. New York: Academic Press.

Fiske, Susan T., and Mark Pavelchak. 1986. Category Based versus Piecemeal-Based Affective Responses. In *The Handbook of Motivation and Cognition: Foundations of Social Behavior,* ed. Richard Sorrentino and E. Torry Higgins. Reading, Mass.: Addison-Wesley.

Fiske, Susan T., and Janet Ruscher. 1989. On-Line Processes in Category-Based and Individuating Impressions: Some Basic Principals and Methodological Reflections. In *On-Line Cognition in Person Perception,* ed. John Bassili. Hillsdale, N.J.: Lawrence Erlbaum Associates.

Fiske, Susan T., and Shelley E. Taylor. 1991. *Social Cognition.* New York: McGraw-Hill.

Fitts, Paul, and Michael Posner. 1967. *Human Performance.* Belmont, Calif.: Brooks/Cole.

Flanigan, William, Wendy Rahn, and Nancy Zingale. 1992. Dynamics of Voter Decision Making. Paper presented at the 1992 Annual Meeting of the American Political Science Association, September, Chicago, Illinois.

Ford, Kevin J., Neal Schmitt, Susan L. Schechtman, Brian M. Hults, and Mary L. Doherty. 1989. Process Tracing Methods: Contributions, Problems, and Neglected Research Questions. *Organizational Behavior and Human processes* 43:75–117.

Frank, Michael W., and Charles S. Taber. 1991. The Calculus of Voting Reconsidered: A Solution to the Downsian Paradox Based on Prospect Theory. Paper presented at the annual meeting of the Midwest Political Science Association, Chicago, Illinois.

Friendly, Michael L. 1977. In Search of the M-Gram: The Structure of Organization in Free Recall. *Cognitive Psychology* 9:188–249.

————. 1979. Methods for Finding Graphic Representations of Associative Memory Structures. In *Memory Organization and Structure,* ed. C. Richard Puff. New York: Academic Press.

Funder, David C. 1987. Errors and Mistakes: Evaluating the Accuracy of Social Judgment. *Psychological Bulletin* 101:75–90.

Gamson, William A., and Kathryn E. Lasch. 1983. The Political Culture of Affirmative Action. In *Evaluating the Welfare State,* ed. Shimon E. Spiro and Ephraim Yaar. New York: Academic Press.

Gamson, William A., and Andre Modigliani. 1987. The Changing Culture of Affirmative

Action. In *Research in Political Sociology.* Vol. 3, ed. Richard D. Braungart. Greenwich, Conn.: JAI Press.

Gant, Michael, and Dwight Davis. 1984. Mental Economy and Voter Rationality: The Informed Citizen Problem in Voting Research. *Journal of Politics* 46:132–53.

Garand, James C., and George Ruiz. 1987. The Simple Act of Voting: A Respecification of the Kelley-Mirer Decision Rule for Voting. Paper presented at the annual meeting of the Southern Political Science Association, Charlotte, North Carolina.

Gardner, Howard. 1985. *The Mind's New Science: A History of the Cognitive Revolution.* New York: Basic Books.

Glucksberg, Sam, and Michael Mcloskey. 1981. Decisions About Ignorance: Knowing That You Don't Know. *Journal of Experimental Psychology: Human Learning and Memory* 7:311– 24.

Goldberg, Arthur S. 1969. Social Determinism and Rationality as a Basis of Party Identification. *American Political Science Review* 63:5–25.

Goldstein, William, and Jane Beattie. Forthcoming. Judgments of Relative Importance in Decision Making: The Importance of Interpretation and the Interpretation of Importance. In *Frontiers in Mathematical Psychology,* ed. David Brown and Jonathon Smith. New York: Springer-Verlag.

Gorn, Gerald J. 1975. The Effects of Personal Involvement, Communication Discrepancy, and Source Prestige on Reactions to Communications on Separatism. *Canadian Journal of Behavioral Science* 7:369–86.

Graber, Doris A. 1976. *Verbal Behavior and Politics.* Urbana, Ill.: University of Illinois Press.

———. 1988. *Processing the News: Taming the Information Tide.* New York: Longman.

Granberg, Donald. 1985. An Anomaly in Political Perception. *Public Opinion Quarterly* 49:504–16.

Granberg, Donald, and Edward Brent. 1974. Dove-hawk Placements in the 1968 Election: Application of Social Judgment and Balance Theories. *Journal of Personality and Social Psychology* 29:687–95.

———. 1980. Perceptions of Political Candidates. *American Scientist* 68:617–25.

Granberg, Donald, and Soren Holmberg. 1986. Political Perception Among Voters in Sweden and the U.S.: Analyses of Issues with Specific Alternatives. *Western Political Quarterly* 39: 7–28.

Granberg, Donald, and R. Jenks. 1977. Assimilation and Contrast Effects in the 1972 Election. *Human Relations* 30:623–40.

Granberg, Donald, and John Seidel. 1976. Social Judgements of the Urban Unrest and Vietnam Issues in 1968 and 1972. *Social Forces* 55:1–15.

Hahn, Harlan. 1970. The Political Impact of Shifting Attitudes. *Social Science Quarterly* 51:730–42.

Hamill, Ruth, and Milton Lodge. 1986. Cognitive Consequences of Political Sophistication. In *Political Cognition,* ed. Richard Lau and David O. Sears. Hillsdale, N.J.: Lawrence Erlbaum Associates.

Hamill, Ruth, Milton Lodge, and Frederick Blake. 1985. The Breadth, Depth, and Utility of Class, Partisan and Ideological Schemata. *American Journal of Political Science* 29:850–70.

Hamilton, David L. 1981. Illusory Correlation as a Basis for Stereotyping. In *Cognitive Processes in Stereotyping and Intergroup Behavior,* ed. David L. Hamilton. Hillsdale, N.J.: Lawrence Erlbaum Associates.

———. 1989. Understanding Impression Formation. In *Memory: Interdisciplinary Ap-*

proaches, ed. Paul R. Solomon, George R. Goethals, Colleen M. Kelley, and Benjamin R. Stephens. New York: Springer-Verlag.

Hamilton, David L., Roger Fallot, and Jack Hautaluoma. 1978. Information Salience and Order Effects in Impression Formation. *Personality and Social Psychology Bulletin* 4:44–47.

Hamilton, David L., Lawrence B. Katz, and Von O. Leirer. 1980. Cognitive Representation of Personality Impressions: Organizational Processes in First Impression Formation. *Journal of Personality and Social Psychology* 39:1050–63.

Harris, Richard. 1981. Inferences in Information Processing. In *The Psychology of Learning and Motivation,* ed. Gordon Bower. New York: Academic Press.

Hastie, Reid. 1981. Schematic Principles in Human Memory. In *Social Cognition: The Ontario Symposium.* Vol. 1, ed. E. Tory Higgins, Charles Herman, and Mark Zanna. Hillsdale, N.J.: Lawrence Erlbaum Associates.

———. 1986. A Primer of Information-processing Theory for the Political Scientist. In *Political Cognition: The 19th Annual Carnegie Symposium on Cognition,* ed. Richard R. Lau and David O. Sears. Hillsdale, N.J.: Lawrence Erlbaum Associates.

———. 1987. Information Processing Theory for the Survey Researcher. In *Social Information Processing and Survey Methodology,* ed. Hans J. Hippler, Norbert Schwarz, and Seymour Sudman. New York: Springer-Verlag.

———. 1988. A Computer Simulation of Person Memory. *Journal of Experimental Social Psychology* 24:423–47.

Hastie, Reid, and Purohit Kumar. 1979. Person Memory: Personality Traits as Organizing Principles in Memory for Behaviors. *Journal of Personality and Social Psychology* 37:25–38.

Hastie, Reid, and Bernadette Park. 1986. The Relationship between Memory and Judgment Depends on Whether the Task is Memory-Based or On-Line. *Psychological Review* 93:258–68.

Hastie, Reid, Bernadette Park, and Renee Weber. 1984. Social Memory. In *Handbook of Social Cognition.* Vol. 2, ed. Robert S. Wyer and Thomas K. Srull. Hillsdale, N.J.: Lawrence Erlbaum Associates.

Hastie, Reid, and Nancy Pennington. 1989. Notes on the Distinction Between Memory-Based versus On-Line Judgments. In *On-Line Cognition in Person Perception,* ed. John Bassili. Hillsdale, N.J.: Lawrence Erlbaum Associates.

Heider, Fritz. 1958. *The Psychology of Interpersonal Relations.* New York: Wiley.

Helm, Charles J. 1979/80. Party Identification as a Perceptual Screen: Temporal Priority, Reality and the Voting Act. *Policy* 12:110–28.

Hendrick, Clyde. 1972. Effects of Salience of Stimulus Inconsistency on Impression Formation. *Journal of Personality and Social Psychology* 22:219–225.

Herstein, John A. 1981. Keeping the Voter's Limits in Mind: A Cognitive Process Analysis of Decision-making in Voting. *Journal of Personality and Social Psychology* 40:843–61.

———. 1985. Voter Thought Processes and Voting Theory. In *Mass Media and Political Thoughts: An Information-Processing Approach,* ed. Sidney Kraus and Richard M. Perloff. Beverly Hills, Calif.: Sage.

Higgins, E. Tory, and G. A. King. 1981. Accessibility of Social Constructs: Information-Processing Consequences of Individual and Contextual Accessibility. In *Personality, Cognition and Social Interaction,* ed. Nancy Cantor and John F. Kihlstrom. Hillsdale, N.J.: Lawrence Erlbaum Associates.

Hippler, Hans J., Norbert Schwarz, and Seymour Sudman. 1987. *Social Information Processing and Survey Methodology.* New York: Springer-Verlag.

Hodges, Bert H. 1974. Effect of Valence on Relative Weighting in Impression Formation. *Journal of Personality and Social Psychology* 30:378–81.

Hoetler, Jon W. 1985. The Structure of Self-Conception: Conceptualization and Measurement. *Journal of Personality and Social Psychology* 49:1392–407.

Hogarth, Robin M. 1981. Beyond Discrete Biases: Functional and Dysfunctional Aspects of Judgmental Heuristics. *Psychological Bulletin* 90:197–217.

———. 1987. *Judgment and Choice: The Psychology of Decision.* New York: Wiley.

Hogarth, Robin M., and Hillel J. Einhorn. 1992. Order Effects in Belief Updating: The Belief-Adjustment Model. *Cognitive Psychology* 24:1–55.

Holtz, Rolf, and Norman Miller. 1985. Assumed Similarity and Opinion Certainty. *Journal of Personality and Social Psychology* 48:890–98.

Hovland, Carl I. 1960. Computer Simulation of Thinking. *American Psychologist* 15:687–93.

Howard-Pitney, Beth, Eugene Borgida, and Allen M. Omoto. 1986. Personal Involvement: An Examination of Processing Differences. *Social Cognition* 4:39–57.

Howell, Susan E. 1981. Short-term Forces and Changing Partisanship. *Political Behavior* 3:161–80.

Hudson, Valerie. 1991. Scripting International Power Dramas: A Model of Situational Predisposition. In *Artificial Intelligence in International Relations,* ed. Valerie Hudson. Boulder, Colo.: Westview Press.

Hymes, Robert W. 1986. Political Attitudes as Social Categories: A New Look at Selective Memory. *Journal of Personality and Social Psychology* 51:233–41.

Iyengar, Shanto. 1979. Television News and Issue Salience: A Reexamination of the Agenda Setting Hypothesis. *American Politics Quarterly* 7:395–416.

———. 1990. Shortcuts to Political Knowledge: The Role of Selective Attention and Accessibility. In *Information and Democratic Processes,* ed. John A. Ferejohn and James H. Kuklinski. Chicago: University of Illinois Press.

Iyengar, Shanto, and Donald R. Kinder. 1987. *News That Matters: Television and American Public Opinion.* Chicago: University of Chicago Press.

Jaccard, James, and Michael A. Becker. 1985. Attitudes and Behavior: An Information Integration Perspective. *Journal of Experimental Social Psychology* 21:440–65.

Jacobson, Gary. 1992. *The Politics of Congressional Elections.* 3d ed. New York: Harper Collins.

Jacoby, Jacob, James Jaccard, Alfred Kuss, Tracy Troutman, and David Mazursky. 1987. New Directions in Behavioral Process Research: Implications for Social Psychology. *Journal of Experimental Social Psychology* 23:146–75.

Jamieson, Donald, and William Petrusic. 1977. Preference and Time to Choose. *Organizational Behavior and Human Performance* 19:56–67.

Jennings, M. Kent, and Gregory Markus. 1984. Partisan Orientations over the Long Haul: Results from a 3-wave Political Socialization Panel Study. *American Political Science Review* 78:1000–1008.

Johnson, Eric J., and John W. Payne. 1985. Effort and Accuracy in Choice. *Management Science* 31:395–414.

Johnson, Joel T., and Charles Judd. 1983. Overlooking the Incongruent: Categorization Biases in the Identification of Political Statements. *Journal of Personality and Social Psychology* 45:978–96.

Jordan, Nehemiah. 1969. The "Asymmetry" of "Liking" and "Disliking": A Phenomenon Meriting Further Reflection and Research. *Public Opinion Quarterly* 29:315–22.

Judd, Charles M., Roger Drake, James Downing, and Jon Krosnick. 1991. Some Dynamic

Properties of Attitude Structures: Context-Induced Response Facilitation and Polarization. *Journal of Personality and Social Psychology* 60:183–202.

Judd, Charles M., and Joel T. Johnson. 1981. Attitudes, Polarization, and Diagnosticity. *Journal of Personality and Social Psychology* 41:26–36.

———. 1984. The Polarizing Effects of Affective Intensity. In *Attitudinal Judgment,* ed. J. Richard Eiser. New York: Springer-Verlag.

Judd, Charles M., David A. Kenny, and Jon Krosnick. 1983. Judging the Positions of Political Candidates: Models of Assimilation and Contrast. *Journal of Personality and Social Psychology* 44:952–63.

Judd, Charles, and Jon Krosnick. 1989. The Structural Bases of Consistency Among Political Attitudes: Effects of Political Expertise and Attitude Importance. In *Attitude Structure and Function,* ed. Anthony Pratkanis, Steven Beckler, and Anthony Greenwald. Hillsdale, N.J.: Lawrence Erlbaum Associates.

Judd, Charles, and James Kulik. 1980. Schematic Effects of Social Attitudes on Information Processing and Recall. *Journal of Personality and Social Psychology* 38:569–78.

Judd, Charles, and Cynthia Lusk. 1984. Knowledge Structures and Evaluative Judgments: Effects of Structural Variables on Judgment Extremity. *Journal of Personality and Social Psychology* 46:1193–207.

Judd, Charles M., and Bernadette Park. 1988. Out-group Homogeneity: Judgments of Variability at the Individual and Group Levels. *Journal of Personality and Social Psychology* 54:778–88.

———. 1993. The Definition and Assessment of Accuracy in Social Stereotypes. *Psychological Review* 100:109–28.

Judd, Charles M., Carey S. Ryan, and Bernadette Park. 1991. Accuracy in the Judgment of In-group and Out-group Variability. *Journal of Personality and Social Psychology* 61:366–79.

Jussim, Lee. 1991. Social Perception and Social Reality: A Reflection-Construction Model. *Psychological Review* 98:54–73.

Kagay, Michael, and Greg Caldeira. 1975. I Like the Looks of His Face: Elements of Electoral Choice, 1952–1972. Paper presented at the annual meeting of the American Political Science Association, September, San Francisco.

Kahn, Barbara E., and Robert J. Meyer. 1991. Consumer Multiattribute Judgments Under Attribute-weight Uncertainty. *Journal of Consumer Research* 17:508–22.

Kahneman, Daniel, and Amos Tversky. 1972. Subjective Probability: A Judgment of Representativeness. *Cognitive Psychology* 3:430–54.

———. 1979. Prospect Theory: An Analysis of Decision Under Risk. *Econometrica* 47:263–91.

Kahneman, Daniel, Paul Slovic, and Amos Tversky. 1982. *Judgement Under Uncertainty: Heuristics and Biases.* New York: Cambridge University Press.

Kanouse, David E., and L. Reid Hanson. 1986. Negativity in Evaluations. In *Attribution: Perceiving the Causes of Behavior,* ed. Edward Jones, David E. Kanouse, Harold H. Kelley, Richard E. Nisbett, Stuart Valins, and Bernard Weiner. Hillsdale, N.J.: Lawrence Erlbaum Associates.

Kantowitz, Barry. 1985. Channels and Stages in Human Information Processing: A Limited Analysis of Theory and Methodology. *Journal of Mathematical Psychology* 29:135–74.

Kaplan, Howard B. 1980. *Deviant Behavior in Defense of Self.* New York: Academic Press.

Katz, D., and K. Braly. 1933. Racial Stereotypes in One Hundred College Students. *Journal of Abnormal and Social Psychology* 28:280–90.

———. 1965. Verbal Stereotypes and Racial Prejudice. In *Basic Studies in Social Psychology,* ed. Harold Proshansky and Bernard Seidenberg. New York: Holt, Reinhart, and Winston.

Kelley, Stanley. 1983. *Interpreting Elections.* Princeton, N.J.: Princeton University Press.

Kelley, Stanley, and Thadeus Mirer. 1974. The Simple Act of Voting. *American Political Science Review* 61:572–91.

Kendall, Patricia, L. 1954. *Conflict and Mood: Factors Affecting Stability of Response.* Glencoe, Ill.: Free Press.

Kernell, Samuel. 1977. Presidential Popularity and Negative Voting: An Alternative Explanation of the Midterm Congressional Decline of the President's Party. *American Political Science Review* 71:44–66.

Kessel, John H. 1972. Comment: The Issues in Issue Voting. *American Political Science Review* 68:572–91.

———. 1984. *Presidential Parties.* Homewood, Ill.: Dorsey Press.

———. 1992. *Presidential Campaign Politics.* 4th ed. Pacific Grove, Calif.: Brooks/Cole.

Kessler, Ronald, and David Greenberg. 1981. *Linear Panel Analysis: Models of Quantitative Change.* New York: Academic Press.

Key, V. O. 1966. *The Responsible Electorate.* Cambridge, Mass.: Harvard University Press.

Kinder, Donald R. 1978. Political Person Perception: The Asymmetrical Influence of Sentiment and Choice on Perceptions of Presidential Candidates. *Journal of Personality and Social Psychology* 36:859–71.

———. 1986. Presidential Character Revisited. In *Political Cognition,* ed. Richard R. Lau and David O. Sears. Hillsdale, N.J.: Lawrence Erlbaum Associates.

Kinder, Donald R., and Susan T. Fiske. 1986. Presidents in the Public Mind. In *Political Psychology,* ed. Margaret Hermann. San Fransisco, Calif.: Jossey-Bass Publishers.

Kinder, Donald R., and D. Roderick Kiewiet. 1979. Economic Discontent and Political Behavior: The Role of Personal Grievances and Collective Economic Judgments in Congressional Voting. *American Journal of Political Science* 23:495–527.

Kinder, Donald R., and Thomas R. Palfrey, eds. 1993. *Experimental Foundations of Political Science.* Ann Arbor, Mich.: University of Michigan Press.

Kinder, Donald R., Mark D. Peters, Robert P. Abelson, and Susan T. Fiske. 1980. Presidential Prototypes. *Political Behavior* 2:315–37.

Kinder, Donald R., and Lynn M. Sanders. 1990. Mimicking Political Debate with Survey Questions: The Case of Opinion on Affirmative Action for Blacks. *Social Cognition* 8:73–103.

Kinder, Donald R., and David O. Sears. 1985. Public opinion and political action. In *Handbook of Social Psychology.* 3rd ed. Vol. 2, ed. Gardner Lindzey and Eliot Aronson. Reading, Mass.: Addison-Wesley. 659–741.

Klatzky, Roberta. 1980. *Human Memory: Structures and Processes.* San Francisco, Calif.: Freeman.

Klayman, Joshua. 1983. Analysis of Predecisional Information Search Patterns. In *Analyzing and Aiding Decision Processes,* ed. Paul Humphreys, Ola Svenson and A. Vari. New York: North-Holland.

Klein, Jill K. 1991. Negativity Effects in Impression Formation: A Test in the Political Arena. *Personality and Social Psychology Bulletin* 17:412–8.

Knower, Franklin H. 1936. Experimental Studies of Changes in Attitude-III: Some Incidence of Attitude Change. *Journal of Applied Psychology* 20:114–27.

Kramer, Gerald H. 1971. Short-term Fluctuations in U.S. Voting Behavior, 1896–1964. *American Political Science Review* 65:131–43.

Krosnick, Jon A. 1988a. Attitude Importance and Attitude Change. *Journal of Experimental Social Psychology* 24:240–55.

———. 1988b. The Role of Attitude Importance in Social Evaluation: A Study of Policy Preferences, Presidential Candidate Evaluations, and Voting Behavior. *Journal of Personality and Social Psychology* 55:196–210.

———. 1989. Attitude Importance and Attitude Accessibility. *Personality and Social Psychology Bulletin* 15:297–308.

———. 1990a. Americans' Perceptions of Presidential Candidates: A Test of the Projection Hypothesis. *Journal of Social Issues* 46:159–82.

———. 1990b. Government Policy and Citizen Passion: A Study of Issue Politics in Contemporary America. *Political Behavior* 12:59–92.

———. 1991. The Stability of Political Preferences: Comparisons of Symbolic and Nonsymbolic Attitudes. *American Journal of Political Science* 35:547–76.

Krosnick, Jon A., and Robert P. Abelson. 1991. The Case for Measuring Attitude Strength in Surveys. In *Questions About Questions: Inquiries into the Cognitive Bases of Surveys,* ed. Judith M. Tanur. New York: Russell Sage Foundation.

Krosnick, Jon A., and Laura Brannon. 1992. The Impact of War on the Ingredients of Presidential Evaluations: George Bush and the Gulf Conflict. Paper presented at the Conference on the Political Consequences of War, February, Washington, D.C.

Krosnick, Jon A., David S. Boninger, Yao C. Chuigan, and Matthew K. Berent. 1993. Attitude Strength: One Construct or Many Related Constructs? *Journal of Personality and Social Psychology* 44:1127–43.

Krosnick, Jon A., and Lee R. Fabrigar. 1993. *Designing Questionnaires to Measure Attitudes: Insights from Cognitive and Social Psychology.* New York: Oxford University Press.

Krosnick, Jon A., and Donald R. Kinder. 1990. Altering the Foundations of Popular Support for the President through Priming. *American Political Science Review* 84:497–512.

Krosnick, Jon A., and Michael Milburn. 1990. Psychological Determinants of Political Opinionation. *Social Cognition* 8:49–72.

Krosnick, Jon A., and Howard Schuman. 1988. Attitude Intensity, Importance, and Certainty and Susceptibility to Response Effects. *Journal of Personality and Social Psychology* 54:940–52.

Kruglanski, Arie W. 1989. The Psychology of Being "Right": The Problem of Accuracy in Social Perception and Cognition. *Psychological Bulletin* 106:395–409.

Kuklinski, James, Robert Luskin, and John Bolland. 1991. Where is the Schema? Going Beyond the "S" Word in Political Psychology. *American Political Science Review* 85, 4:1341– 56.

Kunda, Ziva. 1990. The Case for Motivated Reasoning. *Psychological Bulletin.* 108:48.

Lachman, Roy, Janet Lachman, and Earl Butterfield. 1979. *Cognitive Psychology and Information Processing: An Introduction.* Hillsdale, N.J.: Lawrence Erlbaum Associates.

Lakoff, George. 1987. *Women, Fire, and Dangerous Things: What Categories Reveal about the Mind.* Chicago: University of Chicago Press.

Lau, Richard R. 1982. Negativity in Political Perception. *Political Behavior* 4:353–77.

———. 1985. Two Explanations for Negativity Effects in Political Behavior. *American Journal of Political Science* 29:119–38.

———. 1986. Political Schemata, Candidate Evaluations and Voting Behavior. In *Political Cognition,* ed. Richard R. Lau and David O. Sears. Hillsdale, N.J.: Lawrence Erlbaum Associates.

———. 1989a. Construct Accessibility and Electoral Choice. *Political Behavior* 11:5–32.

———. 1989b. Information Search During a Political Campaign. Paper presented at the 85th Annual Meeting of the American Political Science Association, Atlanta.

———. 1990. Political Motivation and Political Cognition. In *The Handbook of Motivation and Cognition,* ed. E. Tory Higgins and Richard Sorrentino. New York: Guilford Press.

———. 1991. Negative Voting and Negative Voters in Presidential Elections. Paper presented at the annual meeting of the American Political Science Association, Washington, D.C.

———. 1992. Searchable Information During an Election Campaign. Unpublished manuscript, Rutgers University.

Lau, Richard R., and Jack S. Levy. 1993. Contributions of Behavioral Decision Theory to Research in Political Science. Unpublished manuscript, Rutgers University.

Lau, Richard R., and David P. Redlawsk. 1992. How Voters Decide: A Process Tracing Study of Decision Making During Political Campaigns. Paper presented at the 88th Annual Meeting of the American Political Science Association, Chicago.

Lau, Richard R., and David O. Sears. 1981. Cognitive Links between Economic Grievances and Political Responses. *Political Behavior* 3:279–302.

Lau, Richard R., Richard Smith, and Susan T. Fiske. 1988. Policy Interpretations and Political Persuasion: Cognitive and Attitudinal Processes. Paper presented at the Annual Meeting of the American Political Science Association, September 1-4. Washington, D.C.

Lazarsfeld, Paul, Bernard Berelson, and Hazel Gaudet. 1944. *The People's Choice.* New York: Columbia University Press.

Lessler, Judith T. 1984. Measurement Error in Surveys. In *Surveying Subjective Phenomena,* ed. Charles F. Turner and Elizabeth Martin. New York: Russell Sage Foundation.

Lichtenstein, Meryl, and Thomas K. Srull. 1987. Processing Objectives as a Determinant of the Relationship Between Recall and Judgement. *Journal of Experimental Social Psychology* 23:93–118.

Lieberman, Akiva, and Shelly Chaiken. 1991. Value Conflict and Thought-Induced Attitude Change. *Journal of Experimental Social Psychology* 27:203–16.

Lindsay, Peter, and Donald Norman. 1977. *Human Information Processing: An Introduction to Psychology.* New York: Academic Press.

Lingle, John, and Thomas Ostrom. 1981. Principles of Memory and Cognition in Attitude Formation. In *Cognitive Responses in Persuasion,* ed. Richard Petty, Thomas Ostrom, and Timothy Brock. Hillsdale, N.J.: Lawrence Erlbaum Associates.

Linville, Patricia W. 1982. The Complexity-Extremity Effect and Age-Based Stereotyping. *Journal of Personality and Social Psychology* 42:193–211.

Linville, Patricia W., Gregory W. Fischer, and Peter Salovey. 1989. Perceived Distributions of Ingroup and Outgroup Members: Empirical Evidence and a Computer Simulation. *Journal of Personality and Social Psychology* 57:165–88.

Lippman, Walter. 1922. *Public Opinion.* New York: Macmillan.

Lodge, Milton, David Cross, Bernard Tursky, and Joseph Tanenhaus. 1975. The Psychophysical Scaling and Validation of a Political Support Scale. *American Journal of Political Science* 19:611–49.

Lodge, Milton, and Ruth Hamill. 1986. A Partisan Schema for Political Information Processing. *American Journal of Political Science* 80:505–19.

Lodge, Milton, and Kathleen M. McGraw 1991. Where Is the Schema? Critique. *American Political Science Review* 84:1357–64.

Lodge, Milton, Kathleen M. McGraw, Pamela Conover, Stanley Feldman, and Arthur Miller. 1991. Where Is the Schema? Critiques. *American Political Science Review* 85:1357–80.

Lodge, Milton, Kathleen M. McGraw, and Patrick Stroh. 1989. An Impression-driven Model of Candidate Evaluation. *American Political Science Review* 83:399–419.

Lodge, Milton, Marco Steenbergen, and Shawn Brau. 1993. The Relationship Between Memory and Candidate Evaluation over Time. Political Psychology Monograph, Department of Political Science, SUNY at Stony Brook.

Lodge, Milton, and Patrick Stroh. 1993. Inside the Mental Voting Booth. In *Explorations in Political Psychology,* ed. Shanto Iyengar and William McGuire. Durham, N.C.: Duke University Press.

Lodge, Milton, Patrick Stroh, and John Wahlke. 1990. Black Box Models of Candidate Evaluation. *Political Behavior* 12, (1):5–18.

Loeber, Rolf, and Thomas J. Dishion. 1983. Early Predictors of Male Delinquency: A Review. *Psychological Bulletin* 94:68– 99.

Loftus, Elizabeth F., Steven E. Fienberg, and Judith M. Tanur. 1985. Cognitive Psychology Meets the National Survey. *American Psychologist* 40:175–80.

Lopes, Lola L. 1987. Between Hope and Fear: The Psychology of Risk. *Advances in Experimental Social Psychology* 20:255– 95.

Lord, Frederick, and Michael R. Novick. 1968. *Statistical Theories of Mental Test Scores.* Reading, Mass.: Addison-Wesley.

Lord, Charles G., Lee Ross, and Mark Lepper. 1979. Biased Assimilation and Attitude Polarization: The Effects of Prior Theories on Subsequently Considered Evidence. *Journal of Personality and Social Psychology.* 37:2098—2109.

Losco, Joseph. 1985. Evolution, Consciousness and Political Thinking. *Political Behavior* 7:223–47.

Lui, Layton, and Marilyn Brewer. 1988. Recognition Accuracy as Evidence of Category-Consistency Effects in Person Memory. *Social Cognition* 2:89–107.

Lusk, Cynthia, and Charles M. Judd. 1988. Political Expertise and the Structural Mediators of Candidate Evaluations. *Journal of Experimental Social Psychology* 24:105–26.

McClosky, Herbert, and John Zaller. 1984. *The American Ethos.* Cambridge, Mass.: Harvard University Press.

McCombs, Maxwell E., and Donald Shaw. 1972. The Agenda-Setting Function of the Mass Media. *Public Opinion Quarterly* 36:176–87.

McCordock, Pamela. 1979. *Machines Who Think.* San Francisco: W. H. Freeman.

McDonald, Stuart E., Ola Listhaug, and George Rabinowitz. 1991. Issues and Party Support in Multiparty Systems. *American Political Science Review* 85:1107–31.

McGraw, Kathleen M., Milton Lodge, and Patrick Stroh. 1990. On-line Processing in Candidate Evaluation: The Effects of Issue Order, Issue Importance, and Sophistication. *Political Behavior* 12:41–58.

McGraw, Kathleen M., and Neil Pinney. 1990. The Effects of General and Domain Specific Expertise on Political Memory and Judgment. *Social Cognition* 8:9–30.

McGraw, Kathleen M., Neil Pinney, and David Neumann. 1991. Memory for Political Actors: Contrasting the Use of Semantic and Evaluative Organizational Strategies. *Political Behavior* 13:165–89.

McGuire, William J. 1983. A Contextualist Theory of Knowledge: Its Implications for Innovation and Reform in Psychological Research. In *Advances in Experimental Social Psychology.* Vol. 16, ed. Leonard Berkowitz. New York: Academic Press.

———. 1989. The Structure of Individual Attitudes and Attitude Systems. In *Attitude*

Structure and Function, ed. Anthony R. Pratkanis, Steven J. Breckler, and Anthony G. Greenwald. Hillsdale, N.J.: Prentice-Hall.

McKelvey, Richard D., and Peter C. Ordeshook. 1986. Information, Electoral Equilibria, and the Democratic Ideal. *Journal of Politics* 48:909–37.

McKoon, Gail, and Roger Ratcliff. 1992. Inference During Reading. *Psychological Review* 99(3):440–66.

McPhee, William N. 1963. *Formal Theories of Mass Behavior.* New York: Free Press.

McPhee, William N., and Robert B. Smith. 1962. A Model for Analyzing Voting Systems. In *Public Opinion and Congressional Elections,* ed. William N. McPhee and William A. Glaser. New York: Free Press.

Madsen, Daniel B. 1978. Issue Importance and Group Choice Shifts: A Persuasive Arguments Approach. *Journal of Personality and Social Psychology* 36:1118–27.

Marks, Gary, and Norman Miller. 1982. The Effects of Certainty on Consensus Judgements. *Personality and Social Psychology Bulletin* 11:165–77.

Markus, Gregory B. 1982. Political Attitudes in An Election Year: A Report of the 1980 NES Panel Study. *American Political Science Review* 76:538–60.

Markus, Gregory B., and Philip Converse. 1979. A Dynamic Simultaneous Equation Model of Electoral Choice. *American Political Science Review* 73:1055–70.

Markus, Hazel, and Robert B. Zajonc. 1985. The Cognitive Perspective in Social Psychology. In *Handbook of Social Psychology.* Vol. 1, ed. Gardner Lindzey and Elliot Aronson. New York: Random House.

Marquette, Jesse, John Green, and Mark Wattier. 1991. A General Theory of Voting. Paper presented at the annual meeting of the Midwest Political Science Association, Chicago.

Martin, Leonard, and Abraham Tesser. eds. 1992. *The Construction of Social Judgments.* Hillsdale, N.J.: Lawrence Erlbaum Associates.

Massaro, Dominic, and Nelson Cowan. 1993. Information Processing Models: Microscopes of the Mind. *Annual Review of Psychology* 44:383–425.

Mayhew, David. 1974. *Congress: The Electoral Connection.* New Haven, Conn.: Yale University Press.

Meng, Xiao-Li, Robert Rosenthal, and Donald B. Rubin. 1992. Comparing Correlated Correlation Coefficients. *Psychological Bulletin* 111:172–75.

Millar, Murray G., and Abraham Tesser. 1986. Thought-Induced Attitude Change: The Effects of Schema Structure and Commitment. *Journal of Personality and Social Psychology* 51:259–69.

Miller, Arthur H., and Warren Miller. 1976. Ideology in the 1972 Election: Myth or Reality? *American Political Science Review* 70:832–49.

Miller, Arthur H., and Martin P. Wattenberg. 1985. Throwing the Rascals Out: Performance Evaluations of Presidential Candidates, 1952–1980. *American Political Science Review* 79:359–72.

Miller, Arthur H., Martin P. Wattenberg, and Oksana Malanchuk. 1986. Schematic Assessments of Presidential Candidates. *American Political Science Review* 80:521–40.

Miller, George. 1956. The Magical Number Seven, Plus or Minus Two: Some Limits on Our Capacity for Processing Information. *Psychological Review* 63:81–97.

Morin, Richard. 1991. Two ways of Reading the Public's Lips on Gulf Policy: Differently Phrased Questions Seem at First Glance to Yield Contradictory Results. The *Washington Post:* a9.

Morrow, D., S. Greenspan, and Gordon Bower. 1987. Accessibility and Situation Models in Narrative Comprehension. *Journal of Memory and Language* 26:165–87.

Moser, C. A., and G. Kalton. 1972. *Survey Methods in Social Investigation.* New York: Basic Books.

Mueller, John E. 1970. Presidential Popularity from Truman to Johnson. *American Political Science Review* 64:18–34.

Mullen, Brian, and Carolyn Cooper. 1989. The Privileged Position of Person Categories: A Comment on Sedikides and Ostrom. *Social Cognition* 7:373–88.

Murphy, Martin D. 1979. Measurement of Category Clustering in Free Recall. In *Memory Organization and Structure,* ed. C. Richard Puff. New York: Academic Press.

Neely, James. 1977. Semantic Priming and Retrieval from Lexical Memory: Roles of Inhibitionless Spreading Activation and Limited Capacity Attention. *Journal of Experimental Psychology: General* 106:226–54.

Neisser, Ulric, ed. 1987. *Concepts and Conceptual Development: Ecological and Intellectual Factors in Categorization.* Cambridge: Cambridge University Press.

Neuman, W. Russell. 1986. *The Paradox of Mass Publics: Knowledge and Opinion in the American Electorate.* Cambridge, Mass.: Harvard University Press.

Newell, Allen, and Herbert Simon. 1972. *Human Problem Solving.* Englewood-Cliffs, N.J.: Prentice-Hall.

Newman, Leonard, and James Uleman. 1989. Spontaneous Trait Inference. In *Unintended Thought,* ed. James Uleman and John Bargh. New York: The Guilford Press.

Nie, Norman H., Sidney Verba, and John Petrocik. 1976. *The Changing American Voter.* Cambridge, Mass.: Harvard University Press.

Nimmo, Dan, and Robert Savage. 1976. *Candidates and Their Images: Concepts, Methods and Findings.* Santa Monica, Calif.: Goodyear Publishing.

Nisbett, Richard, and Lee Ross. 1980. *Human Inference: Strategies and Shortcomings of Social Judgment.* Engelwood Cliffs, N.J.: Prentice-Hall.

Nisbett, Richard, and Timothy Wilson. 1977. Telling More Than We Know: Verbal Reports on Mental Processes. *Psychological Review* 84:231–59.

Norpoth, Helmut, and Milton Lodge. 1985. The Difference Between Attitudes and Nonattitudes in the Mass Public: Just Measurement. *American Journal of Political Science* 29:291–307.

Oden, Gregg C., and Norman H. Anderson. 1971. Differential Weighting in Integration Theory. *Journal of Experimental Psychology: General* 89:152–61.

Olshavsky, R. W. 1979. Task Complexity and Contingent Processing in Decision Making: A Replication and Extension. *Organizational Behavior and Human Performance* 24:300–16.

Osgood, Charles, George Suci, and Percy Tannenbaum. 1957. *The Measurement of Meaning.* Urbana, Ill.: University of Illinois Press.

Ostrom, Thomas. 1984. The Sovereignty of Social Cognition. In *The Handbook of Social Cognition,* ed. Robert S. Wyer and Thomas Srull. Hillsdale, N.J.: Lawrence Erlbaum Associates.

———. 1987. Bipolar Survey Items: An Information Processing Perspective. In *Social Information Processing and Survey Methodology,* ed. Hans J. Hippler, Norbert Schwarz, and Seymour Sudman. New York: Springer-Verlag.

———. 1988. Computer Simulation: The Third Symbol System. *Journal of Experimental Social Psychology* 24:381–92.

———. 1989. Three Catechisms for Social Memory. In *Memory: Interdisciplinary Approaches,* ed. George R. Goethals, Colleen M. Kelley, and Benjamin R. Stephens. New York: Springer-verlag.

Ostrom, Thomas M., John Lingle, John Pryor, and Neva Geva. 1980. Cognitive Organization of Person Impressions. In *Person Memory: The Cognitive Basis of Social Percep-*

tion, ed. Reid Hastie, Thomas Ostrom, Ebbe Ebbensen, Robert Wyer, David Hamilton, and Donald Carlson. Hillsdale, N.J.: Lawrence Erlbaum Associates.

Ostrom, Thomas M., John B. Pryor, and David D. Simpson. 1981. The Organization of Social Information. In *In Social Cognition: The Ontario Symposium on Personality and Social Psychology,* ed. E. Tory Higgins, Charles P. Herman, and Mark P. Zanna. Hillsdale, N.J.: Lawrence Erlbaum Associates.

Ostrom, Thomas M., John B. Pryor, Thomas P. Pusateri, and Mark L. Mitchell. N.d. Judgmental Consequences of Person Organization. Unpublished manuscript, Ohio State University.

Ottati, Victor C. 1990. Determinants of Political Judgements: The Joint Influence of Normative and Heuristic Rules of Inference. *Political Behavior* 12:159–79.

Ottati, Victor C., and Robert S. Wyer. 1990. The Cognitive Mediators of Political Choice: Toward a Comprehensive Model of Political Information Processing. In *Information and Democratic Processes,* ed. John A. Ferejohn and James H. Kuklinski. Urbana, Ill.: University of Illinois Press.

Pachella, Robert. 1974. The Interpretation of Reaction Time in Information Processing Research. In *Human Information Processing: Tutorials in Performance and Cognition,* ed. Barry Kantowitz. Hillsdale, N.J.: Lawrence Erlbaum Associates.

Page, Benjamin I. 1977. Elections and Social Choice: The State of Evidence. *American Political Science Review* 21:639–68.

———. 1978. *Choices and Echoes in Presidential Elections.* Chicago: University of Chicago Press.

Page, Banjamin I., and Richard A. Brody. 1972. Policy Voting and the Electoral Process: The Vietnam War Issue. *American Poltical Science Review* 66:979–95.

Page, Benjamin I., and Calvin C. Jones. 1979. Reciprocal Effects of Policy Preferences, Party Loyalties and the Vote. *American Political Science Review* 73:1071–89.

Page, Benjamin I., and Robert Y. Shapiro. 1992. *The Rational Public: Fifty Years of Trends in Americans' Policy Preferences.* Chicago: University of Chicago Press.

Palmer, S. E., and R. Kimchi. 1986. The Information Processing Approach to Cognition. In *Approaches to Cognition: Contrasts and Controversies,* ed. T. J. Knapp and L. C. Robertson. Hillsdale, N.J.: Lawrence Erlbaum Associates.

Park, Bernadette. 1986. A Method for Studying the Development of Impressions of Real People. *Journal of Personality and Social Psychology* 51:907–17.

———. 1989. Trait Attributes as On-Line Organizers in Person Impressions. In *On-Line Processes in Person Perception,* ed. John N. Bassili. Hillsdale, N.J.: Lawrence Erlbaum Associates.

Park, Bernadette, and Charles M. Judd. 1990. Measures and Models of Perceived Group Variability. *Journal of Personality and Social Psychology* 59:173–91.

Park, Bernadette, and Myron Rothbart. 1982. Perception of Out-Group Homogeneity and Levels of Social Categorization: Memory for the Subordinate Attributes of In-Group and Out-Group Members. *Journal of Personality and Social Psychology* 42:1051–68.

Park, Bernadette, Corey S. Ryan, and Charles M. Judd. 1992. The Role of Meaningful Subgroups in Explaining Differences in Perceived Variability for In-Groups and Out-Groups. *Journal of Personality and Social Psychology* 63:553–67.

Patterson, Thomas E. 1980. *The Mass Media Election.* New York: Praeger.

Pavelchak, Mark A. 1989. Piecemeal and Category-based Evaluation: An Idiographic Analysis. *Journal of Personality and Social Psychology* 56:354–63.

Payne, John W. 1976. Task Complexity and Contingent Processing in Decision Making: An information Search and Protocol Analysis. *Organizational Behavior and Human Performance* 16:366–87.

————. 1982. Contingent Decision Behavior. *Psychological Bulletin* 92:382–402.

Payne, John W., James R. Bettman, and Eric J. Johnson. 1988. Adaptive Strategy Selection in Decision Making. *Journal of Experimental Psychology: Learning, Memory and Cognition* 14:534–52.

————. 1990. The Adaptive Decision-Maker: Effort and Accuracy in Choice. In *Insights in Decision-Making*, ed. Robin Hogarth. Chicago: University of Chicago Press.

————. 1992. Behavioral Decision Theory: A Constructive Processing Perspective. *Annual Review of Psychology* 43:87– 131.

Payne, John W., and M. L. Braunstein. 1978. Risky Choice: An Examination of Information Acquisition Behavior. *Memory and Cognition* 22:17–44.

Petrusic, William, and Donald G. Jamieson. 1978. Relation between Probability of Preferential Choice and Time to Choose Changes with Practice. *Journal of Experimental Psychology: Human Perception and Performance* 4:471–82.

Petty, Richard E., and John Cacioppo. 1979. Issue Involvement Can Increase or Decrease Persuasion by Enhancing Message Relevant Cognitive Responses. *Journal of Personality and Social Psychology* 37:1915–26.

————. 1986. *Communication and Persuasion: Central and Peripheral Routes to Attitude Change.* New York: Springer-Verlag.

Petty, Richard E., and Jon A. Krosnick. Forthcoming. *Attitude Strength: Antecedents and Consequences.* Hillsdale, N.J.: Lawrence Erlbaum Associates.

Plott, Charles R., and M. E. Levine. 1978. A Model of Agenda Influence on Committee Decisions. *American Economic Review* 68:146–60.

Pomper, Gerald, and Mark Schulman. 1975. Variability of Electoral Behavior: Longitudinal Perspectives from Causal Modeling. *American Journal of Political Science* 19:1– 18.

Popkin, Samuel, John Gorman, Charles Phillips, and Jeffrey Smith. 1976. Comment: What Have You Done for Me Lately: Toward an Investment Theory of Voting. *American Political Science Review* 70:779–805.

Popkin, Samuel L. 1991. *The Reasoning Voter.* Chicago: University of Chicago Press.

Popper, Karl R. 1968. *The Logic of Scientific Discovery.* New York: Harper and Row.

Powell, Larry. 1977. Satirical Persuasion and Topic Salience. *Southern Speech Communication Journal* 42:151–62.

Powell, Linda. 1989. Analyzing Misinformation: Perceptions of Congressional Candidates' Ideologies. *American Journal of Political Science* 33:272–93.

Pratkanis, Anthony. 1989. The Cognitive Structure of Attitudes. In *Attitude Structure and Function*, ed. Anthony Pratkanis, Steven Breckler and Anthony Greenwald. Hillsdale, N.J.: Lawrence Erlbaum Associates.

Pratto, Felicia, and Oliver P. John. 1991. Automatic Vigilance: The Attention-Grabbing Power of Negative Social Information. *Journal of Personality and Social Psychology* 61:380–91.

Pryor, John B., Teri L. Kott, and Gregory R. Bovee. 1984. The Influence of Information Redundancy upon the Use of Traits and Persons as Organizing Categories. *Journal of Experimental Social Psychology* 20:246–62.

Pryor, John B., and Thomas M. Ostrom. 1981. The Cognitive Organization of Social Information: A Converging-operations Approach. *Journal of Personality and Social Psychology* 41:628–41.

Pryor, John B., Thomas M. Ostrom, Janet M. Dukerich, Mark L. Mitchell, and John A. Herstein. 1983. Preintegrative Categorization of Social Information: The Role of Persons as Organizing Categories. *Journal of Personality and Social Psychology* 44:923– 32.

Pryor, John B., David D. Simpson, Mark Mitchell, Thomas M. Ostrom, and John Lydon. 1982. Structural Selectivity in the Retrieval of Social Information. *Social Cognition* 1:336–57.

Puto, Christopher P. 1987. The Framing of Buying Decisions. *Journal of Consumer Research* 14:301–15.

Quattrone, George, and Amos Tversky. 1988. Contrasting Rational and Psychological Analyses of Political Choice. *American Political Science Review* 82:719–36.

Quillian, M. Ross. 1969. The Teachable Language Comprehender: A Simulation Program and Theory of Language. *Communications of the Association for Computing Machinery* 12:459–76.

Raaijmakers, Jeroen G., and Richard M. Shiffrin. 1980. SAM: A Theory of Probabilistic Search of Associative Memory. *The Psychology of Learning and Motivation* 14:207–62.

Rabinowitz, George, and Stuart Elaine Macdonald. 1989. A Directional Theory of Issue Voting. *American Political Science Review* 83:93–121.

Rahn, Wendy M. 1990. Perception and Evaluation of Political Candidates: A Social-Cognitive Perspective. Ph.D. Diss., University of Minnesota, Minneapolis.

———. 1991. Evaluating Political Debate: The Roles of Political Sophistication and Information Processing Context. Paper presented at the annual meeting of the Midwest Political Science Association, Chicago.

———. 1992. Political Candidate Evaluation in Complex Information Environments: Cognitive Organization and Memory Processes. Paper presented at the annual meeting of the Midwest Political Science Association, Chicago, Ill.

———. 1993. The Role of Partisan Stereotypes in Information Processing about Political Candidates. *American Journal of Political Science* 37:472–96.

Rahn, Wendy M., John H. Aldrich, and Eugene Borgida. 1992. Individual and Contextual Variations in Political Candidate Appraisal. Unpublished manuscript, University of Wisconsin.

Rahn, Wendy M., John Aldrich, Eugene Borgida, and John Sullivan. 1990. A Social-Cognitive Model of Candidate Appraisal. In *Information and Democratic Process,* ed. John Ferejohn and James Kuklinski. Chicago: University of Chicago Press.

Rahn, Wendy M., Jon A. Krosnick, and Marijke Breuning. 1992. Rationalization and Derivation Processes in Political Candidate Evaluation. Paper presented at the annual meeting of the American Political Science Association, Chicago. 3–6 September.

Rapoport, Ronald B., Kelly L. Metcalf, and Jon A. Hartman. 1989. Candidate Traits and Voter Inferences: An Experimental Study. *Journal of Politics* 51:917–32.

Reder, Lynne M., and John R. Anderson. 1980. A Partial Resolution of the Paradox of Interference: The Role of Integrating Knowledge. *Cognitive Psychology* 12:447–72.

Redlawsk, David P. 1992. Using Hypermedia to Develop a Political Science Simulation. Paper presented to the 25th Annual Conference of the Association of Small Computer Users in Education (ASCUE), Myrtle Beach, S.C.

Reed, David. 1990. Candidate Perception and the Structure of Trait Accessibility. Paper presented at the annual meeting of the American Political Science Association, San Fransisco.

Reeder, Glenn, and Michael Coovert. 1986. Revising an Impression of Morality. *Social Cognition* 4:1–17.

Reeder, Lynne M. 1982. Plausibility Judgments versus Fact Retrieval: Alternative Strategies for Sentence Verification. *Psychological Review* 89:250–80.

Reichman, Rachael. 1985. *Getting Computers to Talk Like You and Me: Discourse Context, Focus, and Semantics.* Cambridge, Mass.: MIT Press.

Repass, David. 1979. Issue Salience and Party Choice. *American Political Science Review* 65:389–400.

Reyes, Robert M., William Thompson, and Gordon Bower. 1980. Judgmental Biases Resulting from Differing Availabilities of Arguments. *Journal of Personality and Social Psychology* 39:2–12.

Reynolds, H. T. 1974. Rationality and Attitudes toward Political Parties and Candidates. *Journal of Politics* 36:983–1003.

Rhine, Ramon J., and Laurence J. Severance. 1970. Ego-Involvement, Discrepancy, Source Credibility, and Attitude Change. *Journal of Personality and Social Psychology* 16:175–90.

Riggle, Ellen D. 1992. Cognitive Strategies and Candidate Evaluations. *American Politics Quarterly* 20:227–46.

Riker, William H., and Peter C. Ordeshook. 1973. *An Introduction to Positive Political Theory.* Englewood Cliffs, N.J.: Prentice Hall.

Rivers, Douglas. 1988. Heterogeneity in Models of Electoral Choice. *American Journal of Political Science* 32:737–57.

Roberts, Fred S. 1976. *Discrete Mathematical Models.* Engelwood Cliffs, N.J.: Prentice Hall.

Roenker, Daniel L., Charles P. Thompson, and Sam C. Brown. 1971. Comparisons of Measures for the Estimation of Clustering in Free Recall. *Psychological Bulletin* 76:45–48.

Rokeach, Milton, and Peter Kliejunas. 1972. Behavior as a Function of Attitude-toward-Object and Attitude-toward-Situation. *Journal of Personality and Social Psychology* 22:194–201.

Rosch, Eleanor. 1978. Principles of Categorization. In *Cognition and Categorization,* ed. Eleanor Rosch and Barbra Lloyd. Hillsdale, N.J.: Lawrence Erlbaum Associates.

Rosch, Eleanor, and C. Mervis. 1975. Family Resemblances: Studies in the Internal Structure of Categories. *Cognitive Psychology* 7:573–605.

Rosen, Larry D., and Paul Rosenkoetter. 1975. An Eye Fixation Analysis of Choice and Judgment with Multiattribute Stimuli. *Memory and cognition* 4:747–52.

Rosenberg, Milton. 1956. Cognitive Structure and Attitudinal Effect. *Journal of Abnormal and Social Psychology* 53:367– 72.

———. 1968. Hedonism, Inauthenticity, and Other Goals Towards Expansion of a Consistency Theory. In *Theories of Cognitive Consistency: A Sourcebook,* ed. Robert P. Abelson et al. Chicago, Ill.: Rand McNally.

Rossi, Peter. 1956. Four Landmarks in Voting Research. In *American Voting Behavior,* ed. Eugene Burdick and Arthur Brodbeck. New York: Free Press.

Rothbart, Myron. 1981. Memory Processes and Social Beliefs. In *Cognitive Processes in Stereotype and Intergroup Behavior,* ed. David L. Hamilton. Hillsdale, N.J.: Lawrence Erlbaum Associates. 145–82.

Rugg, Harold. 1941. Experiments in Wording Questions. *Public Opinion Quarterly* 5:91–92.

Rumelhart, David, and David Norman. 1983. Representation in Memory. In *Handbook of Experimental Psychology,* ed. Richard Atkinson, Richard Hernstein, Gardner Lindzey, and R. Duncan Luce. New York: Wiley.

Rumelhart, David, and Andrew Ortony. 1977. The Representation of Knowledge in Memory. In *Schooling and the Acquisition of Knowledge,* ed. Richard C. Anderson, Paul J. Spiro, and William E. Montague. Hillsdale, N.J.: Lawrence Erlbaum Associates.

Russo, J. Edward, and Barbara A. Dosher. 1980. Cognitive Effort and Strategy Selection in Binary Choice. Technical Report, Center for Decision Research, Graduate School of Business, University of Chicago.

———. 1983. Strategies for Multiattribute Binary Choice. *Journal of Experimental Social Psychology: Learning, Memory, and Cognition* 9:676–96.

Russo, J. Edward, and Larry D. Rosen. 1975. An Eye Fixation Analysis of Multialternative Choice. *Memory and Cognition* 3:267–76.

Sanbonmatsu, David, Steven Sherman, and David Hamilton. 1987. Illusory Correlation in the Perception of Individuals and Groups. *Social Cognition* 5:1–25.

Sanford, Anthony. 1987. *The Mind of Man: Models of Human Understanding.* New Haven, Conn.: Yale University Press.

Saris, Willem E., and Bas Van Den Putte. 1988. True Score or Factor Models. *Sociological Methods and Research* 17:123– 57.

Savage, Leonard J. 1954. *The Foundations of Statistics.* New York: Dover.

Schank, Roger. 1982. *Dynamic Memory: A Theory of Reminding and Learning in Computers and People.* New York: Cambridge University Press.

Schneider, Walter, and Richard M. Shiffrin. 1977. Controlled and Automatic Human Information Processing: Vol. 1, Detection, Search, and Attention. *Psychological Review* 84:127–90.

Schoemaker, Paul J. H. 1982. The Expected Utility Model: Its Variants, Purposes, Evidence, and Limitations. *Journal of Economic Literature* 20:99–118.

Schrodt, Philip. 1987. Pattern Matching, Set Prediction and Foreign Policy Analysis. In *Artificial Intelligence and National Security,* ed. Stephen J. Cimbala. Lexington, Ky.: Lexington Books.

Schuman, Howard, J. Ludwig, and Jon A. Krosnick. 1986. The Perceived Threat of Nuclear War, Salience, and Open Questions. *Public Opinion Quarterly* 50:519–36.

Schuman, Howard, and Stanley Presser. 1981. *Questions and Answers in Attitude Surveys: Experiments on Question Form, Wording, and Context.* New York: Academic Press.

Schumpeter, Joseph. 1950. *Capitalism, Socialism, and Democracy.* New York: Harper & Row.

Schwarz, Norbert, and Hans J. Hippler. 1987. What Response Scales May Tell Your Respondents: Informative Functions of Response Alternative. In *Social Information Processing and Survey Methodology,* ed. Hans J. Hippler, Norbert Schwarz, and Seymour Sudman. New York: Springer-Verlag.

Scott, William A., D. Wayne Osgood and Christopher Peterson. 1979. *Cognitive Structure: Theory and Measurement of Individual Differences.* Washington, D.C.: Winston and Sons.

Sears, David, Leonie Huddy, and Lynitta Shaffer. 1986. A Schematic Variant of Symbolic Politics Theory, as Applied to Racial and Gender Equality. In *Political Cognition,* ed. David O. Sears and Richard R. Lau. Hillsdale, N.J.: Lawrence Erlbaum Associates.

Sears, David O., and Richard R. Lau. 1983. Inducing Apparently Self-Interested Political Preferences: An Experiment. *American Journal of Political Science* 27:223–52.

Sears, David O., Richard R. Lau, Tom R. Tyler, and Harris M. Allen, Jr. 1980. Self-Interest vs. Symbolic Politics in Policy Attitudes and Presidential Voting. *American Political Science Review* 74:670–84.

Sebald, Hans. 1962. Limitations of Communication: Mechanisms of Image Maintenance in the Form of Selective Perception, Selective Memory and Selective Distortion. *Journal of Communication* 12:142–49.

Sedikides, Constantine, Patricia G. Devine, and Robert W. Fuhrman. 1991. Social Perception in Multitarget Settings: Effects of Motivated Encoding Strategies. *Personality and Social Psychology Bulletin* 17:625–32.

Sedikides, Constantine, Nils Olsen, and Harry T. Reis. 1993. Relationships as Natural Categories. *Journal of Personality and Social Psychology* 64:71–82.

Sedikides, Constantine, and Thomas M. Ostrom. 1988. Are Person Categories Used When Organizing Information about Unfamiliar Sets of Persons? *Social Cognition* 6:252–67.

———. 1990. Persons as Privileged Categories: A Rejoinder to Mullen and Cooper. *Social Cognition* 8:229–40.

Sentis, Keith, and Eugene Bernstein. 1979. Remembering Schema Consistent Information: Effects of a Balance Schema on Recognition Memory. *Journal of Personality and Social Psychology* 37:2200–2211.

Shaffer, William. 1972. *Computer Simulations of Voting Behavior*. New York: Oxford University Press.

Shanks, J. Merrill, and Warren E. Miller. 1991. Partisanship, Policy and Performance: The Reagan Legacy in the 1988 Election. *British Journal of Political Science* 21:129–97.

Shannon, Claude. 1961. A Mathematical Theory of Cognition. In *Cybernetics, or Control and Communication in the Animal and the Machine.* 2d ed, ed. Norbert Wiener. Cambridge, Mass.: MIT Press.

Shapiro, Michael J. 1969. Rational Political Man: A Synthesis of Economic and Social-psychological Perspectives. *American Political Science Review* 52:349–66.

Sherif, Carolyn W., Muzafer Sherif, and Roger E. Nebergall. 1965. *Attitude and Attitude Change.* Philadelphia: W. B. Saunders.

Sherif, Muzafer, and Hadley Cantril. 1947. *The Psychology of Ego-involvement.* New York: Wiley.

Sherif, Muzafer, and Carl I. Hovland. 1961. *Social Judgment.* New Haven, Conn.: Yale University Press.

Sherman, Stephen J., Kim Zehner, Joel Johnson, and Edward R. Hirt. 1983. Social Explanation: The Role of Timing, Set, and Recall of Subjective Likelihood Estimates. *Journal of Personality and Social Psychology* 44:1127–43.

Sherman, Steven, Kim Zehner, and James Johnson. 1983. The Role of Timing, Set, and Recall on Subjective Likelihood Estimates. *Journal of Personality and Social Psychology* 48:863–75.

Shiffrin, Richard M., and William Schneider. 1977. Controlled and Automatic Human Information Processing: Vol. 2. Perceptual Learning, Automatic Attending, and General Theory. *Psychological Review* 84:127–90.

Shively, W. Phillips. 1979. The Development of Party Identification among Adults: Exploration of a Functional Model. *American Political Science Review* 73:1039–54.

Shugan, Steven. 1980. The Cost of Thinking. *Journal of Consumer Research* 7:99–111.

Sigel, Ruth S. 1966. Image of the American Presidency. *Midwest Journal of Political Science* 10:123–37.

Simon, Herbert A. 1955. A Behavioral Model of Rational Choice. *Quarterly Journal of Economics* 69:99–118.

———. 1957. *Models of Man.* New York: John Wiley and Sons.

———. 1978. Rationality as a Process and Product of Thought. *American Economic Review: Proceedings* 68:1–16.

———. 1979a. Information Processing Models of Cognition. *Annual Review of Psychology* 30:363–96.

———. 1979b. *Models of Thought.* New Haven, Conn.: Yale University Press.

———. 1981. *The Sciences of the Artificial.* 2d ed. Cambridge, Mass.: MIT Press.

———. 1985. Human Nature in Politics: The Dialogue of Psychology with Political Science. *American Political Science Review* 79:293–304.

———. 1986. Rationality in Psychology and Economics. In *In Rational Choice: The Contrast Between Economics and Psychology,* ed. Robin M. Hogarth and Melvin W. Reder. Chicago: University of Chicago Press.

———. 1992. Alternative Representations for Cognition: Search and Reasoning. In *Cognition: Conceptual and Methodological Issues,* ed. Herbert L. Pick, Paulus Van den Broek, and David C. Knill, 121–42. Washington, D.C.: American Psychological Association.

Skowronski, John J., and Donal E. Carlson. 1987. Social Judgement and Social Memory: The Role of Cue Diagnosticity in Negativity, Positivity, and Extremity Biases. *Journal of Personality and Social Psychology* 52:689–99.

———. 1989. Negativity and Extremity Biases in Impression Formation: A Review of Explanations. *Psychological Bulletin* 106:131–42.

Slovic, Paul. 1972. From Shakespeare to Simon: Speculations—and Some Evidence—About Man's Ability to Process Information. Oregon Research Institute Monograph, 12. Eugene, Or.

Slovic, Paul, and Douglas MacPhillamy. 1974. Dimensional Commensurability and Cue Utilization in Comparative Judgement. *Organizational Behavior and Human Performance* 11:172–94.

Smith, Edward, and Douglas Medin. 1981. *Categories and Concepts.* Cambridge, Mass.: Harvard University Press.

Smith, Eliot R. 1988. Category Accessibility Effects in a Simulated Exemplar-Based Memory. *Journal of Experimental Social Psychology* 24:448–63.

———. 1989. Procedural Efficiency and On-Line Social Judgments. In *On-Line Cognition in Person Perception,* ed. John N. Bassili. Hillsdale, N.J.: Lawrence Erlbaum Associates.

Smith, Eliot R., and Miriam Lerner. 1986. Development of Automatism of Social Judgments. *Journal of Personality and Social Psychology* 50:246–59.

Smith, Eric R. A. N. 1989. *The Unchanging American Voter.* Berkeley: University of California Press.

Smith, Tom W. 1984a. The Subjectivity of Ethnicity. In *Surveying Subjective Phenomena,* ed. Charles F. Turner and Elizabeth Martin. New York: Russell Sage Foundation.

———. 1984b. Nonattitudes: A Review and Evaluation. In *Surveying Subjective Phenomena,* ed. Charles F. Turner and Elizabeth Martin. New York: Russell Sage Foundation.

Sniderman, Paul M., Richard A. Brody, and Philip E. Tetlock. 1991. *Reasoning and Choice: Explorations in Political Psychology.* New York: Cambridge University Press.

Sniderman, Paul M., Robert Griffin, and James M. Glaser. 1990. Information and Electoral Choice. In *Information and Democratic Processes,* ed. John A. Ferejohn and James H. Kuklinski. Urbana, Ill.: University of Illinois Press.

Sostek, A., and A. Sostek. 1981. Impressions of Presidents: Effects of Information, Time and Discrepancy. *Bulletin of the Psychonomic Society* 17:187–89.

Spellman, Barbara A., and Keith J. Holyoak. 1992. If Saddam Is Hitler Then Who Is George Bush? Analogical Mapping between Systems of Social Roles. *Journal of Personality and Social Psychology* 62:913–33.

Srull, Thomas K. 1983. Organizational and Retrieval Processes in Person Memory: An Examination of Processing Objectives, Presentation Format, and Self-Generated Retrieval Cues. *Journal of Personality and Social Psychology* 44:1157–70.

———. 1984. Methodological Techniques for the Study of Person Memory and Social Cognition. In *Handbook of Social Cognition,* ed. Robert S. Wyer and Thomas K. Srull. Hillsdale, N.J.: Lawrence Erlbaum Associates.

Srull, Thomas K., and Robert S. Wyer. 1986. The Role of Chronic and Temporary Goals in Social Information Processing. In *Handbook of Motivation and Cognition: Foundations of Social Behavior*, ed. Richard M. Sorrentino and E. Tory Higgins. New York: Guilford Press.

————. 1988. Person Memory and Judgment. *Psychological Review* 96:58–83.

Stasser, Gerald. 1988. Computer Simulation as a Research Tool: The DISCUSS Model of Group Decision Making. *Journal of Experimental Social Psychology* 24:393–422.

Stephan, Walter G. 1989. A Cognitive Approach to Stereotyping. In *Stereotyping and Prejudice: Changing Perceptions*, ed. Daniel Bar-Tal, Arie W. Kruglanski, and William Stroebe. New York: Springer-Verlag.

Stoker, Laura. 1993. Judging Presidential Character: The Demise of Gary Hart. *Political Behavior* 15:193–223.

Strack, Fritz, and Leonard L. Martin. 1987. Thinking, Judging, and Communicating: A Process Account of Context Effects in Surveys. In *Social Information Processing and Surveys Methodology*, ed. Hans J. Hippler, Norbert Schwarz, and Seymour Sudman. New York: Springer-Verlag.

Stroh, Patrick K. 1989. Candidate Ambiguity and Voter Projections. Paper presented at the 1989 Annual Meeting of the American Political Science Association, Atlanta, Ga.

Stroh, Patrick K., and David Moskowitz. 1992. Choosing Candidates: Behavioral Decision Theory and the Preference Reversal Phenomena. Paper presented at the 1992 Annual Meeting of the American Political Science Association, Chicago, Ill.

Strube, Gerhard. 1987. Answering Survey Questions: The Role of Memory. In *Social Information Processing and Survey Methodology*, ed. Hans J. Hippler, Norbert Schwarz, and Seymour Sudman. New York: Springer-Verlag.

Sullivan, John L., John H. Aldrich, Eugene Borgida, and Wendy Rahn. 1990. Candidate Appraisal and Human Nature: Man and Superman in the 1984 Election. *Political Psychology* 11:459–84.

Sundstrom, Gunilla A. 1989. Information Search and Decision Making: The Effects of Information Display. *Acta Psychologica* 65:165–79.

Svenson, Ola. 1979. Process Descriptions of Decision Making. *Organizational Behavior and Human Performance* 23:86–112.

Swann, William B. 1984. Quest for Accuracy in Person Perception: A Matter of Pragmatics. *Psychological Review* 91:457–77.

Sylvan, Donald A., Ashok Goel, and B. Chandrasekaran. 1990. Analyzing Political Decision Making from an Information Processing Perspective: JESSE. *American Journal of Political Science* 34:1–30.

Taber, Charles S. 1992. POLI: An Expert System Model of U.S. Foreign Policy Belief Systems. *American Political Science Review* 86:888–904.

Taber, Charles S., Tse-Min Lin, and Michael W. Frank. 1990. Specification of the Kahneman-Tversky Probability Weighting Function. SUNY at Stony Brook. Photocopy.

Taber, Charles, and Marco Steenbergen. 1992. A Simulated Comparison of Models of Electoral Decision Making. Paper presented at the annual meeting of the Midwest Political Science Association, Chicago, Ill.

Taber, Charles S., and Richard Timpone. Forthcoming. Pictures in the PC: Computational Modeling and Political Psychology. In *New Directions in Political Psychology*, ed. Michael X. Delli Carpini, Leonie Huddy, and Shapiro Y. Shapiro. Greenwich, Conn.: JAI.

Tajfel, Henri. 1969. Cognitive Aspects of Prejudice. *Journal of Social Issues* 25:79–98.

Tajfel, Henri, and Charles J. Turner. 1986. The Social Identity Theory of Intergroup

Behavior. In *Psychology of Intergroup Relations,* ed. Stephen Worchel and William G. Austin. Chicago, Ill.: Nelson-Hall.

Tannenbaum, Percy H. 1956. Initial Attitudes toward Source and Concept as Factors in Attitude Change through Communication. *Public Opinion Quarterly* 20:413–25.

Taylor, Shelley E. 1981. The Interface of Cognitive and Social Psychology. In *Cognition, Social Behavior, and the Environment,* ed. John H. Harvey. Hillsdale, N.J.: Lawrence Erlbaum Associates.

Taylor, Shelley E., and Jennifer Crocker. 1981. Schematic Bases of Social Information Processing. In *Social Cognition: The Ontario Symposium.* Vol. 1, ed. E. Tory Higgins, Charles Herman, and Mark Zanna. Hillsdale, N.J.: Lawrence Erlbaum Associates.

Tedin, Kent L. 1980. Assessing Peer and Parental Influence on Adolescent Political Attitudes. *American Journal of Political Science* 24:136–54.

Tesser, Abraham. 1978. Self-Generated Attitude Change. *Advances in Experimental Social Psychology* 11:289–338.

Tesser, Abraham, and C. Leone. 1977. Cognitive Schemas and Thought as Determinants of Attitude Change. *Journal of Experimental Social Psychology* 13:340–56.

Thaler, Richard. 1985. Mental Accounting and Consumer Choice. *Marketing Science* 4:199–214.

Thorngate, W. 1980. Efficient Decision Heuristics. *Behavioral Science* 25:219–25.

Thurstone, L. L. 1927. A Law of Comparative Judgment. *Psychological Review* 34:273–86.

Tolman, Edward C. 1937. *Purposive Behavior in Animals and Men.* New York: Century.

Tourangeau, Roger. 1984. Cognitive Science and Survey Methods. In *Cognitive Aspects of Survey Methodology,* ed. Thomas B. Jabine, M. L. Straf, J. M. Tanur, and Roger Tourangeau. Washington, D.C.: National Academy Press.

Tourangeau, Roger, and Kenneth A. Rasinski. 1988. Cognitive Processes Underlying Context Effects in Attitude Measurement. *Psychological Bulletin* 103:299–314.

Tourangeau, Roger, Kenneth A. Rasinski, Norman Bradburn, and Roy D'Andrade. 1989a. Belief Accessibility and Context Effects in Attitude Measurement. *Journal of Experimental Social Psychology* 25:401–21.

———. 1989b. Carryover Effects in Attitude Surveys. *Public Opinion Quarterly* 53:495–524.

Tourangeau, Roger, Kenneth A. Rasinski, and Roy D'Andrade. 1991. Attitude Structure and Belief Accessibility. *Journal of Experimental Social Psychology* 27:48–75.

Tufte, Edward. 1975. Determinants of the Outcomes of Midterm Congressional Elections. *American Political Science Review* 69:812–26.

Tversky, Amos. 1969. Intransitivity of Preferences. *Psychological Review* 76:31–48.

———. 1972. Elimination by Aspects: A Theory of Choice. *Psychological Review* 79:281–99.

Tversky, Amos, and Daniel Kahneman. 1974. Judgements under Uncertainty: Heuristics and Biases. *Science* 185:1124–31.

———. 1986. Rational Choice and the Framing of Decision. *The Journal of Business* 59 (Part 2): S251–78.

———. 1990. Cumulative Prospect Theory: An Analysis of Decisions under Uncertainty. Unpublished manuscript. Stanford University.

Tversky, Amos, and Samuel Sattath. 1979. Preference Trees. *Psychological Review* 86:542–73.

Tversky, Amos, Samuel Sattath, and Paul Slovic. 1988. Contingent Weighting Judgment and Choice. *Psychological Review* 95:371–84.

Uleman, James, and John Bargh. 1989. *Unintended Thought.* New York: The Guilford Press.

Von Neumann, John, and Oscar Morgenstern. 1944. *Theory of Games and Economic Behavior.* Princeton, N.J.: Princeton University Press.

Wahlke, John. 1991. Rational Choice Theory, Voting Behavior, and Democracy. In *Hierarchy and Democracy,* ed. Albert Somit and Rudolf Wildenmann. Nomos Verlags Gesellschaft.

Warr, Peter. 1974. Inference Magnitude, Range, and Evaluative Direction as Factors Affecting Relative Importance of Cues in Impression Formation. *Journal of Personality and Social Psychology* 30:191–97.

Watts, W. A., and William McGuire. 1964. Persistence of Induced Opinion Change and Retention of the Inducing Message Contents. *Journal of Abnormal and Social Psychology* 68:233–41.

Weber, Renee, and Jennifer Crocker. 1983. Cognitive Processes in the Revision of Stereotypic Beliefs. *Journal of Personality and Social Psychology* 45:961–77.

Westlye, Mark C. 1991. *Senate Elections and Campaign Intensity.* Baltimore, Md.: John Hopkins University Press.

Whittman, Donald. 1991. Contrasting Rational and Psychological Analyses of Political Choice. In *The Economic Approach to Politics: A Critical Assessment of the Theory of Rational Action,* ed. Kristin Monroe. New York: Harper Collins.

Wiley, David E., and James A. Wiley. 1970. The Estimation of Measurement Error in Panel Data. *American Sociological Review* 35:112–16.

Wilkins, Leslie T. 1967. *Social Deviance.* Engelwood Cliffs, N.J.: Prentice-Hall.

Wilson, Timothy, Dana Dunn, Dolores Kraft, and Douglas Lisle. 1989. Introspection, Attitude Change, and Attitude-Behavior Consistency: The Disruptive Effects of Explaining Why We Feel the Way We Do. In *Advances in Experimental Social Psychology.* Vol. 23, ed. Leonard Berkowitz. New York: Academic Press.

Wilson, Timothy, and Sara Hodges. 1992. Attitudes as Temporary Constructs. In *Construction of Social Judgment,* ed. Leonard Martin and Abraham Tesser. Hillsdale, N.J.: Lawrence Erlbaum Associates.

Wilson, Timothy, and John Schooler. 1991. Thinking Too Much: Introspection Can Reduce the Quality of Preferences and Decisions. *Journal of Personality and Social Psychology* 60:181–92.

Winter, Lorraine, and James Uleman. 1984. When are Social Judgments Made? Evidence for the Spontaneousness of Trait Inferences. *Journal of Personality and Social Psychology* 49:904–17.

Woll, Stanley, and Arthur Graesser. 1982. Memory Discrimination for Information Typical or Atypical of Person Schemata. *Social Cognition* 1:287–310.

Wright, George. 1984. *Behavioral Decision Theory: An Introduction.* Beverly Hills, Calif.: Sage.

Wright, Peter, and F. Barbour. 1977. Phased Decision Strategies: Sequels to an Initial Screening. In *Studies in the Management Sciences.* Vol. 6, ed. Milan S. Starr and M. Zeleny. Amsterdam: North Holland Publishing.

Wyer, Robert S., Thomas Lee Budesheim, and Alan J. Lambert. 1990. Cognitive Representation of Conversations about Persons. *Journal of Personality and Social Psychology* 58:218–38.

Wyer, Robert S., Thomas Lee Budesheim, Sharon Shavitt, Ellen D. Riggle, R. Jefferey Melton, and James H. Kuklinski. 1991. Image, Issues, and Ideology: The Processing of Information about Political Candidates. *Journal of Personality and Social Psychology* 61:533–45.

Wyer, Robert, Alan Lambert, Thomas Lee Budesheim, and Deborah Gruenfeld. 1992. Theory and Research on Person Impression Formation: A Look to the Future. In *The Construction of Social Judgments,* ed. Leonard Martin and Abraham Tesser. Hillsdale, N.J.: Lawrence Erlbaum Associates.

Wyer, Robert S., and Thomas K. Srull. 1980. The Processing of Social Stimulus Information: A Conceptual Integration. In *Person Memory: The Cognitive Bases of Social Perception,* ed. Reid Hastie, Thomas M. Ostrom, Ebbe B. Ebbesen, Robert S. Wyer, David L. Hamilton, and Donal E. Carlston. Hillsdale, N.J.: Lawrence Erlbaum Associates.

———. 1986. Human Cognition in Its Social Context. *Psychological Review* 93:322–59.

Young, Jason, Eugene Borgida, John Sullivan, and John Aldrich. 1987. Personal Agendas and the Relationship between Self-Interest and Voting Behavior. *Social Psychology Quarterly* 50:64–71.

Zajonc, Robert. 1968. Attitudinal Effects of Mere Exposure. *Journal of Personality and Social Psychology, Monograph Supplement* 9:1–27.

———. 1980. Feeling and Thinking: Preferences Need No Inferences. *American Psychologist* 35:151–75.

Zaller, John R. 1986. Analysis of Information Items in the 1985 Pilot Study. Memorandum to the N.E.S. Board of Overseers. Ann Arbor, Mich.

———. 1990. Political Awareness, Elite Opinion Leadership, and the Mass Survey Response. *Social Cognition* 8:125–53.

———. 1992. *The Nature and Origins of Mass Opinion.* New York: Cambridge University Press.

Zaller, John R., and Stanley Feldman. 1992. A Simple Theory of the Survey Response: Answering Questions versus Revealing Preferences. *American Journal of Political Science* 36:579–616.

Zaller, John R., and Vincent Price. 1990. In One Ear and Out the Other: Learning and Forgetting the News. Paper presented at the annual meeting of the Midwest Political Science Association, Chicago, Ill.

Contributors

Matthew K. Berent, Department of Psychology, Ohio State University

G. Robert Boynton, Department of Political Science, Iowa State University

James W. Downing, Department of Psychology, University of Kansas

Stanley Feldman, Department of Political Science, State University of New York at Stony Brook

Charles M. Judd, Department of Psychology, University of Colorado

Jon A. Krosnick, Department of Psychology, Ohio State University

Richard R. Lau, Department of Political Science, Rutgers University

Milton Lodge, Department of Political Science, State University of New York at Stony Brook

Kathleen M. McGraw, Department of Political Science, State University of New York at Stony Brook

Wendy M. Rahn, Department of Political Science, University of Wisconsin

Marco Steenbergen, Department of Social and Decision Sciences, Carnegie-Mellon University

Patrick K. Stroh, Department of Social and Decision Sciences, Carnegie-Mellon University

Charles S. Taber, Department of Political Science, State University of New York at Stony Brook

Name Index

Abelson, Robert P., 119, 143, 144, 145, 187, 205, 237, 266
Abramowitz, Alan I., 149
Achen, Christopher H., 251, 253, 262, 269, 270
Ajzen, Icek, 148, 150, 175
Aldrich, John H., 93
Alker, Hayward R., 247
Allison, Graham T., 185
Allport, Gordon W., 66
Anderson, John R., 2, 4, 16, 23, 95, 116, 117, 121, 175, 180, 203, 233, 236, 240
Anderson, Norman H., 114, 117, 118, 119, 120, 126, 127, 132, 133, 134, 148, 155, 157, 158, 256, 261
Andrews, Frank M., 262
Asch, Solomon, 134

Bailar, Barbara A., 270
Banerjee, Sanjoy, 247
Bargh, John, 21, 49, 128, 129, 260
Barsalou, Lawrence W., 4
Bartlett, Frederick, 1
Bassili, John N., 128, 215, 224
Beach, Lee R., 189
Behr, Roy L., 225
Bell, David E., 158, 171
Belmore, Susan, 117
Belson, William A., 256, 262
Berelson, Bernard, 141, 176, 179
Berent, Matthew K., 3, 6, 12, 18, 23, 41, 91, 93, 94, 104
Bettman, James R., 51, 54, 56, 160
Billings, R. S., 186
Bishop, George, 251, 266

Bloom, Howard S., 149, 177
Blumer, Jay G., 211
Bockenholt, Ulf, 55
Bodenhausen, Galen V., 260
Boninger, David S., 107
Borgida, Eugene, 93
Born, Richard, 149, 177
Bowen, Terry, 211
Boyton, G. Robert, 3, 8, 12, 121, 130, 138, 229, 236, 244, 245, 247
Brady, Henry, 19, 88
Branford, J., 129
Brent, Edward, 69
Brewer, Marilyn, 66, 67, 116, 121, 123
Brody, Charles A., 251
Brody, Richard, 155
Brown, Steven R., 25
Budge, Ian, 176, 226

Campbell, Angus, 78, 88, 141, 149, 158, 177, 179, 182, 187, 194, 197, 210, 211, 212, 226, 228
Cantor, Nancy, 128
Cantril, Hadley, 92, 93
Carbonell, Jamie G., Jr., 145
Carmines, Edward, 210, 211
Carpenter, Patricia A., 129
Carroll, John S., 143, 144, 148, 150, 185, 205
Chaiken, Shelly, 23, 33, 34
Chapman, Randall, 213
Clore, Gerald L., 93
Cohen, Claudia E., 115, 215
Collins, Allen, 4, 16, 94, 117, 145, 233
Conover, Pamela J., 69, 70, 99, 172, 175
Converse, Jean M., 250, 255, 267, 269

Subject Index